Death of a Suburban Dream

POLITICS AND CULTURE IN MODERN AMERICA

Series Editors: Margot Canaday, Glenda Gilmore,
Michael Kazin, and Thomas J. Sugrue

Volumes in the series narrate and analyze political and social change
in the broadest dimensions from 1865 to the present, including ideas
about the ways people have sought and wielded power in the public
sphere and the language and institutions of politics at all levels—local,
national, and transnational. The series is motivated by a desire to
reverse the fragmentation of modern U.S. history and to encourage
synthetic perspectives on social movements and the state, on gender,
race, and labor, and on intellectual history and popular culture.

Death of a Suburban Dream

Race and Schools in Compton, California

Emily E. Straus

PENN

UNIVERSITY OF PENNSYLVANIA PRESS

PHILADELPHIA

Published by
University of Pennsylvania Press
Philadelphia, Pennsylvania 19104-4112
www.upenn.edu/pennpress

Printed in the United States of America on acid-free paper
10 9 8 7 6 5 4 3 2 1

A Cataloging-in-Publication Record is available from the Library of Congress
ISBN 978-0-8122-4598-1

for Todd

Contents

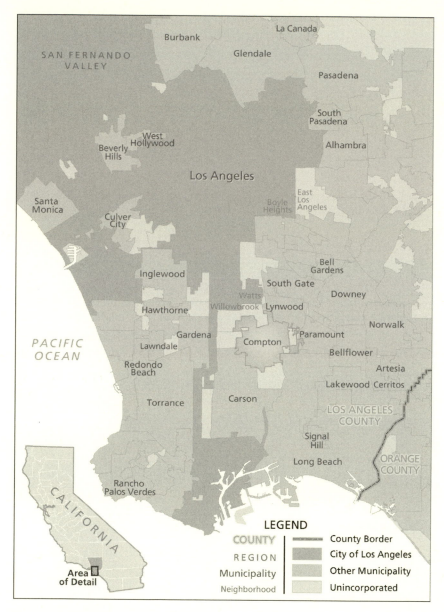

Figure 1. Section of Los Angeles County.

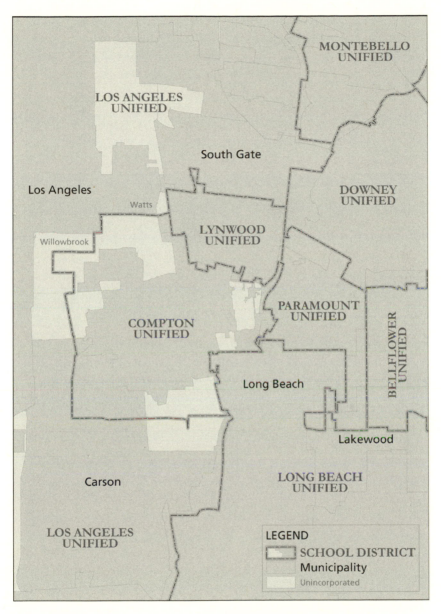

Figure 2. The borders of Compton Unified and its surrounding school districts are not coterminous with town borders.

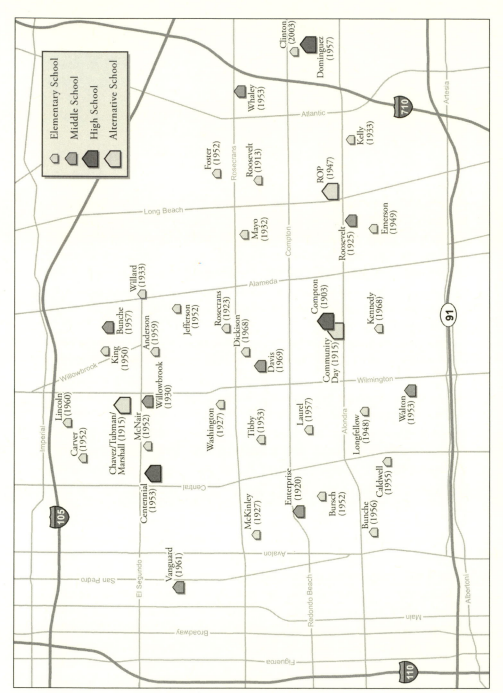

Figure 3. Compton Unified School District schools, with the year of their founding.

Introduction

Marlene Romero watched as her son struggled in school. In his five years at McKinley Elementary in Compton, California, her child had worked hard to master basic math but, according to Romero, he had received no extra help from his teachers. In fact, by her count, "her son has had just one effective teacher in his five years at McKinley."[1] Feeling that her son was "trapped" in the school, Romero signed a petition demanding change and, working with a Los Angeles organization, Parent Revolution, she organized other parents to sign the petition as well.[2]

The group's efforts bore fruit. In December 2010, 61 percent of the parents at McKinley voted no confidence in their neighborhood elementary school, activating California's new "parent trigger" law. According to the state statute, when a majority of parents signed a petition to define their school as "failing," the district had three options: replace staff or teachers, close the school, or give the school over to an independent organization to establish a charter school. In this case, the parents of 275 of McKinley's 442 students demanded a charter school.[3] It became the first use of such a law in the United States.

It is not surprising that this battle over school failure happened in Compton, a Los Angeles area suburb where public schools have a particularly abysmal history. Indeed, in many ways the district's schools have come to symbolize the larger national problem of educational bankruptcy. In 1993, seventeen years before the legislature enacted the trigger law, the district became the first in California to be taken over by the state for both financial and academic failure. After decades of neglect and corruption, the Compton Unified School District was left with dilapidated school plants and enormous debt. It had the worst test scores in the state and the lowest paid teachers in Los Angeles County.[4] Students and educators in Compton went without up-to-date textbooks, adequate supplies, and comfortable classrooms. In addition to these problems, and in many ways because of them, Compton could not attract the best teachers, retain many of the strong teachers it had, or replace those that left in any consistent manner.

Compton's debt became so overwhelming that, by March 1993, the district could neither pay its teachers for the rest of the school year nor afford to open the schools in the fall. Out of sheer desperation, the district requested a $20 million emergency loan from the state, opening the door to a takeover by the state government. California agreed to lend the district $10.5 million and took Compton Unified into receivership, seizing the powers of the district's elected board of trustees and relegating it to an advisory role. A few months later the state added to its charge improving the academic performance of Compton Unified students.[5]

The presence of a state administrator in Compton prompted debate among local residents over who should hold power, as well as what constituted academic performance and what it meant to elevate it. Race played a central role in the debate over the takeover. Some residents deemed this involvement racist, claiming that the state seized power only because African Americans controlled the district of approximately 28,000 pupils, almost all of whom were black or Latino. Others in Compton's black community claimed state officials had ignored the corruption, neglect, and academic failure in Compton precisely because it was a minority-run district. Surely, they argued, if Compton were a white district, the state would have intervened earlier. The state takeover indeed highlighted a deep connection between racial discrimination and educational opportunity. Local district officials did not regain full control until eight years later, in December 2001, only to have residents request state intervention at McKinley again in 2010.[6]

I first encountered Compton during the state receivership. On graduating from college in the mid-1990s, I joined Teach For America and was hired to teach middle school students in Compton Unified. During my time as a teacher in the district I came to know the students, parents, and educators. They not only opened a classroom to me but also entrusted me with their concerns about and desires for their children, schools, and community. Together we shared many hopes and frustrations—and there was much about which to be frustrated. Even under state control, problems still pervaded every aspect of the district. I felt this daily. Each of my classes had forty preteens, all of whom scored below the 35th percentile on statewide standardized tests and most of whom could neither read an early elementary school primer nor write a complete sentence. Along with these academic challenges, my students and I had to contend with a run-down physical plant that inhibited learning. The students sat in dilapidated furniture discarded by a private school. Our classroom ceiling had a gaping hole. On clear days we could see the sky, and on rainy days water streamed into the room.

Many of the questions that first arose for me as an educator in Compton have remained with me as a scholar. What caused the school crisis in Compton? And what was the relationship between the problems I witnessed within the schoolhouse walls, the challenges facing the community, and the problems in society at large? The answers lie at the heart of this book and call into question basic assumptions that many Americans hold about the urban-suburban divide, public school problems, and their potential solutions. Compton's school crisis was not created solely within schoolhouse walls; it was not simply about bad teachers, uncaring principals, or neglected students, though these were certainly part of it. Rather, the crisis evolved over time from the complex, intertwined relationships among racial inequality, economic opportunity, community culture, and educational policy. The educational crisis in Compton, as in so many places across the country, has deep and far-ranging historical roots, and while shifting control of McKinley Elementary School may help Marlene Romero's son with his math, individual school reform will not lead to sustained improvement. Instead, anyone concerned with the plight of American public schools must take a broader and longer view of the structural causes of the problem and use that history to make informed decisions about the present and the future.

Compton's school crisis also illustrates a hidden history of suburban crisis. A more subtle definition of suburbia reveals that Compton's suburban nature itself helped create its particular problems. Scholars and policymakers alike have drawn distinctions between urban centers and their suburban peripheries, but this is a false dichotomy. Suburbia was not monolithic, and the school crisis was not only an urban phenomenon. Suburbs were not—and are not—all the same. While some were affluent, many were not. Defining the American school crisis as "urban" has limited the scope of inquiry into school failure and ignored the connection between schooling and geography.[7]

Labeling a place as urban or suburban brings with it a set of cultural assumptions: the city is the center of crisis and the suburb is the embodiment of the American dream. Suburbs and their schools represented a prosperous, white paradise, an escape from minority-populated cities and their failing schools. The flip side of this racialization of space characterizes urban places and urban schools as centers of violence and family breakdown.[8] Disentangling these basic assumptions about the character of cities and suburbs reveals how demographic changes, political conflict, and lack of economic development combined to put this suburb and its school district in crisis.

Compton's educational crisis is not at heart a crisis of schooling. It is, rather, a long-term crisis of suburban development, in which the schools both inherited and perpetuated the larger community problems. In this larger context, three principal issues, which bear on Compton's specific history but also reach beyond Compton and its school district, come to the fore. First is the fraught history of race, ethnicity, and educational equity. In Compton and elsewhere, residents' needs and expectations of the schools went hand-in-hand with demographic transitions, but the schools' policies remained a step behind. Second is the complicated intersection of schooling and municipal economies. Compton's working-class origins and lack of an industrial tax base played key roles in creating the school crisis. Third is the relationship between schools and place. The particulars of Compton, as well as people's different attachments to or assumptions about it, shaped the suburb and its schools. These three areas illuminate Compton's school crisis as a problem whose solution must not focus solely on the schools themselves.

Located in the geographical center of Los Angeles County just ten miles from downtown Los Angeles, Compton serves as an ideal vantage point from which to examine the history of place, race, and education. California classifies all municipalities as cities and in 1888 local residents politically incorporated Compton as such. Originally a farming town, Compton became a suburb, an identity its residents came to embrace as suburban living became an important social marker after World War II. Levittown, New York, symbolized the postwar suburban dream, and Compton had similar attributes, including single-family houses, an easy commute to a booming metropolis, and, quite significant to a generation that would increasingly focus on youth, a public school system "unsurpassed in Southern California."[9] Compton, like many of its contemporaries in southeast Los Angeles County, was laid out around industry and transportation hubs, but was residential, the great majority of its land occupied by single-family homes.

Compton is neither wholly suburban nor purely urban, and this spatial identity lies at the heart of its educational crisis. Like most suburbs, Compton depended on residential property taxes to fund municipal services, but Compton's modest, single-family homes on small lots did not have the property values necessary to generate adequate income. In this way, Compton was an inner-ring suburb, similar to other locations around the country, such as East Cleveland, Ohio; River Rouge, Michigan; Cicero, Illinois; and Yonkers, New York. Inner-ring suburbs developed next to central cities as primarily single-use, residential-only subdivisions.[10] They lacked strong business districts, which limited their commercial potential, and had aging housing stocks, which limited their desirability for higher-income earners. Without these revenue streams, inner-ring suburbs like Compton did not have the fiscal capacity to fund public schools, and they stood vulnerable.

By the mid-twentieth century, insufficient taxes, scarce metropolitan resources, and little interest from outside businesses plagued Compton. Residents had already strained their meager tax base, investing the limited funds in rebuilding from a 1933 earthquake that had destroyed much of the town, including ravaging the school system's infrastructure. These structural and internal problems continued. As a result, the town never came to look like the stereotypical affluent suburb, and its schools diverged from that model as well. The history of Compton demonstrates that the mid-century suburban ideal was just that—an ideal, one that proved unreachable for the town's residents. Even so, for the residents, living in an inner-ring suburb still represented a step up the social ladder.

Upward mobility was predicated on the power of exclusion, and the most elite suburbs were ones that could prevent those deemed "undesirable" from moving in.[11] Compton was never an elite suburb, yet still its residents tried to control who would be their neighbors, and often part of controlling Compton included defining the town on racial lines. Like residents in Levittown, Comptonites maintained a white enclave. Beginning in the first half of the twentieth century, Compton's whites employed and enforced racial covenants, deed stipulations that barred the sale of properties to nonwhites, though the town always maintained a small Latino population. Counted as white by the U.S. census, this privilege of "whiteness" allowed Latinos to avoid the racial restrictions used to prohibit blacks' residency. Though permitted to live in Compton, the Latino population was not completely accepted as white and remained mostly separate; prior to the late 1950s most Latinos resided on the west side or in a small "barrio" in the north-central area of the town, which bordered on the racially identified areas of Willowbrook and Watts.[12] The Latino population would grow significantly in the later part of the twentieth century.

Despite white residents' efforts, Compton's majority population turned over three times in the course of the twentieth century: from white in the 1950s, to black in the 1970s, to Latino in the 1990s. An examination of why these demographic shifts occurred reveals social and political changes at the local, metropolitan, state, and national levels, including white flight, black suburbanization, Latino immigration, and deindustrialization. Compton shows how all these structural factors converged to create a climate with multiple determinants for disinvestment in schools and conflicts over how they would be run. As such, Compton's history also reveals shifts in educational debates and policies, including the role of charter schools and state intervention.

Even so, Compton's deterioration was not inevitable; local residents shaped their town and their schools. Given difficult structural conditions and their own perceived self-interests, residents did not always make the right choices. As a result, their ill-fated policy decisions for and mismanagement of schools exacerbated Compton's structural disadvantages and ultimately led to many of the town's problems, including job scarcity, economic inequality, and vitriolic race relations. In this way, Compton's experiences also illuminate the way local officials and residents alike thought about race, place, and education.

Along with the dream of homeownership, postwar suburbs became intimately associated with good schools, and the dream was no different in Compton. The link between suburbs and educational superiority had not always been clear; as historians have shown, the best schools were once in the cities, not in the outlying areas.[13] In the postwar era, cities lost their middle class, lured in part by real estate boosters' promises of better schools, and urban schools thereby lost their tax base. For many white families in this era, the superiority of suburban schools lay not only in the strength of educational experiences but also in the possibility that the schools could remain racially segregated.[14] With residential patterns determining school attendance, white Compton parents strove to control who lived in their town, while African Americans in south Los Angeles saw Compton as a step up the ladder from Watts and Willowbrook. Watts had been multiracial from the 1910s and heavily black and Latino after World War II, with Willowbrook becoming majority black soon afterward. When housing covenants based on race became unconstitutional, whites lost grip of residential segregation, blacks moved into previously prohibited areas, and schools became contested ground.

The schools did more than just mirror Compton's municipal maladies;

they also exacerbated the town's problems. As scholar and policymaker Myron Orfield has shown, schooling is both the first victim and a powerful perpetuator of the metropolitan polarization that occurs with changes in demographic, political, and economic circumstances.[15] The politics of public schools are part of a broader local political system that is at the same time subject to larger state and national forces. Compton and its schools exemplify these dynamics. As its economic base deteriorated, so did the town's schools, which further jeopardized its economic base, resulting in a cycle of deterioration that made it increasingly difficult to improve either the town's economy or its education. As Compton's status grew more tenuous, control over the schools grew more important as a political and economic prize. Area residents held firmly onto local control of town resources. Schools were the biggest employer and the center of power in Compton, and as a result, battles over education played central roles in the economic, social, and political decisions and conflicts in this town.

Conflicts with external agencies also developed as various groups and politicians attempted to reform Compton and its school system from outside the town's limits. Compton was in perennial need of assistance from public and private agencies, and yet residents persisted in asserting local control. In Compton, however, suburban localism shifted from being an asset—a source of strength and resources in the early years, when the lack of metropolitan wealth sharing protected local resources—to a hindrance, as the lack of metropolitan wealth sharing became a barrier to meeting local needs. Residents resisted outside help in order to hold onto home rule, even when that local control presided over very limited resources. Residents believed local control was important because of the demographic pressure for racial integration.

Historians have begun to study the economic and racial diversity across suburbia as a whole, but Compton shows how diversity within a suburb unfolds, beginning in the mid-twentieth century. Demographic change did not happen overnight. Rather, over time white residents' efforts at maintaining a racially exclusive enclave broke down. As in other inner-ring suburbs, Compton's population changed racially, while at the same time becoming more uniform in its poverty.[16] After the Supreme Court declared racial covenants unconstitutional in the 1948 *Shelley v. Kraemer* decision, African Americans began to move into the town. Whites defied the decision by continuing to draw racial boundaries across their town rather than around it.[17] Despite white resistance to integration that occasionally included violence, blacks continued to settle there, and whites began moving out en masse. As African

Americans came in and whites left, housing values declined, allowing less well-off blacks to move in. By the 1970s, Compton had a reputation as a black town, which in turn caused commercial exodus and municipal service reductions. As poor African Americans moved in and opportunities opened up in other suburbs, middle-class blacks also moved on. The town became a center of poverty. In 2000, 28 percent of the residents lived below the poverty line, double California's 14.2 percent and more than twice the national 12.4 percent.[18] The books about black suburban experiences tend to focus largely on the black upper middle class. Compton, on the other hand, gives a glimpse into the lives of black poor and working-class suburbanites, offering a critical perspective on suburban diversity.[19]

Each group of migrants to Compton had a different view of what Compton meant for them, but a few desires, for quality education, homeownership, and control over resources, remained constant. For successive waves of whites, blacks, and Latinos, moving to suburbia meant living in a smaller community and inheriting all the costs and benefits that came with it. Given its location at the center of Los Angeles County, the town offered relatively affordable housing stock and, as a result, often became the place people could buy their first homes. Through homeownership, residents gained independence and status for their families. As in other suburban areas, Compton residents' identity was linked to their physical location.[20]

This affordability and accessibility separated Compton from the typical suburban model and made it a candidate for racial turnover. Compton's place as a black working-class suburb offers important insights into the residential, institutional, and political values of African Americans during the civil rights era, as well as the development, meaning, and decline of black political power in many United States metropolitan areas. In 1969, Compton became the largest town west of the Mississippi to have a black mayor, a fact that garnered enormous national attention.[21] Since that time, African Americans have come to hold most of the elected and appointed positions of power in the town and school district. Employment in the public sector played an important role for the black middle class and those aspiring to the middle class. Schools were important for educating children, but they also became an important source of jobs.

As Compton became poorer, it also became more violent, and, like other inner-ring suburbs, in this way it came to resemble an urban ghetto. Cultural representations perpetuated this image. The 1988 release of the music group NWA's *Straight Outta Compton* vaulted the town into the national consciousness as a symbol of urban gang violence. Portraying Compton as brutal and lawless, the double-platinum album's song lyrics, accompanying music videos, and cover art emphasize lessons from the streets and the area's shattered economy. The title track begins with rapper Ice Cube identifying himself as a member of a Compton gang, boasting: "When I'm called off, I got a sawed off, squeeze the trigger, and bodies are hauled off."[22] In their music videos, NWA prominently and proudly display the streets and back alleys of their town; only in fleeting images does the viewer see homes. On the album's cover, the six members of NWA stare into the camera, while group leader Eazy-E points a gun at the viewer. The members' physical positions and facial expressions, as well as the pointed gun, contrasted strongly with the crisp blue California sky overhead. The album's enormous popularity, as well as John Singleton's 1991 Academy Award nominated movie *Boyz n the Hood*, transformed the area into a potent symbol of west coast black gang culture.[23] The dream of Compton's mid-century boosters—suburban tranquility, strong schools, and middle-class material abundance—had gone seriously awry.

Of course, like the image of the suburban idyll of the 1940s, the harsh jungle of the 1980s was a caricature. Boosters may have sold postwar Compton as the perfect middle-class, white community, but things were not perfect even then, and its later use as a symbol of gang culture shaped late twentieth-century Compton in equally complicated ways. Still, in many respects, the real Compton of the 1980s and 1990s did embody and bolster its mythology. Each election cycle seemed to usher in a new set of dishonest politicians while racial and ethnic strife dominated the evening news.

This news coverage, along with songs and films, constituted much of what outsiders knew about Compton. This was problematic because outsiders of many kinds asserted the right to control Compton's schools, and were surprised to encounter resistance. Understanding Compton's schools required more than recognition of the consequences of white flight and economic change: it required an appreciation for how ordinary citizens used, supported, and criticized the schools in their own terms.

In searching out Comptonites' own views of their schools, I found that some voices did emerge from traditional sources, but many remained unheard. At points those silences spoke volumes about the social and political power dynamics in Compton. For example, in Compton's *Herald American* newspaper, racist assumptions lurked only slightly below the surface, while in others it lay at the more foundational level. To hear from individuals whose voices were often absent from the written record, I employed oral histories, primarily through interviews I conducted, supplemented by those of other researchers. Time and again, Compton residents, past and present, described Compton as their home. Despite the town's problems, historical and contemporary, it always remained a place where people live and experience everyday moments of happiness as well as important occasions and life milestones. The oral histories pushed me to remember those moments when thinking and writing about Compton.[24]

Unveiling the lived experiences of Compton's suburbanites—white, black, and Latino—also provides an important opportunity for the examination of the multi-ethnic struggles within a suburban town and its schools. A study of black-Latino relations in Compton expands beyond the white-black binary that dominates scholarship on race in the United States. While historians are beginning to explore interactions between blacks and Latinos, they tend to focus on urban stories.[25] Compton offers a case study of an inner-ring suburb as African Americans and Latinos began to compete for limited resources in the suburban schoolyards, school administrations, and communities more broadly.[26]

Latino immigration transformed Compton, as it did southern California and the nation at large. In Compton, antagonism developed as two historically disenfranchised populations resisted sharing power in a context of scarcity. School disputes pitted long-time residents against newcomers—white and black, black and Latino—in tumultuous battles for control over public resources. Given Compton's waning financial resources amid larger economic changes, decision-making positions in the school district became a source of political clout. As the largest employer in the town, schools functioned not just to provide children with an education but as a major source of jobs for adults, leading to issues of security and patronage.[27] In fact, in the summer of 2010, nine years after the state had returned local power to the district, a state audit found the district continued to have a focus on "adult needs as a priority before student needs."[28] While the schools remained the arena for myriad battles over equal access to education and political power, the political discourse of this audit is too simplistic to understand a situation like Compton's, a place where schools served as complex community institutions.

Compton's history emphasizes the role of public schooling in the civil rights struggles beyond urban centers. Studies of the civil rights movement in communities outside the South expand our understanding about race, space, and inequality by examining the effects of housing discrimination, urban renewal, and job discrimination.[29] Understanding schooling is a key component of understanding any community, because schools indicate that community's present and future health. Schools act as this marker because when they hit a certain threshold of poverty, middle-class families move out. In conjunction with this, when black and Latino students make up a certain percentage of the population in a school, white homebuyers perceive that the community is in decline and choose not to buy there. Soon, whites in that community begin to move away. A community's children are by and large its next generation of adults, and thus school quality has a dramatic long-term impact on a community's overall well-being.[30]

Compton's history must be understood by reconciling local, state, and national contexts. By analyzing structural and internal causes, this book untangles the questions of how and why Compton arrived at its current state. An examination of the town's mixture of population changes, political conflict, and economic dynamics reveals how race, place, and schools are interwoven. It explains the process that has produced a notorious cultural icon—the Compton mythologized today, a place of frequent drive-by shootings as well as demoralized teachers and poorly educated students.

The nature of suburbs is changing, as we see a reverse migration of wealthier residents from suburb to city and the rise of additional poor, inner-ring suburban areas. Compton's suburban nature opened the door for racial and ethnic turnover as well as the rise of poverty within its borders, and limited the town's response to poverty's effects. In recent years researchers from the Brookings Institution have documented a nationwide rise in suburban poverty and immigration, along with the inadequate safety nets in suburban jurisdictions.[31]

While Compton's history is particular to the town, it may also serve as an advanced preview of the plight of public schools in the age of government austerity. As local and state entities cut their education budgets to make ends meet, Compton's story of budget shortages, both systemic and prescribed, offers a cautionary tale. In the eyes of many, including the State of California and the parents at McKinley Elementary School, Compton's schools have failed their students. Is our cherished tradition of public education headed the way of Compton? Compton's story is still unfolding, but even now its history is instructive.

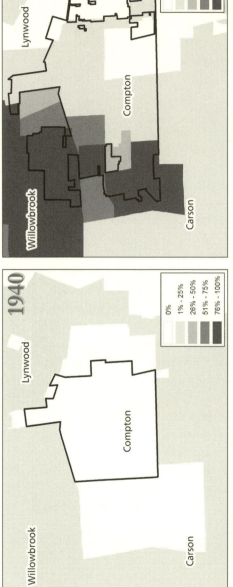
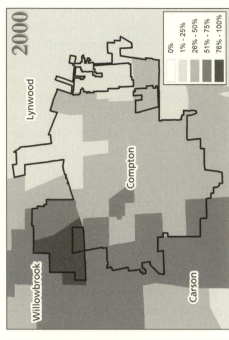
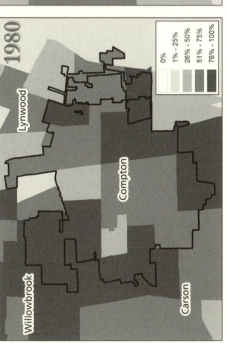

Figure 4. Percentage of population who were African American in 1940, 1960, 1980, 2000. U.S. Census.

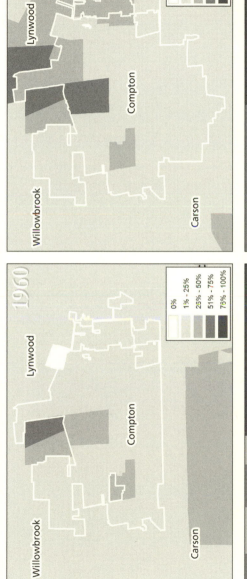
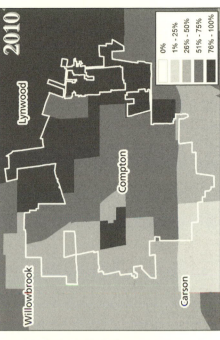
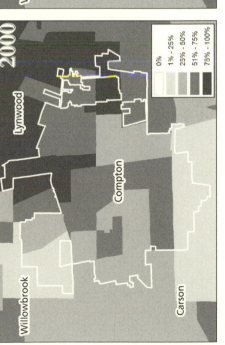

Figure 5. Percentage of population who were Latino in 1960, 1980, 2000, 2010. U.S. Census.

Chapter 1

On Shaky Ground

Early in the evening on Friday, March 10, 1933, ten-year-old Ruth Ashton was sitting by her radio in her Compton home listening to one of her favorite serials when the ground began to shake.[1] Windows shattered, doors collapsed, and stores "burst open." Brick chimneys were "snapped off," roofs "caved in," and walls "buckled," as people ran for safety from their homes and businesses.[2] The brutal earthquake rattled California's southland for thirteen long seconds. Though the epicenter lay off Newport Beach's shore, Southern Californians from Ventura to San Diego felt the initial tremor. At 6.3 on the Richter scale, seismologists did not consider it a major shock. Residents felt otherwise. The quake left 118 people dead and caused more than $40 million in property damage over a twenty-mile radius.[3]

According to engineers who surveyed the area, the earthquake hit hardest in Compton, then a small residential community of just over four-and-a-half square miles that housed fewer than fifteen thousand people, the vast majority of whom were white and working class. The earthquake "either razed or severely damaged" almost all of Compton's three thousand stores, offices, and residences. Long Beach, a port city just south of Compton, suffered the greatest loss of life and greatest total damage, but Compton suffered the greatest proportionate damage.[4] Compton's police station and city hall lay in ruins. Fearful for the integrity of the remaining buildings, many residents refused to reenter their homes, opting instead to pitch tents or move furniture into vacant lots where they cooked over open fires. Amid the chaos, sailors, marines, police officers, deputy sheriffs, and American Legion members guarded the town to keep the peace.[5] Yet all of this assistance did not translate into a quick recovery. Even when most students in Los Angeles County returned to school, Compton was one of three locales with unsafe educational facilities. The quake had shattered their town.[6]

The earthquake was a tremendous setback for Compton, but it alone did not put the town and its schools on shaky ground. In addition to external factors such as the quake, the way Comptonites were developing their town would have ramifications down the line. From early on, Compton's residents valued local control over drawing boundaries and residential growth, and they resisted building industry. As a result, by the time of the earthquake, the town already had a tenuous infrastructure. Compton was a working-class bedroom community with a low tax base, and Compton schools thus had precious little financial safety net. Once the quake hit, the suburb did not have the resources to rebuild and accrued deep debts that would plague the town and its schools for decades to come.

In its formative years Compton faced in quick succession two major crises: an economic depression and a natural catastrophe. Both of these strained Compton's meager tax base, resulting in an ill-supported infrastructure. When confronting these combined pressures, services—such as schooling—suffered. The demographic, political, and economic changes created uneasy footing on which Comptonites navigated their educational opportunities.

Life Before the Quake

Compton began as a small farming town. On December 6, 1866, Francis Temple and Fielding Gibson purchased a portion of the Rancho San Pedro from Spanish colonizers.[7] Less than a year later, a small band of approximately thirty disappointed gold seekers from the San Joaquin Valley, led by Griffith D. Compton and William Morton, established Compton on this land, making it the second oldest "American" community in the area. These Anglo-American settlers were Methodists, who sought arable farmland and a permanent home where they could maintain their traditions and mores. Founded by devout people, Compton retained its religious tone, even after other denominations moved in.[8]

Compton soon became known for its farms. An 1887 *Los Angeles Times* article included the town in its report on "prosperous agricultural settlements," and described its bounty of corn, pumpkins, and alfalfa.[9] In 1893 local farmer Amos Eddy sent seven cuttings of alfalfa to be placed on exhibit at the 1893 Chicago's World Fair. The height of the crop was so astonishing that Eddy included a sworn affidavit, in order to curb any doubts of its authenticity.[10] Agricultural successes like Eddy's and affordable land drew people to Compton. Savannah Chalifoux's father moved to the town in 1906 because he was able to buy a farm. His family had recently moved to California from Illinois, after spending some time in St. Louis and Nebraska. Compton fulfilled his dream of owning land. Though the land was "a bad piece of property" for farming, it supported sugar beets, and the family could make a living.[11]

Compton residents also raised poultry and hogs and produced dairy products. By the end of the nineteenth century, Compton had the largest cheese factory in Southern California, and, due to the town's proximity to multiple markets, its cheese and butter gained "a wide reputation."[12] A 1909 travel article encouraged tourists in Los Angeles to visit Pasadena, "a thriving business city and health resort"; Santa Monica, "a popular seaside resort"; and Compton, "the center of the dairy district."[13] Agriculture and the tourist industry played the leading roles in Los Angeles County's early economy, and while each town had its strengths, Santa Monica's and Pasadena's proved more resilient as the region evolved into a more urbanized area.[14]

Settlers in Los Angeles County established independent communities. At first, most were loosely knit agricultural settlements, with the exception of the tourist attractions and harbor communities.[15] Compton and Pasadena were two of the earliest, and a comparison of the two offers insight into Compton's development.[16] Built in the same era, Compton diverged from Pasadena in significant ways, not the least of which was that, unlike Pasadena, Compton did not attract regular outside visitors. While Pasadena's founders immediately set out orange and lemon groves, they also turned the town into a resort community. Pasadena became a favorite place for land speculation, and as a result its population mushroomed during the Southern California land boom of 1886–88.[17] The rapid influx of new residents settled into a comfortable stream by 1890. Pasadena's boosters continued to take advantage of both the town's stop on the railroad and its isolation from city life, attracting winter visitors with hotels, shops, attractions, and restaurants. Hoteliers built inns and boarding houses, as well as grand hotels in the 1890s, bringing in wealthy patrons. The grand hotels thrived in the warm winter months, serving both overnight guests and locals who sought a night out at a concert, ball, or a multitude of other high society gatherings. Indeed, many of the seasonal residents were millionaires, who spent their time in mansions they had built on and off Orange Grove Avenue.[18] By the 1920s, Pasadena had

the wealthiest per capita population in the country because of this concentration of extreme wealth.[19] The majority of the residents, though, were unable
to afford these mansions and instead resided in quintessential Southern California bungalow homes. Pasadena's incorporation of different classes set it
apart from towns like Compton, which never had a wealthy tax base. From
these foundations, Compton and Pasadena would take dramatically different
directions in their development.

Though Compton did not attract the same number of tourists as Pasadena, a small business district did exist to serve the immediate community.
In 1887, Compton's establishments included a "fair-sized" hotel, two drug
stores, two dry goods and grocery stores, one "fancy" grocery, and a jewelry
shop. The town also supported hardware, harness, wagon, and blacksmith
shops.[20] The business district remained minimally developed, however, because it served as a destination for locals only. At the turn of the century,
Compton's population remained small, making it unnecessary to expand the
downtown area.[21]

Figure 6. In 1887, Compton had a block for businesses, including hardware and
grocery stores. Courtesy Archives & Special Collections, California State University,
Dominguez Hills.

Compton's location could have helped make it a business hub, but instead it became an affordable place to live for those who worked elsewhere. The small town bordered Los Angeles and Long Beach, the two largest cities in Los Angeles County, and because of their proximity Comptonites did not depend solely on the local economy for their livelihoods. The Southern Pacific Railroad gave Compton residents easy access to both cities, while two major truck highways, Alameda Avenue and Long Beach Boulevard, traversed Compton as they linked downtown Los Angeles with the ports. Compton's proximity to these modes of transportations made it geographically desirable for working-class residents.[22]

Many Compton residents worked in Los Angeles or Long Beach. Beginning in the last part of the nineteenth century, both cities had grown rapidly. In 1880, with a population of only 11,000 residents, Los Angeles did not rank as one of the top hundred most populous places in the country. By 1920, however, it had risen to tenth among the country's urban places, the largest city in California with a population of over 575,000. Just ten years later, the City of Angels had over 1.2 million residents, and the population continued to rise as did the city's physical size. Through a series of annexations the city grew by approximately 80 square miles. The county population rose from just over 900,000 in 1920 to over 2.2 million in 1930, an average of 350 newcomers a day for ten years.[23] Los Angeles had gone from a rural outpost to the West's leading financial, entertainment, and industrial center.[24]

Long Beach also transformed during this period. Founded as a seaside resort in 1881, the town came to attract vacationers from across the United States. Among Southern California beach towns, Long Beach came to have it all: a municipal auditorium to host gatherings; upscale and affordable hotels; and a streetcar to transport visitors to the rest of the Los Angeles area.[25] The city's wealth boomed with the discovery of oil, first in 1910 and then with the famous 1921 Signal Hill strike. With oil came increases in real estate prices and land speculation. Like neighboring Los Angeles, the city grew in population and size, as it annexed adjoining land. The business district expanded and the city became more urbanized, with paved streets and large buildings.[26]

Unlike Long Beach and Los Angeles, Compton was built as a rural town and had little civic infrastructure. Little changed even when, in May 1888, Compton became the seventh town in Los Angeles County to incorporate. This incorporation developed as a response to the Los Angeles region's real estate boom in the 1880s; Compton residents looked to manage their community and keep its identity in the face of regional change. Incorpora-tion gave residents some measure of power over development and taxes. Res-idents incorporated the town as a sixth class city, meaning it could elect a mayor and raise municipal revenues, because they wanted "a more efficient government" and believed the county was providing "inadequate control."[27] Residents wanted internal improvements, better police and fire protection, and limits to itinerant peddlers and outside merchants. Desires did not al-ways match reality, however. The town's central district began the new cen-tury without paved streets or public utilities. It also lacked a city hall and fire and police stations.[28]

Most Comptonites were white, and Compton workers wished to define who worked in their town on racial and ethnic lines, but the town's govern-ment failed to tackle this issue. In 1893, eleven years after the enactment of the federal Chinese Exclusion Act of 1882, which barred the entrance of Chinese workers to the United States, the issue of nonwhite workers in Compton came to a head, culminating with "an incipient riot."[29] In this case, white locals de-manded a rancher dismiss his thirty Chinese employees. When the rancher refused to "discharge the heathens," the whites threatened violence.[30]

Racial violence targeted against Chinese workers affected other places as well. Most notably, an anti-Chinese riot rocked Los Angeles in October 1871, twelve years before the uprising in Compton. Another such example was in Pasadena. Though a majority white town, Pasadena was also home to small populations of Latino, Japanese, Chinese, and black residents. With the rail-ways complete, many Chinese laborers found themselves unemployed. The Chinese in Pasadena toiled in low-income jobs such as working in the laun-dry business and in grocery stores. Accused of taking jobs from whites, the Chinese became the target of rioters in 1885, after which they moved to a segregated area of town where they lived with Latino, African American, and Japanese residents. Pasadena, like Compton, would remain an ethnically seg-regated town for years to come.

Along with maintaining the town's racial lines, Comptonites also encoun-tered numerous stumbling blocks, with municipal government even ceasing operation for fifteen years around the turn of the twentieth century.[31] In an extraordinary move, the government dissolved itself after residents, for all practical purposes, unincorporated their town by removing the majority of the land from city limits. Accounts differ as to why the residents took this ac-tion. In one rendition, residents withdrew their land from the town because they did not wish to be part of a community in which liquor was sold.[32] A more widely reported version credited residents' disinclination toward taxes as the reasoning behind the dissolution. In this explanation, soon after residents' incorporated Compton, the town leaders realized that it was in financial difficulties; license fees had not netted the town much funds, and the town quickly spent that money on salaries, leaving little for public improvement. To deal with the shortfall, the board of trustees proposed a municipal tax. Despite widespread opposition to this plan, the board passed the unpopular levy.[33] Regardless of the precipitating event, residents tried to unincorporate their town, but once they realized that they couldn't, they withdrew more than 80 percent of the land from Compton, making a practical disincorporation by excluding territory from the boundaries of incorporation.[34] By the end of the ordeal only a small corner of the town was left incorporated.

Dissolution or disincorporation was rather rare, but some other municipalities, such as Long Beach, also went to such lengths. In 1891 some residents of Long Beach also circulated a petition to disincorporate their fledgling town, which had only been incorporated for four years. After debate among residents and after years of stalling, the California Supreme Court granted the disincorporation petition in spring 1897. Almost immediately on disincorporation, a set of Long Beach residents looked to reincorporate the town, which they successfully completed in December 1897, with a vote of 237 to 27.[35]

As in Long Beach, Compton's disincorporation was not permanent, though it did last longer. At the end of 1906, Comptonites petitioned the governor to reincorporate.[36] They soon discovered that a small part of Compton had remained incorporated and as a result, they only had to re-annex the land. The town soon began supporting municipal improvements, including a city hall, public library, and public park. Enhancement of infrastructure would continue sporadically.[37] Yet, even as Compton underwent these conversions, what remained constant was residents' wish for home rule, a common sentiment among late nineteenth and early twentieth century urban reformers, and one that would extend both spatially and temporally.[38]

Though municipal politics did not always run smoothly (or at all), Compton provided schooling throughout this period; indeed, Compton's school district was one of the oldest in Los Angeles County. The early settlers brought with them their Protestant values, including education.[39] They built a one-room elementary schoolhouse within two years of their arrival, and just three years later in 1872 they erected a two-story grammar school to serve the first eight grades. Ninth grade instruction began in 1891 and instruction extended through the twelfth grade beginning in 1896, when residents formed the Compton Union High School District to serve the surrounding areas. Compton established a high school over a decade before Californians voted to provide annual state funds for them.

While California did not provide state funding for high schools until 1902, it did have a constitutional guarantee of public education. The first state constitution, written in 1849, required common schools for at least three months of the year and provided for a Superintendent of Public Instruction. It also provided for a means to raise money so that the state could help fund education. The second state constitution, adopted in 1879, changed the minimum three-month school term to six months and gave local school district governing boards more power, a direction that was partially reversed a few years later when in 1884 the State Board of Education was founded. Perhaps more importantly, the 1879 Constitution codified the state's philosophical commitment to education, asserting as the first section of the article on education: "A general diffusion of knowledge and intelligence being essential to the preservation of the rights and liberties of the people, the Legislature shall encourage by all suitable means the promotion of intellectual, scientific, moral, and agricultural improvement."[40]

The state legislature passed a series of laws to support public schools. In 1851 it passed the first school governance and finance act, which required each district to raise at least a third of the operating budget for its schools using local property taxes and other means if it wished to get state aid.[41] That same year California's first free public schools opened in San Francisco. In 1874 the state passed its compulsory education law for children eight to fourteen and guaranteed state aid for each school based on the number of children in the district, not the number of students who actually went to school. This distinction would not be changed in California law until 1911.

Even with the expansion of state oversight, Compton bore the burden of funding its schools, and its expansion of educational offerings meant incurring new expenses. Though the number of students in all Los Angeles area school districts remained quite small despite California's passage of a compulsory school act in 1903 (in 1910 the county's second and third largest districts, Long Beach and Pasadena, graduated 82 and 72 students respectively), increasing the number of grades still meant increasing the number of students.[42] More students meant hiring more teachers, buying more supplies, and expanding the physical plant. Local residents took on all these expenses. In the same month that the compulsory school act passed, March 1903, local residents overwhelmingly approved a bond issue of $15,000 to build a separate high school building. Over the next two decades Compton's high school added administration, gymnasium, shop, science, music, commerce, and home economics buildings to meet the needs of the area's swelling population.

California aided its school districts through state property taxes and other state resources when needed. Property assessment practices varied throughout the state, however. This resulted in inequities of the levies. A 1906 Report from the Commission on Revenue and Taxation recommended a separation of state and local levies, with the local government taxing property and the state collecting on such things as inheritance, insurance, and corporations. These recommendations became codified in a 1910 constitutional amendment, allowing for the levying on property, if need be. Even with the legal change, the state did nothing. Instead, state funding in education slowed and a greater burden fell on local property taxes.[43] In 1921 California officially turned over the task of setting their own budgets and taxes to the local school boards.

The Compton area had especially high taxes because it supported several school districts. Independent of municipal governments and not necessarily coterminous with municipal boundaries, California school districts administered elementary and secondary schools, including junior colleges as part of the secondary school system. At its founding, Compton Union High School District consisted of three feeder grammar school districts: Compton, Enterprise, and Lugo (later renamed Lynwood.) Over the next three decades the number of component districts would expand to eight, adding Clearwater, Graham, Palomar (later renamed Paramount), Watts, and Willowbrook to the original three. These districts provided schooling through the sixth grade and would send their students to the centralized high school district.

Each district had its own elected board of trustees and its own bureaucracy. The Compton Union board of trustees oversaw the junior highs and high school (and eventually the junior college, established in 1927), while each elementary school district administered itself. Local residents contended that these multiple districts gave more power to their communities and were "economical and efficient."[44] While the districts allowed for local control, they also repeated a lot of the same functions. As such, these multiple bureaucracies would in fact prove costly for the community, becoming more acute as the population grew. While residents periodically put forth proposals to merge the school systems, several school boards continued to govern Compton area schools.[45] Some changes did occur, most notably the withdrawal of Clearwater and Watts from Compton Union. In 1926, Watts was incorporated as part of the city of Los Angeles and became part of its school district. Not all proposed withdrawals happened, however. There was also a movement to remove the Willowbrook and Enterprise districts from Compton Union to Los Angeles City School District. Compton opposed this action and no movement happened.[46]

The maintenance of multiple districts was common across Los Angeles County—and was not limited to schools. In 1900 Los Angeles had 105 school districts and 38 road districts. The county also had some special districts to provide services such as libraries and drainage to unincorporated areas. Towns also joined forces in some districts to provide services such as water across their borders.[47] The degree of fragmentation was not unusual in the Sunbelt because residents needed to form service districts or have counties

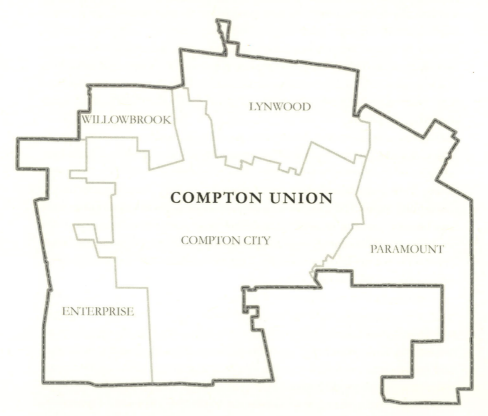

Figure 7. The Compton Union High School and Junior College District was split into component elementary school districts.

fund services for unincorporated areas. Towns cooperated regionally over water because of both its scarcity and its need for massive infrastructure.

While towns joined forces for a variety of services, home rule remained particularly important in schools for a variety of reasons, not the least of which was that it gave locals sway over the curriculum. Compton educators also changed the structure of the schools using progressive educators' models. Progressive educators, as exemplified by American philosopher John Dewey, valued a child-centered education, and their ideas about schooling influenced educational policies across Los Angeles County from the 1890s through the 1940s.[48] Compton's school districts configured their schools, dividing students into what seemed more appropriate age clusters to facilitate student-centered learning. Beginning in the 1930s, Compton's school systems ran on a progressive 6-4-4 plan, which grouped the grades in an unconventional way. Elementary school students attended school in their local districts through grade six.[49] They then attended area junior high schools for grades seven through ten, continuing to high school for the last two years of secondary school and first two years of college. The final two years, grades 13 and 14, were junior college and as such were not mandatory. They were, however, open to all students in the district and were funded by taxpayers.

Other Los Angeles area school systems also adopted this unconventional structure. Starting in the late 1920s, the progressively modeled Pasadena schools also ran on the 6-4-4 system, which, according to historian Michael James, "took political will and pedagogical know-how coupled with strong community support. It also took money—a lot of it."[50] While Compton may have had the community support and knowhow, unlike Pasadena, it did not have the same tax capacity. Rapid population growth coupled with the Great Depression and rebuilding from the 1933 earthquake would expose Compton's problem with school funding.

The passage of the federal 1915 National Defense Act and the 1917 Smith-Hughes Act signaled greater federal involvement in public schooling as they, respectively, established funds for a Reserve Officers Training Corps program and for vocational education. But local property taxes along with county and state monies still supported schools.[51] In 1920 California voters used the initiative process to decide on the funding of schools. The process for having a proposition, referendum, or recall was established in 1911 after Progressive Era reformers, supported by the labor movement, advocated for it as a way to bypass the state legislature, which appeared corruptible to big business. The initiative process allowed the voters to propose and adopt or reject amendments to the state's constitution. Since the ballot measures circumnavigated the legislature, the courts served as the only way to check the process. California was the tenth state to implement such a process and became a leader in using it for a variety of measures.

The 1920 Proposition 13 (which was not related to the more famous 1978 Proposition 13) mandated an annual state contribution to public education and also mandated county tax levies to, at minimum, match the state contribution for elementary schools and double the state appropriation for secondary and technical schools. Even with these mandated funds, however, the majority of the money came from local sources and, because of Compton's small tax capacity, the town schools suffered.

The Compton Area Transforms

The 1920 discovery of oil on nearby Dominguez Hill and the accompanying development of industry changed Compton. Recognizing the new possibilities for the real estate market, development firms began to buy up farms and divide them into parcels for home building. At the same time, Compton began to annex undeveloped county land, increasing development within its limits.[52] The Compton Board of Realtors and the Chamber of Commerce also started advertising campaigns to lure new residents, touting Compton's central location and vast tracts of affordable land. With the two railroad lines that stopped in town, Compton promised to become a conveniently located yet affordable suburb.[53] The largest development company, Ramsey and Bemus, declared in 1923: "What Harlem is to New York, Compton will be to Los Angeles."[54] Both were affordable residential areas in near proximity to the city center. While their positions seemed like positives for Harlem and Compton, the intertwined relationship with the metropolis would have unforeseen consequences for both.

Compton's relationship to the larger metropolitan region evolved along with the development of Los Angeles County. The county's industrial boom of the 1910s and 1920s changed Compton's economic landscape; farming no longer served as its main occupation. In 1913, the Panama Rubber Company built a factory for manufacturing automobile tires and accessories in Compton.[55] The factory brought more workers to the town and prompted more home construction.[56] Though this particular manufacturing plant did not remain in Compton and its successor would end up filing for bankruptcy in 1915, other firms replaced it and expanded production.[57]

Compton also gained more residents, in part because of the increasing prevalence of automobiles, which made the once-remote farming town more accessible. People could now live in Compton and commute to other places in Los Angeles County for work.[58] Compton and its surrounding community supported a variety of other industries, including pickle, brick, and glass factories, as well as petroleum companies, with their wells and refineries.[59] Many of these companies located just outside Compton's city limits and, while Compton did not get their taxes, their growth affected the town. Residential rent was high in Los Angeles and Long Beach, and, like South Gate and other blue-collar suburbs, Compton became an affordable option for many workers.[60] As a result, Compton's population expanded rapidly; between the end

Figure 8. Aerial view of Compton, 1920. Courtesy Archives & Special Collections, California State University, Dominguez Hills.

of 1920 and the beginning of 1926 the town population grew from just under 1,500 to approximately 13,500.[61]

Whites comprised the majority of new residents, including a small population of Latinos, who were counted as white. Most Latinos lived near the northernmost border of Compton, in the Walton Villa Tract subdivision, which was constructed in 1917. One reason for the homogeneity was that Compton and other Los Angeles area suburbs enacted restrictive covenants barring African Americans from settling in their towns. Beginning in 1921 Compton had racially defined legal provisions written into property deeds. Developers built Compton to be an affordable blue-collar suburb, which would have made it an option for blacks. In 1930, the median value for an owner-occupied home in Compton was $4,471 while in more affluent suburban areas like South Pasadena and Santa Monica the values were $9,538 and $7,131 respectively. Compton hovered near, but was not at the bottom of the list. For example, in South Gate and Azusa median home values were $4,264 and $3,589 respectively.[62]

Like many whites across the country Comptonites believed blacks made "poor neighbors," and as a result, they did not want blacks as their neighbors or as classmates for their children.[63] In taking these preventive measures, Compton homeowners united to implement successfully their slogan "Keep the Negroes North of 130th Street."[64] In other words, keep them in Los Angeles and out of Compton. A 1927 survey of realtors identified Compton's local creed: "never sell to an undesirable."[65] Defining their community meant racial exclusion, which in turn, helped white residents form a cohesive community.[66]

The Great Depression bolstered the context in which whites focused on racially segregating neighborhoods. Two Depression-era agencies, the Federal Housing Administration (FHA) and the Federal Home Loan Bank Board, underwrote millions of loans in the interest of stabilizing the national real estate market. The agencies aggressively disseminated their underwriting guidelines, stressing that white neighborhoods were less risky.[67] The federal Home Owners Loan Corporation (HOLC) also used race to inform its decisions about loaning money. Local practices coupled with federal agencies' policies led to a focus on racial homogenization.

The attempts to maintain racial segregation extended to the schools. A decade after white Comptonites called for drawing the line at 130th Street, some called for a new school district boundary in Willowbrook to be drawn at 120th Street, so that the district's black and Latino students would attend schools in Los Angeles instead.[68] At the time Willowbrook had two elementary schools, which the black periodical the *Los Angeles Sentinel* described as: "one largely attended by Negroes and Mexicans, and the other a new school where Negroes are frankly told that their children are not wanted."[69] The proposed boundary change would leave only one black family in the district. While the recommendation gained significant backing from whites in Willowbrook, the board members of the Los Angeles district quickly shot down this idea.[70] When the plan backfired, school administrators and teachers allegedly urged black students to seek transfers to Los Angeles schools, a technique whites would later use themselves as a means to leave Compton area schools.[71]

Comptonites depended on each other when the Great Depression hit, forming a number of cooperative associations to address their desperate need for food, clothing, and other necessities. One disabled Spanish War veteran, William "Shorty" Burchfield, started a new trend: he took a sack on his back and went to the vegetable fields around Compton. At night he and the people who joined him in picking, dubbed the Veterans' Relief Association of Compton, donated the vegetables they gathered to other residents.[72] Like Burchfield, many Comptonites proved their ingenuity in creating communal self-sufficiency. The Association placed baskets in local stores for donations during the winter of 1931–32 and distributed the proceeds among their most destitute neighbors.[73]

Residents sought to institutionalize this community spirit. Just one month before the earthquake, locals formed the Compton Unemployed Relief Association. Within a few months of its inception, the group listed 2,500 families in its records and passed out tons of food daily through its commissary. The group also had an impact beyond the town's borders. According to economist Clark Kerr, the Compton unit stimulated the organization of many similar associations and provided the essential outlines for early barter activity in California. Throughout the state, people involved in the cooperative movement considered the Veterans' Relief Association of Compton the "mother of them all."[74]

In addition to the cooperative associations, early in the Depression, Compton residents used their town government to protect the interests of their fellow citizens. On March 9, 1933, the day before the earthquake, the city council passed an emergency resolution prohibiting employment of "laborers, artisans, mechanics, contractors or their helpers" who were not residents of Compton. Locals sought to control the labor in their town to protect their limited employment opportunities. Unlike in Long Beach, which had sufficient local laborers, the earthquake challenged Compton's ability to do so as local labor would prove insufficient for the amount of rebuilding they were facing. A few weeks later, in the aftermath of the earthquake, the council amended the ordinance, affording the city manager the power to use his discretion in giving permission to laborers to work inside the town limits if they resided in the elementary school district and trading area of Compton.[75] New construction after the earthquake required additional workers. After the quake, Compton reluctantly entered into a more dependent relationship with outsiders.

Rebuilding Compton During the Great Depression

After the 1933 earthquake, the Southland was in disarray. The tremor broke lines of communication in the entire Long Beach area. Refugees soon crowded public parks and highways trying to escape the demolished buildings. Four thousand marines and sailors from the United States battle fleet, along with local police officers and firefighters, guarded Long Beach and the southern towns. Experts found much of the towns' infrastructures unfixable.[76] The earthquake had flattened nine of Compton's ten elementary schools, and the tenth eventually had to be destroyed because of irreparable structural damage. Given the faulty construction of Compton's schools, it was a mere stroke of luck that the earthquake hit after school hours; the death toll could have been far more severe.

Comptonites banded together to heal their damaged community. Town leaders commended the chief of police for his "efficient work" and recognized the "heroic effort" of the firefighters.[77] Compton residents quickly moved to reestablish their public school system. Within two weeks of the quake, the school district reopened with classes held in warehouses, frame buildings, and tents.[78] Despite the physical obstacles created by the tremors, by the end of the school year every class had completed the year's work, and the seniors graduated with their diplomas.[79] Years later, a report on Compton's schools fondly recalled the first few days and weeks after the earthquake as "an epic of community cooperation, indomitable courage, and civic unity."[80]

The devastation of the quake required outside financial assistance. As a working-class bedroom community, Compton did not have the capacity to deal with such an emergency. Already struggling to provide basic services

Figure 9. Compton Boulevard after March 10, 1933, earthquake. Courtesy Archives & Special Collections, California State University, Dominguez Hills.

under the best conditions, Compton residents needed to accept aid from beyond their town's borders. The quake's disaster necessitated this outside intervention even though it countered Comptonites' desire to have local control. The aid opened up a path to closer and, at times, more dependent, relationships with nonlocal agencies.

Aid flowed into the Southland, despite "the financial distress that [had] brought hunger and misery to many thousands." The *New York Times* reported that "the country [paused] to sympathize with Southern California" after the devastating earthquake.[81] Moving beyond mere commiseration, Americans sprang to action. Within five days after the trembler, the Salvation Army was feeding upward of one hundred thousand people in affected towns daily.[82] The Red Cross made an appeal for a half-million dollar fund for rehabilitation and reported receiving responses from many citizens across California and the Pacific Northwest.[83] The State Dental Association and the

Dental Reserve Corps provided emergency dental work to alleviate pain for earthquake survivors.[84] And Jewish welfare organizations held a two-day "Town Fair" for thousands of guests, featuring a "brilliant program of entertainment and merrymaking," to benefit the Compton earthquake victims.[85] All levels of participation—from local individuals to statewide organizations to the federal government—were integral to Compton's recovery.

The federal government's involvement was notably broad, supplementing the work of everyday citizens and relief organizations. Roused in the early morning by the news of the earthquake, President Franklin Delano Roosevelt immediately ordered "every facility of the Federal Government" to be put behind relief work.[86] He directed the army, navy, and public health service to give all possible assistance and the USS *California* dispersed 230 men to Compton. The Department of the Treasury authorized California banks to advance cash to relieve the devastation and provide food, medicine, and other necessities of life.[87] Two weeks later, the president signed a $5 million relief resolution for immediate repairs and restoration of damaged buildings in the earthquake area.[88]

Federal aid in times of crises had precedents, but this time, due to the international economic crisis, the federal funds did not cover the materials and labor necessary for the rebuilding, causing stress among local officials.[89] At an Enterprise School District board meeting, the trustees worried that the district would have "very little opportunity of securing any Public Works money"—which would have only amounted to about 30 percent of the rebuilding—because, according to secretary of the interior Harold Ickes, who oversaw the funds, the Pacific states had already received more than their year's quota.[90] Though the earthquake brought national attention and sympathy, federal funds could serve as only one piece of the effort needed for the area's recovery.

The State of California also offered help. On learning of the quake, Governor James Rolph, Jr., hurried onto an airplane from Sacramento to Los Angeles, where he surveyed the distressed area with his emergency relief work committee. Pheba Crawford Splivalo, state director of social welfare, established a missing persons and welfare bureau in Long Beach and ordered all available welfare workers in San Francisco and Sacramento to report there for duty.[91] Through their immediate response and ongoing efforts, California state agencies helped the quake area citizens in their recovery process.

No single entity could fix Compton alone. The combination of self-help activities and outside aid rebuilt the town. Within a few months of the March quake, parts of the town were running again. In fact, in September, just five months later, residents held a three-day celebration for their rapid recovery. While the Compton event could not compare to Long Beach's much larger fundraising celebration, "Neptune's Electrical Extravaganza," Comptonites took time to dedicate the new county office building, to listen to the lieutenant governor's lauding of the town, hold a mutt dog derby, dance in the street, and watch a vaudeville performance. Topping off the events, a "mystery student rider" crashed a speeding motorcycle through a flaming half-inch board wall.[92] Even though their town remained in shambles, residents found ways to celebrate, exhibiting their close communal ties.

Not all the recovery happened within the first few months. City hall did not reopen until April 13, 1934, when Comptonites dedicated it on the site of the original building, destroyed thirteen months earlier. The construction operations for city hall cost approximately $50,000 for which the Federal Civil Works Administration supplied all the labor and a portion of the materials. The town itself spent approximately $17,000 to provide a substantial and attractive building of "modern design of which its citizens could be proud."[93] The new building was designed in the classic, and widely reproduced, New Deal modern architectural style. Some of the rebuilding after the quake improved the town, while other new structures would prove to be false façades.

As Compton's school districts attempted to rebuild their decimated infrastructure, they encountered severe difficulty finding the money to complete these projects. During the Depression, California had already cut spending on public education. The constitutionally guaranteed funds became a target when James Rolph became governor in 1931. Citing the crippling economic circumstances, the new governor beseeched the legislature to cut costs everywhere and to amend the California Constitution to lessen state school appropriations. While the legislature maintained the constitution, lawmakers did cut school allocations and the department of education's budget. In a March 1933 article published by the department, Vierling Kersey, superintendent of public instruction, posed the pressing question: "Shall public schools in California be closed?" In the article, he explained that the demands for relief from taxes, strengthened by local taxpayers' associations, resulted in a decrease of almost $10 million in public school expenditures for the 1931–32 school year. The next school year saw an even more dramatic decrease, close to an additional $50 million. Some California districts could not afford to keep their school doors open for the shortest required term. Others required teachers to instruct large classes with minimal supplies.[94] In response to this obvious crisis in school financing, California voters passed a constitutional amendment in June 1933. The amendment eliminated county taxes for funding public education, instead sending that money to the state's general fund to be apportioned out.

The Depression opened new roles for government intervention, and the earthquake compounded the economic problems, further changing the relationship of local communities to the state and national governments. For example, the quake ushered in a new set of regulations for all California school buildings, not just those directly hit. After the earthquake, the state investigated all its schools and found, in the words of Southern California scholar and resident LaRee Caughey, "an object lesson proving how not to build in earthquake country."[95] Geologist William Putnam discovered that schools across California were particularly vulnerable because of their poor construction and design flaws. In most schools, "wide spans were used for classroom floors in multistory buildings and at the same time outer walls were weakened through the extensive use of large windows."[96] Making these structures sound became a priority in the rebuilding efforts and required more funds. In response, the state legislature passed the Field Act in 1933, ending conventional building practices. This law "required all new public school construction to be highly earthquake resistive and provided for competent professional supervision and inspection of construction."[97] Hiring supervisors was removed from local hands. In May 1933, California legislators also passed a law creating regulations for buildings other than schools.

The Field Act altered California in terms of both safety codes and political structures. The legislature—and many of the voters—felt that these new regulations benefited Californians in the long run. First, the new buildings were stronger and, second, the regulations preemptively prevented an entire community from having to rebuild. The new legislation also relocated more power to Sacramento by giving the state the power to control new building construction and placing supervisory powers with the State Division of Architecture. In conjunction with the 1933 Civil Service Act, which required that only state-employed engineers and architects work on state projects, the laws mandated that the management of these projects and jobs be squarely under state control.[98]

In order to afford rebuilding to these higher standards, Compton's school districts needed external help, and in turn the districts became drawn into deeper dependent relationships with state agencies, the federal government, and private creditors. The state provided funding through emergency Average Daily Attendance funds.[99] The federal government funneled money to Compton through the State Emergency Relief Administration (SERA), and later through its successor the WPA. Responsible for the entire state of California, only a portion of these agencies' money and labor could go to rebuilding the school districts that served Compton.[100] Yet, though limited, the external aid continued to help pay for the schools' rehabilitations. In 1936, Compton City School District planned to spend almost $30,000 on beautification programs for school grounds, with all but $2,315 of that money coming from the WPA.[101] The federal Reconstruction Finance Corporation also provided funds to erect the school buildings as well as other facilities such as athletic fields.[102] In providing funds and labor for Compton's public school needs, the federal government became a much-needed ally. In 1937 the people of Compton renamed Compton Junior High School as Roosevelt Junior High to honor the administration that had been generous with assistance after the earthquake.[103]

Despite the national attention and outside aid, the reconstruction of many of the schools did not happen as quickly as some of the other rebuilding, and the slow process affected Compton area students. According to the Compton Union High School and Junior College yearbook, local sports teams and the marching band were "hampered somewhat by inadequate playing fields" and the drama club no longer had the "fine stage and auditorium" in which to perform, instead having to use a converted old annex as the playhouse.[104] One photo caption in the 1934 yearbook read, "All is wreckage, everywhere the same pile of debris, silent but staunch witness to the tremendous forces of nature. Here students once laughed, were gay, and went forth into life with high spirit. Now only rocks, bricks, steel and desolation!"[105] After paying for the prom and other expenses, the surplus in the student treasury dues was "generously added" to the student body assistance in the rebuilding of the school plant.[106] In spring 1934, a little over a year after the earthquake, the editors of the annual acknowledged that the earthquake acted as a "severe deterrent" to the progress of the school, which they believed had previously been "one of the best equipped schools and most beautiful grounds in the state."[107]

The students endured the destruction of their learning environment. In the 1934 yearbook, the students at the high school and junior college designed their chronicle around the reconstruction because "the tearing down of the demolished structures on the campus and the consequent rebuilding of them into new and modern edifices provided them with an unusual opportunity to portray this as it applied to student life." A hand-drawn picture of the revamping introduced each section of the annual because the editors wished to "call attention to the inevitable progress in construction." The editors saw parallels between the reconstruction and their lives as students: "Students in the progressive age are continually tearing down old and obsolete ideas and beliefs and are replacing them with constructive aid to the perpetuation of the life which we live."[108] Despite the positive outlook of the editors, Compton students had to withstand the realities of the earthquake destruction and the lack of funding for rebuilding. The effort promised students that their lives—both academic and personal—would no longer be "hampered" by the effects of the quake.

Even with the problems in funding, construction on Compton High School and Junior College buildings was completed in 1936, and local residents inaugurated the buildings with much fanfare.[109] Before the new plant even opened, many observers held in high esteem its architecture and planning. Contemporary columnist Lee Shippey credited these achievements to the combination of government aid, SERA labor, and local funds, arguing that the amalgamation of these sources allowed for the construction of a "much handsomer and better equipped school than [Compton] could have afforded otherwise." Not only was the façade of Compton's new school more aesthetically pleasing, but the inside was "scientifically planned for best results in lighting, ventilation, helpful and artistic color schemes and convenience."[110] The new facilities could actually mirror, and even enhance, the district's progressive plan for education. In the earthquake's wake sprung some positive results.

Though Shippey and others heralded the fruits of federal and state funds, in reality these sources were insufficient to complete the rebuilding of all Compton's schools, and the districts had to take out large loans. While seemingly unavoidable, these debts would prove debilitating for the town. Almost immediately local leaders looked for ways to escape the albatross. In 1937, the *Compton Herald* reported that Compton City School District appealed to the federal government to forgive some of its debt. Due to the combination of preexisting bonds and those issued for reconstruction after the earthquake, the district was almost $1 million in the red, a deficit it had to pay off from the proceeds of taxes on only $12 million of assessed valuation.[111] School board member Harry Billings spearheaded an unsuccessful campaign to have the state excuse a portion of the bonds to help relieve the financial crisis.

Figure 10. The new school plant for Compton Union High School and Junior College District. Courtesy Archives & Special Collections, California State University, Dominguez Hills.

The situation appeared dire, and board members' hands seemed tied—they could not get their unpaid bills forgiven and as a result had to incur new ones. Even with the already enormous debt, district officials asked voters less than a year later to pass a $400,000 bond for construction of auditoriums and other classrooms, as well as improvements on existing buildings. Though voters rejected the bond measure, its very presence on the ballot indicated the magnitude of the community's financial predicament as well as administrators' desperation to find solutions.[112]

The town's lack of commercial revenues affected the financing of Compton's public school systems. In 1937 the Compton Chamber of Commerce conducted a survey to discover why Compton housewives shopped in Los Angeles rather than locally. The survey found that Compton stores did not carry enough stock.[113] By shopping elsewhere, Compton residents starved their town and their schools of a sufficient tax base.

The state legislature had tried to restructure the tax system because the

Great Depression caused a crisis in collecting revenues. The state needed to offer relief for the overburdened residents since property taxes remained high even though property values had dropped. This mismatch led to foreclosures that in turn led to dwindling revenues on the county level. The state also needed additional funds. In June 1933 California voters enacted the Riley-Stewart plan, which more than doubled state support for schools and lowered local property taxes. Throughout the 1930s, the plan ushered in a series of other state levies, including a corporation income tax and a private car tax. It also introduced a sales tax, which was instrumental in funding California's public schools during the Great Depression. But even this new source of income fell short and as a result in 1935 the state added several new levies, including a personal income tax. California looked to taxation as a means for relief from the depths of the staggering economic emergency. Once the economic crisis passed, local property taxes would carry the burden once again.

Even with state aid, Comptonites needed to offset the difference. By 1939, Compton had the highest tax rate for large school districts in California.[114] One year later, Compton topped the list of Los Angeles' forty-five municipalities. Compton's rate was $6.33, while twenty-five miles northeast, West Covina stood at the bottom with a total rate of only $3.58, and "only four or five" had rates in excess of $6.00. While the town government's own rate was lower than many others, it also boasted a record-high school tax rate and multiple other levies, a red flag for potential migrants.[115] Compton's deficient commercial base and its recovery from the earthquake caused it to have high property and school taxes, distinguishing it negatively from the rest of Los Angeles County's towns.

Despite state and federal assistance, Comptonites and their school districts remained burdened for years by the massive debts accrued from their schools' reconstruction. Looking to outside help while desperately trying to hold onto local control, residents struggled to define Compton—who would live there, how community funds would be spent, and how public schools would progress. But when community resources proved insufficient, Comptonites accepted assistance from state and federal agencies. This relationship would expand during World War II, but then residents would push back on the implications of taking that aid.

Most important in this period, Compton's financial burdens persisted. Almost twenty years after the 1933 earthquake, the *Los Angeles Examiner* reported that Compton's school officials had been "'buying a dead horse' . . .

paying back the loans and adding to their outmoded classrooms with bunga-lows and war surplus buildings."[116] Compton's schools stood on shaky ground due to a confluence of the earthquake and the economic crisis. The tensions between preserving local control and desiring outside assistance further ex-acerbated the situation. These issues would become even more pronounced during World War II.

The Fastest Growing Town

Ron Finger was born in 1941 in Jefferson, Iowa, where his father worked as a plant manager for Economy Forms Corporation, a company that made steel forms for buildings, bridges, and concrete work. In 1948 the company needed a supervisor for its newly opened Los Angeles office. Los Angeles was exploding in building development, and Economy Forms wanted to be a part of that surge. The Finger family were also drawn to LA's postwar boom and the opportunities it opened for them. Soon, Ron, his younger brother, and their parents were packing their bags to move to California. Their first stop was a duplex rental house in the Los Angeles County suburb of Bell Gardens. It soon became apparent, though, that the house would be woefully inadequate for their needs, as it shared its only bathroom with another family. So after a year the family moved to Compton, where they rented half of a two-family stucco house on West Spruce Street. The home sat on a corner lot and, Ron recollected, had a "very, very small front yard," a "good-sized backyard," and "a few flowers along the house." The house had two bedrooms, a kitchen, and dining and living areas. It was modest, but after Bell Gardens it seemed ideal.[1]

Pamela Grimm's parents also saw moving to Compton as a step up the social ladder. Living temporarily in Oregon after leaving their native South Dakota, Grimm's parents soon left for California's Southland, first living in downtown Los Angeles, then in the suburb of Lynwood, and finally settling in Compton. They chose Compton because they heard it was "the place to be," and so they "moved up." Once there they realized the town had a lot to offer their young family other than just status. Families filled the neighborhood and the children often played outside together. It was also affordable; the family could live on one salary. Pam's father worked at Northrop Aircrafts in nearby Hawthorne, which was not surprising since, according to Pam, "everybody's family had parents who worked in aircrafts." Pam's mother was a homemaker and a stay-at-home mother while her children were in their formative years, but once they reached secondary school she began a career selling real estate.[2]

Shirley Holmes Knopf also grew up in Compton at mid-century, and she remembered her childhood town as "idyllic," because, despite the rapid development of the town, vacant lots remained where Shirley and her friends could "build forts and throw dirt clods." She enjoyed the security that came from living in a small community. Her family became particularly well known as they became deeply involved with local sports, something on which many Compton residents prided themselves. Her father taught at local schools: first at Lynwood High and then at the combined Compton High School and Junior College, after which he became director of athletics at the junior college when it got its own campus. Shirley's mom stayed home with her children until they entered secondary school and then she too taught in Compton schools.[3]

In many ways, these three young families exemplified Compton residents at mid-century. Moving to California for employment, they settled in the town because it offered the opportunity to live in a small community, with all the benefits of a major metropolitan center. For some, like Shirley's parents, Compton was the place of their employment, but for most it was not. Instead, its housing stock and geographic proximity to the more industrialized and commercialized areas of Los Angeles County made it a bedroom suburb. Compton residents commuted easily to a number of industries that boomed in Los Angeles and in doing so, they maintained Compton as a traditional suburb, a place of homes and parks, separate from the metropolitan center.

Living in a suburb carried social cache and moving to a town like Compton was often part of establishing one's family on a higher rung of the social ladder. This social mobility was marked in several ways. First, the actual act of moving outside city bounds served as a meaningful emblem. Living in a house was also important. Though the Fingers, Grimms, and Knopfs were not all homeowners, they approximated the suburban dream as best they could, renting a home rather than an apartment in a complex. The families were also white, and an important factor in choosing Compton was that it was an overwhelmingly white town. During and after World War II, Compton's location just south of Watts put it in the pathway of an expanding black community, and the town's white residents bolstered their cohesion by blocking the migration of African Americans into their town. Comptonites took pride in their white residential suburb that served as a hub to surrounding industrial areas. Compton residents struggled to preserve and protect this identity. Compton was a place where people could afford this dream.

Compton's affordability was also a curse. Though Southern California experienced a boom during and after World War II, Compton did not benefit in the same way as other parts of the metropolitan area because it did not house large industries from which to raise tax revenues. The war resurrected the United States economy, but it created mixed social and economic results on the home front.[4] Compton exemplified this point: the defense industry offered new employment opportunities for residents, but unchecked expansion sometimes offset these gains.

Population growth put a strain on Compton schools. With more residential properties came less money and more children to serve. Moreover, Compton's modest houses did not generate much revenue for the town. As a result, with the return of soldiers, annexation of land, and increase in births, Compton's population growth became unmanageable. The town expanded rapidly, earning the title of fastest growing municipality in California's Southland in 1949.[5] To provide even the most basic educational services, the Compton area school districts needed to add more facilities, but the town and districts' fiscal capacity was insufficient for the task. In order to increase the number of school plants and playgrounds, Compton issued bonds, raised tax rates, and accepted state and federal aid. These measures were a way to address the town's problems, but they were hardly solutions as they added to the already existing debt and put pressure on the local populace.

The domestic results of World War II—including the broad patterns of job-related migration, exacerbated racial tensions, and the changed relationships among federal, state, and local governments—created local battles at home, work, and school. From its founding, Compton was an insular community, and this bigotry became even more acute as it developed a more dependent relationship with the outside world. Residents' sense of community—a positive force in rebuilding after the 1933 earthquake—became negative in responding to newcomers. The desire to preserve local power led voters to retain many aspects of the existing government structure, including the multiple overlapping school districts.[6] This inefficient bureaucratic organization handicapped local leaders' ability to address the town's rapid changes. The maintenance of separate districts added to the existing economic difficulties and facilitated the segregation of racial groups. Compton area voters overlooked the ways in which unification could have alleviated the pressures of their overcrowded schools and declining tax revenues, electing instead to act defensively by shoring up segregated schooling.

The West at Mid-Century

Even before America's entry into the war, the West profited from the U.S. policy of "cash and carry," which permitted the Allies to purchase war materials from American manufacturers on condition that they pay cash and carry the goods on their own ships. This program particularly enhanced aircraft manufacturers in Los Angeles because they could safely expand their factories with the money from the prepaid aircraft.[7]

This investment in western industries heightened during the war, when more than $40 billion (most of it from the federal government) flowed into the region. Wartime mobilization created millions of jobs in the West, with the greatest employment expansion occurring in aircraft, shipbuilding, petroleum, steel, and electrical manufacturing. The opportunities prompted a mass migration, and the area grew four times faster than the rest of the nation. The population of California, Oregon, and Washington swelled by more than a third between 1941 and 1945. From 1939 to 1945, the number of industrial workers in the region increased 280 percent. Industrial establishments climbed from 5,594 to 7,500, and the average number of employees per plant rose from twenty-seven to seventy-seven.[8] Aircraft employment went from 15,930 at the end of 1938 to over 120,000 when the United States entered the war in December 1941.[9]

Los Angeles became the West's leading city, spurred by $11 billion in war contracts between 1939 and 1945, representing 10 percent of the nation's entire war production, but all parts of the metropolitan area did not benefit equally. Though Los Angeles was a "young" area prior to World War II, it housed several industries before the war. It was during the war, however, that the city achieved a "world rank." LA became second only to Detroit in auto assembly, and second only to Akron in tire and rubber production.[10] But minimal industry opened in Compton specifically, so the town's tax capacity did not grow. The town's residential character and proximity to industry did affect it, however. The passage of Title IV of the 1941 Housing Act allowed for the federal government to give loans to home builders in areas close to defense industries. During the program's first year, California received over one-quarter of the funds.[11]

Defense industries that had taken root in Southern California during World War II remained perfectly aligned to meet postwar manufacturing demands. With the beginning of the Korean War and the heightening of the Cold War, federal defense spending increased, speeding the pace of urban development in both the West and the South. Scared of being vulnerable to attack because of concentrating too many resources in one area and cognizant of the increasing clout of these regions, the federal government, in the words of historians Robert Self and Thomas Sugrue, "rewrote the geography of American industry."[12]

While much of Los Angeles manufacturing was connected to the military-industrial complex, it was not exclusively so. Los Angeles remained strongly open shop and its anti-union right-to-work laws attracted a variety of companies to the region. After the war, Los Angeles experienced the flourishing of the aircraft, motion picture, automobile, rubber, petroleum, furniture, food processing, and electronics industries. As a result, during this period, Los Angeles County became the nation's largest manufacturing county; the City of Angels rivaled New York and Chicago as a leading U.S. industrial center.[13]

The availability in job opportunities, low property taxes, and cheap land resulted in the Los Angeles area's continued population growth and housing crunch. Federal spending also changed the region as it had funded the interstate highway system, facilitating the mass movement of Americans, and established Social Security, aiding people in retiring comfortably in warm weather areas. Like most cities across the country, Los Angeles experienced a severe housing shortage, with the return of military personnel and formerly interned Japanese Americans. Though Angelenos did not embrace the returning internees with open arms, they did welcome the veterans. County towns like Compton offered veteran services such as aid in securing housing and jobs.[14]

Due to the mushrooming population, the Los Angeles region needed to multiply its housing construction. In 1947 Los Angeles city proper became the "busiest builder," with its number of construction permits dwarfing those in New York and Chicago.[15] By 1948, the city's building program surpassed those of "nine of the largest western cities combined," but even with this colossal push, the city could not meet the demand for housing.[16] Developers looked to unoccupied land, such as that in and around Compton, for space for new houses.

Federal policies fueled the housing boom. The Federal Housing Administration (FHA) gave developers mortgage insurance and extended repayment periods, which allowed real estate developers to create vast new subdivisions of affordable, single-family homes. As a result, new housing developments covered the Southern California landscape. The federal government also helped people afford to buy houses through the FHA, Home Owners' Loan Corporation (HOLC), and Veterans Administration (VA). The VA guaranteed a portion of each loan, which made many veterans eligible as well as protected the lender's investment. The HOLC also helped families avert foreclosures by buying old mortgages and giving out new loans to homeowners. The FHA issued mortgages on its own, nearly a million between 1945 and 1949 and increasing those numbers in the 1950s. Prior to these programs, the price of buying a home was simply prohibitive for most Americans.[17]

Not everyone benefited equally from these programs. Aid for home buying went on racial lines, with agencies deeming African Americans risky loan recipients. Across the country, realtors drew red lines around black areas, marking these parcels as no-loan territories.[18] These racial lines extended to Los Angeles's rental market. As a result of the housing discrimination, at mid-century, most of the Los Angeles black population was confined to three communities—the Central Avenue district (south of downtown), Watts (seven miles south of downtown), and West Adams area (five miles southwest of downtown). Latinos were similarly relegated to segregated barrios. As the waves of new migrants saturated these areas, however, African Americans and Latinos pushed for more housing opportunities.[19] Furthermore, as the regional economy contracted, blacks were the first fired from industrial employment, resulting in an increased number of blacks in poverty, which in turn affected the areas in which they lived. Those who could afford to, thus, tried to move from the increasingly poverty-stricken neighborhoods. Given Compton's geographic location and its relatively affordable suburban living, it was not surprising that blacks pushed against the town's racial restrictions. It was equally predictable that Compton's white residents would hold their ground.

As part of the Los Angeles boom, Compton and its population swelled. Developers expanded the town outward, incorporating almost 1,500 acres through fifty-one annexations between 1940 and 1950. Though almost completely vacant when incorporated, the land soon became developed for residential use.[20] According to the Compton Chamber of Commerce, local residents frequented the town's two banks, rode the two bus lines in the city, worshipped at the forty-five churches, participated in sixty-two clubs and organizations, and read one weekly and one semiweekly local newspaper.[21]

Compton's business district did not grow enough, and as a result, its stores could not adequately supply the enlarged populace. In April 1942, residents complained about Compton's overcrowded business district and advocated shopping in areas with fewer crowds.[22] Though the town's retail sales skyrocketed, once again Compton's inadequate infrastructure caused the town to lose out on the potential financial benefits of population growth. Shoppers spent their money—including the sales tax—elsewhere. In Los Angeles County, sales and property taxes went to local towns to pay for schooling. So other towns collected Compton residents' sales tax and Compton's growing population could not use it for their needs.

An increase in housing mirrored the population boom. In 1940 Compton had 5,118 dwellings. By 1950 that number had increased almost threefold. Though numbers increased, the characteristics of the dwellings remained the same. In 1940, the vast majority—84 percent, 4,293 structures—were single-family detached homes, with only 367 (7 percent) designed for more than two families. Even the few apartment buildings were small; no apartment buildings for more than twenty families existed within town limits.[23] According to the 1950 census Compton had 14,743 dwelling units. The census reported information for all but 400 of these homes. Out of this number, only 5,285 (37 percent) were built before 1940, with the remaining 63 percent built after. Of that group, 43 percent (6,165 dwellings) were constructed after 1945: 30 percent were renter-occupied, with the vast majority of the rest (a handful remained vacant and for sale) occupied by their owners.[24] The figure on leasing was a bit deceiving, as renting was uncommon in the town; Victory Park, the federally constructed housing project, comprised most of the town's rental property.[25] Rental or owner-occupied, most of Compton's hous-

Table 1. Compton Population Growth, 1940–50

Year	Population	Increase over 1940 population (%)
1940	16,198	—
1944	23,460	45
1947	32,254	99
1948	42,789	164
1950	47,991	196

Sources: 1940 Census; "Special Census of Compton, California, April 21, 1944"; "Special Census of Compton, California, October 7, 1947"; "Special Census of Compton, California, October 28, 1948"; 1950 Census.

ing was new and family-occupied. Once dominated by farms, Compton's parcels were now covered by homes.

While new home construction increased municipal and school budgets, the needs of the growing population stretched the coffers. The state had begun to take on some of the burden of funding public education, but with the improved economic conditions following the Great Depression and World War II, local property taxes once again provided the largest share of school support. In order to raise funds, Compton's city council passed a tax on theater and dance hall tickets. When the District Court of Appeals ruled that this ordinance needed resident approval, the council put it before the voters and it passed. Compton also requested five special censuses between 1946 and 1955, in order to receive a larger allotment of the state's gas tax.[26] The growth in population meant more aid. With each special census taken, and each significant addition in population recorded, the State Department of Motor Vehicles increased Compton's gasoline tax allotment, with which Compton could improve its infrastructure. These allotments, however, were small compared to the changes needed as a result of the population growth.

The town wanted this money to fulfill a large demand for public works projects and municipal agencies. New homes meant new streets that needed sewers, cleaning, and lights. More people and more houses also required more police officers and firefighters. Even the town's building department grew in order to handle the traffic of people requesting construction permits. Though clearly in need of increased services, the town could not pay to support them, and as a result many necessary public works projects lagged. In 1949, Compton city manager K. B. Douglass thanked the city council and mayor for finally making the projects possible as "many of which have been neglected for years."[27] That year, and for the next few years, the town spent 65 percent of its budget on public safety and public works projects.[28]

Compton's class composition remained similar to that of the previous decade. Reflecting national trends, the education level of residents rose between 1940 and 1950, with, for the first time, the majority of people attaining high school diplomas. Even so, Compton remained a blue-collar town, with only a small portion of the population employed as professional workers.[29] Almost 60 percent of the population held "working-class jobs," which included the census categories of craftsmen, foremen, operatives, service workers, and farm workers. Among Los Angeles metropolitan suburbs with a population of over 15,000 at the time, Compton had the third highest percentage of working-class residents, behind only Belvedere and South Gate.[30] In both the

1940 and 1950 census reports, the largest percentage of Compton workers were employed in manufacturing, with 22 percent and 30 percent respectively.[31] A survey of the Compton Union High School and Junior College District found that the majority of employed persons worked in "some phase of industrial, commercial, or service occupation allied to industry." Most of these workers commuted to work outside the town's limits.[32] Compton was a blue-collar bedroom community, which carried a desirable sociocultural marking but not a deep tax base to go along with it.

Maintaining Local Control

Compton residents tried to control their town's types of housing. Three motives shaped their preference for single-family homes. First, this style of house defined suburbia, while high-rise buildings were its antithesis. Second, Comptonites worried about the bottom line. Single-family homes meant better property values and taxes than multifamily residences and also meant Compton's new residents would come from a higher economic status. Third, the number of people who could be housed in a large apartment building would surely stretch the town beyond its means.

While city council members recognized the need for more housing in 1942, they disagreed with Washington about the types of residences that best suited their community: the federal government wanted to build high-rise apartment buildings; Compton residents desired single-family homes. In January 1942, at a city council meeting, federal administrators P. E. Edwards and Ed Criley presented maps and plans of the proposed Compton housing project for defense workers. According to Edwards and Criley, the government would build multifamily units, all without "garages or individual fencing." The council members unanimously agreed that this building type was "very undesirable" because the new homes would not be up to community standards and therefore would lower the value of the community.[33] As much as was in their power to do so, the members of the Compton city council tried to block construction of these units.

Though dependent on external aid, city council members sought to maintain some semblance of control over their community. Just one month after the approval of the defense housing, city council members unanimously passed a resolution opposing another set of proposed government housing. In order to protest the federal government plan, city attorney Ralph Pierson traveled to Washington to meet government officials. Federal commissioners assured him that five- and six-hundred unit projects would not be located in Compton.[34] Previously Compton residents and the federal government had built a reciprocal relationship, but in this case Compton residents bristled against outsiders' influence.

Tension also appeared when the city manager traveled to San Francisco with Mayor Tarleton and City Attorney Pierson to interview federal officials regarding the proposed housing units. At a Compton city council meeting, City Manager Park reported on the agreement reached up north: no federally funded buildings would be erected on one of the disputed properties, but, Compton and federal administrators disagreed on the other. According to Park, the Compton representatives had tried to persuade the federal bureaucrats to obtain property west of the still-contested land for the unit, but federal officials would not concede to such a proposition because of the delay it would cause in construction. They did agree, however, to a change in architectural design that would give the houses pitched roofs instead of the flat type proposed previously.[35]

Despite their resolve, residents could not completely control their town's residential construction. The fact remained that war workers needed housing. As a result of the overpopulation, in June 1942, city hall issued the largest building permit in the history of Compton: $1,565,000 to cover construction of homes for defense workers at the FHA Victory Park housing complex. Completed and dedicated in March 1944, Victory Park's eighty acres of bare land turned into a community of five hundred units, housing 1,900 people. Designed to house a regiment of war workers in the "Arsenal of Democracy," the project also included an $88,000 administration building and school.[36] The federal government also designed Victory Park to house three teachers' families, four classrooms, and a kindergarten.[37] The small allotment of teachers revealed the federal government's minimal support for the broader community.

Yet even Victory Park could not alleviate Compton's acute housing shortage. Just a year and a half after the announcement of the housing development, another big subdivision for war workers was publicized. The new development raised all of the ordinary suspicions of white Comptonites' concerns over maintaining the character of their town, and added another volatile issue to the mix. The new Palm Lanes Homes federal public housing project planned for the area of Willowbrook would house black families. Willowbrook's white residents fiercely fought emergency war worker housing

Figure 11. Exterior of Victory Park housing development, circa 1940. Courtesy
Huntington Library.

in their community. They declared their community would remain white at
all cost and even proposed annexing their unincorporated area to Compton
in order to keep the housing out.[38]

The announcements of these housing developments were made during
the height of Los Angeles wartime anxiety. During this period, racialized
fears heightened due to a combination of increased xenophobia and racism;
Los Angeles experienced migration of blacks from the South, and of Latinos
from Mexico. The black population more than doubled from 1940 to 1946—
from 63,000 to over 133,000. In 1940, however, more than 84 percent of the
black population lived in the area of poorest housing in the city.[39] Los Angeles exemplified the West's increasing diversity and changes that ran headlong
into the deeply ingrained prejudices that also defined the region.[40]

In 1942, the same year that the United States interned 120,000 Japanese
Americans from the West Coast, local newspapers blamed Latino youths for
the death of José Diaz, a Mexican national, in Los Angeles. Linking the murder to a supposed crime wave, local police enforcement targeted Latino

Figure 12. Students in the Victory Park School, circa 1940. Courtesy Huntington Library.

youths, arresting hundreds of these youngsters and prosecuting twenty-two for Diaz's death. Known as the Sleepy Lagoon case, this trial exemplified the racist attitudes of many white Angelenos. An all-Anglo jury convicted three Latinos of first-degree murder, nine of second-degree murder, and five of assault. Defense attorneys immediately appealed the verdicts, which a judge overturned in October 1944.

The Sleepy Lagoon case has been considered a pre-cursor to the June 1943 disturbances, now dubbed the Zoot Suit riots. For four days, white servicemen and civilians beat and stripped black and Latino youths. The Zoot Suiters, with their unique style of dress, represented a challenge to social and cultural norms and, as such, were tagged as troublemakers. For the black and Latino youth who chose this style, "the zoot suit symbolized a generation filling the streets, taking up more than the space allotted them," according to scholar R. J. Smith.[41] While Latinos and blacks had suffered racial discrimination in California for a long time, World War II caused a rapid increase in both groups' population as Los Angeles as a whole mushroomed. Having a more noticeable presence in the job force, the schools, and the streets made both groups appear as larger threats to white workers' jobs, housing opportunities, and class status. That year, in Los Angeles, Detroit, and communities across the United States, racial anxieties played out on the streets.[42]

Compton residents were especially anxious about the threat represented by black migrants. The announcement about Palm Lanes was made just six months after the Zoot Suit riots. One month after Palm Lanes was proposed, Gordon Corey, a representative of a group of Compton residents, addressed the Compton city council regarding the situation. He expressed dismay that blacks would be living nearby. City Attorney Pierson thought the situation was serious enough that Comptonites should protest. He also suggested that the city officials check deeds to see if racial restrictions were included and still valid. City Treasurer Adams volunteered to obtain the information regarding racial requirements in the tracts in the northwest part of the city. Pierson further suggested that all the town's property deeds be obtained from a title company.[43] One week later, after checking the records, Adams reported that all restrictions had expired on the lots lying in the northwest part of the town, except for the racial limitations, which were perpetual. Adams thought that approximately fifty to sixty tracts in the town contained no guidelines, however. The members of the city council unanimously authorized to have all properties in Compton reviewed so that they could renew any expired restrictions.[44]

Despite Comptonites' efforts, the Palm Lane homes opened as planned, bringing African Americans into the vicinity, and more important, into the area's schools. The housing development had 300 units, shelter for 600 adults and approximately 1,250 children. Of the adults, 80 percent were from the southern states of Louisiana, Oklahoma, Arkansas, Mississippi, Alabama, and Texas.[45] Their children, starting in junior high school, attended classes with the students of Compton, the very situation white residents had worked aggressively to prevent.

Area residents had better luck in blocking another federal housing project intended to house African Americans. In January 1945, officials made an announcement of a new National Housing Agency project, which would serve 1,200 black families. Location of the new project placed it in close proximity to Compton and Lynwood. Private contractors would construct the dwelling for qualified war workers only and the units would be of one, two, and three bedrooms. M. H. Driggers, local National Housing Agency head, added fuel to the fire of opposition by stating, "While it is expected that these homes will be rented or sold to Negroes, other developments in the future may meet similar housing needs of Chinese, Mexicans, and possibly American Japanese."[46]

Compton residents wanted a white town, and this suggestion shocked them. Even though the *Compton Journal* asserted that opposition centered on the tax exempt status of federal housing projects, the two main arguments that defined the opposition were that property values would be adversely affected, and inadequate transportation facilities existed.[47] The area's Chambers of Commerce, Junior Chambers of Commerce, and civic, fraternal and professional organizations mobilized to block the development. White residents wanted federal support, but they wanted it on their own terms. While they did not stop the construction of these houses, they exerted authority over how their town would look. And, more important, by stopping the federally supported large apartment complexes, Comptonites essentially regulated the area's socioeconomic and racial demographics. They wanted jurisdiction over who would be their neighbors and with whom their children would attend school. Given such efforts, it was no coincidence that despite the large increase in population, Compton remained a vastly working-class white town.

Challengers to the projects believed it was unnecessary to build the war homes in the Compton and Lynwood area and instead argued the neighborhood of Watts was more appropriate because it had better transportation and more immediate access to war plants where African Americans worked. In March 1942 the Southern Pacific Railroad had begun providing free transportation to three thousand blacks who were employed as section hands.[48] Inevitably many of these black workers lived in the Watts community. The area was becoming decisively more black, but as late as 1940, the population of Watts was still ethnically integrated, with 50 percent white (including Mexican Americans), 35 percent black, 13 percent Mexican immigrants, and 1.5 percent Asian.[49] In Compton the number of nonwhite residents declined from seventy-two in 1940, to only six in 1944—three men and three women. The principal cause of this decrease was the relocation of persons of Japanese descent, sixty-nine of whom lived in Compton in 1940.[50] According to the 1940 Census, the "other races" comprised less than 1 percent of Compton's population, but the presence of a few black residents in Northwest Compton, along with its proximity to Watts, threatened further infiltration, according to 1939–40 HOLC survey maps.[51]

Racial segregation extended to the Latino population in Compton. While town and national population figures did not include Latinos as a separate category and instead counted them as white, Compton residents were clear on whom they considered white and the segregation in Compton's housing reflected this attitude. Prior to 1940, the vast majority of Compton's Latino population resided in one area on the northernmost boundary of the town. A 1927 survey of real estate agents noted that "a few Mexicans and Japanese lived in the old part of the city."[52] There were forty-four families with Spanish surnames in the Compton barrio in 1936, sixty-two in 1940, and eighty in 1946. After 1940 there was some evidence of Latino "infiltration" into the western half of Compton.[53]

Project adversaries used popular assumptions about race to frame their rhetoric. They complained that the decision to place the houses in the Compton and Lynwood areas "appears calculated to create racial tensions deliberately and to do so without regard for established residential and property areas and is a policy blind to the decline of property values that would be visited upon small home owners in the affected area."[54] The residents of Compton had strictly controlled *who* lived in their town. They resented the government's challenge to these restrictions. Unstated in Comptonites' advocating for Watts to be the new home was the effect on the schools. The Los Angeles City School District served Watts, unlike its neighboring Willowbrook. Compton residents accepted federal money in building homes when it fit into their social structure and pushed against federal intervention when it defied the conformity.

Local residents' vocal protests caught the attention of federal administrators. Recognizing the local area's opposition to the establishment of the National Housing Agency project, the federal government considered the community's ideas. Local people aired the problems surrounding the contemplated housing project at a meeting spearheaded by representatives of the Compton Chamber of Commerce. At the conclusion of the meeting, government officials agreed that no project would be built south of Watts at that time.[55] Compton residents accepted this arrangement. While Watts neighbored Compton, and African Americans would live nearby, the threat of children mixing in their schools did not exist.

Suburbia meant having local control, and Compton residents continued to define this in racial terms, as they prided themselves for living in a " 'lily-white' community."[56] In order to ensure a continuation of this, white Comptonites resorted to a variety of measures. In 1947 the Compton Chamber of Commerce and local realtors sought to bind their entire area with 99-year racial covenants. The groups claimed that the FHA backed their efforts, though administrators at the federal agency denied any agreement. Even so, the chamber and the realtors continued to use the FHA as cover for their actions. The Los Angeles area National Association for the Advancement of Colored People (NAACP) along with other groups such as the United Steelworkers challenged the chamber and realtors' assertion that occupancy by blacks depreciated real estate values, citing surveys by the National Association of Real Estate Boards and government housing statistics.[57] Even when confronted with these facts, white Comptonites resisted demographic change in their town; for example, in September 1948 the African American Whitley family found their newly purchased home in Compton vandalized with oil poured across their front yard and "KEEP OUT NEGRO" painted in red on their house.[58] Bottles filled with paint were routinely thrown at homes occupied by blacks and at homes where whites had indicated that they would sell to blacks.[59]

Reinforcing the Dependent Relationship

Changing demographics stood among other concerns. The dearth of funds coupled with the increase of students also burdened the area school districts. As early as 1940, the Compton City School District (still in debt from the earthquake) had to authorize the building of new classrooms.[60] In 1941, the Enterprise School District presented a request for the construction of two more bungalows at Roosevelt Junior High School.[61] So overcrowded were Compton's junior high schools that in November 1943 superintendent O. Scott Thompson announced that more than four hundred students were being instructed in auditoriums and cafeterias.[62] For the 1943–44 school year, pupil enrollment in Compton Union was 18,895, up from 15,291 in 1941–42.[63]

Finding funding for all the necessary construction became a Herculean task. In many cases, the area's school districts sought federal government aid, which was available because area families were connected to national defense. In 1942, the Enterprise School District received just over $19,000 to pay operating costs and teacher salaries.[64] At the beginning of the next school year, to meet expenditure increases brought on by the "unprecedented influx" of war workers to Compton, the Compton City School District collected $38,000 in federal funds.[65] That same year, the federal government agreed to grant a $13,000 lunch subsidy in the same district.[66] Nine months later, superintendent of Compton City School District Ardella B. Tibby announced an appropriation of $68,597 to the Compton school administration, bringing a total of $301,297 to eleven Compton elementary schools. The largest grant compensated the school district for the education of the hundreds of war workers' children.[67] A similar appropriation the next year again covered the education for those students.[68] Many Comptonites gladly accepted this aid for two reasons: first, it fit their requests and second, it did not challenge their social fabric.

Compton school districts also required money to modernize their school facilities. Charles Bursch, chief of the California Department of Education, Division of Schoolhouse Planning, estimated that a million dollars was necessary to revamp the five junior high schools—Roosevelt, Clearwater, Lynwood, Willowbrook, and Enterprise—and Compton High School and Junior College. He emphasized the existing facilities' inadequacies. "I was shocked at what I found," he told his audience of five hundred pupils receiving instruction in the junior college auditorium in 1945. He discovered the building needs throughout the district's schools were "serious." He continued: "Kitchens in the cafeterias are congested and difficult to work in. There is not enough storage space. Administration facilities are crowded. The boys' and girls' physical education facilities, especially showers, dressing, and rest rooms, form an outrageously inadequate situation with, in one instance, 280 pupils being crowded into one exercise hour in one cramped quarters and without provision to change their clothes." He was most appalled with "the science situation," which he considered "an emergency situation." He explained: "You are taking too great a risk by having chemicals in such close quarters."[69] The federal government did provide the district and its component districts with some funds, but these monies did not even approximate the necessary amount.[70] In consequence, Compton simply did not have the money to pay for the essential additions to its public school systems.

The state and federal assistance in response to the massive in-migration did not cover Compton's needs, and, as with the rebuilding from the quake, residents shouldered the burden. In 1943, Compton City School District applied for just over $50,000 for its maintenance and operation fund but only received $34,500 in federal aid.[71] To supplement the federal monies, the residents of the area school districts assumed further debt. In 1944, the Lynwood Elementary School District passed a $250,000 bond issue by a majority of 411 votes, with only 37 residents voting against it. Of this amount, $130,000 went for an expansion program to relieve the overcrowded condition of elementary schools. The remaining $120,000 provided for retirement of the 1933 debt, still on the books from the quake.[72]

The wartime population boom beset the schools with more problems. The rapidly growing population only worsened the school districts' already dire financial situation. Not surprisingly, Compton area districts' expenditures per pupil continuously ranked at the bottom of those in Los Angeles County. As soon as the Compton City School District administrators learned of the possibility of new homes, they contacted the Department of Defense Public Works asking about the federal government's plans for assisting the district. At a school board meeting in January 1942, school administrator Stevens reported on district officials' "considerable correspondence" and meetings with government bureaucrats, pleading with the federal government to provide funding for additional school facilities and supplies that would become necessary if the new homes were built.[73] Administrators had learned from past lessons: their community would shift, and they had to act early to ensure that they received what their schools needed. Unable to provide the necessary materials themselves, district administrators lobbied outside agencies.

In addition to creating a new financial burden, World War II also influenced the daily activities and curriculum of California school districts, as it necessitated an increase in vocational education. The war deepened the relationship between public schools and federal government, a connection that caused uneasiness among Californians. Compton schools were a prime example of both. The army selected Compton Junior College for a "STAR unit," for servicemen from all over the country. Compton Junior College housed, fed, and educated 1,933 soldiers. In addition, Compton Junior College conducted a flight training school. The college also added war production classes, featuring such subjects as first aid, machine shop, welding, carpentry, sheet metal, and radio, to prepare workers for employment in defense plants in surrounding areas.[74]

Compton Junior College students worked on campus in war jobs through a partnership with the Firestone Tire and Rubber Company. Firestone used one school building for manufacturing self-sealing gas tanks for the army air corps.[75] Originally, Firestone designed the project for only one summer, when approximately one hundred young men worked in the factory eight hours a day under the supervision of Compton Union. It soon became understood, however, that at the beginning of the school year the students would split their time between school and work. This was not the only change. Firestone also enlarged the program to include young women. Hundreds of students went to school for the minimum of four hours and worked in the factory for four hours. The company paid the students and covered the cost of renting, operating, and maintaining the buildings.

The partnership altered the students' education. When Firestone proposed this extension into the school year, superintendent of Compton Union O. Scott Thompson stated that the district would do it to help the war effort—and to give students one "side of education sadly lacking in our schools—firsthand experience for youth on a real job, under real work conditions."[76] While students engaged in war work and learned real-life skills, they also lost time from their formal schooling. In addition, the war established a system of reciprocal obligation between the Compton community and the federal government. The citizens of Compton contributed to war production, and the federal government subsidized their endeavors.

Younger students in the Compton area participated in the war effort, too. In cooperation with the town and chamber of commerce "Food for Victory" program, faculties and students of Roosevelt, Enterprise, and Willowbrook junior high schools launched plans for extensive student participation. Through its garden classes each school signed up every student for at least one type of activity. Students could raise victory gardens, fowl, or small animals; can, dry, or preserve fruit or vegetables; or work for a farmer, dairyman, or other food producer. Students also sold war bonds and stamps. In April 1943, three schools—Kelly, Abbott, and Rosecrans—each sold enough bonds and stamps to buy a Jeep, and the Mayo school reported purchase of four Jeeps.[77]

For some in Compton schools, involvement in the war was more immediate. Faculty, students, and alumni fought overseas. Eighteen teachers at Compton Junior College and High School went on active duty in the army, navy, or marines. In addition, approximately seven hundred students who would have been attending some level of Compton Junior College left school to perform war-related work. During the early days of U.S. involvement, faculty members registered students under the Selective Service Act and, for the war's duration, a military advisor remained on campus to counsel students about entering the armed services.[78] The war changed the fabric of Compton's school community and played an everyday part in students' lives.

Military service coupled with the astronomic growth of the student population caused a teaching shortage in the Compton area school districts. At a regular meeting of the Enterprise School District, the members of the school board waived for the duration of the armed conflict the requirement that all district employees live within district borders.[79] A few months later, the director of the junior college broached the problem of loss of teachers to war service, particularly from the physical science department. He indicated that if any more of these teachers were drafted, he could neither replace them nor continue their classes. After a long discussion of the problem, the board suggested that he file requests for deferment, known as 42-A forms, with regard to these particular teachers.[80] At the same time, the members of Compton City School District board of trustees worried about having enough classrooms to fit all the new residents. At a Compton City board of education meeting, the superintendent reported that it was necessary to employ at least ten new teachers to meet increased enrollment.[81] The district had a hard time retaining these teachers because, in addition to war service, many left for better paying districts.[82] Compton's relatively limited funds and small tax capacity coupled with its preexisting debt and rapid growth created a spate of nearly insolvable problems.

After the war the Compton Union High School and Junior College School District labored to serve this ever-growing citizenry, serving Compton and the other four component elementary districts. For the 1948–49 school year, the total area of the high school and junior college district covered roughly twenty-five square miles and had a population over 160,000, the third largest district in the county, exceeded only by Los Angeles and Long Beach. The average daily number of students was 16,304 in the elementary school district and 5,487 in the junior high and high schools.[83] A 1949 report described Compton Union: "the schools are overcrowded, buildings and equipment are inadequate, personnel is limited, classes are large and the demands for new educational services for more individuals in more courses are increasing daily. The district faces increasing enrollments and increasing demands for added educational services for an unpredictable number of years ahead."[84] In 1949, the Enterprise School District held twenty-four double-session classes and had only forty-seven teachers for 1,229 students.[85] The Willowbrook School District had only twenty-eight classrooms and predicted a need for eighty by 1952.[86] The Compton City School District used six converted residences for classrooms and even this was not enough to alleviate the overcrowding. Washington Elementary School in Compton, originally built to accommodate 550 students, by 1949 had a registration of 1,350. Compton City superintendent Ardella Tibby told state senators that when she first went to Compton there were "acres of vegetables, but now—in their place—we have acres of children."[87] In fact, between 1940 and 1950, Compton Union had the greatest population increase in California.[88]

Due to the funding structures, none of the districts in (and including) Compton Union could competently accommodate the area's many students. As in districts across Southern California and the country, the physical facilities did not match the unceasing population growth, and school administrators perpetually asked for more funds simply to keep school doors open. Unfortunately the money did not flow easily, and Compton's debt multiplied. Dealing with the brimming, inefficient school system meant continually requesting government funds and accumulating debt. In the immediate postwar years, all the area school districts procured money and supplies from a variety of sources, just as they had in the years following the earthquake and during the war. In 1947 and subsequent years, the state government allocated funds for general maintenance and operation of schools. The voters also looked inward, approving bond issues.[89] The districts approved using the funds for construction, for both new buildings and additions to existing structures.[90]

Federal assistance was limited, however. Despite the fact that the issue of direct federal aid to public education had been raised periodically, it consistently failed to pass Congress.[91] Even with lobbying efforts from national organizations, such as the powerful National Education Association, the federal government continued its abstinence from funding public schools in the immediate postwar years, though Compton received federal aid other ways. For example, in 1947, Compton Union received twenty-two war surplus buildings from the Federal Works Progress Administration. The already burdensome financial crisis persisted in the immediate postwar years. By continuously assuming debt, Compton voters essentially mortgaged the town's future.

Maintaining Separate Schools

Growth was not the only change for Compton's population. Its demographics changed over the decade, despite residents' continued efforts to keep their town a white space. In 1950 whites comprised the vast majority of the town's population, with 95 percent of residents identifying themselves as white and 4.5 percent (2,180) identifying themselves as black. Though the number of African Americans remained small compared to the town's overall population, this figure represented a significant change, since no African Americans had lived in Compton in 1940. The shift over the decade did not reflect a loosening of racial discrimination, but resulted from Compton's annexation of territories in which black families already lived as well as building new housing on that land and selling those houses to blacks.[92]

Housing patterns created segregated elementary schools, as the residents of the Compton City School District remained predominantly white.[93] In 1949 Compton elementary schools served only sixteen black children, twelve of whom were students at the Washington School, on Compton's west side. While in 1880 California law ended de jure segregation of black and Native American children in schools, many districts continued practices of separation. Furthermore, many California school districts, including Pasadena, maintained separate schools for children of Mexican descent. Others, like Compton and Los Angeles, used attendance zones to produce segregation. Although in 1946 California courts in *Mendez et al. v. Westminster* struck down laws that required segregation of Mexican students in California, residential segregation in places like Compton meant that they too attended separate schools.[94] As the Washington School exemplified, school administrators drew school zones based closely on neighborhoods, and therefore racial restrictions prevented young residents from attending racially integrated schools. Administrators justified these zones because "parents, naturally and understandably, [were] inclined to keep their boys and girls as near to them as possible that they may watch over and safeguard their development," according to Lloyd Morrisett, the author of the 1949 survey of the Compton area schools.[95] While many reasons existed to want students to go to neighborhood schools, such as convenience and the role of the school in building community, in suburban Compton "safeguarding" their children also became a not-so-veiled code for segregating by race.

In school politics residents also used the language of home rule to maintain a segregated school system. To do so, residents held onto their structure of multiple school districts despite their costly inefficiencies. Defining their community required controlling their schools. The 1949 survey of the districts found that if the separate elementary and secondary districts were to serve their populations effectively, they would need a "well-developed overall plan of budgeting both revenues and expenditures, and the cooperation of the several governing boards." The report also explained that "in the past no such plan has been developed or followed."[96] In an area with low fiscal capacity, the structure of maintaining multiple districts became an impediment in handling the communities they served.

Residents could not, however, prevent the integration of the high school and junior college because the entire area fed into Compton Union. Los Angeles's black population was growing and African Americans pushed away from overcrowded and neglected housing available within city limits. The demographic shift affected the high school district. Neighboring areas to Compton, including the Willowbrook and Enterprise neighborhoods and school districts (which fed into the Compton Union), became increasingly black. Enterprise first enrolled African Americans in spring 1947. By 1948, it had 117 black students.[97]

The Willowbrook School District integrated earlier. Willowbrook was an unincorporated area that included some five thousand residents. In 1941 the district was 80 percent white, 10 percent Latino, and 10 percent African American. White inhabitants were alarmed by the shift and tried unsuccessfully in 1945 and 1946 to restrict migration of blacks from Los Angeles by incorporating the area. Instead, Willowbrook became one of the places where developers built tracts of single family houses specifically for blacks to buy, including the Carver Manor tract of 250 homes.[98] While the district included African Americans at the beginning of the 1940s, the black population more than doubled in the last few years of the decade. Willowbrook served 254 African American students in the 1945–46 school year and 510 by February 1949.[99] This did not translate into integrated schools, however. The district had an "open policy of segregation" with "inferior opportunities" afforded to black students, according to the *Los Angeles Sentinel*.[100]

The schools became means for increasing social distance between groups within the community, as well as a forum for fighting it. African Americans confronted the discrimination and inequalities through a variety of avenues. In 1946 an African American ran for the first time for a seat on the board of trustees of the Willowbrook district.[101] In February 1947 black students walked out of Compton Junior College during an assembly when the scheduled program depicted an African American in a stereotypical manner.[102] According to Morrisett's 1949 study, "the moving of negro families into a previously all-white neighborhood create[d] certain problems and tensions."[103] These tensions would increase as the proportion of the minority population increased. As students came of age they entered Compton High School. Many of the white parents in the union district reacted angrily to this prospect.

Willowbrook also stood out as home to residents of different socioeconomic classes. According to Morrisett's report, many Willowbrook residents had recently migrated from the South. The parents of Willowbrook Junior High School pupils had educational levels lower than for the Compton Union

High School District as a whole. The Willowbrook School District also had a much lower percentage of parents working in professional jobs. That year, less than 2 percent of employed fathers in Willowbrook and just over 2 percent of employed mothers worked in professional positions. The district's junior high school pupils reported that 32 percent of their fathers were skilled workers, 23 percent semiskilled, and almost 15 percent unskilled laborers. The 1.9 percent of fathers employed in some professional vocation was the smallest in the high school district.[104]

As Willowbrook, and, to some extent, its neighboring area of Enterprise, became increasingly poor, residents required expanded social services. A 1946 survey instituted by the Welfare Council of Metropolitan Los Angeles, a department of the Los Angeles Community Welfare Federation, classified Willowbrook and Enterprise as "areas of low social rank," in which the investigators found "concentrated juvenile and adult delinquency, high transiency, high tuberculosis rates, high incidence of other diseases, poor housing and many other factors of social disorganization."[105]

Due to whites' desire to maintain racially and economically homogeneous schools, Compton Union soon became embroiled in a problem of reorganization. At the end of 1949, the overwhelmingly white Lynwood School District considered creating its own unified district. For years many Lynwood residents had resented "being attached to Compton's coat tails," according to long-time Lynwood resident and politician J. Jack Willard.[106] Proponents argued that the realignment would give them better control over their children's schools and prevent students above the tenth grade from traveling to school outside their own community.[107] Opponents contended that the current high school district operated efficiently and that the change would result in financial and operational turmoil for it, especially because Lynwood's assessed valuation was greater than those of the other districts except Compton City. Despite opposition from the board, Lynwood residents voted in 1949 to withdraw in July 1950 from Compton Union and to create their own unified district, with its own junior and senior high schools. At the time of its secession, Lynwood was approximately 3.5 square miles with a population of more than 26,000. Another component district, Paramount followed suit three years later.[108]

Lynwood's withdrawal from the high school district raised a number of immediate and difficult organizational problems. The district administrators first tackled the issue of where the teachers would work. Would they stay in Compton or go to Lynwood? Furthermore, in which district, or both, did they have seniority rights? After some debate, administrators permitted the teachers to choose the district in which they wished to teach. Many remained in the Compton schools to retain their seniority rights.[109] Administrators also had to deal with the students who resided in Compton City School District and who under past practice would have attended Lynwood Junior High School. The union district administrators decided "under no circumstance" to let these students attend the new Lynwood district because losing students meant forfeiting state funds.[110] Last, there was the issue of the new junior high school that Compton Union had built in Lynwood in 1940. After countless arguments over the ownership of the building and its contents, Compton Union stripped the building of its furnishings, causing Lynwood to raise its tax rates to refurbish the school.[111] The hostile split between the districts created more difficulties for the already beleaguered Compton Union district.

Union district administrators' biggest problem was the junior college. Compton Junior College, like the high school, had been serving Compton, Lynwood, Willowbrook, Paramount, and Enterprise. When the districts for the junior college and high school were coterminous it was possible for them to have a single administration. This changed, however, when Lynwood created its own unified school district: while Lynwood seceded from the high school district, it remained under the junior college's jurisdiction. As a result, in 1950 the Compton Junior College had to establish its own separate district with its own governing board.[112] Already inefficient because of its many administrations, the Compton area schools added yet another bureaucracy.

The reorganization of the districts' administrations brought under scrutiny the schools' educational structure. When it did, critics condemned the 6-4-4 structure. Under that configuration, the first six years were governed by the boards of the component elementary districts and the last eight by the union district.[113] The main argument in favor of this configuration was that it provided "better articulation" between the several units. The problem with implementing this system in the Compton area was that it would require "most favorable and cooperative relationships" among the school districts. The 1949 survey found that Compton schools needed more cooperation because "under existing conditions of community rivalries, lack of staff and faculty coordination, the problem of articulation [was] a major impediment to a good school program."[114] Because each district governed its own curriculum and monitored its own teachers, opponents of the system felt that the 6-4-4 configuration created discontinuities and gaps in the educational program. One school district, they argued, would allow a more coherent curriculum.

Critics also rebuked the system for its top-heavy administration. In 1950, the *Compton Herald American* argued in a boldly titled editorial, "Crisis in Schools," that the multiple-district organization remained unnecessarily expensive and confusing. Having five separate districts—four elementary and one high school—required five different school boards, five superintendents, five supervisory and administrative staffs, five purchasing departments, and five operational staffs. The article called for district unification to simplify the school system, which in turn would alleviate exorbitant costs, provide a more standardized education, and facilitate easier public cooperation and understanding. Opponents also asserted that having multiple districts meant that each could encumber more bonds and levy its own taxes, which they labeled "excessive." On top of what they paid to town, state, and federal governments, residents paid taxes to their elementary, secondary, and junior college districts separately. Since all these districts had financial strains, each taxed at a high rate. Critics advocated unifying the districts to promote "efficiency and economy."[115]

Progressive era reformers across the nation had sought to centralize educational systems. Often the initial cry for reform came after the discovery of corruption, believing that centralization could promote efficient and honest school administrations. Others adopted the rhetoric of educational innovation as means for justifying reorganization. Either way, school districts across the country reorganized their administrations.[116]

Not everyone disparaged the 6-4-4 plan. L. V. Koos, professor of secondary education at the University of Chicago, called Compton secondary school education "the bright spot of America" when addressing Compton's Rotary Club in February 1949. His praise continued: "I have studied the 8-3-3 and 8-4-2 plans but have found the 6-4-4 program at Compton to be the best." According to Koos, educators around the country could learn from Compton, because, he believed, "the educational problems of Compton are not only of this city and the state of California but they fit the nation. In other words, when the educational problems of Compton are solved, the school problems of the nation are solved."[117] For Koos, the 6-4-4 was a model of pedagogical and developmental enlightenment because it grouped students in what he deemed a more educationally appropriate manner, allowing students at both the early junior high years (grades seven and eight) and the early high school/junior college years (grades eleven and twelve) to be exposed to more advanced students and better trained teachers.

Raw politics contributed to the difficulties in the school districts in other ways too, as seen in the case of the hiring and firing of Willowbrook's super-intendent in the early 1950s. At the April 15, 1953 meeting of the Willow-brook board of trustees, trustee member Dr. Smith asserted that the board had already asked Superintendent L. B. Jones to resign because it "seems ut-terly impossible for him to make the efficient head that we find so necessary at this time to help our children." According to Smith, "Mr. Jones was brought here for political reasons" and made "certain commitments to get the posi-tion." Smith continued by listing a series of actions he construed as "gross incompetency . . . [and] they certainly were not for the good of the school district." Another board member, Mr. Lundy, insisted on the record showing that Dr. Smith did not speak for the entire board.[118] This kind of political in-fighting and inept leadership further hindered area school districts already overwhelmed by enormous debts and inefficient bureaucracies.

Taxing the School Systems

While locals wrangled over school politics, over-enrollment continued to plague the districts in the postwar years, leaving many elementary schools operating on half-day sessions, with half the students attending school in the morning and half in the afternoon. In the secondary schools the student-to-teacher ratio was "excessively high" with classes "too large to allow attention to be given to individual pupils."[119] Although Compton Union had the great-est population increase of any area in the state from 1940 to 1950, during this time the voters of the secondary school district repeatedly voted down school bond issues.[120] Comptonites became unwilling to take on yet more debt be-cause they were already in the red.

Hesitancy to owe more money did not necessarily translate into aloofness toward schools, and not all Compton residents remained complacent with their school districts. The founding of Compton's Citizens Committee exem-plifies the community involvement. One day in 1950, two residents of Comp-ton, William Holland, a car dealer, and W. Howard Day, a real estate broker, sat in Day's car waiting to drive his daughter home from school. The two men became appalled as they watched the girl leave her overcrowded school and wade through the mud to the car. In response to the "chaotic school condi-tions," the two men organized the committee, where they were joined by businessmen, union members, doctors, and clubwomen.[121] These disparate factions coalesced because improving their schools meant improving their suburb. Better schools meant more than better education. It also meant better home values, which would attract more affluent neighbors. As a result, the town's fiscal capacity would grow, the schools would improve, and the cycle would continue.

The committee made tangible improvements to the districts. By conducting a cost analysis, the group uncovered the need for a $10 million school expansion program. Together the members fought to get a $7.6 million school bond passed, eventually getting the state to agree to give the remaining $2.4 million. Members also worked to change the school administrators for the first time in twenty-five years. They believed that fresh blood could invigorate the overtaxed educational systems. For all the committee's hard work, *Look* magazine named Compton an "All-America City" in January 1953, because, like the other ten honored recipients, Compton's citizens had improved their town.[122]

The initiative inspired by Holland and Day allowed school administrators to address the overwhelming problems of the secondary district and build new schools for the first time since the earthquake rebuilding in the 1930s. In 1951 Compton Union began construction on Centennial High, a second comprehensive senior high school, and on Whaley Junior High, in order to eliminate the double-day sessions at Roosevelt Junior High. Other building projects quickly followed, including a $3.5 million campus for the junior college, which had previously shared space with Compton High. During the late 1940s and early 1950s, Compton residents would see the building of six new elementary schools, two junior highs, and one new high school.[123] These developments did not happen equally across all the area districts, however, because some districts remained poorer than others. For example, in 1954, in response to a one year student population increase of 26 percent, the cash-strapped Enterprise School District was forced to ask its voters for yet another tax rate increase.[124]

Overcrowding created more than the need for buildings. It also produced a teacher shortage. In this case, Compton area districts were desperate enough to go beyond the societal norms to hire male elementary school teachers. In 1951, the heavy student load forced the Willowbrook School District to try "a new experiment," hiring a male teacher for a second grade class.[125] Male elementary teachers were extremely rare in the mid-twentieth century because men were deemed more appropriate for content-oriented classes on the secondary level. Teaching at the elementary level was sex-typed as woman's work and few contemporaries objected.[126] But Willowbrook was in a bind. Finding teachers was difficult and Willowbrook paid its teachers less than many other Los Angeles districts, making it even harder to attract qualified candidates.

Naturally, all these new construction projects and new hires required funding. Still in debt from both the earthquake repair and the rapid expansion during the war era, Compton residents paid for some of the work by floating even more bonds and asking for more state and federal aid.[127] Help did come. Compton received an allotment of funds from a 1949 statewide $250 million state school aid bond issue. Additional federal allocations came after Congress passed Public Law 874, which provided assistance to communities where activities by the federal government, particularly in regard to military production, created an extra load on the schools.[128]

While Holland and Day had improved the schools, they did not accomplish everything they had set out to do—they could not get the districts to unify. Brought to the forefront by the secessions of Lynwood and Paramount elementary districts, unification remained a persistent and contentious debate for many years to follow.[129] Opponents also questioned whether the people living in the areas that would be unified had "similar problems, community interests, background and aspirations?"[130] This not so thinly veiled language referred directly to the differing racial compositions of the different component areas. White Comptonites worked aggressively to maintain the segregated districts. The issue of federal funds arose in the perennial debate over unification. Receiving federal funds became a key argument against unifying Compton's school districts. Opponents of unification argued that districts received more funds as separate entities than they would as one, while proponents advised that running four districts cost much more than running one. The structure of school funding became an impediment to lowering school districts' budgets and simplifying their administrations.

Maintaining separation came with a price. Managing Compton's municipal services, especially the school districts, remained problematic because of financial troubles. Despite the already high tax rates, in 1954, the Compton Union board of trustees ordered a special election to secure approval for an additional assessment that would more than double the amount ordinarily authorized by law without such an election. The current tax rate for the secondary district was 30 cents on each $100 of taxable income, and the board members proposed to add 60 cents more. This levy was only one of many borne by Compton residents who also were responsible for taxes by the Compton City School District, as well as an obligation to retire district bond issues and repay money borrowed from the state for construction purposes. According to the board members, Compton Union needed to increase its tax rate because the assessed valuation of property in the district was the lowest of the eighteen high school districts in Los Angeles County and the monies collected were insufficient for the schools' needs. In turn the district had to tax property more heavily to amass the same amount of money and provide similar programs because, as tax revenues fell, student population increased, provoking an unprecedented financial crisis.[131]

The board members issued a statement appealing for a sizable amount because the district's "financial plight" was a "serious one." To justify their request, they pointed to the 1953–54 school year, during which the high school district shortened its school day from six to five periods, reduced the number of teachers, and slashed the available supplies and materials.[132] Board members also claimed that "teachers in the schools have on numerous occasions approached the board to urge the calling of an election to increase the tax rate in order that they might do a better job of teaching." Board members explained that the teachers did not make these requests out of self-promotion; teachers were not asking for salary increases "even though salaries here are not as high as in most surrounding districts."[133] In a record turnout of seven thousand, Compton voters approved, by a margin of only thirty-one votes, the increase in the maximum tax rate.[134] Even in this moment of real crisis, Compton voters divided almost equally over whether to aid their schools. In garnering this vote, the board of trustees blamed the financial problems on the Lynwood and Paramount withdrawals, but clearly the fiscal strains had begun much earlier.

In order to deal with the financial woes and to assuage the tax burden, many area residents continued to argue for district unification. In November 1954, Compton Union and City school boards authorized a survey to determine whether the formation of a single school district would save money for the taxpayers. Fourteen months later, the California Taxpayers' Association found that joining the districts was not a clear-cut issue. The arguments for unification continued to be the same: a standardized, continuous curriculum and more efficient and economical expenditure of school funds. Opponents of the change doubted that the process would result in these benefits. Their reasoning against amalgamation continued to center on the loss of local control as well as a desire to avoid the complicated reorganization process.[135]

What was unique about this round of fights was that this time resistance to unification came from *both* white and black parents. At the same time that many African Americans nationally celebrated the Supreme Court's decision in *Brown v. Board of Education* for outlawing segregated schools, the parents of the majority-black Enterprise and Willowbrook elementary school districts resisted unification. Of course, being opposed to integration was not necessarily the same thing as being for segregation. Rather, black parents, teachers, and community leaders in the Enterprise School District, and across the country, understood the costs of integration on jobs, students, and schools, and they felt that community control was the way to protect their interests on all three fronts, even though home rule required the districts to take the maximum state aid.[136]

Local control was a longstanding theme in the history of Compton and the history of black education. In Boston in the nineteenth century, and in the post-emancipation South, African Americans sought control over their schools as part of a larger trend in black political history to retain independence and institutional control.[137] The debate over whether to push for equalization or integration continued in the mid-twentieth century and would reappear in the late 1960s and 1970s when African Americans felt that the emphasis on desegregation had compromised the education of their children. In New York City, for example, a group of black parents and community members clamored for community control of schools.[138] Support for community control in the Enterprise and Willowbrook districts did not occur in the framework of these two major flash points. Rather, the resistance to integration in Compton area schools occurred over a decade before the disillusionment from *Brown* fully developed.

Parents felt Enterprise placed a higher priority on education than did other districts. They saw this difference in the variation of money spent among the three component elementary school districts. In the school year of the report, 1955–56, the assessed valuation per Average Daily Attendance (ADA) in the largely black populated Willowbrook was $1,662, while in the white Compton City it was $4,781. But, in Enterprise, ADA was the most, $9,458 per student. In the 1953–54 Willowbrook had the lowest assessed valuation per pupil in its category. Once again, Enterprise was heads above the other districts in the area. It was tenth on the list while Compton was twenty-third. In 1955–56, Enterprise again budgeted more per pupil than Willowbrook or Compton City.[139] This high spending would change with unification because during that process, the assessed valuations would equalize the elementary districts to the level of the high school district, which ranked below its equivalent districts.[140] Due to a combination of factors, including the disparity of assessed valuation and expenditures, the Compton area districts did not unify.[141] Despite the same outcome, this round of unification fights differed because the involved parties' had shifted their rhetoric.

Expenditures were not the only reason black residents wished to remain autonomous. Enterprise parents' and board members' eagerness to retain a separate district also stemmed from the desire to maintain a black-run school district, one that could highlight and promote black educational accomplishments. This priority emerged a couple of years later when the Enterprise school board named its new elementary school after Ralph J. Bunche, a black academic and civil rights leader. The choice of Bunche was no small decision and was clearly significant in monumentalizing the achievements of a black educator. Among the nominated names not chosen were Washington Irving, Dwight Eisenhower, and Jonas Salk.[142] When the district dedicated the school, the presiding dignitaries pointed out that the name chosen had "become a worldwide symbol for understanding between people."[143] Further showing the district's commitment to promoting and celebrating black accomplishment, the district also mandated that all social studies curriculum include African American history, an innovative plan for its time.[144] Met with an entrenched white power structure, blacks sought to change Compton and its schools in order to fulfill suburbia's promises for their own community.

In the decade following World War II, the Los Angeles metropolitan area continued to grow. People flocked to the region as it became an industrial center *and* a place of suburban growth. Compton became the fastest growing community in the metropolis. Compton residents built on their already strong sense of community and carried with them their expectations of what a suburb *should* be. Suburbia meant a single-family home, quality schools, and safe streets, all in a racially homogeneous space.

At the same time that Compton residents held strongly to their racialized definition of the town, Los Angeles's black population swelled, outgrowing its neighborhoods. Looking for better housing and for a piece of the suburban dream, blacks pushed the limits of racial discrimination. Backed by Supreme Court decisions outlawing racial covenants and emboldened by desires to have their own piece of the dream, African Americans pushed against the region's proscribed racial boundaries. First stop would be Los Angeles's inner-ring suburbs, like Compton, which offered relatively affordable housing stock and the suburban lifestyle.

Whites' racialized vision of suburbia butted squarely against blacks' efforts to move out of the overcrowded city and into the suburbs. In order to stop this flow, or at least to lessen the impact of the shift, white Compton residents looked to protect their suburban dream. As blacks moved into Compton, whites drew the battle lines within their town and used a variety of means to enforce racial separation.

Chapter 3

Separate and Unequal

While picketing the freshly built Compton Crest development, a black GI and his friend a white GI, both just two weeks back from Korea, argued with the white residents. "We're fighting for you—we're facing bullets for you—why can't we live here?"[1] Irate white homeowners told the *California Eagle*, a black newspaper, "We fought all the way from Normandy to the Battle of the Bulge! We have a right to these homes. When we bought 'em—there were big signs all through this Compton tract, 'Highly Restricted!'—that's the way we bought and that's the way it's going to stay!"[2] Though the advertisements for the 535-home tract called out to veterans, the developers never intended to include all of them. Compton Crest, like the rest of the town in 1950, was explicitly meant for whites.[3] Like blacks across the country, African Americans in the Los Angeles area did not accept Compton's racial lines, and, along with some white allies, actively challenged the development's restrictions. In the debates that arose over integrating Compton Crest, both proponents and opponents used their status as veterans to justify their position on residential segregation. Integration was coming to Compton, but not easily.

As they began to reap the benefits of full citizenship after serving their country in wartime, African Americans sought their own suburban dream, and it was no coincidence that they settled in Compton. Like their white predecessors, they desired homeownership, quality schools, and safe streets. Having been segregated into a few overcrowded Los Angeles neighborhoods with the worst housing stock, blacks pushed against decades-long practices of racial discrimination and pursued the promise of the suburbs.[4] While Compton was not an upper-middle-class area, it offered relatively affordable houses and was, both culturally and physically, a step out of the ghetto and toward that middle-class dream.

Though Compton was an improvement from their previous neighborhoods, the full promise of the suburban good life eluded many of the town's black residents. First, African American migration to Compton caused anxiety among some of the white residents, who linked their physical location to their class identity. Yet, while whites resisted, this is not a merely a story of blacks moving in and whites moving out, because not all whites could afford to leave Compton. As a result, this inner-ring suburb became contested ground. Comptonites fought vigorously over where people lived, who got jobs, and what schools children attended. At first whites' racial discrimination kept Compton's black population segregated on the west side of town. This restriction took its toll as it fostered racial prejudices in the school districts, which played out in the classrooms and schoolyards. Community leaders drew school boundaries to reinforce racial lines and the boundaries helped create social divisions. The stratification affected Comptonites' daily lives as schools helped define the physical, cultural, and discursive divisions of the town. The segregation also proved costly for the already financially strapped suburb.

Compton's financial and social status became further threatened as white flight to other suburbs increased. Compton became a more racialized space, carrying all the assumptions that came along with being a minority town. As Compton got blacker, it lost its already precarious toehold on economic stability. Compton's whites took their businesses with them as they left, and new businesses failed to invest in Compton. The black Compton suburbs were not the white Compton suburbs.

Testing the Barrier

Changes in the Los Angeles social geography as well as the 1948 *Shelley v. Kraemer* and the 1953 *Barrows v. Jackson* Supreme Court decisions to eliminate racial covenants directly affected Compton.[5] Many black families earned double incomes, allowing them realistically to set their sights on moving for "an opportunity, a step up."[6] Compton became this step. From 1947 through 1953, Compton annexed a little over two-and-a-half square miles, aiming to increase its tax base through residential and industrial growth.[7] Much of this land was on the town's western edge, adjacent to black communities. Tract developers took advantage of the unrestricted land and built houses that they sold to African Americans.[8] As a result, Compton began to shift away from a virtually all-white citizenry, with a small Latino population, to include a growing population of middle-class African Americans, many from the increasingly impoverished area of Watts. African Americans comprised 17 percent of Compton's community in 1955, and 40 percent just five years later. The town experienced the most profound racial change of any municipality in Los Angeles County during the 1950s precisely because as a working-class area it was within the means of some blacks.

Along with the town's affordability, African Americans were attracted by the suburban promises of a better educational environment for their children and a higher-class status for their families. Even though Compton schools were overcrowded and underfunded, they seemed like an improvement (or at least an equivalent) to what migrating blacks had in their former neighborhoods. Los Angeles city schools were racially gerrymandered and willfully neglected by the local government.[9] Compton's districts were smaller and parents ostensibly could have more of a say in their children's education.

Lifelong Compton resident (and future Compton mayor) Omar Bradley reflected that "living in Compton in the fifties and sixties signaled a successful step toward economic prosperity." He explained that "most blacks who lived there were working-class folk who'd begun their California saga in Watts or Willowbrook," and once they developed "greater economic resources," they moved to the "green and well-manicured" neighborhoods of Compton.[10] According to Bradley, unlike Watts and Willowbrook, Compton became home to an upper class of African Americans who "inspired poorer black families to do better."[11] Another black resident remembered, "for once, the Negro did not move into slums; for once he came into good housing."[12] Compton did not mean that one had fully attained middle-class status, but it was a definite step toward it.

Individual family stories support this notion that the town offered blacks the chance to pursue the suburban American dream. Maxcy and Blondell Filer left Arkansas for California (by way of Indiana) to find a place where they could buy a house with "grass in our front yard."[13] When they moved, in 1953, Compton was one of the few suburbs in the county where blacks settled. Linda Allen's family moved to Compton that same year. When they first settled in Compton there were only three other black families on Caswell Street. Linda attended the local elementary school, Charles Bursch, where most of her classmates and teachers were white.[14]

Fred Cressel was born in Ashdown, Arkansas, a small town near the Texas border. In 1955, at seventeen, Fred visited family in Compton, a vacation that convinced him to stay in California. Once settled, he found a job as a welder (he had already completed trade school) and attended academic classes at night, finishing high school in California. As a welder, Fred worked at Douglas Aircraft, becoming "the first black person hired off the street" for that position. Douglas employed him for fourteen years, during which time he learned how to work with all the "exotic" metals, even becoming one of thirteen specialists who made "all the boosters that go to the moon."[15]

Sylvester Gibbs's experience also demonstrated the early stages of Compton's racial change. In 1952, he bought his first house, and it was in Compton. When he first moved to Southern California he resided in Wilmington, in what they called "the Army barracks" because "veterans had the first privilege for those." As he looked to buy a home in the suburbs, he realized his options were limited. He recalled: "when you looked out in Lakewood, they'd say we only sell to whites. So I moved into Compton in a place that was a corn fields and they built tract homes so mostly blacks moved in and a couple of Mexicans and a few whites."[16]

Lorraine Cervantes's family exemplified this interracial mix. Lorraine's mother was of Mexican descent while her biological father's family came from England. The first few children in the family came from this pairing. After that relationship dissolved, Lorraine's mother began seeing the man Lorraine would come to consider her father, even taking his name as her own. He was African American and he and Lorraine's mother had six children together. At home Lorraine and her family spoke both Spanish and English.

In December 1952, Lorraine moved with her parents and siblings to the Compton area from East Los Angeles, a majority Mexican American area. She was in the middle of sixth grade when her mother and her stepfather bought their first home. Having only rented previously, they jumped at the opportunity to move their large family to 124th Street, between Willowbrook and Wilmington Avenues, in the unincorporated county area of Willowbrook, which Lorraine recalled as being a relatively integrated neighborhood: "White, black, Mexican and Japanese. And there was one Filipino, who was married to a Mexican. A Filipino woman married to a Mexican guy." As a result, the schools were moderately integrated though the teachers remained mostly white. By the time Lorraine reached high school in 1955, her neighborhood school, Centennial High, was "just blacks and Mexicans," however. White families had moved on.[17]

Guarding Homes

Not all Compton's white residents could afford to, or wanted to, leave. Compton was their home, and they wished to protect the space they called their own. The town's relatively affordable housing stock made it a place where people could buy a house. Through homeownership, the residents gained independence and status for their families. And those who stayed often defended their social standing. This experience was not unique to Compton. Historian Thomas Sugrue explains: "rapidly changing neighborhoods in northern cities, particularly those whose white residents could not afford to pick up and move easily, became bloody battlegrounds."[18] Compton shows that this was not just an urban phenomenon but also happened in inner-ring suburbs.

The town's newcomers worried many of Compton's white residents. White resident Pam Grimm first became aware of her family's racial prejudice after she attended a week at a local day camp. During that week she "palled up with a little black girl," and when Pam got home she wanted to call the girl to make a play date. In response her parents called a "family meeting" with her uncle and grandmother to figure out what they were going to do with her. In Grimm's words: "They were scared because they didn't even know her. She was a nice girl . . . they were in alarm, really in alarm." The family forbade Grimm from playing with the black girl.[19]

Some white Comptonites' behavior made Grimm's family look civil by comparison. Despite the claims by town leaders like city manager Harry Scott that Compton was "one of the friendliest cities in a state that is noted for its hospitality to the newcomer," white Compton residents' actions told a different story. Whites employed a variety of tactics—from real estate restrictions, to school zoning plans, to violence—to prevent African Americans from becoming their neighbors or their children's schoolmates.[20] Their targets included both blacks who wished to move to Compton and whites who aided them in the process. In February 1953, several white property owners were beaten and threatened for listing their properties with South Los Angeles Realty Investment Company, a real estate company that sold to both whites and blacks. The *California Eagle*, Los Angeles's black newspaper, called it "a reign of terror," and cited observers on the scene that "certain sections of Compton resembled an armed camp as home owners in the area, goaded on by the Compton Chamber of Commerce, the *Compton Daily Press* and the Ku Klux Klan elements in the district, seemed determined to keep their neighborhood lilly-white [sic] by force and violence."[21] Also citing unnamed members of the community, the *Eagle* noted that white residents had been organizing for some time, holding meetings in homes as well as in the Long-fellow School about how to circumvent the outlawing of racial covenants.[22] The use of the home and the school lent both physical space and rhetorical weight to the protests. Both represented the heart of the community, what residents wanted to defend.

Whites' defense of community continued. In March a group of home-owners dug up a law against peddlers, using it as a basis for arresting two black real estate brokers and three of their salespeople. Despite being on the books for years, the ordinance had never been used against white real estate agents.[23] In response to these actions the *Eagle* ran an editorial declaring "we've got news for Compton." The news: "Compton must face the fact that the Constitution, with its guarantee of equality for all citizens, covers that city, too."[24] The arrests signaled trouble for all real estate agents, not just black agents, and as a result, the fight against the use of the Compton ordinance went beyond the black community. In response to the arrests, locals working in real estate formed the Brokers Protective Committee to defend the rights of licensed property brokers and salespeople to solicit listings.[25] The defendants were acquitted.[26]

Still, whites' hostile behavior continued. In April 1953, unidentified "vandals" left a "vile note" for the Whittaker family who moved to Reeve Street, which was part of the "'forbidden' area south of Olive Street."[27] In May 1953, black homeowners in Compton had to guard their homes as white residents picketed another house on Reeve Street, where a black family had recently moved.[28] According to the *Eagle*, Reeve was a "quiet, nice street of new two and three bedroom homes" inhabited by working-class whites who labored in Los Angeles area shipyards, defense plants, and factories.[29] Comptonites may have tolerated integration in their workplaces, but they actively resisted having it in their neighborhoods and their schools. In fact, the president of the Compton Crest Improvement Association, Joe Williams, was a member of the United Auto Workers, an integrated union that "unconditionally condemned" and ultimately censured him for his actions in picketing the homes of African Americans.[30] Despite the union's pressure, Williams continued. He and other Compton residents would not accept at home and in school what they would allow on the job. Their dislike translated into a constant threat of violence for their new neighbors.

Williams's behavior exemplified the types of conflicts that were occurring across the nation. Whites created homeowners' associations to secure their neighborhood from integration and protect their status as middle-class Americans.[31] At the very same time the battles raged in Compton, the U.S. Supreme Court was still resolving aspects of the case against racial covenants.[32] But, as the clashes on Reeve Street displayed, these encounters had high stakes. While for African Americans moving to the suburbs meant asserting a new class status, for many whites, like the parents of Pam Grimm, having black neighbors meant losing theirs.

The women of Compton, both black and white, actively defended their social standing, their homes, and their families. When Luquella Jackson, the mother in the black family that moved to Reeve Street, put her eleven-year-old daughter Jacqueline to sleep she did so with "a .45 Colt in her cotton dress pocket."[33] And, when a group of white "banner-carrying housewives" marched up and down in front of her home with signs that read such things as "protect our children's homes," Jackson kept her own children inside the house "with a shotgun within easy reach."[34] Promises of peace and security defined the suburban lure and, ironically, that ideal was worth fighting for.

The stories of Compton Crest's integration never made it into the local Compton newspaper or the *Los Angeles Times*. Perhaps the papers' editors did not consider the threats to African Americans newsworthy because such efforts to intimidate were so common, or perhaps it was because they thought their readers would not find the story compelling. The stories did run quite prominently, however, in the *California Eagle*, whose editors clearly saw the battles in Compton Crest as momentous. In spring 1953, the *Eagle* ran a series on Compton's housing battles, with each issue featuring a banner headline as well as numerous pictures and articles. It also published a series of editorials, even calling out the leading Compton newspaper as "leading the agitation for this racial residential segregation."[35]

Yet the *Eagle* hesitated to blame local white residents' racism entirely. The newspaper's writers and editors defined Compton's situation was "an involved one" and they chronicled the nuances of the story. The paper identified Compton as the site where African Americans sought homes and a community where residents "nursed on the myth" that black homeownership destroyed property values. Compton was both a place where a property owners' association "concocted a fantastic scheme of secret mortgages to penalize neighbors who sell to Negroes" and a place where residents made a "sincere, conscientious attempt . . . to put out the fires of racial prejudice before they flare[d] into violence." The molding of Compton's story, however, went beyond its own borders; banks and financial institutions acted "hand in glove with attempts to restrict credit and limit Negro occupancy of homes in Compton." [36] Redlining shaped Compton like it did in many other American cities and suburbs.

Ultimately, according to the *Eagle*, the problem of Compton was "the story of men and women, white and Negro, who [were] caught up in a population trend and who [were] bewildered by what [was] happening." [37] Throughout the town "general fear and panic prevailed [because] everyone thought Compton would become a shantytown overnight," according to a merchant group. [38] White residents fretted that the very presence of African Americans would turn their neighborhoods into ghettos and they did not have to look too far for an example: the nearly all-black neighborhood of Watts stood as a nearby and constant reminder. Once an ethnically and racially integrated space, South Central Los Angeles became increasingly black. During the 1950s, this area, once two separate communities of Watts and South Central, housed approximately 94 percent of the city's black population. [39] As such, the area, in the words of historian Eric Avila, "became synonymous with the black ghetto." [40] For whites, this new conceptualization defined not only Watts but also their own white spaces. They viewed suburbs, like Compton, in opposition to the metropolis. Consequently, many whites rushed to sell their homes at the first sight of a black family moving in down the street. [41] White and black real estate brokers fueled the fire by engaging in the practice of blockbusting, inducing homeowners to sell their property in a panic at prices below market value, usually by exploiting racial prejudices.

Some white, local realtors sought to protect their community from black newcomers. African American Douglas Dollarhide recalled that when he and his family wanted to move to Compton in 1956, he needed a lawyer to help him find a home because a local real estate agent refused to sell him one. Once they bought the house and moved to Compton, the violent prejudice heightened, as, he explained, white Compton residents "would paint swastika stickers on my door." [42] This type of behavior sprung up around the country. "Cross burnings, arson, window breakings, and mobs," as historian Thomas Sugrue has shown, "greeted black newcomers to white neighborhoods in nearly every major northern city between the 1920s and the 1960s." [43] Compton was no different. In June 1953, Mr. and Mrs. Herman White and their two-and-a-half-year-old daughter Francia moved to South Dwight Street in Compton. South Dwight was covered by the Longfellows Homeowners Association, a group of approximately two hundred families dedicated to

Compton, Please Note

Figure 13. Cartoon from *California Eagle*, June 25, 1953.

keeping their neighborhood racially exclusive. A week after they moved in a cross was burned in front of their house. Two days later a rock smashed through one of the home's front windows. Wrapped around the rock was a note saying "You're not wanted" and signed "KKK."[44] That Saturday night "threatening crowds," including a band of "white teenage hoodlums," milled in front of and circled the block around the South Dwight home until three in the morning.[45] In response the *Eagle* ran an editorial cartoon asserting that the "decent citizens" of Los Angeles would beat back "race hate."[46]

The *California Eagle* continued to spotlight incidents in Compton. It reported on both the actions of the attackers and the inaction of the Compton police. On June 25 the *Eagle* asked "Why No Action, Compton Police?"[47] The next week the *Eagle* reported that "while police looked the other way, Compton vandals struck again in two sneak attacks."[48] In one case someone inserted a hose into a mail slot of a house at 502 Aprilla Street when the residents were away. The water flooded the hardwood floors. Whites owned this home and had listed their property with a black real estate broker. In a separate incident at a home owned by a black family, 2504 West Cypress Street, a brick crashed through a kitchen window. At the same home two days later white teenagers threw garbage on and tossed insults toward a ten- and an eleven-year-old playing in the yard. In each case, the residents called the Compton police, who did nothing, claiming the wave of attacks was just the "work of youngsters and pranksters."[49] The *Eagle* perceived the inaction of police as purposely allowing for impunity of whites.

Fear and violence also erupted in Compton's schoolyards. In January 1953, white and black youths fought at the gate of Enterprise Junior High. White youths were stabbed and the police took seventeen black Comptonites into custody, ten of whom were later found guilty of the assaults. Black parents protested the sentencing of four black students to "indeterminate terms in lumber camps," asserting that the black teenagers were singled out unjustly and were being used as an example while the whites involved were allowed to go free.[50] While the court eventually suspended the sentences, those charged still protested the unequal treatment.[51] According to police records and school officials, the white teenagers did not provoke the fight. Rather, the fight occurred when three carloads of black students randomly stopped and beat up the white students. Writers at the *California Eagle* remained skeptical about the purposelessness of the fight, however, and contended it reflected the larger tensions between whites and blacks in Compton.[52] For the white media, racial tension remained unworthy of reporting: the local Compton paper and the *Los Angeles Times* continued their silence. In the next decade, however, racial tensions would become more difficult to ignore.

A few months after the incidents on Reeve and South Dwight Streets and outside Enterprise Junior High, the United States Supreme Court in *Barrows v. Jackson* rejected the use of racial covenants by realtors in Los Angeles. The *Barrows* ruling meant that blacks could move into all-white neighborhoods and towns.[53] The decision had a profound impact on areas close to Watts. Between 1952 and 1955, the nonwhite population of Compton nearly doubled, from 11.6 to 37.6 percent of the town's population. White Comptonites' weak hold on their neighborhoods grew more tenuous, but, despite what the law said, many tried to strengthen their control over Compton.[54]

Behind these numbers lay the fact that, even with the threat of violence, Compton still provided one of the few opportunities for African Americans to move out of the awful living conditions in Los Angeles's historically black neighborhoods. African American migrant Mary Cuthbertson recalled that her husband felt proud of his home in Compton. In her words: "It was a very old house, but being the first house he owned in his lifetime, it just meant a lot to him to *own your own house.*"[55]

Though Compton was a rung above, it still did not completely fulfill the promise of suburbia. When just a boy, for example, Omar Bradley lived with his parents and six siblings in a three-bedroom house in Compton. The bedroom he slept in with his brothers barely accommodated five beds. Even though his family lived in extremely tight quarters, they still saw it as a step up from the "Sardine Days" of their prior living arrangement. The highlight of the Compton house was its "spacious backyard full of thick green grass surrounded by a tall pink brick fence." It was a place the Bradley family could call its own. Bradley recalled: "It was our private playground, a place where we'd turn into Army men or cowboys and Indians. My brother and sisters taught me how to crawl and walk there."[56]

"An Us/Them Thing in Our Town"

Increased population numbers did not translate into integrated schools. Racism manifested in the purposeful racial segregation in the schools. White politicians and school officials strategically zoned the schools and located new school facilities to ensure racial segregation. Originally, Compton High served the entire district. But as the general population grew in the town, and as the school became more integrated, the district opened Centennial High in 1953 to serve Compton's growing black community on the west side. Centennial would serve black students and Compton High would serve whites. Soon this new facility was not enough to keep Compton High segregated, however. As the black population crept toward the town's east side, Compton High was once again integrated. In response, the district opened Dominguez High in 1957 on the east side to serve the white community. Despite its low tax capacity, the town continued to build new facilities.

Segregation affected the students. Grimm remembered: "there was a lot of prejudice among the kids I grew up with. When Compton High came over for our baseball games . . . their drill team was great. It was cool. I mean, they really had the moves and, you know, they were really jazzy. But I remember everybody laughing at them and calling them 'jungle bunnies' and all of that." She continued: "It was an us/them thing in our town, and I don't know how they felt."[57]

White resident Shirley Holmes Knopf recalled that her elementary school was nearly "a hundred percent white," with maybe a couple of black students. By the time she went to Compton High in 1956, she had a few black and Latino classmates. In fall 1958, Knopf's senior year, Compton High had its first black homecoming queen, Nadine "Naddie" Smith. Smith was one of five candidates, competing against three whites and one Latina. The three white candidates split much of the white vote, allowing Smith, the most unlikely candidate, to seize the title, and the Latina candidate to be the runner-up. This is not to say that only African Americans voted for Smith, because, as white resident Shirley Knopf recalled, "Naddie was one of the top people. She was in [the select and exclusive service club] the Chimettes and everything else." [58] The local branch of the NAACP saw the election as worth reporting back to the organization's West Coast field secretary.[59]

Despite Smith's reputation, Knopf remembered her winning as "just a shock to everyone."[60] The evening Smith received her crown at a Compton-Lynwood football game, a white youth reportedly hurled derogatory remarks about her race and "a group of boys of her race allegedly tried to mop up the street near Compton High stadium with him," according to the *Los Angeles Sentinel*.[61] Ron Finger, who was a senior at Compton High that year, remembered that on the day after Smith was elected queen, "on Compton stadium in bright red painting was 'We don't want your nigger queen.'"[62] While Smith's election may have indicated that attitudes were changing slowly among the younger generation (or it may have indicated that the white vote was indeed split), the reaction to her election showed that racism endured in Compton.

The practice of racial segregation occurred in school districts across Los Angeles County and California. Residency determined school zones and neighborhoods were largely segregated. The Los Angeles city board of education purposely placed both schools and students based on race. Even in racially mixed areas, the school district maintained white schools even if it meant students' traveling. This policy, along with residential segregation, ensured racially segregated schools across the district. Furthermore, the conditions of the schools reflected their racial composition. Not surprisingly, the school district was less likely to maintain a school that was predominantly black or Latino.[63]

Other Los Angeles County school districts also maintained segregated schools. Pasadena school district sustained such practices. Although most of the district's residents were affluent middle- and upper-class whites, Pasadena had always had a small black population who worked in the town's resort hotels or as domestics in the town's mansions. During World War II, Pasadena's black population grew alongside Southern California's defense-related economy.[64] As in Compton, white residents of Pasadena resisted the integration of their schools by enforcing racial segregation. As a result, blacks and Latinos lived in the densely populated northwest section of Pasadena.

The racial segregation also reflected class differences; Pasadena's black residents were significantly less affluent than white residents. Whites who recently moved up into the middle class populated the sections bordering the minority-populated northwest, while upper- and upper-middle class whites lived in older sections of Pasadena.[65] The wealthier residents could afford to send their children to private school or to move to other, more segregated, towns if integration encroached on their children's schools. Unlike their richer neighbors, Pasadena's newly minted middle-class whites could not afford either option, however, and as such carefully protected the racial composition of their children's schools, in turn protecting their own tenuous class status.

Racial and class prejudices played into the Pasadena school board's desire to segregate schools. In addition to residential patterns, the board wielded another weapon of segregation; since the 1930s, the Pasadena school district allowed parents to request transfers within the district.[66] White parents used this policy as a ticket to an all-white school. The district maintained such overtly separate schools that the NAACP had even considered including

Pasadena as one of the cases that would eventually comprise *Brown v. Board of Education*, whose 1954 Supreme Court decision would declare it illegal to segregate public school students by race.[67]

While the NAACP did not ultimately involve the west coast suburb in the landmark case, it did, along with black churches, support black residents' continuous protests against school segregation.[68] The NAACP vigorously organized, holding mass meetings and threatening a lawsuit when the school board proposed building new classrooms at the overcrowded all-white Arroyo Seco School, while classrooms stood empty at the neighborhood Garfield School. The overcrowding occurred largely due to the school board's approved transfer of white children out of the Garfield School where the pupils were predominantly black, Latino, and Japanese.[69] In response, the school board redrew neighborhood boundaries and put an official end to intradistrict transfers. Racial segregation continued, however, as parents used means such as fake addresses to get their children into the schools they desired.[70]

Parents' resistance to integration before and after *Brown* was a national phenomenon. *Brown*'s most notorious test came in 1958 in Little Rock, Arkansas, where Governor Orval Faubus ordered the Arkansas National Guard to prevent black students' entrance into the city's Central High School. Eyes focused on Little Rock as television cameras caught white Arkansans' violent reactions. While extreme, their response to integration was not unique, and could be seen in districts across the country, including some in California, like Pasadena and Compton.

Eventually a lawsuit challenged Pasadena's school assignment policies. In this 1963 suit, *Jackson v. Pasadena City School District*, the California Supreme Court applied *Brown* and found that Pasadena intentionally segregated its schools. The court required the district "to alleviate racial imbalance in schools regardless of its cause."[71] By framing its decision in such a way, the court mandated that Pasadena eradicate both the de jure gerrymandering and the de facto segregation that came through housing patterns built on discrimination. By this time, the California State Board of Education was moving toward a similar doctrine, and after the *Jackson* decision the board asked the state attorney general whether it could begin to identify students by race to balance school attendance. The attorney general ruled that districts could consider race and ethnicity in formulating desegregation plans, a decision that opened the door for a statewide racial census.[72]

Like school districts across the country, Pasadena found ways to abide by the court's decision while circumventing its intent. In order to comply, the school district adopted a voluntary, open enrollment plan, allowing blacks to leave segregated schools on a space-available basis.[73] The plan only included certain "white" schools, leaving others completely segregated. Like many of its southern counterparts, the majority conservative Pasadena school board implemented a purposely ineffective desegregation plan, successfully forestalling any immediate outside intervention. Its ineffective plan would lead, however, to later court battles.

As in Pasadena and other districts across California, Compton's schools were separate and unequal. In August 1958, a letter declared Centennial graduates unqualified to attend major colleges in California and asked that the board change the curriculum and academic standing of the school.[74] One week later, a group of voters from the Centennial area, a predominantly black neighborhood, sent a different letter to the board of the Compton Union High School District, protesting the school's lack of facilities—specifically an auditorium, swimming pool, football stadium, baseball facilities, or gymnasium—and complaining of the low grade averages of Centennial graduates. Two weeks after that, Centennial's principal, Benjamin Jamison, reported to the board of trustees that he had written to each 1958 graduate to impress on them the importance of attending college for the sake of the school. In this analysis, the students' personal decisions and achievements not only reflected on themselves but also served as a marker for the success of the school. At the same meeting, he also informed the board he intended to review the grading procedure of the school and "that the students and teachers alike would be imbued with the fact that the school is an educational and not a social institution."[75] While suburbia was supposed to offer strong educational opportunities, some of Compton's schools were not fulfilling this dream for black residents.

Population growth did necessitate that the districts build some new schools, and district officials planned them to be segregated. In 1958 Compton Union opened another junior high school to serve the black community. Ironically the district chose to name the school after civil rights leader Ralph J. Bunche. Enterprise had named an elementary school a few years back for Bunche, but this did not dissuade the high school district from doing the same. Bunche himself attended the school's opening, giving the dedication speech. In his remarks he did not explicitly mention the fact that the school would mostly serve black students but a tacit acknowledgment came as he reflected on the possible benefits of a school bearing his name. He noted that he was "mindful, of course, of the helpful effect on race relations in the country resulting from any meritorious recognition accorded an individual Negro." He continued: "It is also true, that such recognitions serve as sources of hope and inspiration to young Negroes and encourage them to aspire and strive and improve despite the discouragements and frustrations of racial handicap."[76] While the law books did not condone the segregation policy, it was an open secret, so much so that even the students were aware of the planned segregation. "We all talked, each new school year, 'oh, they moved the [school] boundaries again,'" recalled Grimm.[77] While population growth made the new facilities necessary, their placement highlighted the white establishment's desire to thwart integration and maintain the segregated status quo.

The segregation of black and white residents in schools and neighborhoods helped further racial tensions. During Grimm's senior year at the traditionally all-white Dominguez High, she served on the student government. One day the cabinet held a special meeting because the school was "getting

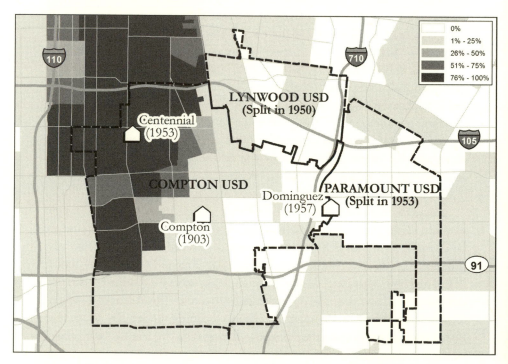

Figure 14. Compton's 1960 African American population and high school construction.

our first black boy." The cabinet was charged with watching out for the student. While, according to Grimm, there was "no scene," they were all very "conscious" that there very well could have been.[78] Compton's whites had shown a strong resistance to integration and Dominguez High remained one of the last strongholds.

At times the tension manifested in both subtle and overt ways. One example of the friction was that black children stayed away from youth dances because it was "commonly held that Negro youths would not be welcomed as members of either of the dance clubs. The absence of membership from Centennial High School (whose enrollment [was] entirely Negro) would support this impression."[79] Though not overtly barred, black children were simply not integrated into the fabric of the greater Compton community. Some whites' actions were harsher. Bradley recalled that whites made it clear that they did not want blacks in their side of town at night, even if it meant giving up some business. He recollected: "blacks were encouraged by the all-white Compton Police Department to 'get out of the east side before sunset.' If the white cops didn't get the ugly message across, the storeowners, employees, and a Compton-born-and-bred street gang known as the Spook Hunters sure as hell did."[80]

Blacks and whites were separate in both housing and schooling, the very idea that would later be expressed by the 1968 Kerner Commission, which in the wake of a series of riots concluded: "Our nation is moving toward two societies, one black, one white—separate and unequal."[81] But, Comptonites' experiences complicate that narrative in two ways. First, the Kerner Report diagnosed this divide as white suburban affluence versus black urban poverty.[82] Compton was a suburb that was neither all white, nor affluent. Second, Compton experienced the divide within its own borders.

Living in the same town, whites and blacks fought over resources. School districts' hiring practices exemplified this. Schools were the largest employer in Compton, and white residents held tightly to their control of the hiring process. As black resident Maxcy Filer recalls, "We didn't have one black teacher when I came here, or one black administrator. We didn't even have a custodian in the schools when I moved here, nor the city."[83] The high school district had hired its first black employee in 1950, but even into the 1960s the hiring policies for ethnic groups came under scrutiny. At a June 1963 board of trustees meeting, Compton Union superintendent Rae Cargille asserted that "assignment policies of the Compton Union High School District could be open to criticism from the fact that there are no full time Negro teachers assigned to Roosevelt, Whaley and Dominguez Schools," three schools in Compton's predominantly white east side.[84]

At the same meeting in which he conceded a viable critique of district assignment practices, Cargille also explained away one of Compton's black community's main complaints, which centered on the districts' promotional policy regarding ethnic groups. Cargille stood by the district policy, saying that "if logic is applied rather than emotion our policy concerning administrative openings in the district is sound." It took an average of nine years before administrators received their first administrative assignment in Compton Union and an additional eight years before receiving principalships, and, Cargille reasoned, because the district had only employed African Americans for thirteen years, they could not have at that time reached the top positions of power.[85] According to this logic, all job candidates regardless of color began the job ladder on an even rung and moved up equally based solely on competency and seniority; the lack of African Americans in certain positions was due to standard operating procedures, rather than to any systemic discrimination. The reality of Compton's community contradicted this theory as whites continued to deny African Americans access to jobs.

For the black community, the barriers to job opportunities "fostered a feeling of frustration and lack of confidence in decisions reached by these municipal and civic bodies," according to a report by the Welfare Planning Council.[86] One member of the Compton Community Center board explained: "The innumerable and subtle barriers to full participation in community life for the Negro in Compton might well make him feel completely hopeless."[87] All members of the board agreed that "the iniquitous effects [were] wide-spread, particularly in the feeling of being unwelcome, and in the form of increased school drop-out, crime, and delinquency."[88] The educators and administrators did not improve the situation, tending either to talk around issues of race and class or to aggravate anxieties.

African Americans created communities that would aid them in fighting these problems. According to Bradley "the unity was apparent in our neighborhoods." He explained that the "cohesion was borne of two inalterable conditions," living in crowded neighborhoods and attending the same schools. "Everybody knew everybody's business," he continued, and as a result, if you did something wrong, you were easily "snitched out" when the "elders got together at church, PTA, or the grocery store."[89] Kelvin Filer had a similar experience. In his immediate vicinity lived ten children all around his age, and "we all grew up together, this is from elementary school on, so we all hung out together. We were all friends. Our parents all knew each other so you really had the community feeling, particularly with the parents. I mean, there was nothing . . . if I did something wrong, there was no problem with Mrs. Simmons snatching me, Mrs. Kelly snatching me and you know, 'I'm going to tell your dad.' That was the same thing, they were all with my parents. They had the same areas of responsibility and they had the same expectations in terms of how they wanted to be treated so we were all real close. And to this day, really, still are close. So that was the neighborhood feeling. We all played together. We all played Little League, football. We went to the same church."[90] Pamela Samuels-Young also recalled growing up in a supportive environment, which she defined as "church, school, and parents." Her mother was one of the founding members of the Community Baptist Church in Compton, which became a center point for Samuels-Young, just as the church had done for African Americans across the country. From there, and from school, she built her social circle.[91]

Building from this community, Maxcy Filer, along with some other residents, organized the Compton chapter of the NAACP and local teenagers established a youth branch. The chapter initiated local actions as well as supporting the organization's actions on the regional, state, and national level. In 1958, the Compton branch urged its members to participate in a voter registration drive as well as a boycott of Budweiser beer, a campaign initiated by the Los Angeles branch and endorsed by the regional and national offices. The local chapter also sought to establish fair employment practices in Compton and supported both financially and ideologically the establishment of a statewide commission to enforce such practices.[92]

While recognizing its role in regional and national struggles, and at times taking a page from their playbook, the branch also publicized its own "home grown problems." In the March 1958 newsletter the local NAACP reminded its readers: "We don't have to go to the South to cure the evils of prejudice and discrimination. The defeat of the civil rights ordinance in our own Compton City Council, the subsequent rebuff by the Compton Chamber of Commerce in refusing to discuss FEP [Fair Employment Practices] with our Labor and Legislation Committee, the reports of inadequate education of our young people, the lack of employment opportunities in Compton."[93] Mirroring the actions of southern chapters, the members of the Compton branch picketed city hall, the school district, and private businesses such as Sears and Woolworths, in order to protest their discriminatory hiring practices and pressure them to hire African Americans.[94] In 1958, the Compton group fought for fair employment at the town's branch of Bank of America as well as the local Sears store. The branch's newsletter urged black women with office experience or training to apply at the two businesses because "the managers of both these institutions have indicated their hiring policy was one of non-discrimination and at the same time have said that they have had few Negro applicants for such positions." The newsletter went on to note that "opportunities in most Compton businesses are limited," and the NAACP's goal was "equal opportunity to work where we live."[95] Similar tactics were used across the Los Angeles region to combat segregation in schooling, housing, and hiring, with varying degrees of success.[96]

The Compton branch's campaign against Bank of America illustrates African Americans' ability to organize and sustain protests against Compton's white power structure. In addition to urging black women to apply for jobs, NAACP members distributed fliers urging folks to speak with the bank manager either by phone or in person, requesting that he discontinue the discriminatory practices. They also asked patrons to withdraw their funds from the bank until it hired black employees. According to the flier, the bank manager used such excuses for the practices as, " 'if I hire a Negro, my white employees will quit'; 'when Compton becomes predominantly Negroid, I will consider it'; [and] 'I have lived in Compton twenty three years and I am not going to be pressured by the NAACP to do anything.' "[97] His resistance worked for awhile, but as Filer recalled "after about a year or so picketing, the manager came out and said, 'Maxcy, you could put your picket sign down now, we have a black working in Bank of America.' . . . And, I said, 'Where, where, where?' And, he said, 'There she is.' Well, she was fair skinned, blond hair, blue eyes, but they called her black and she was."[98] Despite the manager's obvious attempts to placate the black activists by manipulating understandings of race, the group considered the battle against Bank of America a victory.

The local chapter of the NAACP also monitored employment gains. In March 1958 the Los Angeles County Sheriff's Department was changing hands and the local chapter commended the outgoing sheriff on his fair employment practices. The chapter, however, feared that the sheriff-elect would return to "the old trend of hiring negroes last and firing them first."[99] The local chapter also monitored the school districts. In 1959, the leaders of the Compton NAACP joined with parents and other civic groups to protest the firing of Vivian Thomas, the librarian at Centennial High School. School principal Benjamin Jamison recommended her contract not be renewed on the grounds of incompetency. In doing so Jamison sparked a heated controversy and charges that his own actions were unethical and unprofessional, which eventually led to the board removing him from his principalship.[100] With these and other campaigns, Compton's local branch of the NAACP grew quickly, reporting approximately five hundred members in October 1959.[101]

As it grew in number and action, Compton's NAACP received threats. In October 1960, in response to the group's picket lines in front of the town's Woolworth stores, the NAACP local office had swastikas painted on its windows and received menacing letters.[102] A month later someone threw a brick through the office window with a note attached, stating "Get the hell out of town."[103]

Tensions became so palpable that in June 1961 Compton established the Council on Human Relations to create a "wholesome community atmosphere."[104] While the establishment of the committee showed some movement toward addressing the town's problems, it was not a cure-all.[105] Only a few months later two "hoodlums" fired thirteen shots into the glass window of the Compton NAACP's office.[106] Violence between black and white students also erupted on some of Compton's school campuses. In February 1962 three African American Compton High students clashed with four white Dominguez High students after an interschool basketball game. A white student ended up hospitalized with a fractured skull. The booster club at the predominantly white Dominguez High discussed canceling, or at least moving to the daytime, all future basketball games against the predominantly black Compton High.[107]

The local newspaper, the *Compton Herald American*, already notorious for its racist commentary on blacks as well as stirring up tension between black and white Compton residents, called the attacks "brutal and savage." The paper, using charged language, described the African Americans as part of a "gang."[108] The newspaper's polemic framing of the incident may have led to its continued interest in the story. It reported that in the wake of the skirmish, three black students were arrested, with fourteen more soon to follow. The fissures between Compton's black and white residents grew deeper, and their segregated schools embodied their disunion.

The Consequences of White Flight

The spread of Latinos also affected Compton's social fabric. Latinos were always a portion of Compton's population but by 1957 they lived throughout the town.[109] This dispersal meant that Latinos attended several of Compton's schools, but the majority remained within the Willowbrook and northern Compton schools.[110]

As blacks and Latinos moved into an established white neighborhood, whites moved out. In the period between 1955 and 1960, the white population of Compton decreased by 19 percent, while the nonwhite population increased by 165 percent.[111] The flight of Compton's whites was part of a movement occurring nationally. For example, between 1950 and 1960, 700,000 whites moved to Philadelphia's suburbs, while the city lost 225,000 whites and gained 153,000 blacks.[112] During the 1960s roughly 60,000 whites fled Atlanta, and during the 1970s another 100,000 would follow.[113]

While similar to the big cities' stories, Compton deviated from the norm. Unlike traditional white flight, from city to suburb, Compton's whites fled first from one part of Compton to another, and then from one suburb to the next. In 1961, white resident Ron Finger's parents also moved out of Compton because "the neighborhood by then had pretty much become black." For his parents and their white neighbors, "it was kind of like the first [African American] family that moved in was okay. The second family moving in, then it was like 'there goes the neighborhood,' and so people started selling their houses." By the time his parents left, there were only a few white families left on the block.[114]

White Comptonites also worked to keep neighborhoods segregated, with whites on the town's east side and African Americans on its west. A 1962 study by the Welfare Planning Council found "'two Comptons'—essentially white and non-white, segregated rigidly," with the commercial Alameda Boulevard as the line of demarcation between two residential areas.[115] As in other cities during these years, this segregation was not coincidental: white developers and residents played active, and important, roles in creating and maintaining the two Comptons.[116] While the new developments were open to anyone who could afford to buy, mostly blacks and Latinos moved in.

The suburban space of Compton no longer provided the desired social markers. In 1962, Katherine Nelson, an African American nurse, moved with her family to the town's west side. She recalled, "[the neighborhood] was all white. I think we were the first African American family to move there. And, my husband said, the next morning when he woke up, we woke up, that there were signs in everybody's yard that said 'House for Sale.' "[117] White Comptonites' responses were both overt and swift, as they relocated to nearby suburbs that, unlike Compton, had remained overwhelming white.

Pam Grimm's was another such family that fled to outer-ring suburbs. She heard her mother's racism "every night at the dinner table," as she and her father discussed the influx of African Americans into Compton. She recalled: "When we were at the dinner table every night, 'we have to get out.' It's called white flight. Everybody talked about it." The fear wasn't limited to talk. Grimm explained that her cousins "had this brand new house, maybe four, five years old and they didn't like black people and they were moving in. And the next time I went over [to their house,] there was a 'for sale' sign in almost every yard in the block." When African Americans moved closer to her own neighborhood, Grimm's parents moved their family to the nearby, almost exclusively white suburb of Lakewood.[118]

Just north of Long Beach, and east of Compton, Lakewood was a planned community formed by developers, who mapped out a town with single-family homes on individual lots and used principles of mass production in forming the new community. Like its east coast cousin Levittown, Lakewood was built in a deliberate and efficient multistep process. Plans for the development began in 1950, and by 1952 ten thousand homes already stood.[119] In describing Lakewood's houses, scholar Alida Brill observed, "despite the promotional rhetoric to the contrary about exterior trim styles and different floor plans, to the untrained eye they looked identical."[120] These identical rows of homes sat on a grid system of streets, which typified the efficiency model of the community.

The town's population mirrored the homogeneity of its houses. Lakewood became the fashionable locale, not simply because of its new homes, but also, and perhaps more important, because it was a white district in a metropolitan region that was becoming increasingly integrated. Lakewood's realtors touted the town as the county's new white enclave and denied African Americans home applications, steering them instead to Los Angeles' South Central district.[121] As blacks moved into inner-ring suburbs like Compton, whites fled farther out. Civil rights attorney Loren Miller noted in 1955 that Lakewood was "a bean field ten years ago, a thriving metropolis today—lily white, made white, kept white by builders with the active consent of the FHA."[122] According to the 1960 census, of Lakewood's 67,126 residents, only 75 were classified as nonwhite.[123]

Lakewood soon became its own town. In order to stave off annexation by Long Beach (and to avoid that city's tax rate and retain its own retail taxes and home values), the development company and local residents fashioned the "Lakewood Plan," in which Los Angeles County contracted services such as fire and police to Lakewood, which thus did not have to develop and pay for its own. Lakewood residents paid for these services at a low rate, which as scholar Mike Davis points out, was "indirectly subsidized by all county tax-payers."[124] Under this plan, residents could control local decisions, such as zoning, while avoiding public expenditures required by providing public services. Outsourcing services represented a major difference between Lakewood and the older suburbs like Compton, which shouldered the burden of the vast majority of its municipal services.

Incorporated in 1954, Lakewood became the model for other towns that wanted to keep down their tax rates. The Lakewood Plan inspired a wave of municipal incorporations across Los Angeles County.[125] By 1961, all cities and towns contracted some of their services from the county. Not surprisingly, the county provided the fewest services to Los Angeles and Long Beach, only assessment and collection of taxes for the former and the final map check of subdivisions for the latter, as well as election services for both. The county supplied Compton with six services and Lakewood with thirty-four.[126] Lakewood with its lower tax rates became an attractive alternative to the heavy tax burdens of the original suburbs.[127]

Lakewood, and other surrounding suburbs, affected Compton's economy by providing other retail and manufacturing centers. In the postwar years, Compton had grown in population and geographic size, but its new construction centered solely on residential housing and school plants. No new manufacturing plants were erected in Compton during this period and industry settled in neighboring towns.[128] The anemic industrial base lessened the potential income from property taxes and, as a result, the town relied disproportionately on monies from its sales tax. Unfortunately for the town's coffers, Compton's retail sector also struggled to bring in funds. In the early 1950s, the stores in Compton's central business district served people from both inside and outside the town. When agricultural towns around Compton became less rural, they developed their own shopping areas and relied less on Compton's. Furthermore, developers created new retail centers in other Los Angeles County areas, such as Lakewood and Torrance. The Lakewood Center, the largest shopping center in the country at that time, embodied many of the postwar changes. In fact, when the developers built Lakewood, they first constructed the shopping center and then built the houses around it.[129] The 100-store outdoor mall stood in the middle of a vast parking lot, which unlike traditional downtown areas, like the one in Compton, accommodated the rising car culture of the 1950s.[130] These areas contributed directly to the decline of business activity in Compton. Peaking in 1958, Compton's retail sales, along with their taxable portion, plunged at the end of the 1950s, further depressing the tax base.[131] In terms of financing the schools, all the component elementary school districts were mainly residential and therefore had a small tax capacity.[132]

The demographic shifts also had economic implications for Compton. As Davis shows, new suburbs under the Lakewood plan "gave suburban homeowners a subsidized 'exit option' as well as a powerful new motive for organizing around the 'protection of their home values and lifestyles.'"[133] Scholar Michan Connor concurs: "Lakewood's settlers had made significant capital and social investment in their homes, and quite sensibly viewed the politics of incorporation as a means of protecting those investments."[134] Lakewood was a good deal—it had new homes, a retail tax base, a low property tax rate, and firm racial lines, which promised to keep housing values high. The contracting of services in Lakewood and other municipalities like it allowed residents to reject metropolitan political and residential integration.[135]

These new developments and incorporations helped widen Los Angeles County's racial and income divides. These effects could be seen clearly in Compton. In 1949, when the town was predominantly white, the residents were for the most part middle and working class, with 83 percent in the middle brackets, just over 15 percent below the poverty line and almost 2 percent in the high wage bracket.[136] As the proportion of blacks and Latinos increased, the town's income level decreased, because discrimination in educational and employment opportunities often relegated nonwhites to lower-paying jobs.

Racial segregation in Southern California became even more acute, spreading from the center of Los Angeles to its outskirts, like the San Fernando Valley, as well as to other areas, not least of which was Los Angeles County's neighbor, Orange County. Both the San Fernando Valley and Orange County exploded in population and money during and after World War II, and their rise affected Los Angeles's older suburbs like Compton. The new suburbs' expansion added to the racial segregation and economic stratification in Southern California as a whole. The aerospace industries had been suburbanizing for years, and in the early 1950s, they moved even farther from the central city and its surrounding communities to the more far-flung Valley. Between 1950 and 1960 the Valley's population more than doubled as companies worked with housing developers to sponsor planned communities for their workers, leading to further suburbanization of its workforce.[137] Developers and realtors systematically excluded blacks even after this type of practice was ruled unconstitutional.[138] Because residency determined school zones, schools remained racially segregated, and during this period more than a hundred new public school sites were built in the Valley.[139] In 1960, fifteen of the sixteen towns in the Valley had a black population of less than 1 percent.[140] Moving to the Valley ensured racially segregated neighborhoods and schools.

A similar pattern occurred in Orange County, where defense money brought job opportunities and a flood of new residents. In 1950, Orange County housed 216,224 residents and by 1970, nearly 1.5 million people called it home.[141] African Americans comprised less than 0.5 percent of the county's 1960 population of 703,935.[142] When white residents in older suburbs like Compton failed at keeping their areas racially segregated, they had options as to where to move.

In March 1959, recognizing the intertwined fates of towns, Edmund "Pat" Brown, governor of California, commissioned a study for recommendations on problems in the state's metropolitan areas. The study identified the crux of the issue as "whether California can maintain a suitable working and living environment for future urban growth."[143] The report analyzed the metropoles, recommended action programs, and identified areas for further research. Many of the issues, such as the concepts of local government and home rule, had been plaguing Compton for years. Many of the identified problems such as the economic and social structure of the metropolis were reasons people left Compton.

Living with Economic Disparities

Wage disparities across ethnic lines held true even after California's 1959 creation of the Fair Employment Practices Commission (FEPC).[144] In 1960, the median family income in Compton was $6,256, with 22 percent of the families having incomes under $4,000; 52 percent of employed male residents were in the craftsman, foreman, operatives and kindred workers category. Professional and related categories accounted for 14 percent of the employed males. With 12 percent of Compton's population, the west side, which was majority African American, had about 20 percent of the unemployed persons in the labor force. Less than half as many neighborhood residents were working in technical, professional, and proprietor type jobs; most people were semiskilled or unskilled.[145] Moreover, Compton's proportion of youth rose, lowering the number of wage-earners (and their tax dollars) while simultaneously necessitating greater city spending for their education. The Willowbrook School District also had a large number of youths. In 1960, there were proportionately more children twelve and under in the Willowbrook School District than in Los Angeles County as a whole.[146]

Compton struggled with raising the essential money for financing all its municipal services. Dividends from sales, use, and property taxes comprised most of the town's funds. Compton's bonded debt meant that the town could not dedicate enough of its tax revenues to schools, police, and other municipal responsibilities.[147] Compton's tax problems did not end with its bonded debt, however. The suburb lacked a base because its citizens valued living in a bedroom community. Town leaders' annexation policies reflected this desire as they emphasized annexing residential rather than industrial areas. Large industries that could normally support such an area located outside the municipality. Only small firms settled in the suburb and they did not generate generous tax revenues.[148]

Even the land zoned for industry was used for other purposes and little vacant land existed for industrial development. In 1964, there were about 2.3 acres of land per thousand population used for commercial purposes in the city of Compton, compared with 3.5 acres per thousand in all Los Angeles County. Compton had less commercial development for its population than surrounding communities or the county as a whole.[149] This meant that for the most part Compton residents worked outside the town. Between 1950 and 1960 the Compton labor market doubled its number of employees, but increased its employment opportunities by only 50 percent.[150]

Recognizing the detrimental effects of a weak tax base, Compton boosters hoped to attract more industry and produced a booklet in 1959 entitled "Compton: Industrial Heart of the California Southland." The brochure promised that land in Compton would become available for development but, while it showcased the town's machine shops, manufacturing plants, and retail stores, the pamphlet also confessed that Compton lacked any "industrial 'giants.'"[151] While aiming to remedy this, the authors also made sure to quell the fears of any potential homebuyer who might have doubted whether a town with industry could also provide a suburban existence. The authors claimed the contrary: "Industry has accepted a responsibility to the community as a whole. Not only do the more recently constructed Compton plants refrain from defacing a landscape: they beautify it."[152] They also highlighted Compton's suburban amenities, such as a summer recreation program that included children's baseball leagues, which in 1958 had over 1,200 players who participated in over 700 games.[153] Though not the authors' focus, these types of activities and facilities remained central to Compton. Despite boosters' efforts to court businesses and their claim of Compton as the "hub city," Compton remained a residential suburb, and its residents went elsewhere for work.

Due to their financial shortcomings, the component elementary districts and the high school district took on more debt. Some of the monies came as direct loans, and when the loans came due, the voters approved bond issues to pay back some of these debts. Furthermore, the districts issued more bonds to pay for construction of new schools and additions to existing ones.[154] Compton area schools continued to spend less on their pupils and have bigger class sizes than other Los Angeles County schools.[155] Due to financial restraints, Compton students lost out. While much had changed in Compton since the 1930s, the financial problems that challenged the community persisted and deepened.

Faced with tight funds and threatened by newcomers, Compton's white leaders continued to discriminate against blacks by controlling access to both education and jobs. African Americans pushed against these limits. In November 1964, Ted Nelson, a representative of the Parent Teacher Action Group, NAACP, and Congress of Racial Equality (CORE), submitted a letter to the Compton Union board of trustees beseeching the district to make seven major changes "to insure an equal educational opportunity for all our children and fair and equitable working conditions for all district employees, certified and classified." In terms of improving the educational component of the schools, the groups implored district officials to implement "an enriched educational program, compensatory education, and a crash program to discourage drop outs in the ghetto." They also appealed for smaller classes and "adoption of textbooks that represent the multiracial and multicultural conditions of our society." Regarding racial divisions in the schools, Nelson and the groups demanded immediate integration and "a stop to boundary changes that perpetuate school segregation." Concerning employment, they asked for a written statement of district policy of hiring, promotions, and transfers as well as an issuance of "a directive for placement of all teachers regardless of race or creed in all schools."[156] Met with an entrenched white power structure, African Americans sought to change the community and its schools.

A Change Is Coming

Some political change did come to Compton. In 1963, U.S. Representative Clyde Doyle died, opening his seat for a special election. City council member Delwin "Del" Clawson was elected to Congress, vacating his council position. In its own special election, Compton elected Douglas Dollarhide its first black council member by a mere 73 votes.[157] Dollarhide ran on the platform of encouraging more businesses to locate in Compton and more representation for blacks on boards and commissions of the town government. He called for closer scrutiny of the oral portions of the civil service examinations, as they were used to discriminate against blacks.[158]

African Americans soon gained political power in Compton as a whole. In July 1963, Jesse Robinson became the first African American to sit on Compton Union's school board when he was appointed to fill a vacancy left by the death of Ramon Gonzales.[159] The next month Ross Miller was appointed to the town's Parks and Recreation Commission and Foster Ricardo Sr. was appointed to the Compton City Planning Commission.[160] Some positions came through elections as well. Two years later, Compton voters elected Doris Davis as city clerk. Davis, an African American, defeated incumbent Clyde Harland and another white candidate. Compton's black residents had won victories, increasing their political power. These triumphs were harbingers of changes yet to come.

Nevertheless, these elections did not mean Compton had rid itself of discrimination. They indicated that blacks were growing in numerical strength, not that white voters had fundamentally changed. The same year Ross Miller was appointed to the town's commission, he and his wife also moved to the town's predominantly white east side. A day after taking possession of their new house, the Millers found part of their lawn burning in the shape of a cross. Ironically Miller was at a Human Relations Committee meeting at the time of the incident.[161] In another example, shortly after his election, newly selected U.S. Representative Del Clawson, who served Compton as well as other white working-class suburbs, conducted a district-wide survey by sending one hundred thousand surveys to registered voters in his district, twenty-five thousand of which were returned. According to Clawson, the survey responses indicated that "racial prejudice is far deeper than we had anticipated."[162] Respondents, for the most part, rejected the idea that the government had the right to prohibit discrimination, whether in integration of public schools, hiring for job opportunities, or selling homes. Clawson followed his constituents' lead and vowed to vote against any civil rights bill, a promise he followed through on when in February 1964 he became one of five representatives from California who voted against the federal civil rights bill.[163]

The California state government, however, sought to tackle certain manifestations of racial discrimination. In 1959, the state legislature created the FEPC to enforce equal employment opportunities and enacted the Unruh Civil Rights Act, which required equal access to any business. The California Supreme Court decided in a series of cases that the law included real estate brokers and housing developers, forbidding them to discriminate.[164] The court drew a line at the private homeowner, saying real estate brokers and developers were not responsible for a homeowner's discrimination. As a result, fair housing advocates looked to establish new legislation that did prohibit such bias.[165] Assemblyman William Byron Rumford led the charge in the legislature, and in June 1963 the California legislature passed a law bearing his name, the Rumford Fair Housing Act, which prohibited racial discrimination in private housing financed by any public source and any housing with five or more units. Though the legislation did not cover all the state's housing, it covered a large percentage and empowered the FEPC to investigate and adjudicate discrimination complaints.[166] California joined fourteen other states that passed some version of open housing legislation enforceable by an administrative body.

Immediately after the bill's passing, the real estate industry spearheaded a movement to overturn it. In response to the law, they placed an initiative, which became known as Proposition 14, on the November 1964 ballot. If passed, this statewide initiative would amend the state constitution to repeal the Rumford Act and prevent enactment of any similar fair housing measures on the state or local level.[167] The Compton Council on Human Relations vigorously supported the Rumford Act and worked to save it, as did other groups across the state.[168]

Proposition 14 was a bellwether, as it became "a virtual referendum on civil rights." In framing the language of the proposition its authors avoided racial language, yet its proponents justified their campaign as opposing special privileges for minorities.[169] Instead, they employed the language of rights—such as the right to private property—as the language of their campaign to overturn the Rumford Act, framing it as a decision between "freedom of choice" and "forced housing."[170] Using this logic, white residents became the victims of discrimination.

The debate over the initiative gave California residents a means to discuss federal civil rights legislation, as the election came on the heels of the passage of the Civil Rights Act of 1964. After President John F. Kennedy's assassination in November 1963, his successor Lyndon Baines Johnson called for enactment of the civil rights bill as a memorial for Kennedy. Johnson signed the bill into law in July 1964. The passage of the Civil Rights Act all but ensured that California's Proposition 14 would be found unconstitutional, yet California voters wanted their opinions heard.[171]

And heard they were. Proposition 14 passed with 65.4 percent of California voters in favor and 34.6 percent opposed. In Los Angeles County, 67 percent voted for repeal, while, paradoxically, Johnson received 58 percent of the county's vote.[172] This vote was consistent with what had been happening in Compton for years, as white Compton residents had sought to prevent African Americans from moving into their town and their school districts. For over two decades prior to the passage of Proposition 14, white Comptonites protected their middle-class suburban dream by enforcing racial covenants, refusing to unify their school districts, and, when all else failed, moving out of their homes and neighborhoods. All these efforts compounded existing financial, organizational, and political strains on Compton and its school districts. They also created enormous tensions between blacks and whites in Compton.

The vote on Proposition 14 indicated that something was different in Compton, however. The city council had unanimously opposed the proposition on the basis it would amend the state constitution to legalize discrimination.[173] More people in the town voted against its passage. The vote—10,888 for and 15,259 against—reflected a political shift that had already begun to occur, even though Compton was only 40 percent African American at the time.[174] The white population, however, still included Latinos. While a demographic and political shift had happened in Compton that change served as a model of what could happen in other places and for many California voters that possibility was scary.

These tensions were not unique to Compton as racial and economic segregation seemed ever more entrenched with the passage of Proposition 14, which stoked the alienation of African Americans in South Los Angeles.

Already feeling pressure from the stark economic realities of chronic under-employment and unemployment, many African Americans felt discouraged by its passage. For many blacks, California, and Los Angeles in particular, represented the promise of a better life. The national Urban League had rated sixty-eight American cities and found that Los Angeles offered Afri-can Americans the most opportunities.[175] Though better than other cities, Los Angeles, particularly the Watts section, where the vast majority of black Angelenos lived, was no paradise. Residents faced overcrowded neighbor-hoods, filthy streets, and troubled schools. As journalist Ethan Rarick writes, the people of Watts cared little about how they compared to other cities be-cause "they were Californians; they wanted the California life."[176] California had represented employment and housing opportunities, but the passage of Proposition 14 crushed many of these interrelated dreams as it limited fair housing and exposed racial fissures.[177] Though the California Supreme Court would later overturn Proposition 14 and the United States Supreme Court would uphold that decision, the passage of the proposition remained an indelible mark. Within a few months, this alienation would ignite Los Angeles and bring the struggles of black communities into the glare of the national spotlight.

The growth and shifts in demographics reconfigured control over political power in Compton. As African Americans moved in, many white Compton residents resisted the demographic changes in their neighborhoods, sometimes violently, but more often simply by leaving. The white exodus left black Comp-tonites with a series of problems—high taxes, low revenues, poorly structured school districts, and overcrowded schools. These problems, along with Comp-ton's growing status as a black town, left the residents with a troubled legacy. As infrastructure costs skyrocketed, whites fled to outer suburbs, and the inner-ring suburbs experienced the stresses and decay of the central city.

In the decade from the mid-1950s to the mid-1960s, Compton was es-sentially an intermediary suburb, one that was home to working-class whites and blacks aspiring to the same ideals of the suburban dream that dominated the popular culture and discourse. Both sought to live in a nice town with nice schools. But Compton's spatial boundaries of the suburban city made it difficult to achieve and maintain these suburban dreams for whites. Comp-ton was a working-class suburb, and as such could not avoid integration. The invalidation of racial covenants and the modest housing prices made it al-most impossible to prevent racial transition as residents from the neighboring minority neighborhoods of the Los Angeles moved into the once vastly white town. In this middle ground between the central city and the elite suburbs, African Americans and whites took a step toward the middle-class suburban dream and each group fought ferociously to protect their access to that dream.

Chapter 4

Becoming Urban

Kelvin was the third of seven children born to Maxcy and Blondell Filer, who moved to California in 1953. Like many Americans, they sought out suburbia, but as African Americans they had limited options. When they moved to the west side of Compton, it was one of the few suburbs in Los Angeles County where African Americans could settle, and it became the Filers' new home.[1]

Like all the Filer children, Kelvin attended Compton public schools: Rosecrans Elementary School, Walton and Davis Middle Schools, and Compton High School. When Kelvin began his formal education, the vast majority of the teachers were white. Most of his classmates were black, though some white and Latino students attended the local district schools. By the time he reached Compton High in 1970, however, his school was almost all black and was run by an African American principal, Aaron Wade. During Kelvin's elementary school years, demographic changes in Compton also drove a political transformation, as blacks became the voting majority in the town and secured power over Compton's offices and institutions.

Compton offered a strong sense of community, which for Kelvin came from his experiences in the public schools. Kelvin loved attending Compton High, which he characterized as the "flagship school of the Compton school district." The school buzzed with students interested in sports and academics. Focusing on good grades and playing the trumpet made Kelvin "what people would consider a square."[2] Still, he thrived. He graduated thirteenth in his class of over 750 and matriculated at the University of California, Santa Cruz.

Once in college, Kelvin realized that Compton schools perhaps did not offer "the best education." When competing with other students who also had graduated at the top of their high school classes, Kelvin found himself "falling down and literally failing." Shocked, he wrote to Compton school administrators saying he wanted "to sue the school district because they deprived me of my quality education." While hindsight softened his opinion, Kelvin still admitted that "I should've been pushed a little bit." He recalled, for example, how, in his first college term paper, on Karl Marx, he spelled the philosopher's name with a "C." When he got his paper back, and all the Carls were circled, he was greatly embarrassed. Through hard work, Kelvin overcame his knowledge deficiencies. He became a lawyer and returned to Compton to serve his community as a member of the school board. He eventually became a judge in the Compton branch of the Los Angeles County Superior Court.

The Filers were one of the many black families who moved to Compton in search of suburbia's promises, but during Kelvin's childhood Compton took on many characteristics traditionally considered urban. Between 1965 and 1970 many businesses left the downtown area and the storefronts stayed empty. While remaining lower than in the neighboring areas of Watts and Willowbrook, the unemployment rate for black men in Compton increased from 8.7 percent in 1960 to 10 percent in 1970.[3] The crime rate also rose and the schools faltered. Beginning in the 1950s and extending into the 1960s, Compton transitioned from a white to a majority-minority town. Despite civic leaders' assertion that Compton was "the Beverly Hills of the Black Belt," the economic composition of the town soon changed: as it reached a black majority, affluent and middle-class black families began to leave for other suburbs.[4]

Compton's racial and economic changes further hampered an already burdened school system. As the town's population became increasingly poor, students came to school with a wide range of issues. With whites' departure, Compton evolved into a differently racialized place, as people started to think of it as a black town, a label that would add to its marginalization. Compton residents reacted to these changes with locally sponsored activism and programs, and appealed for state and federal aid. These responses proved inadequate for a place that was, in symbol and reality, becoming "urban."

Following Watts

On Wednesday, August 11, 1965, the California Highway Patrol pulled over African American motorist Marquette Frye on suspicion of drunk driving in the nearby Watts section of Los Angeles. The circumstances around Frye's arrest, fueled by pent up anger over what many blacks viewed as years of police abuse, precipitated six consecutive days and nights of looting, arson, and violence. While the unrest occurred in pockets throughout Los Angeles County, including Pasadena, Venice, and Monrovia, the violence most deeply affected the South Central region of Los Angeles, home to two-thirds of Los Angeles County's black population.

Poverty, police brutality, and lack of employment opportunities laid the groundwork for the unrest. Jobs, along with large grocery and department stores, had moved to the suburbs. In Watts, unemployment rates held at double those of the Los Angeles metropolitan region and the state of California. Local residents who were employed usually occupied the bottom of the pay scale; only 4 percent of employed men in the southern part of Los Angeles worked in professional and technical occupations.[5] Police brutality was also rampant in the area. Between 1963 and 1965 police officers killed sixty African Americans, twenty-five of them unarmed and twenty-seven shot in the back.[6]

The unrest created ruinous results. The physical outcomes included thirty-four deaths, more than a thousand injuries, almost four thousand arrests, and an estimated more than $45 million in property damage, an enormous amount by contemporary standards. The psychological consequences ran deep as well. Whether viewed as an uprising, rebellion, or riot, those six days and nights terrified an onlooking nation. The violence brought to the forefront the rage over economic and political inequity felt by many African Americans not only in the Los Angeles area but across the United States.[7] Though it was not the first violent race conflict, the coverage of Watts would change the country as a whole and neighboring Compton in particular.

And yet the effects on Compton were not immediate. At the time of the uprisings, there were only a few violent incidents in Compton, even though the town bordered on the riot areas. This was not coincidental. When the strife began, Comptonites stood at the edge of the suburb and refused the rioters entry. Residents—white, black, and Latino—took pride in their town and worked hard to protect it from the spreading destruction. Despite Compton's long history of racial discrimination, Compton's black residents experienced more upward mobility than those in the surrounding areas. In 1960 unemployment in Compton was less than a third of that in Watts.[8] Though still a deeply problematic space for its black residents, Compton served as a step out of the ghettos of Watts and Willowbrook. Furthermore, by the time of the riot, African Americans had begun working in some of Compton's downtown businesses, knocking holes in the previously impervious wall of job discrimination. They had won hard battles in Compton and were not about to lose that. The opportunities they had won put some distance between the experiences of blacks in Watts and those in Compton. Kelvin's father, Maxcy, recalled, "When the Watts situation happened, it was something that we didn't suffer as much discrimination."[9] Though labor, residential, and educational discrimination persisted in Compton, the town's black residents were not subject to the same level of desperation as the residents of the riot-torn areas.

Though blacks in Compton experienced some level of achievement, the town's schools on the whole did not effectively educate their students. Following the uprisings, Edmund "Pat" Brown, the governor of California, named a commission, whose findings were summarized in the McCone Report. The commission offered three major recommendations to solve the problems associated with poverty, and in turn to ease the underlying tensions: increase employment opportunities, mend public education, and bolster crime prevention. Though the McCone Commission had its critics, a close look at its recommendations still offers some insight into the state of affairs in Compton, especially the local schools.[10]

Here, in these recommendations, Compton was indicted. The McCone Report cited the Los Angeles schools for ill-preparing their students and, as a result, limiting the students' future opportunities and fostering a sense of hopelessness and frustration. Compton's educational system was also implicated because Willowbrook, one of the main centers of rioting, was one of the component districts to the Compton Union High School District. The population of Willowbrook, like Watts, was majority black and vastly poor, with almost 19 percent of families living at or below the poverty level, many of them "chronic and consistently unemployed residents."[11] Willowbrook's population was 31,750, with 1,100 white (3.5 percent), 26,740 black (84.2 percent), 3,910 Spanish surname, and others (12.3 percent). The average family income for Willowbrook was $4,990 in 1965 and $5,607 in 1969, a growth of 9.9 percent. Meanwhile, the county average income rose 31 percent, from $7,045 to $10,205.[12] Students from Willowbrook attended junior high and high school with students from the other two component districts, Enterprise and Compton.[13] If part of the solution dictated improving education, then Comptonites had a task to complete.

Perhaps most significantly, the uprising in Watts incited demographic shifts throughout the region. It prompted the exodus of many whites from South Los Angeles and the Watts-Willowbrook area, as well as from the afflu-ent and middle-class neighborhoods of Ladera Heights and Baldwin Hills.[14] African Americans also migrated to Compton because many wished to leave the strife-torn area to the north. In the 1970 census Compton became the first majority black town in Los Angeles County, with 71 percent of its popu-lation reporting as black.[15] Just three years later, all but one of Compton's forty-one schools were over 90 percent black, twenty-seven of them being 99 to 100 percent black. The other school reported that 80–89 percent of its stu-dents were African American.[16] Not only did the town's population become predominantly black, but African Americans governed the majority of the public services, including the school districts. Due to these changes, Comp-ton became known as a black town.

Compton's racial shift was part of a larger transition in Los Angeles Coun-ty's social geography. Between 1950 and 1970, the county became increasingly black, going from 5.5 percent to 10.7 percent African American. This shift did not occur uniformly throughout the county, however. Most of the increase was concentrated in the city of Los Angeles and a few inner-ring towns like Pasa-dena and Inglewood. In 1970, over 73 percent of the county's African Ameri-cans lived in Los Angeles and Compton, though their population was only 41 percent of the county.[17] The flip side of this concentration was also true. As certain inner-ring suburbs became increasingly black, other towns retained their racial boundaries. Between 1950 and 1970, the proportion of the county's population living in racially exclusive towns rose.[18] Out-migration also hap-pened to Los Angeles's neighboring counties. Between 1960 and 1970 Orange County's population more than doubled, and between 1960 and 1980 Ventura, Kern, Riverside, and San Bernardino counties grew by almost 100 percent.[19]

Increased residential segregation furthered school segregation. Even though the schools throughout the county were already segregated they be-came even more so. Some of this segregation in Los Angeles city schools re-sulted from white families moving to the suburbs and some was connected to white parents' pulling their children from their neighborhood public school and enrolling them in private schools. In the wake of Watts, between 1966 and 1970, the Los Angeles Unified School District lost nearly 80,000 white students.[20] Increased residential segregation played a central role in that pro-cess. Blacks not only found a home in Compton, but whites also used the black space as a contrast to their own experience. Compton became an easy place against which whites could measure themselves.

Compton no longer seemed such a step up. Instead, other southland towns, like the neighboring suburb of Carson, which incorporated in 1968, drew black property owners from Compton and Los Angeles. Like Compton, Carson had once been a racially restricted community that was the province of blue-collar whites. Once it incorporated, after many failed attempts, Carson offered high levels of municipal resources with no property tax, and white-collar African Americans moved to the town. Poor blacks could not afford to move to Carson because the town refused to build any form of low-income housing. At the end of the 1960s, blacks in Carson had a higher income and lower unemployment and poverty rates than those for Carson's total population.[21] With middle-class residents' departure, among both whites and blacks, poverty in Compton became more pronounced. During this period Compton went from a community with some income-class heterogeneity to one that was homogeneously lower-income.[22] This shift led to an even greater depletion of resources and an increase in crime.

With poverty came gangs, crime, and drugs. In December 1965, the *Compton Herald American* reported that four "youth gangs" merged into two opposing "social clubs" and "Compton once again erupted into gang violence."[23] While the paper, under the longtime leadership of white owner and publisher Colonel Smith, had a clear dislike for the black in-migration and tended to use inflammatory language describing the town's new residents, it was not the only documentation of increased crime. That same month official crime numbers revealed that Compton ranked third in Los Angeles County for major felony offenses, trailing only the much more populated cities of Los Angeles and Long Beach.[24] Crime, often a reason people moved to the suburbs, was becoming a problem that would continue to plague the town, in both direct and indirect ways.

While crime numbers appeared on the rise, the perception of increased crime also rose, engendering both a cause and effect for Compton's businesses to deteriorate or leave the town altogether. The racialization of Compton as a black space added to the criminalization of the town. Many whites had come to see a concentration of African Americans as threatening and Compton fit that mold.[25] Company owners did not wish to invest money into a town they saw as floundering. By 1966, according to a report on Compton's business district, "the appearance of the town is bad ... the street itself is filthy" and "any plan [for improvement] seems hopeless unless you can get someone to spend money."[26] The town itself had little money to invest in the necessary repairs and private enterprises proved unwilling or unable to take up the slack. As a result, the few businesses remaining in Compton sought escape routes, and when they succeeded they took employment opportunities with them, helping set the stage for further increases in crime and decreases of tax revenue. As such, Compton was increasingly taking on quintessential urban characteristics. These changes countered the very definition of suburbia, a middle-class haven, safe from the crime-ridden, dirty streets of the city. Yet, ironically, Compton's suburban nature would make reversal difficult.

The Mixed Blessing of Government Aid

Schools stood vulnerable to the storm of problems hitting Compton because they lacked the funds to improve their academic offerings and educational environment. Compton area districts spent below average per child, with only one district in Los Angeles County spending less. Students were increasingly poor and brought with them poverty-related difficulties. Comptonites responded to these changes by tapping into a variety of federal programs, but the interventions could not curb Compton's woes, and they served to enhance public perception of Compton as a town with "urban" troubles.

Federal support for poor school districts like Compton reigned in the mid-1960s. The publication of such books as James Conant's 1961 *Slums and Suburbs* and Michael Harrington's 1962 *The Other America* had exposed the problems of poverty and its link to education.[27] Liberal lawmakers and the administration of President Lyndon Johnson believed that the customary practices of public schools had to change to meet the needs of disadvantaged students. Improving education for poor and minority students became the centerpiece of Johnson's Great Society legislation and served as the rationale for Congress's authorizing the first program of general aid to schools, the 1965 Elementary and Secondary Education Act (ESEA). At the heart of ESEA was Title I, which allocated federal funds based on a school's enrollment of low-income children to meet the needs of those who were "educationally disadvantaged."[28] Beginning then, the federal government directly aided local school districts and Title I dominated policy discourse.[29]

The rhetoric around disadvantaged youth swirled in several national policy arenas in the mid-1960s. One of the most influential and controversial was "The Negro Family: The Case for National Action," most commonly known as the Moynihan Report, written in March 1965 by sociologist and assistant secretary of labor Daniel Patrick Moynihan. Intended as an internal document for President Johnson, the report addressed the perceived crisis of the breakdown of black families, defining the problem in historical context. Another was the highly publicized critique of liberal education policies put forth in *Equality of Educational Opportunity*, commonly known as the Coleman report. Commissioned by the U.S. Office of Education in accordance of the Civil Rights Act of 1964 to determine the availability of equal educational opportunity, sociologist James Coleman and his research team completed the nation's first large-scale assessment of academic achievement in 1966. They challenged the belief that schools could make a difference in the lives of poor and minority students. Among their findings was the judgment that schools had not, and could not, overcome the "initial deficiency" of the early upbringing that most poor, particularly black students had when they entered school.[30] The public by and large understood this conclusion to mean that schools could not make a difference in these students' lives and therefore extrapolated that pumping money into public schools was a waste. The Coleman and Moynihan reports became prime justifications for a growing resentment against funding struggling schools.

Other strong signs appeared that suggested the prevailing liberalism was beginning to wane. The Watts uprising converged with the backlash against college campus upheavals, the rise of the black power movement and increases in state spending and taxes to foster a growing grassroots conservative movement. This conservatism became an especially potent force in California politics and vaulted conservative Republican Ronald Reagan to defeat incumbent Democratic Governor Brown in California's 1966 gubernatorial election.[31] The conservative revolution would prove enduring in California and would soon starve the state's public schools of state financial support. Both revolts would serve as road maps for other states and the country as a whole.

While conservatism gained momentum, liberal programs remained. In 1968, the federal government accepted Compton and Willowbrook as part of the Model Cities program, which government policymakers had designed to address urban and economic problems. Model Cities sought to coordinate federal, state, and local resources, develop innovative programs, and involve local residents in the planning and development process. Programs included such initiatives as neighborhood health clinics, job training, and "slum" clearance. Though local employees conducted the programs, federal funding from the U.S. Department of Housing and Urban Development was their engine.[32]

Compton officials welcomed the opportunity to receive federal Model Cities funds, eagerly embarking on the first step of writing a planning grant. William Jones, Compton's director of community development, expressed this sentiment in a letter to the Los Angeles Federal Executive Board Steering Committee on Critical Urban Problems, in which he explained, "the enlistment of Anglo liberal economical support appears to be the only hope for Compton Citizens to achieve full equality and first class citizenship."[33] Local political power was only one step toward having equal political clout.

Compton's application for the Model Cities program documented the town's grim reality. This application, along with the government's support, added to the public's perception of Compton as a place of urban problems. Of course, the grant writers did not invent the town's woes. In the whole of the suburb, about 13 percent of families had annual incomes less than $3,000 and almost 20 percent earned less than $4,000. On Compton's solidly black west side, residents fared worse, and as a result this area became the proposed Model Cities neighborhood. In west Compton, 18 percent of families earned less than $3,000 per year.[34] The report found that the 1969 unemployment rate in Compton was more than a full percentage point higher than that of the greater Los Angeles-Long Beach metropolitan area. Even the employed residents did not hold high paying positions. Less than 20 percent of the civilian labor force reported work in white-collar jobs and the percentage of skilled craftsmen and foremen was about 15 percent. Just over 14 percent of the workers in Los Angeles County were classified as professional, technical, or kindred workers; Compton's figure was a little over 6 percent. In the county, 17.5 percent were classified as clerical or similar, and 8 percent as sales; in Compton the percentages measured 6.5 and 3.[35] A special census also revealed that the majority of Compton's labor force worked outside the town, and therefore other municipalities gained from their payroll taxes.[36] Compton's numbers clearly indicated that the town's residents, and by extension the town, suffered from financial hardship and that there was little hope of imminent relief from the economic distress. Emphasizing these problems strengthened the case for receiving funds, but the downside was that it helped to define Compton's reputation.

The Model Cities application also revealed the state of Compton's schools, which other sources affirmed. In 1968, Compton High had low reading scores and a high pupil to teacher ratio. On July 9, 1968, high school teacher Jacqueline Goldberg addressed the Compton Union board of trustees about her concern that some of her students could not read.[37] A few months later, the parents of Centennial High students sent a resolution to the Compton Union board because they were "gravely concerned" about the level of their children's reading competency.[38] The Model Cities application exposed Compton students' poor scores on state reading tests. First graders in Compton elementary schools ranked in the 26th percentile on a scale of 100 compared to students in Los Angeles (29th), Paramount (32nd), and Long Beach (44th). Tenth graders in Compton's senior high schools ranked in the 23rd percentile compared to students in Paramount (37th), Los Angeles (46th), and Long Beach (57th). Compton's dropout rate was over twice that of Los Angeles County as a whole. Area students were academically impoverished, and the schools had taken on characteristics often associated with urban centers. Better schools were a linchpin in changing the poverty-stricken community, but in these areas a vicious cycle persisted: poverty helped destroy the schools, and the schools helped perpetuate poverty in the community.

The Model Cities program would not ameliorate these problems. Though progressive in the concept of mixing community action with federal funds, all the Model Cities across the nation suffered from insufficient resources. Moreover, public identification of Compton as part of the Model Cities program and other federal programs to deal with urban problems only served to reinforce public perception of Compton as a town with the intractable social and economic problems more commonly associated with urban centers.

The Desegregation Trap

Cutting funding hurt Compton's school districts. With less money, Compton area schools could not match the pay scales of other districts and, as a result, they struggled to hire and retain teachers. In 1964 a local grassroots organization, the Parent Teacher Action Group, produced a list of grievances against districts, including documenting that there were seventh– and eighth–grade geography and history classes with 150 and 175 students per class.[39] There could be no reasonable expectation that students could learn in those classes.

While classes that large would be a nearly impossible situation for any teacher, some of Compton's teachers were underprepared to teach in even a regular-sized class. In the mid-1960s the districts had to take nontraditional routes to fill teaching slots. Compton City was one of 240 California school districts that gained permission from the state to recruit teachers who had not fulfilled the required minimum education for regular classroom jobs.[40] In addition, the Compton Union and Willowbrook districts took part in the National Teacher Corps, a Great Society anti-poverty program that trained liberal arts graduates as teaching interns in public schools serving poor children.[41] While filling the requisite number of teaching slots, these programs put underqualified instructors with the neediest students.

White parents in the Compton City School District used the lack of funds as a justification for asking that their neighborhood school become part of another district. In September 1966, parents requested that the Lynwood and Paramount districts take jurisdiction from Compton City in running the Abbott and Keppel Schools respectively. Adversaries of the annexation pointed out that "Compton City Schools have a student population of 17,000 with approximately 60% of these being Negro children. Keppel School, which has petitioned to go to Paramount, and Abbott School are both all 'white.'" Challengers noted that if the switch transpired much of the white student population would leave the district. Ultimately, they worried: "Would not this be setting a fearful precedent for other areas who are trying to escape the responsibilities incumbent on all citizens to reach a solution of our racial 'problems?'"[42]

Opponents used race—and racial integration—as the arguments for keeping the district together. Like Lynwood's departure from Compton Union in 1950 and La Canada's from Pasadena in 1961, white parents' appeal for annexation took on racial overtones though the parents denied any such motives. Like those in La Canada, the parents who requested the transfer adamantly denied the charges that they wished to maintain a white school and pointed to the fact that "we have had at Abbott School, on two separate occasions, Negro children in attendance. Abbott School had last year in their employ two very fine and most competent Negro Teachers, who will again be in attendance this school year."[43] These numbers did not reflect the demographic changes in the Compton area. Instead, they proved that racial lines persisted in Compton schools, a notion supported by the Parent Teachers Action Group's 1964 list of grievances. The list noted that minority teachers were "frozen in undesirable positions," the district employed only two black and no Latino counselors, and three schools on Compton's east side, Roosevelt, Whaley, and Dominguez, had never had any African Americans on the staff.[44] Yet, as the area became increasingly black, it was progressively more difficult for white parents to maintain racially segregated schools. Black leaders wished to stop whites from leaving the district because a predominantly black district would face harder times.

Fights over integrated schools raged in other pockets of Los Angeles County as well. Pasadena schools were once again prime examples of this struggle. Since the 1963 *Jackson* decision Pasadena's school district had a system of open enrollment that nominally allowed students to choose to attend non-neighborhood schools where empty seats existed. The district did not provide transportation to schools, so only parents who could drive their children could take advantage of the program. In practice, the system served to segregate schools further as whites used it to move from racially tipping schools to ones that were all white. This practice culminated in a 1968 lawsuit in which black and white plaintiffs challenged the district's purposeful racial segregation of students. This case, known as the *Spangler* suit, was the first of its kind west of the Rocky Mountains.

Spangler grew in scope and gained national attention. In 1969 the federal government expanded the suit beyond Pasadena's high schools to include the entire school district. In January 1970, the trial opened, and just two weeks later, in a surprisingly quick decision, the judge ordered Pasadena to integrate its schools fully by the start of the next school year because the district was violating the black students' rights under the Fourteenth Amendment. The decision also found that the district needed to desegregate its staff. Pasadena implemented a system of busing, but it did not have the desired effect of integrating the schools. Instead of participating in the desegregation plan, many white families left Pasadena or sent their children to private schools.[45]

Los Angeles schools also faced desegregation lawsuits. The 1970 *Crawford v. Board of Education of the City of Los Angeles* explicitly expanded the directive for desegregation beyond the South and beyond just integrating whites and blacks. This ruling forced Los Angeles Unified School District to integrate all groups of students, a plan that would require busing students. As it did across the country, busing raised the ire of many white Angelenos, and for years anti-busing groups challenged the decision. In 1976, a California court upheld the decision, and in 1978 Los Angeles began busing forty thousand students as well as implementing a magnet program to retain white, middle-class students in the district.[46]

While the records do not indicate any explicit involvement with the *Spangler* or *Crawford* cases, evidence exists that Compton residents' concern for integrated school districts, and protecting the rights of black students, extended beyond their own districts' borders. In 1970, the Compton branch of the NAACP urged its members to attend a meeting of the California Board of Education to oppose the weakening of the state's desegregation guidelines.[47]

The next year, the Compton NAACP joined with the Western Regional Chapter of CORE, Southern Christian Leadership Conference-West, and Community Resources Council to protest the "racist tactics prevalent in the Lynwood, California School System." The groups assessed that the district was "guilty of maintaining a racist-type administration which is tantamount to a criminal conspiracy to subject Blacks to cruel and undue physical abuse and harassment." The list of offenses ranged from specific classroom occur- rences to more systemic problems. In one documented case, an English teacher called his four black students "clinkers" and, in another, a five-year- old black girl was refused admission to the exclusively white elementary school around the corner from her house. She was forced instead to attend a school almost a mile from her home.[48]

Even as Compton activists looked outward, every aspect of school life and politics in their own town became racially charged with the changes in population. Linda Allen, an African American resident of Compton, recalled tension when attending the still predominantly white Dominguez High in the late 1960s. She recounted, "we [the black students] felt outnumbered . . . I remember they never had a black on the homecoming court at Dominguez until the year after I graduated in '69 . . . and they only had very few blacks on the drill team. . . . You know, so there was a lot of tension then. There re- ally was."[49] The town's remaining white residents populated the east side schools and held onto control of school activities.

The *Compton Herald American* both documented and reflected the con- flicts between black and white residents. The editor barred African Ameri- cans from the society pages. Writer Richard Elman noted, "in Compton, any white person who wasn't in jail or on Welfare could make the society pages, so the absence of Negroes was noteworthy."[50] At other times the paper's edito- rial policy was not as subtle. Maxcy Filer recalled, "the *Herald American* used to just print some of the worst articles in the world about us. 'Negro does this.' 'Negro robs this.' 'Negro robs that.' That was the *Herald American*."[51] When the first African American ran for city council, the *Herald American* printed pictures of both candidates and reminded people to vote.[52] This vi- sual representation helped vault the white candidate to an easy victory.

Black and Latino Power Ascendant

Despite whites' efforts to maintain control of the town and its institutions, African Americans gained political power as the number of black residents surpassed the number of whites. In June 1967 African Americans gained a majority on the Compton city council.[53] Two years later, in spring 1969, voters elected Compton's first black mayor, Douglas Dollarhide. With his selection, the *Los Angeles Times* posited that Compton would become a "test tube for study and analysis" because it was the biggest town west of the Mississippi with black political power in action. The article argued that Compton's becoming a black-run town emerged at a particularly important time as the black power movement was gaining strength.[54]

In the era after the passage of the Voting Rights Act, African Americans made momentous political gains in Compton.[55] In 1969 Compton residents elected blacks to the highest offices in the municipal government and appointed an African American to lead the school district.[56] On the whole, blacks achieved power at Compton by controlling the town's political, cultural, economic, and educational institutions. Compton had experienced a quiet revolution in the ballot box, though its new leaders faced formidable obstacles in running their town and their schools, as they inherited deep debt, community tensions, and an inefficient school system. Focusing on the change in power newspapers nationwide ran the story of Compton's election; this suburb was becoming known nationally as a black city.[57]

Even with these victories at the ballot box, Compton's black residents continued to mobilize to get out the vote. The national NAACP held a voter registration drive in an attempt to affect the 1970 mid-term elections, and the Compton branch eagerly took part in organizing. In a letter to the national director of the drive, chapter president Maxcy Filer explained why the group was enthusiastic to participate: "though we have made great strides here in Compton through the use of the ballot, there is still too much apathy and too many failing to register, or re-register."[58]

The NAACP also tried to influence what was taught in the schools, starting in 1968 to sponsor a "Negro History Week." Each year the local chapter held a special program that highlighted the achievements of Compton's school-age students. The lineup typically had a few performances and speakers as well as an art show. The organization then gave out awards to students from each of the schools. The chapter chose to emphasize educational and athletic achievements because they felt "too much attention is focused on delinquents."[59] In shaping the program in this manner the NAACP achieved two goals: rewarding achievers and spotlighting them to the public.

The NAACP banquets were just one way African Americans extended their influence beyond elected positions to public discourse. In order to put forth black voices silenced in the *Herald American*, in March 1970 Ray Watkins founded *The Bulletin* (later called the *Compton Bulletin*), which printed news about the black community.[60] Articles in the *Bulletin* exposed that even with, and perhaps because of, their increased political power and larger public presence, African Americans continued to face whites' anger. The *Bulletin* published a wide variety of news, including the problems between Compton residents. One July 1970 article described whites' threatening blacks who moved into their neighborhoods, focusing on the experiences of the McCoy family. "Night raiders" drove by the house and threw "bricks and bottles" through the windows. Mrs. McCoy witnessed "white teenage youths urinating against the side of the house," and when she tried to stop them, "they would only say, 'We're going to get you Niggers out of here.'"[61] Though more than a decade after the events on Reeve Street, blacks continued to face whites' hatred when crossing Compton's racial boundaries. With the publication of the *Bulletin*, Compton's black residents now had a place to publicize such experiences.

Maintaining institutions such as newspapers became an important part of the discourse around fixing Los Angeles's economic and political inequality. In spring 1966, in the aftermath of the August 1965 rebellion, the local leadership of the Student Nonviolent Coordinating Committee (SNCC) proposed that Watts along with parts of Compton and Lynwood secede from their municipalities and, with unincorporated Willowbrook and Florence, incorporate as Freedom City. Watts residents felt neglected and dumped on by Los Angeles municipal authorities. Complaints included disproportionate placement of public housing in their area, abusive treatment by police, and inadequate schools. Advocates argued that with home rule residents could more effectively influence political and economic dynamics that affected their lives. While the plan reflected SNCC's embracing of Black Power, more moderate activists also considered the potential of Freedom City.[62]

The case of Watts's neighbor Compton could have served as the argument against a separate Freedom City, as Compton exemplified the limitations of political power without economic development. When Dollarhide became mayor in 1969, it was clear that Compton's fiscal survival depended on the ability to annex industrial tracts. But the all-white County Local Area Formation Commission, which governed annexations in Los Angeles County, systematically discriminated against Compton in annexation decisions while white communities like Carson, Torrance, and Long Beach got the tax base. In one instance Compton, Long Beach, and Carson battled over the right to annex and tax a parcel of industrial land valued at more than $65 million. Dollarhide told the Local Agency Formation Commission that his town had an insufficient tax base and vitally needed the tax revenues the land would provide. Warren Butler, a member of the Compton City Planning Commission, took the argument a step farther and said that if the land was annexed to Long Beach it would amount to "economic segregation" and "a crime against the children of Compton."[63] Compton officials believed that without the increase in funds the annexation of industrial lands promised to provide, their schools were doomed to failure.

The structure of California's school finance dictated the need for increased tax funds because it used a foundation program to allocate revenues to local school districts. The California Department of Education established a minimum acceptable level of expenditure and then calculated the amount of revenue each district needed to raise through property taxes. If the tax revenues, when added to the basic state aid, fell short of the minimum, the state granted additional "equalization" funds to bring the district up to the foundation level. A district that had a higher assessed valuation in property taxes raised larger total revenue than a district like Compton, which brought in less tax revenue.[64] Even with state aid, therefore, Compton remained among the poorest funded districts in California.

The town needed more money for its schools. In the early 1970s, about 40 percent of the school district's general funds came from local taxpayers.[65] It was losing the already meager commercial tax base it had, however, as many of the businesses in Compton closed because of the high rate of violence and crime. The federal government granted funds to revitalize the central business district, but the redevelopment plans failed.[66] Cabot, Cabot & Forbes built an industrial park on the annexed land, promising to bring at least seventy-five new commercial firms and an estimated 6,300 new jobs to the Compton area. By 1973, however, many Comptonites felt duped by the company, asserting that it employed very few blacks from Compton and that most of the facilities were warehouses.[67] In July 1973 the *Compton Bulletin* ran an opinion article that posited that Compton was turning into the proverbial stepchild of Los Angeles County because "too many businessmen are pulling out of downtown Compton because of the high crime rate in our city."[68] Because of the town's crime-ridden image, the shops did not attract customers from other towns. Local residents were struggling financially and could not keep the stores afloat on their own. Furthermore, when Compton residents did spend their money, many chose to shop outside the town's limits because they perceived Compton stores as unsafe and their prices and quality of merchandise as not competitive.[69] John Corcoran, Compton's city manager, reported that a survey of ten nearby cities showed that Compton turned up 28 percent below average in business sales. He said, "What we're doing in Compton is putting iodine on a cancer. We must upgrade retail sales facilities so the sales tax rises sufficiently to support the needs of the city."[70] Compton did not modernize its retail facilities and its stores lost customers to new shopping centers in nearby towns.

A Growing Latino Presence

Compton was not simply black and white. Latinos had lived in Compton when whites were the majority, but they began to spread out from their small *barrio* as African Americans were becoming the majority.[71] Former Compton resident Gilda Acosta-Gonzalez remembers that in the 1960s, "My neighborhood was all African American. They were all African American, but it was African Americans that embraced us because we were the only Latinos . . . . I would say in the radius of five miles there were no more than about ten Hispanic families; and we all knew each other." Even though her family was Latino, she recalls that "the community embraced us. We had the best, best neighbors. . . . They knew we were Mexican. They knew that we cooked different food. And while we were growing up, we noticed that . . . sometimes the kids are mad at you and they called you 'Mexican beaners' and stuff like that. The first time we got called that, we just didn't understand why. It was just pettiness."[72]

Beginning in the 1970s the Latino population expanded as Mexican immigrants moved into the south central portion of Los Angeles County. Much of this migration resulted from the recent radical changes in federal law, the Hart-Cellar Immigration and Nationality Act of 1965. Specifically, the new law abolished the quota system that had governed the nation's immigration policy since the 1920s. The old restrictions gave preference to immigrants from certain European nations and the new law instead gave priority to immigrants who had certain skills or had family relationships with American citizens or residents. Hart-Cellar thus gave immigrants from around the world an equal shot at entering the United States.[73]

The act reshaped California's population. Following its enactment, Asian and Latin American immigrants entered the United States in unprecedented numbers. Mexicans, both documented and undocumented, became the state's largest group of immigrants. In 1960 approximately 1.75 million people of Mexican origin lived in the United States, and by 2000 they exceeded 21 million. California housed about 40 percent of their total population in 2000 and was home to the largest number of undocumented immigrants in the nation.[74] California's non-Hispanic white population dropped from 77 to 48 percent between 1970 and 2000, due to the growth of the Asian and Latino populations.[75]

The increase in population numbers did not mean social integration, however. At that time Acosta-Gonzalez began attending Davis Junior High School, where "we were getting all this mixture, blacks, Latinos, Samoans. So it's always conflict. . . . You would notice blacks here, Latinos here."[76] This separation was also evident at Dominguez High, which by then had become exceedingly black. In Dominguez's 1977 yearbook, members of the senior class awarded a number of titles to their "favorite" classmates. African Americans won all of the honors including "Mr. & Mrs. Personality" and "Most Likely to Succeed." The only categories not held by African Americans were "Mr. & Mrs. Mexican American."[77] Even as a token of inclusion, this prize indicated the extent of segregation among the student body. The racial division caused other problems because, in the words of Acosta-Gonzalez, "the gangs were forming because they needed to protect themselves against the other races."

Latinos played a similar role in the *Compton Bulletin*. Although the newspaper focused on the experiences of blacks in Compton, it also gave Compton's Latino population a small voice in a regular column aptly entitled "Chicano Corner." In one such column, the author complained that in Compton "the Chicano faces a virtual stone wall. For the Black leaders are not too eager about relinquishing any of their newly acquired power; power they fought long and hard in a city boasting of itself now as the largest city West of the Mississippi with a Black Mayor."[78] While allotting space to a Latino writer, the *Bulletin's* editorials and other opinion pieces clearly demonstrated that it was a black newspaper that would marginalize Chicano and white voices. The trend would continue even as Compton's Latino population grew.

The dynamic between blacks and Latinos in Compton needs to be understood in the context of the larger economic changes occurring in the Los

Angeles metropolitan area. Industrial flight had shaped the region's economy as a whole since the mid-1960s. Evident before the Watts riot, the process accelerated in its wake and continued through the 1970s. While the number of traditional, highly unionized, high-wage manufacturing jobs declined, the number of high-technology manufacturing, craft-specialty, and advanced service-sector positions increased. Most of these jobs remained out of reach for Latinos and African Americans because of racial discrimination and education requirements. As a result, they bore the brunt of the decline in manufacturing employment, losing high-wage, stable jobs. By the mid-1970s, the employment situation for blacks in Los Angeles County was the worst it had been since the Great Depression. In Compton, unemployment doubled between 1960 and 1970.[79] Compton, like South Central Los Angeles, was at a "disaster" level of destitution and becoming more and more like its neighbor.[80]

As Compton became a town populated by people of color, it also became a racialized space, and urban ills as well as the specter of federal programs to ameliorate them dominated the discourse about this inner-ring suburb. Crime became central to this dialog as well. A 1972 study by Compton's Special Service Center had declared that the town's residents, businesspeople, and officials viewed crime and delinquency as the community's biggest problems. Earlier statistics had validated their concern—for 1969, Compton held the distinction of having the highest crime rate in California.[81] Drug arrests rose 255 percent between 1964 and 1968. Between 1966 and 1968 juvenile arrests grew 600 percent.[82] Americans had moved to the suburbs to escape crime but crime came to plague the suburbs as well.

The Ironies of Unification

While accepting federal programs, residents also believed that changes on the local level could make a difference in their schools. In 1964 and then again in 1966, local residents proposed unifying the school districts as a solution to the districts' problems, but these proposals butted up against desires for local control and racial separation. In 1964 members of the Enterprise board split over supporting unification, with some favoring the prospect because its coffers were spread thin and others opposing it because the district was willing to tax at a higher rate and pay teachers more.[83] In 1966, the members of the Willowbrook's board of trustees rejected the idea because they believed their district had "much to lose in unification," such as the reduced lunch program and other anti-poverty programs that the district obtained precisely *because of* its level of poverty.[84] Board members instead voted (unsuccessfully) to secede from Compton Union and unify the Willowbrook School District itself, turning it from an elementary district into one that served students in kindergarten through twelfth grade.[85] Board members of the Enterprise School District also unanimously rejected the idea of a Compton Union unification.[86] In addition to protecting the funds, board members in both districts hoped to maintain their power over jobs and classrooms. Other communities around Compton also fought for local control, or home rule. Between 1954 and the 1970s, Lakewood residents worked hard to make this sensibility dominant in Los Angeles metropolitan politics and culture.[87] Political power over such things as a school district served as a root for community identity.

California politics played a role in the school districts. In rejecting unification local residents countered a prevailing trend in California politics, a revolt against taxes. Unification would mean lower taxes, a central tenet of California's rising conservative movement. But even this argument did not succeed with local voters. Despite efforts to maintain local control, unification of some configuration became more likely in 1966 when the state legislature passed the Unruh Reorganization Bill, which, in an attempt to ease the "heavy burdens now being imposed upon local property taxpayers in providing adequate support for the public schools," required non-unified school districts to hold unification elections every two years until a consolidation was accomplished.[88] While these two tenets—anti-tax and local control—would exist in tension, the statewide anti-tax sentiment would win out.

Yet, even with the state mandate, the first round of unification elections in Compton Union proved unsuccessful. While the boards of trustees of Compton Union and Compton City supported their amalgamation as "the most logical form of school district organization for this area," Compton Union voters rejected it twice in 1967.[89] Both times residents in the Willowbrook and Enterprise, the two poorer of the three component elementary districts, headed the charge against the merger. Willowbrook board members once again stressed the fear of losing "local control [that made for] a more effective response to community educational needs and desires" and "local identification," which allowed for closer contact between citizens and school personnel, as well as more individualized attention for students.[90] The black residents of those districts employed the rhetoric whites had used in places as arguments against integration. Similar arguments were made in a subsequent election in spring 1969.

The issue of power continued to dominate the debate. In spring 1969, the Enterprise School District board members argued against unification because they believed that pro-unification forces wanted to consolidate power into the hands of Compton City School District administrators, not improve education. In order to illustrate Compton City's—the majority district's—quest for power, Enterprise's opposition statement pointed to Compton City's refusal to support a unification plan that had equal representation from the districts on the new board, instead advocating for at-large representation. In a joint statement the Enterprise trustees used strong language to describe the unification campaign, calling it an "assault" and asserting it could be viewed "in no other light than as a gigantic <u>POWER PLAY</u>, to take over the lives of an entire area." Officials expressed fear that in a larger district the needs of their area's students would be overlooked.[91]

Enterprise officials also claimed that their residents supported educational improvement more than the other areas' residents because Enterprise voters consistently passed bond issues and willingly carried an extremely high tax rate. In their joint statement, board members asked their constituents: "Can we be assured that the educational level of our children that we, in Enterprise, have taxed ourselves to produce will continue to show achievement and growth? Have the other districts which will be a part of this unification shown the same willingness to support education with their tax dollar? A cursory look at the record will show the answer to be <u>NO</u>!"[92] Enterprise officials did not, however, acknowledge that their district carried long-standing debts that also hindered efforts to improve the schools.[93]

Despite opponents' efforts, in April 1969 the residents of the Compton Union elected to combine the districts. The vast majority in Enterprise voted against unifying, but the majority in Compton and Willowbrook cast their ballots in favor.[94] After years of battles the districts would finally merge into one.

The new unified district became the third largest in Los Angeles County, serving the area's approximately 44,000 students from early childhood to adult classes. It covered eighteen square miles, in which it had twenty-nine elementary schools, with seventeen Head Start and ten child care programs; eight junior high schools; three regular high schools; one continuation high school, with a teen mothers' program; a school for special needs students, elementary through secondary; and an adult school complex. The district employed approximately 3,000 people.[95]

Like other public school districts across the country, including Los Angeles, Chicago, Atlanta, and New York, the newly unified district developed a decentralized form of administration in order to have decision-making in more "locally responsive units."[96] Under this structure the district was divided into three areas, each containing one of the three regular high schools and its feeder schools. An area administrator oversaw the educational and bureaucratic programs in the schools of that region. The school district hoped that breaking up the district into smaller units would bring the school community closer together.[97]

Even with this decentralized structure, the unified district needed one superintendent. The new amalgamated school board chose Alonzo Crim, an African American educator from Chicago, to lead its district for the 1969–70 school year and become the head of the new unified district in July 1970.[98] As one of the first steps in organizing the district, Crim arranged a series of town hall meetings to, in his words, "look at what the system could and should do."[99] Area residents packed the gatherings, with more than a thousand people attending each, showing the new district's leader that the desire for input into the local schools persisted in Compton. By the fourth meeting, the district's mandate became clear: "to improve basic skills of all students, to increase the number going on to postsecondary education, to distribute equitably the resources of the school district, and to maintain communication between the district and the community in general." Holding these meetings and actually developing a plan of action from them increased community support for the new district.

Unification left unsolved the area schools' fiscal problems, however. Crim recalled: "Much of my time in Compton was devoted to the search for additional resources to augment the meager tax base of the district."[100] In fact, while unification could ostensibly weed out the bureaucratic repetition and lessen costs, in reality, it did not make quick changes because the bill that required the merger of schools also placed a two-year moratorium on layoffs. As a result, the new district retained all five districts' nonteaching personnel, which remained costly. Just a couple of months after ratification of the measure, the district became further hampered with economic problems when Enterprise's deep debts were uncovered. Accordingly the newly minted Compton Unified School District had to request an emergency loan to pay its teachers and classified employees.[101]

*   *   *

Unification did not dramatically alter the prospects for Compton and its schools, and problems persisted. From its inception, the new district faced financial crises, as it assumed all of its member districts' expenses, debts, and bonds. The sums unpaid had mounted and proved a continuous financial burden. The long-standing educational and economic problems remained and Compton schools would continue to flounder because they stood on an already anemic financial base and a suburban structure that limited opportunities to build a stronger foundation. Compton plunged into a downward economic spiral: residents became poorer; stores and employers moved elsewhere; and the local economy, property values, and tax revenues declined. In turn, the increase in poverty caused rising crime, lowered student achievement, and created embittered students, teachers, and parents.

Chapter 5

Unyielding Problems

In September 1972, a student shot and killed another student in a classroom at Compton High. Teacher Sydney Morrison recalled the incident: "the third week into school I had gone over to the district office and came back and there was a body covered in a sheet down the hall from my room, two doors down. Apparently one student accosted another student and the kid pulled out a gun and just shot him right there in class."[1] Only two months after the Compton High killing, a school security guard shot and wounded a Dominguez High student, leading to a band of over fifty students running around the campus, breaking windows and throwing trash cans. During the ruckus, several students assaulted a teacher.[2] This violence, and the continuing threat of more violence, showed the school administrators' lack of control.

Morrison said a constant threat of disruption dominated the schools, and, as a result, "the major preoccupation of the administration was maintaining order." The threat and reality of violence drained students and teachers, as Morrison learned firsthand. He recollected, "I remember another time where there was a shooting outside the gates and there was a body outside on the streets. I remember another time where on campus some kid had pulled out a gun on the bus and someone shouted 'gun' and I darted to the ground. That's when I decided that I was going to leave. I said I am not going to die at Compton High after surviving Vietnam."[3] Morrison left the district at the end of the school year. Despite the small number of students causing the problems, the threat of violence pervaded the schools, inside and outside the classroom.

The violence and crime on the schoolyards reflected the disorder in Compton's community as a whole. In 1972, the year of the shootings at Compton and Dominguez High Schools, the town of Compton ranked second only to the city of Los Angeles in the number of reported homicides in Los Angeles County. Compton topped Long Beach in murders even though the latter had five times its population.[4] Though the *Los Angeles Times* claimed that the 1972 crime sheets served as a "shallow or superficial view of a city," it nevertheless painted Compton as a "veritable outlaw sanctuary."[5] Once the vehicle for the suburban dream, Compton had become the trope of the inner city—endemic poverty, inadequate schools, and frequent violence.

At this time, violence in the schools was a major national issue and Compton was an extreme example because of its extreme poverty and endemic problems. Comptonites inherited deep debt, community tensions, and an inefficient school system. As students and families became increasingly poor, Compton's politicians and school administrators needed to provide more services. Already drowning under decades of debt, however, they could hardly afford to furnish them, since the town lacked the booming factories and government contracts that buoyed other towns in the region. Thus, despite higher local taxes, the schools worsened. In time the schools' low performance coupled with these high taxes made Compton a less attractive place to settle for those who could afford to choose.

These failings became a part of a larger web of cynical statewide politics, which culminated in state voters' passing Proposition 13. The referendum forever changed the funding of California's public services, especially its public schools. Already starved of resources and forced to pay its teachers lower salaries, Compton's schools faced the realities of an ever-decreasing tax capacity and an ever-increasing poverty-stricken population. In this way, Compton's schools shaped the community and vice versa.

As Compton experienced these socioeconomic changes, politicians, policymakers, and journalists began to equate the town's problems with "urban blight," and as the town became increasingly poor and black, its categorization as "urban" often took on symbolic meanings—a shorthand for crime, violence, and chaos. Like their white counterparts, middle-class African Americans began to fear that a black majority would diminish suburbia's promise, and just as whites did in other suburban enclaves, the town's new black politicians fought these real and perceived problems through "law and order" and redevelopment campaigns. Existing in a space between city and suburb, Compton exposed the often arbitrary line drawn between the two.

Law and Order in a Black Community

In the wake of Watts, the fear of violence dominated Compton politics. In 1972 Compton had 46 murders, which, in a town of almost 80,000, ranked it first per capita in the nation. That same year Compton had 873 armed robberies, 4,305 burglaries, and 98 rapes.[6] In promising to fix Compton's woes, Doris Davis, Compton's city clerk, was elected mayor in 1973 on a "law and order" platform, declaring: "We're not going to allow a handful of hoodlums to run this city . . . . If I sound like law and order, well that's too bad. I'm not apologizing for it."[7] Compton's black politicians adopted law-and-order rhetoric as a means to place their black town in the American mainstream by showing that black residents also desired police protection.

Both contemporaries and historians have written about the ways white conservative and liberal politicians, policymakers, and pundits framed security as a means to tap into white anxiety about a variety of perceived threats, from street crimes to civil rights protests to antiwar demonstrations.[8] The case of Compton was different, however. In framing her rhetoric in terms of "law and order," Davis, an African American, claimed the term that had served as a racially coded symbol of the conservative movement. Barry Goldwater had used "law and order" as one of his themes for his 1964 presidential run, and Ronald Reagan adopted the term during his 1966 California gubernatorial election. Maintaining law and order became the most important domestic issue in the 1968 presidential campaign and helped fuel Richard Nixon's win over Hubert Humphrey.

Creating a discourse around crime prevention meant appearing tough to a variety of factions: criminals, residents, and outsiders looking in on the suburb. Politicians aimed their battles against Compton's real and imagined lawlessness in order to calm the streets and squash the assumptions that came with being an increasingly racialized place. During her election campaign, Davis reflected that "there is a lot of work to be done in Compton, a city with a high unemployment rate; few new businesses; a high crime rate; and a lack of sufficient police force."[9] She asserted that crime had made many Comptonites "virtual prisoners in their own homes" and promised to fight vice by providing jobs for youth and boosting the quality, size, and pay of the police force.[10] Davis's emphasis in her campaign on a commitment to "law and order" also meant portraying a calmer and safer environment, which Compton politicians hoped would improve their town's prospects for business.

Get-tough rhetoric and the increased police presence targeted gangs, which at the time numbered around twenty. While not new in Los Angeles and Compton, gang formation and activity grew in the late 1960s and 1970s, attracting new members for a variety of reasons including safety, money, identity, and status. Racialized identities and structural constraints also played a major role in gang formation in Los Angeles and it was no coincidence that the resurgence of gangs occurred in the wake of the Watts rebellion in the heavily African American populated areas of South Los Angeles. The first Crip gang formed in South Los Angeles in late 1969 and "sets" of the group quickly cropped up in areas such as Compton, where the first Blood gang, the Compton Pirus, began.[11]

The communities and schools of Compton, Watts, and Willowbrook quickly became overrun by gangs. Kelvin Filer recalled that when he was a student at Compton High from 1970 through 1973 gangs were "becoming an issue." He continued: "That's right about the time that it was starting to impact not only neighborhoods, but the schools. So I was very cognizant of it. But I also knew that it was nothing that I wanted to get involved in and most of the people I, of course, hung around with felt the same way."[12]

Though Compton served as ground zero for the emergence of gangs, Compton police department only started its first full-time gang detail in 1974. Despite the rhetoric of getting tough on crime, Compton's law enforcement failed to address the threats to peace and security in an effective or timely manner. These gangs altered the town and its schools.[13]

Law and Order in the Schools

While the political class talked tough, the actual need for law and order extended to the schoolyards. Unification of Compton area districts had promised to fix the schools' financial, academic, and safety problems but the social and economic impediments to the performance of the school system remained. Schools provided employment, so as a result other needs—such as employment and loyalty—sometimes came before the needs of students, who thus confronted frequent violence, underresourced classrooms, and unprepared teachers. Not surprisingly, parental anger at the system grew, but their critique stood in tension with the larger forces that seriously constrained the schools.

Disorder in the schools dominated headlines in both the *Compton Herald American* and the *Compton Bulletin*. In May 1970, several black students beat a group of Chicano students "beyond recognition" at Whaley Junior High. In a separate incident at Whaley a student was raped.[14] That winter, in a period of just three weeks, two other students were murdered in Compton's schools. The first was seventeen-year-old Robert Rhinehart, a student at Centennial High, where he was killed, and the second was Robert Valdez, a seventeen-year-old Dominguez High student, murdered on the campus of Whaley Junior High.[15]

Parents and students reacted to the violence. Parents held a marathon, "less than orderly" meeting that lasted over four hours. It ended with a call for a boycott of all Compton schools.[16] That Monday, five hundred of Whaley's eleven hundred students stayed out of school, while many students walked out of the district's other campuses. Students wanted officials to "see the urgency of the situation and thus act in a more positive and relevant fashion," according to "Chicano Corner" columnist Jose Ysidro Lopez. But instead, "So far crumbs." Lopez cut to the core, asking, "What kind of school system is the Compton Unified School District running?" For Lopez, and ostensibly the other Compton residents who boycotted the schools, it was "bad enough having second-rate teachers but when the students are being harassed, extorted, molested and killed in the 'halls of learning' the situation has reached a dead end." The district reacted with a classic "law and order" response—adding security guards to the most troublesome school sites.[17] This addition was inadequate, and many parents still feared sending their children to Compton schools.

The lack of law and order affected academics, which also languished. There had been a lot of rhetoric about fixing the schools, but that did not translate into action. A few months after the killings, academic problems took center stage when the district's abysmal test scores were released. For the 1970–71 school year Compton's third grade students scored in the fifth percentile and sixth grade students in the first percentile, as low as any district statewide. High school seniors also scored in the lowest-possible first percentile.[18] While the merits and pitfalls of standardized testing have been debated, especially for students of color, the depth and scope of the education problems clearly indicated systematic failure in the district. Gilda Acosta-Gonzalez remembered that when she went to college she soon realized she "lacked so much education versus the [other] people that were going [to her college.]" She felt like her "writing skills were not up to par."[19] Compton Unified failed to serve its students on two of the most basic levels: education and safety.

In response to the district's glaring problems, parents and students continued to demand improvements in the schools. In fall 1970, approximately fifty Centennial High students organized themselves into the Student Action Committee and picketed a school board meeting, demanding better learning conditions, a more diverse staff, and an improved educational program. At another meeting of the Compton Unified board of trustees, parents from Compton High and Davis Junior High laid out concerns about vandalism and security. Among their demands were the hiring of armed guards and increased police protection for both students and property.[20] They argued that cleaning up the disorder would serve as a step in addressing academic challenges.

Yet, two years later, in 1972, these concerns remained. As the year began, five parent groups in the Compton community combined efforts to present the school district with an outline of problems of student safety, academic programs, and school facilities. Their concern originally stemmed from the condition of Centennial High, where students did not have proper materials for their classes. The consolidated group asserted that the district owned the necessary books but that the materials remained in the warehouse rather than being delivered to the school. In an open letter the parents enumerated a series of reasons for demanding the resignation of Superintendent Crim and several of the district's school board members.[21]

In March 1972, at the request of the teachers' union, the Compton Education Association (CEA), which was started in the 1960s as an affiliate of the National Education Association (NEA), a team of teachers and consultants visited almost half of Compton Unified's forty-one schools. The investigators from the California Teachers Association (CTA) found that "violence and the lack of safety were matters of primary concern to high school teachers."[22] Their report listed a number of violent incidents, including one where three students threw a substitute teacher on the floor in a robbery attempt. The union's report suggested that a minority of the student population set the tone for the schools as a whole. Teachers felt that most students behaved properly, but "thugs" apparently had the upper hand and managed to create a "siege of terror" and vandalism in the high schools.[23]

In addition to investigating the violence, the union report delved into other issues. It documented class size overload in all the schools, including one teacher having fifty-one students in a remedial English class. In another school, due to overcrowding, the library substituted as a classroom. A shortage of playground space and equipment existed in some of the elementary

schools, and teachers cited lack of supplies as a "serious problem." Not surprisingly, the survey team also found teacher morale at a "low ebb" in all
schools it visited.[24]

Compton Unified's administrators challenged the report, saying it was
motivated by teachers' demands for higher salaries. Local municipal officials
also bristled at the union's statement, citing the unfavorable publicity it
brought the city.[25] Compton politicians and officials remained acutely aware
of how these problems affected wider public opinion. The Compton Local
Government Advisory Board—comprised of representatives from the municipal government, Compton Unified, Compton College, Compton Chamber of Commerce, and each of the federal and state agencies working in the
community—voted unanimously to censure the teachers' union for what it
claimed to be a "deliberate" move to "degrade Compton students and the
community." The entire advisory board sided with the sentiments of the
Compton Unified members and said the union's account served only to set
the stage for a new collective bargaining agreement.[26] Compton politicians
and officials remained acutely aware of how these problems would affect
wider public opinion. Whatever the motivations may have been behind the
report, few doubted the veracity of what it revealed.

Recurring violence in the Compton schools certainly reinforced the report's findings. In June 1972, just one month after the Local Government Advisory Board denounced the CTA statement, more than 50 percent of the
teachers at Centennial High called in sick to protest a rash of violence at the
school. With so many teachers absent, students rampaged through the school,
breaking windows, turning over desks, defacing ceilings, and destroying
books and other classroom materials.[27] That same month a substitute teacher
at Dominguez High reported being attacked with an umbrella by a student
after the two disagreed over a disciplinary matter.[28]

Compton was not alone. The 1970s saw an increased wave of school
crime and violence across the country, which provoked national distress. Popular thought associated most of these problems with troubled
inner-city schools. In Los Angeles, for example, several gun incidents in
schools riveted public attention, while Detroit's district administrators admitted it was "impossible" to catalog the number of violent occurrences in
their schools.[29] A 1975 California congressional committee identified a lack
of law and order in schools across the state. The two national teachers' unions,
the NEA and the American Federation of Teachers, both argued that teachers
across the country could not teach amid the prevalence of crime, which often

made victims of teachers. So widespread was the phenomenon, even the academic and social changes experienced in elite public schools raised serious concerns.[30]

The fact that violence plagued districts across the nation does not diminish the real effects it had on Compton Unified. Violence created fear and apathy among the students, some of whom fled the district. Tim Wright, student body president of Compton High, said "we [the students] are afraid in school that we're going to be shot or something."[31] An article in the *Los Angeles Times* reported that such fear caused many students to request transfers to other school districts and that if they did not receive the transfers, they often dropped out of sight—with at least tacit parental consent.[32] Some parents chose, when possible, to send their children to private or parochial schools or move out of the school district altogether. Unable to provide protection for its students, Compton Unified lost many of them.

The 1974 Supreme Court decision *Milliken v. Bradley* ensured that when families moved to other districts, there would not be a court order to integrate across district boundaries. In *Milliken*, the Supreme Court reversed a Michigan desegregation plan that dealt head-on with the problem of school segregation as a result of residential segregation. In order to desegregate the schools, the plan required students to be bused across school district and town boundaries. The Supreme Court ruled this plan unconstitutional, asserting that no evidence existed that showed the suburban districts deliberately segregating their schools.[33] But Compton turned the assumptions in *Milliken* on their head. Compton was a majority-minority suburb. In *Milliken* the suburbs were white and the suburbanites did not want to be integrated with urban areas. This could not be the case with Compton.

When parents and students tried to escape Compton Unified by moving, transferring, or dropping out, these actions produced more trouble for the already beleaguered district. The decline in the number of students created further fiscal strains because state allocations of funds were based on average daily attendance. During the 1972–73 school year, the district lost just over 2,300 students, a loss of almost $1.9 million in revenue. As a result, the county superintendent of schools placed the district in the category "financial difficulty" and notified district leaders if they did not make immediate cuts the district would be forced to close its doors in April.[34] Having struggled financially for decades, Compton's schools had hit a new low.

A state-sponsored stopgap measure plugged the financial hole temporarily, but the effects of poverty continued to ravage the district, resulting in more violence in the schools and an even more disgruntled workforce. Compton's teachers did not sit idle. In April 1973, teachers walked out of Whaley Junior High School after administrators failed to satisfy their demands guaranteeing a safer campus. Whaley's faculty called the protests, citing months of violence, unrest, and undisciplined behavior, in addition to the most recent incidents. The boycott virtually shut down the school for two days.[35] But, even after the teachers agreed to return to Whaley's classrooms, the problems persisted.

Compton's teachers not only faced violence in their schools, they did so for poor pay. While violence was not unique to Compton schools, the district had fewer resources to deal with it. Compton Unified's long-term financial woes worsened at the beginning of 1973–74, when, once again, attendance slipped below anticipated levels. This time the drop in enrollment meant a loss of almost $3 million in state aid. When district officials adopted the new budget, they did not include raising provisions for salaries. Not surprisingly this did not sit well with teachers who were paid 15 percent less than the county average salary.[36] Due to its low pay scale, Compton had scant opportunity to attract or retain the county's best teachers.

Low pay, indifferent students, inadequate supplies, potential violence, and deficient schools continued to take their toll on teachers. In Dominguez High's June 1973 yearbook, the students acknowledged, "at Dominguez to be a good teacher is almost like performing magic tricks for some and slave driving for others because of the lack of materials, but . . . the teachers did what they could to make use of what they have and expected the fact that there wasn't enough materials [sic]."[37] In November 1973, citing all these problems, Compton's teachers struck against the district, demanding increased security, supplies, and pay. The union claimed teachers faced wide-scale violence, classrooms with broken windows and no heating, playgrounds littered with glass, buildings with exposed wiring, and a "drastic" lack of materials.[38] By midday of the strike's first day, all forty-one schools, which served thirty-six thousand students, closed. Walking out of their classrooms, the vast majority of Compton Unified's teachers openly grieved the state of the district. The teachers would stay on strike for over two weeks.[39]

The strike focused attention on the district's conditions, including the overstaffing of administrators, though once again the discussion of Compton's problems was framed in terms of violence. Statistical studies revealed the district retained up to twice as many non-teaching employees in certain categories as others of comparable size. Compton financed fifty-two accounting positions, compared to eighteen in Pasadena, sixteen in Hacienda-La Puente, and fourteen in San Bernardino, each district with similar enrollments to that of Compton Unified.[40] A county report released in the midst of the strike confirmed teachers' allegations of a top-heavy district. The report argued that in order to become fiscally sound Compton Unified would have to close five schools and eliminate many jobs, including slashing administrative personnel, a step which alone would have saved over half a million dollars.[41] At a board meeting during the strike, one teacher called the number of administrators a "type of violence," meaning that the retention of such a top-heavy district showed administrators' disregard for the students and teachers.[42] The lengths of blown-up rhetoric revealed the desperation of the place.

Even after the mandatory retention period required through the unification process, Compton Unified continued to overstaff nonteaching personnel. District administrators resisted downsizing because Compton Unified provided employment for many community members. Superintendent Don Hodes asserted: "One of our main functions in this economically depressed area is to provide jobs, and so you don't go around cutting off people's jobs unless you have a good reason."[43] Hodes understood the district priorities to be twofold, education and employment. As a result, he considered the county task force's criticism of the districts' staffing unfair and misguided.

In Compton, a town devoid of many resources and populated by groups marginalized in the greater Los Angeles and U.S. economy and body politic, the municipal government and public school system became the main employment source in the increasingly beleaguered area. Compton's use of schools as a source of employment for adults was hardly unique. Political scientists have described such districts as "employment regimes" that view the schools primarily as a source of jobs and patronage.[44] Despite the altruistic view of the district's role in community, in actuality Compton Unified did not adequately meet the needs of the majority of students. The problems of debt, under-resourced classrooms, and dilapidated school sites continued to detract from students' educations.

The strike lasted sixteen days before the teachers and the district reached a settlement. The agreement addressed the main issue of the walkout, campus security, with the promise of a three-faceted program: a $200,000 violence control program, establishment of a school action committee to develop antiviolence educational programs, and creation of a protection program at various schools. In addition to gaining increased physical security, teachers obtained pay increases that placed them within the median income of teachers throughout the county schools. The district also promised to provide additional classroom materials and supplies for student educational purposes and additional maintenance on all district campuses.[45] Given the district's financial realities, it was unclear how it would fulfill all these promises.

Meeting the strike agreement became even more difficult when the already impoverished district found itself yet again in deep financial straits; soon after the work stoppage it became clear that the schools would incur an almost $2 million deficit. Ironically, much of the projected shortfall stemmed from money lost during the walkout. The district was deprived of funds based on attendance while continuing to pay most nonteaching employees who remained working. In addition, many of the striking teachers took sick leave during the walk out, making it necessary to pay them for missed days. The deficit caused Compton Unified's board to request a $2 million loan from the county in order to finish the school year.[46] Furthermore, state law required that Compton act conservatively with future plans, mandating that the district give notice to teachers who might be let go because of the district's projected budget. As required, Compton Unified dismissed 325 teachers, counselors, librarians, nurses, and principals, a move which set off a new furor.[47] Teachers had gone on strike to improve their employment situation and in turn helped worsen it.

The teachers' strike had brought the impact of poverty and crime on schools to the forefront and these issues returned to the spotlight a few months later when a special committee of the Los Angeles County Grand Jury convened to examine Compton. During the week of meetings, over one hundred interested citizens and officials addressed the committee.[48] Residents testified to the eleven grand jurors about the lack of available jobs. Seventeen-year-old Dominguez High School student Larry Benjamin stated, "I filled out an application for a job at Jack-in-the-Box and I found 50 other people applying for the same job. It was the only job around here."[49] James Wilson, the city manager of Compton, said that due to the lack of jobs and the inability to sell land in Compton for a decent price, "the Federal government became the source of income" for many residents, continuing "from 60 to 70% of Compton is on relief; AFDC, general relief, food stamps, and Medi-Cal at an average of $8,000 per family."[50] They found that the conditions "were worse than they were at the time of the Watts revolt" and asked that the McCone Commission be reconvened.[51] Despite money invested and promises made, Compton had fallen deeper into crisis.

The grand jury also heard about the schools and recommended the legislature permit the county superintendent of schools to assume jurisdiction for two years over the "mismanaged" school district.[52] Among the information disclosed, the testimony revealed that seventeen of twenty-six typewriters in a typing class were broken, that school buildings were without light and heat on occasion, and that one school had a flea infestation. School officials testified that the dropout rate in Compton was one of the highest in Los Angeles County and that the graduates of Compton Unified were, on many occasions, functionally illiterate. Larry Benjamin testified: "it takes me three weeks to read a short book, and I find it hard to do."[53] The schools, in effect, passed out diplomas simply for attendance, not for achievement. According to the grand jury summary, many residents complained that too much money had been spent on questionable items and on unnecessary trips for officials, some salaries were too high, and the district used favoritism in hiring. Town and district officials denied that the schools were as desperate as portrayed and asserted that the committee's report failed to recognize the financial and educational achievements in the previous two years.[54] Whether these allegations were true was unclear and perhaps irrelevant. Many Compton residents had lost faith that their school district could provide the most basic services, supplies, and facilities for their children, and that in itself was a glaring and elusive problem.

Lack of faith in the district led to parental action. At the beginning of the 1975–76 school year, parents once again requested their school area be annexed out of the Compton Unified, citing the lack of academic support as the reason for the desired change. Stevenson Village in Carson was one such case. This neighborhood's students attended schools in Compton Unified while the majority of Carson's students went to schools in Los Angeles Unified. In their request to transfer their children to Los Angeles Unified schools, parents cited a number of compelling reasons: Compton had the lowest reading scores in California; Compton had higher taxes; parents had been lying about their addresses to send children elsewhere; and Compton provided inadequate learning materials.[55] The complaints of parents ranged from safety to academics, but their bottom line remained the same—Compton Unified did not adequately serve their children.

Clearly in need of help, Compton Unified looked to the federal government for increased aid. In 1976, Compton received $3.5 million in federal emergency school funds. Two years prior the federal government appropriated to the district a mere $250,000. In 1977, the federal government gave the district no federal money (and the district had to lay off about 150 teachers, parent-aides, and para-professionals) because district administrators submitted a poorly written proposal that did not present a strong argument that the district provided programs to meet the needs of the minority students.[56] The inadequate grant application revealed school administrators' incompetency. As a vastly minority district, Compton had no sound reason to have grant applications failing to show how programs would aid black and Latino students. Compton was the very type of district for whom this grant was created and yet district officials managed to get the district's application denied.

Imagining Compton

Compton schools were failing in a variety of realms, and their continuing struggles helped cement public opinion of the town. The town also became progressively racialized, and its image in the popular consciousness changed.[57] Popular media played an integral part in defining Compton as urban in the national imagination. Compton's politicians resisted these characterizations because they would lose the social status of living in a suburb, and their town stood to lose financially.

As Compton became a black town, it became known as an economically depressed area. In 1967, journalist Richard Elman's book *Ill-at-Ease in Compton* chronicled his stay in the suburb. While in Compton Elman lived in a motel (which was mostly used on an hourly basis) and interviewed many area residents. In the book, Elman recorded his observations of the area as well as some narratives from the interviews he conducted. On the subject of race these oral testimonies varied enormously, from a black woman's saying she preferred living in the South where feelings about race were "all out in the open" to a white gentleman saying that he felt whites and blacks should be able to "work together if we gave it half a chance" because "color can't be everything."[58] Even though all the oral history testimonies were not optimistic on the subject of racial harmony, it is with them that historian Josh Sides finds the book's significance. According to Sides, "it was the last publicly known account of Compton that recognized the potential for the city's alternative future" because some residents expressed hope and enthusiasm for living in an ethnically and economically integrated town.[59]

At the time of its publication, however, many residents thought Elman unfairly portrayed Compton as ghettoized. Comptonites resisted these characterizations, recognizing the harmful effects that they carried. The *Compton*

Herald American published a book review by Douglas Dollarhide, who complained that the book dealt only with "the gutter" rather than with the positive aspects of Compton.[60] For Dollarhide, negative depictions threatened both the psyche of Compton residents and the workings of the town itself. Furthermore, unfavorable press could lead to detrimental consequences, such as more affluent people choosing not to settle or invest in Compton. The next week, also in the pages of the *Herald American*, Elman responded that neither Dollarhide nor the newspaper should be trusted to produce an objective book review since both appeared in its pages. Elman emphasized that the debate obfuscated the book's main issue: few people considered Compton their permanent home. The town had become a place that people left once they had the means to do so.[61]

Not all residents and outside observers recognized, or at least acknowledged, Compton's tribulations. In a 1970 *Boys' Life* cover article about Compton High's dominant boys' basketball team, journalist Arnold Hano described the town as having a "fresh look," with a civic center that was "so sparkling clean its looks fabricated by Disney" and the high school as having a look of "openness, green, and tidy." Noting that the town was 70 percent black, with Compton High's population of 2,600 almost entirely African American, Hano asserted that "the usual brutalizing forces of ghetto life have left few marks on Compton."[62] Hano's assessment of Compton varied from the very testimony of many Comptonites but echoed those of Elman's critics. A variety of reasons could explain this discrepancy. Perhaps Hano's publisher or his audience limited his ability to be critical of Compton (*Boys' Life* was a publication of the Boy Scouts of America), or, perhaps, on any given day Compton could appear to an unfamiliar eye to fulfill the suburban dream it had long promised. Or, as Dollarhide had asserted in response to Elman, Compton had positive attributes. For many residents, Compton was their home, and they would gladly show the pride they felt for it.

Compton's elected officials sought to control the image of their town, because they recognized that this cultural discourse had material consequences. Their attempts took on a new furor in 1974 when the local Los Angeles NBC affiliate ran a documentary entitled *Compton: A Restless Dream*, which looked at community members' efforts to overcome unemployment, crime, and inadequate living conditions. Town officials contended that the film negatively depicted daily life in the town. Particularly galling to them was a segment featuring an interview with a young Comptonite purporting to be a gang member. In the film, the man complained that many Compton youngsters turned to gangs because the town did not provide them with anything else to do. In response to the film, the members of the city council voted unanimously to write a strongly worded letter to the station indicating their displeasure at its "negative emphasis," citing the station's "biased reporting and bad faith" in overstating Compton's problems. Council members contended that the documentary caused the town harm and monetary loss, though they could offer no tangible proof.[63]

The council did not stop with the letter. Next, the council unanimously requested the city attorney file legal action against NBC for damages and enjoin the station from further broadcast of the film. The city filed suit against the network, charging malicious intent against Compton, seeking $5.4 million in damages to compensate tax and license revenues allegedly lost as a result of the program. In a troubling foreshadowing of events to come, Compton's public officials tried to benefit personally from the suit, as the mayor and council members sought $600,000 each in damages.[64] While municipal officials feared that media depictions would hurt the town, they also believed battling such portrayals could be personally lucrative. The lawsuit was eventually dropped, however.

City officials also battled negative print depictions. In 1975, the city council wished to fire Thomas Cochee, Compton's police chief, for allowing Bruce Henderson to write the book *Ghetto Cops* based on the town's police department. Cochee had taken the job as police chief in July 1973, becoming the first black police chief in California. Nine months later, Henderson arrived in Compton to chronicle the chief's experiences. In doing so, Henderson inevitably noted his own impressions of the town. He first describes Compton as "a ghetto city with the highest per capita crime rate in the United States."[65] Defining the town solely in terms of its crime statistics indicated Henderson's perspective. Furthermore, and no less significant, Henderson employed loaded language when he chose to define the town as "a ghetto city," two terms that each carried a set of assumptions. Despite the uproar over the book, Cochee kept his job.[66]

The making of Compton's public image came from both whites and blacks. Also in 1973, Doris Davis, the mayor of Compton, penned a strongly worded letter to the West Coast Regional Office of the NAACP, protesting the civil rights organization's characterization of Compton as a "disaster area" in a recent issue of *Ebony* magazine. Davis argued that this language would not be allowed from whites and it was time to stand up to blacks who disparaged other blacks. She wrote: "We have had it, and begin the process of chastising those who would destroy us." She continued: "Please do not believe that this is merely a public relations damage. This is the actual stopping or delaying of federal dollars that were earmarked for this community."[67] The cultural representation of a place linked to its residents' material and social standing. Compton residents had moved to the town as a step out of the ghetto. They fought depictions of their town that challenged this. Yet, despite protests, Compton was becoming known as a black city, with all the spatial and racial monikers. In the case of Compton, the line between city and suburb blurred, making it clear that the very definition of a place was a cultural construction.

Though Comptonites fought to create a positive public image, no lawsuit could erase what truly molded the town's public image: the unyielding problems of poverty. Crime, unemployment, and educational inequity were real challenges. In 1974, Compton experienced the greatest unemployment and crime rates in Los Angeles County, both higher than the national average. The reading scores of Compton students sat at the very bottom of the scale—in the first four school years of the 1970s, Compton's sixth- and twelfth-grade students consistently scored in the first percentile, the only exception being the sixth graders scoring in the second percentile in 1974.[68] Academics had hit rock bottom and the physical structures of the schools also continued to deteriorate. In 1974, a student reported that Compton High's bathroom had no running water, toilet paper, or paper towels.[69] In 1977, four investigative teams from the *Los Angeles Herald Examiner* documented horror stories of students and teachers being assaulted in Compton schools. Compton's impoverished community and school system fueled cultural stereotypes and prejudices more than any book or television show could.

Adopting the prevailing rhetoric of getting tough on crime, municipal leaders declared they would decrease violations and they looked to federal monies to improve the town in order to assure business owners that the town was a worthy investment. In 1975 federal funds provided a third of the police budget. Despite the tough rhetoric and influx of money, business owners thought better than to locate in a town that suffered from a high crime rate. But it took money to fight lawlessness, and Compton could only get that money from aid or from new business' tax dollars.[70] Despite the tough "law and order" stance of Compton's leaders, the town remained stuck in a vicious cycle of crime and economic deterioration, and the leaders hoped that federal funds would make the difference.

Compton's elected officials earmarked economic development and crime prevention as their top two priorities, but one of their major redevelopment

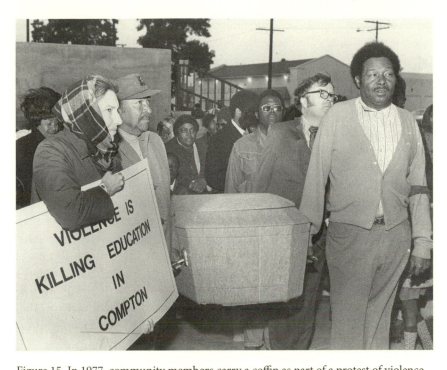

Figure 15. In 1977, community members carry a coffin as part of a protest of violence at Compton schools. Courtesy Los Angeles Public Library Photo Collection.

plans proved corrupt. In July 1975, JC Penney, like many other stores before it, announced that it was closing its Compton store. A month later the Compton redevelopment agency, a group run by the municipality, agreed to buy the property for $700,000, twice its valued price. It soon became clear that the reason the city council willingly paid such a high price was that some elected officials received kickbacks for the sale. Within a few months two council members, Hillard Hamm and Russell Woolfolk, were indicted and convicted of extortion charges. Mayor Doris Davis was also named as an unindicted co-conspirator. Both Hamm and Woolfolk were sentenced to three years in jail and were each ordered to pay a $10,000 fine, as well as serve five years probation.[71] Once touted as a center for showcasing Black Power, Compton became evidence of how power and poverty could corrupt public officials.

Understandably, many Comptonites responded angrily to the news of their council members' criminal acts. Before Hamm and Woolfolk stepped down, incensed residents crowded the city council chamber demanding the two council members immediately resign. Also in response to the extortion convictions, three ministerial groups in Compton merged into a new alliance, the Coalition of Concerned Clergy and Citizens for Social Action. The new amalgamation wielded a lot of influence as it represented twenty churches and ten thousand registered voters. The group helped elect one of the two replacements for Hamm and Woolfolk and showed that Compton citizens would continue to fight to improve their community.[72]

The troubles extended beyond two corrupt politicians, however. Around the time the extortion plot came to light, it also became apparent that city hall had not fully appreciated Compton's dire financial situation. In February 1976, municipal officials told their departments to brace for cutbacks as much as 30 percent. In March, accountants found $100,000 of federal money that an audit had previously reported missing, and, a few months later, another probe indicated that Compton had failed to document cash advances to staff and elected officials, with approximately $75,000 remaining unexplained. When accountant Lionel Cade became mayor in 1977, he ran an audit of the town's finances. Town leaders soon discovered a $2 million debt. Under Cade's stewardship, the town eliminated the deficit in a year, but did so with much cost to the municipal government, cutting their finances and making the town more desperate.[73] Compton's shaky finances only worsened and the people in charge exacerbated an already desperate situation.

In the face of diminished finances and popular support, the city council attempted to fix Compton's problems through redevelopment. After a number of stalled projects, the council focused on the creation of an auto plaza, a mall for cars. Auto dealers had once been important to Compton, but many had relocated in nearby Lakewood. Compton had subsequently suffered as sales tax revenue had failed to keep up with inflation.[74] City officials predicted that the auto plaza would generate up to $1 million annually in sales tax revenue, which Compton's elected officials expected would "effectively reverse economic deterioration."[75] In order to build the car mall the redevelopment agency sold $11 million in bonds. Ultimately though, the auto mall would become another of Compton's failed plans for healing.[76]

Redevelopment resources were only one type of fund that flowed into the town. Despite mishandling of finances, Compton and its school district continued to receive revenues from the state and federal governments. In 1976, Compton gained approval for a $4.7 million block grant under Title I of the Housing and Community Development Act of 1974, which was geared to helping communities provide decent housing for low and moderate income people. That same year, Compton Unified received a $3.7 million allotment from the ESEA, the largest amount received by any district in the United States. Representative Charles Wilson expressed his gratitude that "federal officials have the wisdom to recognize this and have seen fit to apply funding in an area which needs it so desperately."[77] The next year Compton Unified used $4.8 million of its $20 million in public works funds to refurbish many of its school sites, some of which were the oldest school buildings in the state.[78] Yet, even with the influx of funds Compton continued to falter: unemployment remained high, test scores stayed in the bottom percentiles, and almost 50 percent of the residents received some form of welfare.[79] These problems only worsened after the passage of California's Proposition 13.

The Taxpayers' Revolt

Proposition 13 was not the first attempt at equalizing school financing in California or at limiting taxes.[80] As the national political agenda moved from civil rights to poverty, a decade-long debate in the courts over equitable school financing emerged. California had a system in which each school district determined its own revenue as residents voted on their district's tax rates. By the late 1960s the districts were raising more than half their revenue by taxing local property, including commercial, industrial, and agricultural parcels. California was typical in employing this type of system; at the time every state except Hawaii depended on local property taxes to finance schools.[81] The disparities throughout each state were great and, in protest, in 1968, the Western Center on Law and Poverty brought a class action suit against California on behalf of school children in Los Angeles and their parents. The suit became known as *Serrano v. Priest*, named for one of the parent plaintiffs, John Serrano, Jr., and one of the public officials, Ivy Baker Priest, state treasurer. In the 1971 *Serrano* decision, the Supreme Court of California found the state's educational finance system unconstitutional, a ruling upheld in the 1976 appeal.[82] Specifically the court concluded that all property wealth-related spending differences across districts should be reduced to no more than $100 per student (the dollar figure was adjusted later for inflation.) Using the California constitution's equal protection clause, California led the way with using state level courts to declare education as a fundamental right.[83] The California legislature responded to *Serrano* by passing SB-90, which was aimed at narrowing the funding gap. Unfortunately for poor districts like Compton, all the changes were nullified by the 1978 passage of Proposition 13, which required a complete overhaul of the structure of California's educational finance system.

Proposition 13, officially titled People's Initiative to Limit Property Taxation, amended the California constitution in two main ways. First, it capped property taxes at 1 percent of the property's market value as assessed in 1975. This amount could not increase more than 2 percent per year, without a major remodeling or sale of the home. Furthermore, the base value could only change with a sale. The initiative also wrote into the constitution the necessity of a two-thirds majority in both the state house and senate to increase or impose any state tax rates. In 1978, California voters passed the proposition by a two-to-one margin.

The seeds for 1978's Proposition 13 were manifold. During the 1970s, the American economy experienced rapid inflation and California property values underwent tremendous increases. Across the state, residents stood frustrated by this rise, alarmed at the increase in property taxes, and disenchanted with the growth of government. A scandal that caused the high rates particularly angered voters. In 1965 it became known publicly that some of California's elected tax assessors took money to adjust assessments on some business properties. This scandal caused the state legislature to pass a bill requiring that all communities reassess all property within three years. The reforms resulted in the increase of assessments, which then soared beginning in 1974 when California experienced a property boom. The rise of tax obligations coincided with a decrease in faith in the government, which stemmed from the war in Vietnam, the Watergate scandal, and civil strife throughout the United States. Furthermore culture wars over curricula fed into taxpayers' desire to spend less on public schools. The rise of bilingual and sex education helped lead to a backlash and a rise of conservative politics.[84] The combination of these factors, along with the growing surpluses in the state treasury and the aggressive campaign led by anti-tax activist Howard Jarvis, laid the foundation for California's tax revolt.

Overnight the proposition slashed local property tax revenues and altered the political and financial landscape in California. The state tax collection decreased from 2.6 percent of the 1978 market value of homes to one percent of the 1975 values. Prior to the initiative, local towns, counties, and school districts set their own tax rates and local assessors determined a property's value. Proposition 13 revoked the power to make those decisions.

In both the popular and scholarly assessments, Proposition 13 has long been considered a suburban revolt against urban problems. Historian Robert Self argues that Proposition 13 represented a standoff "between revenue-starved older cities, where the majority of African Americans and other communities of color lived, and revenue-rich suburban communities dominated by white-Anglo homeowners."[85] The vote in Compton complicates this poor urban-rich suburban divide, however. Compton was a suburb, but residents did not fit the simple mold. Rather, many Compton residents were poor and as such, their interests aligned with their urban, rather than their suburban, neighbors. Comptonites voted overwhelmingly against the proposition, with 3,433 votes in favor and 9,310 against.[86]

Compton further belies the simple narrative of suburban tax revolt against financing urban programs. Inner-ring suburbs confronted problems akin to the inner city and voters did not make clear distinctions about what place had an urban or a suburban structure. Rather, problems of corruption and violence helped lead to the tax revolt, regardless of where they were located. California voters did not wish to aid troubled places, whether they were urban or suburban. Places like Compton came to represent the bankruptcy of liberal policies and California voters, soon followed by others across the country, reacted against these perceived failings.

While not on a strict urban-suburban divide, the tax limitation measure did increase the social stratification in California. Poorer communities saw their tax revenues slashed and became more dependent on the state making up for those losses. Wealthier communities did not face the same type of deficits in their social services because they could raise money to supplement what they raised in taxes. With the passage of this proposition, Compton residents' ability to bridge the divide became more desperate.

Already a barrier to educational opportunity, the funding for schooling became an even bigger obstacle to equity. "Proposition 13 has been a disaster for public education," observed Sydney Morrison, former Compton educator and president of the California Administrators' Association.[87] Proposition 13 equalized school funding, but equalization of school quality did not follow. Furthermore, in equalizing revenue the proposition leveled the districts down. Districts spent less per pupil and hired fewer teachers, resulting in a large increase in the teacher-pupil ratio. It also hurt the districts in terms of capital outlay, making it difficult to get money to fix buildings.[88]

Proposition 13 hit Compton hard as it starved the school district's already skeletal budget and dismal financial base. Compton Unified lost $14.4

million in revenue from local property taxes. Dipping into its $3.8 billion surplus funds, the State of California replaced nearly 90 percent of the money the district lost that first year. This immediate bailout saved district administrators from ordering massive layoffs and severely curtailing educational programs.[89]

State aid did not come without a price, however. The bailout quickly eroded the state's surplus while simultaneously giving the state legislature a larger role in funding public schools. California school districts' autonomy diminished as the districts became even more dependent on outside sources to keep their educational programs afloat. For decades Compton leaders had looked outside their borders for support while clinging to local control, but Proposition 13 brought this tension to a new level.

While the state subsidized districts in the immediate aftermath of the referendum, the California legislature could not sustain this compensation. Five years after the passage of the proposition, California's schools had approximately 20 percent fewer "real resources" per pupil than in 1978 and overall budgets 25 percent below those of 1978, in real terms.[90] California public schools became desperate for monies to continue the most basic programs. Once in the top tier of public schools in the country, California schools plunged to among the worst.

Compton faced the intertwined pressures of increasing property taxes and rapidly decreasing funds. Solutions put forth, such as increasing tax revenues through redevelopment, and receiving outside funds, did not offer the relief necessary. Rather, the town and its schools, already afflicted for decades, continued into a deeper downward spiral, compounded by its worsening public image. Compton teachers, students, and parents protested district administrators' negligence and mismanagement of funds, resources, and academic affairs often, but to no avail. All these factors combined to create a school district that was less about serving the needs of its students and more about gratifying the corrupt impulses of a segment of the adult population. Outside funds, law-and-order campaigns, and teachers' campaigns did not make up for the systemic impoverishment and frequent violence. Already on shaky footing since the 1930s, the problems of the 1970s only worsened Compton's educational crisis.

Chapter 6

A Rapidly Changing City

Pedro Pallan was a longtime Compton resident and businessperson. In December 1984, the Compton Unified board of trustees appointed Pallan to its personnel commission, a three-member board that oversaw the recruitment, screening, and hiring of approximately 1,900 classified employees. He became the first Latino to serve on the commission, when he replaced African American George Robinson. Ted Kimbrough, Compton Unified's superintendent, applauded Pallan's appointment, stating it showed Compton was "moving in a positive direction."[1] Despite Kimbrough's optimistic declaration, the appointment did not portend a shift toward shared power or equal opportunities for blacks and Latinos. Instead, Pallan's influence in hiring Latinos would remain limited as African Americans held tightly to the reins of Compton Unified.

Pallan's appointment reflected Compton's changing demographics and black's tokenism toward Latinos. In the 1980s, the ethnic composition of Compton and its school district changed from almost entirely African American to include a growing population of Latinos. This shift added new demands to an already troubled district, such as the operation of a bilingual program and the hiring of bilingual teachers. District officials, most of whom were black, resisted meeting the needs of the new Spanish-speaking Comptonites, because investing in bilingual programs and teachers would mean redistributing already scarce resources away from black teachers and students. Nationwide, African Americans historically depended on public-sector employment, including public schools, for economic opportunity and mobility because many white employers had blocked opportunities in the private sector.[2] Not surprisingly, black educators, along with broad networks of organizations, ministers, and politicians, worked to "delay, derail, or diminish initiatives perceived to destabilize the historic *economic* role the school systems have played—and continue to play—in the black community."³

District officials' focus on education as a source of jobs distracted their approaching education as a fundamental civic obligation, a service they owed the community's children regardless of their ethnicity. The district failed to meet the needs of both its Latino *and* black students. Compton Unified's students continued to rank at the bottom of statewide tests while school officials continued to mismanage funds. The animosity between blacks and Latinos, the increasingly poor population, the statewide funding problems, the pressure of state-imposed standardized tests, and the lack of qualified teachers all took their toll on Comptonites' aspirations.

Redeveloping Compton

The quest for local money through sales tax revenue grew out of Proposition 13, which capped local property taxes at 1 percent of their 1975 assessed value. As Compton staggered under continued financial strains, officials sought a variety of solutions. While some sought outside aid, officials also looked to bolster local resources. In the late 1970s and 1980s, consistent with the plans of many other American towns, from its neighboring inner-ring suburb Lynwood to small rustbelt cities like Omaha and Muncie to the country's largest metropolis, New York City, Compton officials funded a series of redevelopment projects to enlarge the tax base and jumpstart the economy.⁴ Instead, the ill-chosen projects damaged the town's already dwindling coffers, and cemented Compton's negative image.

The town found itself in a vicious cycle. In 1979, the federal government refused to guarantee a grant to Compton for its downtown's development without private financial backing, but the town could not attract these nongovernmental funds without the federal grant. Local officials blamed the predicament on Compton's being a "poor, black and extremely redlined community."⁵ Compton appeared to be a bad investment.

Losing the federal grant changed Comptonites' strategy for improving the economy, though it did not squash Compton's redevelopment plans. Shifting focus from the downtown, town leaders pinned much of their hope on the Alameda Auto Plaza, conceived as an "auto mall" that would halt the exodus of new car dealerships from the town. Planners designed the plaza to be in the southern part of town, right off the 91 Freeway, and the municipal redevelopment agency funded it because the agency expected it to generate up to $1 million a year in sales tax revenue. The town willingly invested its funds because, according to Lionel Cade, the mayor of Compton, the auto plaza would "effectively reverse economic deterioration."[6]

From the beginning, the plaza faced numerous hurdles, not the least of which was attracting dealerships. In 1978, the city council charged that Volvo Motors had redlined the town by refusing to allow one of its dealers to move into the auto mall. Hoping to save the floundering plaza, the next year the city council appropriated funds for two more car lots, selling the sites for considerably less than it cost the agency to acquire them.[7] To attract dealerships, Compton officials invested in the future—willing to risk the town's money in the hopes of financial gains and economic stability.

The auto plaza continually faltered, however, and town officials complained that Compton's image as a depressed minority city with a high crime rate contributed to the difficulties in attracting auto retailers. In 1979, with much of the auto mall vacant, Compton's dreams of swift and profitable redevelopment stymied and the town redevelopment agency sold off some of the land for a loss of more than $500,000. In February 1984, one of the three existing auto dealerships filed for bankruptcy, with debts of over $1 million.[8] The land east of Compton was more appealing; the auto plaza in Cerritos had seven dealerships. Compton's politicians had believed that the town's auto plaza would be its salvation, but instead it added to its woes.

Large-scale economic restructuring compounded Compton's financial problems. In the late 1970s, Los Angeles County changed from a highly specialized manufacturing center to a more decentralized and diversified metropolis. Traditional manufacturing firms either closed or moved from the region, throwing about seventy-five thousand Angelenos out of work. In the words of urbanist Mike Davis, in the 1980s the Los Angeles economy was "'unplugged' from the American industrial heartland and rewired to East Asia."[9] As employment opportunities decreased, African Americans across Los Angeles County lost their jobs first.[10]

Some types of employment were increasing, but African Americans did not benefit from these changes. Professional, managerial, and technical employment expanded, but black workers often did not qualify for these jobs because of the legacy of racial discrimination and inadequate schooling. Labor-intensive industries, such as garment manufacturing, and service positions, such as janitors, waiters, busboys, day laborers, and domestic workers, also increased, but Asian and Latino immigrants filled many of these low-paying jobs.[11]

Along with the deterioration of the job market came an increase in crime, particularly the illicit economy of drug dealing. With few other options, the pull of this economy strengthened at the same time that law enforcement agencies enforced stricter drug laws. By 1987, the police estimated that more than half of the crimes in Compton were drug related.[12] The lure of illegality spread when the state and federal governments cut funding for summer jobs for teenagers and many Comptonites found that "there was a lack of things for them to do," according to resident Linda Allen.[13] Between 1985 and 1990, Compton's parks and recreation appropriations decreased by a dizzying 97 percent, while at the same time the police budget increased by an astonishing 195 percent.[14] Drug consumption increased, alternative social programs decreased.

With the defunding of such programs as public recreation and summer youth employment, and with public schooling undermined, street gangs came to dominate the lives of youth. With the chaos in the community, gangs offered "family, excitement, money, protection and peer acceptance," according to Willard McCrumby, an anti-gang program officer in Compton Unified.[15]

Gangs recruited many of their new members from chaotic neighborhoods and in turn made those communities even more tumultuous. While gangs were not new to Los Angeles, as the *California Eagle* had even noted their presence around Los Angeles high schools in the mid-1940s, the focus of the gangs shifted from wars over school-based turf to those over the lucrative drug trade.[16] In the 1980s, the center for cocaine importation changed from Miami to Southern California. Increased drug trafficking meant additional economic gains, resulting in growth in gang violence. Members battled for control over the sale of crack cocaine in their communities. At a U.S. congressional hearing in 1983, Los Angeles County district attorney Robert Philibosian testified that violence in the county had reached "an intolerable intensity" and "rival gang activities have turned some areas of the county into war zones."[17] Compton became the "epicenter" of gang violence and "consistently had the greatest number of gangs of any city in Los Angeles County" other than the much bigger Los Angeles itself.[18]

Many observers considered gangs an activity of young males, but some statistics suggested otherwise. In 1990, the Compton Police Department database listed 10,435 Compton gang members, while the census recorded only

8,558 fifteen- to twenty-five-year-old males living in the town.[19] This disparity of numbers could have reflected a range of different possibilities: the activity of older gang members, the addition of girls in gang activity, problems with census taking, and inclusion of gang members from non-Compton areas (such as the unincorporated Willowbrook) in the database. It also points to the racial profiling of black men as being gang members.

Los Angeles had similar issues identifying gang members. The LAPD also used the flimsiest of evidence, such as the type of clothing worn, nicknames, and places of hangouts, to label and arrest people as gang members. Using this type of evidence led to the implausible conclusion that nearly half the black male population between twenty-one and twenty-four belonged to gangs, as opposed to one-half of 1 percent of white males, 6 percent of Asian males, and 9 percent of Hispanic males.[20] While it was ambiguous exactly who or what these numbers reflected, it is clear that gangs were of wide concern in the Los Angeles metropolitan area.[21]

Gangs became the way of understanding crime in the Los Angeles region, and Comptonites demanded the town government and school district rid their neighborhoods and schools of gangs.[22] Compton's financial problems hindered efforts to address crime, however. Instead, crime further hurt the town and school district financially. In 1979, the *Los Angeles Times* reported that Compton did not have enough money to retain the number of police officers necessary to combat the lawlessness in the town.[23] In the 1978–79 school year, arsonists and vandals damaged an estimated $750,000 worth of district property.[24] Not only was Compton ill-equipped to prevent these offenses, but it also lacked the resources to recover from them.

An increase in crime decreased the value of property and in turn created an increase of absentee landlords who cared little for their properties. In a 1979 lawsuit, Compton resident Anselmo Renoso reported several horrid conditions in his rented apartment, including rat and roach infestations, water leaks, and broken windows. Renoso and the other tenants did not sit idly with their complaints about the premises. Instead, they created an organization, La Hermandad, to advocate for better living conditions and their rights as tenants. As a result, the landlord tried to illegally evict the tenants.[25] The growth of absentee landlords affected the town.

To address the town's pressing needs, municipal leaders continued to search for solutions. In 1980 and again in 1982, in two short-lived schemes, city council members proposed legalizing draw poker and bingo for revenue purposes. In the first go-round, council members withdrew the motion to consider card parlors after they faced strong opposition from a coalition of ministers. Two years later, in a 3–2 vote, the council approved card clubs in the town, but once again a group of ministers and residents put pressure on the politicians, who soon reconsidered their votes. Though some held firm, enough council members broke under public pressure and, in a dramatic reversal, rescinded the card club measure.[26] Though the card club issue would be resurrected, council members' initial rejection left their town without an immediate plan for raising much needed funds.

Compton's efforts took part amid a larger effort to revitalize commercial centers in the southeastern Los Angeles inner-ring suburbs. In the 1970s Lynwood developed a shopping center with a Montgomery Ward store as its anchor. By 1986, however, Montgomery Ward closed its Lynwood store and the entire shopping center closed, remaining abandoned for seven years.[27] The region as a whole was struggling with crime, racial change, and poverty, factors that were making it even harder for Compton to attract investors because of the area's reputation and because the town had to compete for those funders who were willing to invest in the area. Exacerbating these issues were federal cutbacks in aid for renewal efforts. These cuts began under the Carter administration and deepened under Reagan's.[28]

Even so, Compton officials continued to fund renewal projects. In the late 1980s, Compton's municipal leaders invested funds in a hotel and convention center. The project promised to alleviate the town's overwhelming unemployment rate. Leaders such as Anthony Ybarra, deputy director of the Community Redevelopment Agency, hoped the new project would show Compton as a "rapidly changing city."[29] Town officials expected the hotel to bring $320,000 in revenue its first year and by its fourth to generate $640,000 annually.[30] Developers also hoped the new center would change the town's reputation, but they did not realistically assess that image's potential in dooming the project.

Problems plagued the project even before the hotel opened and allegations of cost overruns continually marred construction. In 1988 the town of Compton lent over $5 million to the developers of the Compton Lazben Hotel to keep the project afloat. Six months later developers deemed the loan insufficient and stopped work for five months, saying they needed an additional $3 million. After a series of budget negotiations, monetary loans, and work stoppages, the hotel finally opened in fall 1989, a year and a half behind schedule. Even at its opening, construction remained incomplete, with the top four floors unfinished.[31]

The project developers also broke their promises. In exchange for municipal funds, the hotel was supposed to hire Compton residents as the majority of its employees. The hotel proprietors, however, did not fulfill their pledge. In 1989, they had hired more than one hundred people to work, only twenty-seven of them Compton residents. Of the Comptonites employed, local officials' family members held some of the highest positions. Mayor Tucker's daughter worked as a concierge and the wife of the deputy director of the city redevelopment agency served as an administrative assistant in the hotel's personnel department. Most other local residents held low-level jobs such as housekeepers, security guards, and busboys. To make matters worse, when the construction and opening of the hotel suffered continuous delays, the owners fired many of these workers.[32] Like the auto plaza, the hotel made little positive impact on the community and instead sapped the town of some of its precious financial resources.

Many of Compton's other redevelopment projects, or plans for ventures, also went sour. In 1988, Compton officials had planned on building next to the hotel their own "Bourbon Street," an entertainment and shopping complex with the "flavor and vitality" of the New Orleans French Quarter. Laurence Adams, Compton's director of redevelopment, believed the complex would be large enough to provide enough tax revenue to free the city from financial binds.[33] The project never materialized.

Yet another much needed project that went awry was a plan by the Hub City Urban Developers to build affordable townhouses and provide construction jobs for building them. Between 1978 and 1984, Compton officials steered $2 million to the firm as well as $3 million in direct municipal loans to help set up a factory to manufacture the prefabricated houses. The firm spent the money without producing the houses or creating the jobs. In 1989, the federal government pressured Compton to foreclose on the land and recover the money spent. The developers ended up deeding the land back to the town and returning about half a million dollars.[34] Compton took a big loss on the project.

The auto plaza remained a thorn in the side of Compton's redevelopment. The town gave Brett Mitchell, a Chevrolet dealership owner, title to plaza property in fall 1988, but Mitchell never made a mortgage payment and owed the city more than $100,000 in loans when, in 1990, the court took away his business license for "numerous deceptive and fraudulent practices."[35] The auto plaza continued to struggle and developers proposed new plans for the site. In 1988, city administrators along with a private company looked to place an auto swap meet on the parcel. In order to do this, the town had to spend $1.6 million to pave the vacant lot and construct offices.[36] Despite the high expectations that the plaza would provide the town with financial stability, much of the land remained unoccupied.

The auto plaza had become a money pit and the fate of the land remained controversial in the community. In 1989, city council plans for using the vacant land for business rather than low-cost housing development raised the ire of hundreds of Compton residents, represented by two groups—the South Central Organizing Committee and the United Neighborhoods Organization. The organizations wished to build six hundred townhouses on the lot, but the town leaders wanted to court businesses to increase tax revenues. The housing organizers questioned whether the suburb could pull in business. One of the neighborhood organizers, Reverend William Johnson, expressed this sentiment: "Who does the city council think they are fooling? We have the highest per capita murder rate in the country. Nobody is going to come

Figure 16. South Central Organizing Committee (SCOC), United Neighborhood Organization (UNO) leaders, and 500 community members gathered at the site of the Compton Auto Plaza to rally in support of a proposal to turn the site into 600 low-cost single-family homes. Courtesy Los Angeles Public Library Photo Collection.

shop in a murder capital."[37] In reality, the city council did have trouble entic-
ing businesses to settle in the beleaguered town.[38]

Even so, local officials did not settle for deals they felt hurt the town financially. In December 1989, the city council received two offers for the auto
plaza land. First, the council rejected a $5 million cash offer by community
activists who wanted to develop moderately priced townhouses, claiming
that commercial land was more valuable to the town because it could generate more substantial tax dollars and provide job opportunities. Second, it rejected a $3.7 million offer from a Mack Truck franchise, claiming the price
was not right because the land was appraised at $4.7 million. Mack wished to
put $1 million down, pay the rest over thirty years, and guarantee sales tax
revenues. Although this proposal did not pass the city council initially, some
council members supported the sale; Maxcy Filer and Jane Robbins argued
that the truck enterprise would generate job opportunities for Compton's un-
deremployed residents and tax revenues for the financially strapped town.
Their argument won out and two weeks later the council reversed its position, agreeing to sell the land to the Mack Truck sales and service franchise.
Unfortunately, the truck dealer defaulted six months later.[39]

Though some redevelopment plans were more successful than the auto
plaza, Compton continued to suffer financially. As poverty increased, so did
crime. As crime increased, many businesses did not wish to settle in the area.
Schools were an integral part of this cycle too. Schools were a place where
children could receive aid, but they did not adequately assist the more and
more needy students. No less significantly, the school district increasingly
became an important place of employment for many in the community. In
this way, as Compton moved from a black-majority to a Latino-majority city,
schools became the focal point of pitched battles over power to control them.

The Rocky State of Black-Latino Relations

Compton's struggling redevelopment plans, along with the historical lack of
industrial infrastructure in the town, limited residents' employment opportunities and made the jobs that were available even more coveted. African
Americans who managed both the school district and town hall held tightly
onto control over public sector jobs. In Compton this meant boxing out
whites, Latinos, and other residents including Compton's small—but
concentrated—population of Samoans.[40] Latinos had been a minority in the

town when it was white run and remained so when blacks became the majority. Latino numbers grew, however, when during the 1970s, an enormous number of Mexican immigrants moved into the South Central region of Los Angeles County. Southern California's expanding economy offered job opportunities, and South Central, including Compton, had affordable housing. In 1980, Latinos were 21 percent of Compton's population and growing.[41] This increase accelerated when, in 1982, Mexico suffered a severe economic recession that escalated immigration to the United States in general, and to California especially. Central American migration, particularly from the politically tumultuous countries of Guatemala and El Salvador, also increased significantly throughout the 1980s.[42]

Following the lead of whites, many African Americans left Compton, this time relocating to inland counties San Bernardino and Riverside, as well as to other states. A push and a pull existed as reasons for leaving the area. Some blacks left to find their suburban dream in more likely places, while others found that they could not get jobs in the Los Angeles area.[43] Once a community of homeowners, Compton had become a town where absentee landlords rented homes for relatively low prices. Drawn to an area that offered cheap housing and access to the available jobs, Compton's Latino population grew quickly over the decade.[44]

As African Americans had done before them, the burgeoning population of Latinos pushed for job opportunities. On July 23, 1973, at a city council meeting, Compton resident Lorraine Cervantes remarked that the town had not hired enough Mexican American people and suggested that the council enact a charter amendment to grant extra hiring points for bilingual people to give them an added boost in the application process. Less than a year later, the Grupo Chicano de Acción Afirmativa demanded the city council provide an affirmative action program for Latinos.[45] In 1976, "disenchanted and discouraged" members of Compton's Latino community persuaded city council members to meet with them "to see what could be done" to increase their representation in town government. At the time Latinos comprised approximately 14 percent of the town's population while making up less than 7 percent of the boards and commissions.[46] The talks did not yield a job-sharing compromise, so Latinos criticized more overtly what they termed "discriminatory conditions."[47] Compton's black leaders resisted relinquishing their hold on the town's positions. Widespread racial discrimination in employment existed in the Los Angeles area as a whole, and as a result black power-holders ensured that the vast majority of public-sector jobs in Compton went

Figure 17. During a series of border patrol raids in Southern California, fifty undocumented immigrants were found in a garage of a Compton home. Courtesy Los Angeles Public Library Photo Collection.

to their own friends, neighbors, and kinfolk. In response, to advocate more effectively, some Latino Comptonites formed the Latino Chamber of Commerce, which supported Latino-owned businesses and families.[48]

In Compton, African Americans built their political and social power in opposition to white control, and when Latinos became a significant portion of the population, language and race became easily identifying markers on which to draw the line of resources. That African Americans, not whites, managed Compton and its school district helps explain the interethnic tensions in its borders and its schools. Since whites no longer monopolized the power structure, blacks and Latinos had no common foe to unite against. Rather, as the power holders, blacks had more to lose from an alliance with Latinos than they stood to gain.[49]

The parceling of jobs along racial lines was particularly troubling in the schools because it translated into a failure to serve second-language learners, despite federal mandates for bilingual education. In 1968, Congress found that one of the most acute problems plaguing education in the United States was that of educating children with limited English-speaking ability.[50] To remedy this ill Congress passed the Bilingual Act of 1968, and the federal government began to grant districts the funds to provide services for second language learners. Notwithstanding the passage of the Act, this student population remained underserved nationwide.

Nationally, bilingual education seemingly butted against integration efforts. In order for bilingual education to work, there needed to be a significant number of a particular language group in one school. But *Brown* and subsequent cases, such as *Crawford*, mandated desegregation. Due to their seemingly separationist ideology, advocates of bilingual education made strange bedfellows with conservatives who opposed desegregation. In his 1970 run for reelection as California governor, Ronald Reagan explicitly opposed busing for integration while supporting bilingual education. In doing so, according to historian Mark Brilliant, Reagan exploited the tension between desegregation and bilingual education—"pitting them against one another as a zero sum choice between educational civil rights policies."[51] Both proponents and detractors of bilingual education used the language of the civil rights movement to bolster their positions.

These arguments were made both in policy chambers and courtrooms. In 1974, the U.S. Supreme Court in *Lau v. Nichols* affirmed the right of limited-English students to receive special services. The justices reasoned that without adequate English language instruction, schools denied students "meaningful opportunity to participate in the public education program," which violated the Civil Rights Act of 1964.[52] The same year as *Lau*, California legislators passed the Chacon-Moscone Bilingual-Bicultural Education Act, establishing transitional programs to meet the needs of students with limited English proficiency. Schools needed to provide instruction in two languages (one of them English) in order to build and expand on students' existing language skills.[53] Compton's Latino student population was growing quickly, and despite what state and federal law dictated, Compton Unified's leaders failed to implement an effective, or even viable, bilingual program.

In order to demand equal access to education for Latino students, several groups fought with the black-run school district. In a presentation to the Compton Unified's board of directors, the Chicano Law Students Association cited statistics for the 1971 school year to illustrate the district's failure to "produce students bound towards higher education." The group pointed out that while this failure pertained to both blacks and Latinos, the needs of Latino students went unmet in a variety of ways. For instance, curriculum choices concerned the group. They asserted "the failure to provide intellectually and culturally interesting and exciting curriculum and the inability to engage students in relevant programs and course work also plays a part in creating a deep sense of alienation and resentment on the part of Chicano students." The group was also concerned with the lack of Latino teachers and administrators because the lack of Latino authority figures working alongside blacks in similar positions "contributes to the present situation of tensions." The group even claimed the school system fostered "unhealthy racial attitudes" among students.[54]

Other organizations took action against the school district. In the late 1970s, a group of Compton parents formed the Concerned Parents of the Community. They complained about several injustices, not the least of which was that district officials inappropriately placed some Spanish-speaking students in classes for the mentally disabled because of language issues. When it became obvious that school district officials would continue to drag their feet in addressing their concerns, the group sent a letter of complaint to the federal Health, Education, and Welfare Department Office of Civil Rights. HEW responded by instructing Compton Unified to submit a proposal within ninety days detailing how it would improve its bilingual programs.[55] While school district officials ultimately adopted a bilingual plan, which HEW accepted, their initial recalcitrance in implementing the law indicated a more general aversion toward sharing jobs, funds, and power across racial lines.

Compton school administrators' reluctance to write a plan corresponded with their reticence in implementing it; even after adopting the program, the district continued to understaff it. In the 1979–80 school year Compton Unified had 163 bilingual classrooms but employed only four qualified bilingual teachers. Over the next school year, with "strong prodding" from the State Department of Education, Compton Unified "agreed to comply with state law" and began providing some form of bilingual training for some of its teachers.[56]

Latino protests in Compton occurred in a wider context of Latino civil rights political activism, which was a California-wide phenomenon and had a strong presence in the Los Angeles region. In the late 1960s Latino students in East Los Angeles became increasingly politicized and began organizing around a variety of issues, including inadequacies in the schools. The students demanded such improvements as better physical conditions, Chicano studies classes, bilingual education, college counseling, and increased number of Latino teachers. After feeling ignored by Los Angeles Unified's board of education, Latino students in East Los Angeles staged a "blowout" in March 1968. Over several days hundreds of students from fifteen Los Angeles schools walked out, demanding more attention to student needs.[57]

The students of East LA had made their concerns known, but still, many remained unmet. Some issues, such as the demand for bilingual education, had practical obstacles. Facing increasing numbers of English language learners and the limits of the job applicant pool, most districts in California had trouble attracting enough bilingual teachers. This was true in Compton and few of the district's black leaders had interest in devoting resources to effect change on this front. In September 1988, at a Compton Unified School District board meeting, a group of residents demanded that Latino hiring be made a "top priority," claiming the district systematically discriminated against Latinos in the hiring for managerial positions. To make their case, they pointed to the fact that Latino students made up 42 percent of the district's pupil population, but Latinos held only 3 percent of the certificated management positions. Of the thirty-eight principals, only one was Latino. No Latinos were among the twenty-one assistant principals. In 1987 and 1988, Latinos held only 6 percent of the teaching positions in the Compton Unified School District, while blacks held 79 percent, even though almost 25 percent of Compton Unified's pupil population needed the bilingual skills that Spanish-speaking teachers were able to provide.[58]

Having battled years of discrimination from whites to gain their positions of power, blacks, like their white predecessors, refused to consider affirmative action plans for Latino workers. Their recalcitrance fit with the national understanding of the federal policy. For the purposes of affirmative action and desegregation, the federal government often interpreted "minority" needs as strictly "black" needs. This interpretation boosted opportunities for blacks; it, as well as additions of innovative curriculum that included black history, contributed to the rise of a black middle class.[59] In Compton, African Americans had stepped into positions of school and municipal leadership.

Once reliant on "whiteness" to deliver privilege, Latinos fought to win minority status in order to benefit from the federal government's new mandates. The affirmative action proposal aimed to open opportunities for Latinos as older black employees moved or retired. Board members refused to entertain the plan. "We do not need affirmative action; the majority of employees are minority," argued school board president John Steward.[60] By framing the issue as one of affirmative action, the debate focused on job opportunities rather than serving the needs of bilingual students and community. The use of affirmative action as a defense against including Latinos also spoke to the specific issue of what it meant to have a minority group within a group of historically disenfranchised people.

Latinos also remained underrepresented in municipal jobs and frequently made affirmative action proposals to city hall. In 1989, the Committee on Hispanic Affairs presented an affirmative action plan to the Compton city council. This proposal called for the town to triple the number of Latinos hired over the next five years. Even though one third of Compton's population was Latino, fewer than 10 percent of the full-time municipal employees at the time were Latino, while African Americans represented about 78 percent of the workforce. The proposed affirmative action plan would bring Latino workers to more than 27 percent.[61]

Council members refused to commit to any plan, openly challenging the idea that town leaders had discriminated against Latinos. Former city council member Maxcy Filer explained, "Many times Latinos came to us and said appoint me to such and such a thing. No, I'm sorry. I can't appoint you to that. You have to take the [civil service] test like everyone else."[62] Black leaders created barriers to hiring Latinos because of economic and social motivations. To do so, they used the process of professionalization that had been conceived as a means to protect equal opportunity.[63]

Despite the shortage of jobs, Latinos continued to flow into the town and blacks, who controlled the school district and city hall, continued to resist sharing jobs. This was particularly true in the school district, where bilingual education commanded an increasing share of the district budget. The vast majority of California school districts were ill-prepared to deal with the influx of students, and Compton Unified was no exception. In 1985, Compton Unified made special efforts to recruit Spanish-speaking teachers, but even so, the district remained short fifty bilingual teachers. By 1990, Latino students comprised almost 51 percent of Compton Unified's student population, as compared to 33 percent just five years before. More than eight thousand children spoke little, if any, English, but only forty-six teachers held any bilingual credentials.[64]

In addition to the language barrier, many immigrant students confronted other hurdles in their schooling. First, many of their parents were unfamiliar with the American school system and faced challenges navigating it, a problem sometimes compounded by their legal status. Many parents also had little education in any school system, which has been shown to affect their children's educational attainment. Guatemalans, Salvadorans, and Mexicans had some of the lowest educational levels of all foreign born. Also, students had to deal with family stress around a large number of issues. For example, many of the immigrants did not have secure financial and material situations, as they had left countries that suffered socioeconomically, paid money to enter the United States, and had financial obligations to family members back home. Many also experienced family separation.[65] All these factors affected students' daily experiences in schools as well as their overall performance.

Hiring Latino leadership became a major issue when the school district needed to find a new superintendent in 1990. In the interim, Elisa Sanchez held the position of acting superintendent and Latinos campaigned for the district board to install her in the position permanently. Instead, the board of trustees (of whom six were African American and one was Latino) appointed J. L. Handy, a black educator and assistant superintendent from Sacramento. Latino leaders called Handy's appointment another example of the school board's "systematic discrimination" against Latinos.[66]

Board members disagreed. Kelvin Filer recalled, "I think we did a very good job in terms of being inclusive, I really did. Our school district was one of the first school districts to celebrate Cesar Chavez day, in fact, probably in the nation. We were the first to utilize bilingual presentations of the Pledge of Allegiance, to print things in Spanish and English. We had interpreters at our meetings." The district also closed schools for Cinco de Mayo, a well-intentioned effort to incorporate Latino culture. This gesture belied reality: the Latino population was increasingly from Guatemala and El Salvador. The district's insensitivity caused resentment among Latinos not of Mexican origin.[67]

Cultural inclusion veiled economic interests; while it was palatable to share holidays, it was not as easy to share jobs. Filer explained: "I've had some individuals come up and just basically tell me, 'you have to do this or you have to create a Hispanic seat or give me a job because I'm Hispanic.' No, that's not the way that works. It's just like anything else; you try to be as colorblind as possible." While he believed in affirmative action, he felt "you don't give people things. No one gave anything to the black elected officials. No one gave anything to the black citizens."[68] In Compton, African Americans employed the same logic to exclude Latinos that whites had used to shut out blacks.

Hindering School Performance

Compton Unified was the largest employer in town, and, while it only offered modest salaries, even in comparison to other school districts, it still offered a steady paycheck and benefits. Running the district also meant controlling jobs, and Compton Unified officials doled out jobs along racial and political lines. For example, in 1980, the largely black-run district demoted seven school administrators, all white. The seven sued the district, accusing the district board of trustees of discrimination. District administrators initially claimed that low-performing students and misconduct led to the downgrading of the complainants' jobs, but in his testimony Aaron Wade, Compton Unified's superintendent, said the demotions were not due to misbehavior or mismanagement but rather because he wanted to work with people with whom he was comfortable. A federal judge decided against the district, ruling that the change of job status violated the white educators' civil rights. The judge found the administrators competent and believed Wade's comfort level was based solely on race.[69]

The question of qualifications also emerged in a scandal over district personnel who had received degrees from St. Stephens Educational Bible College. Investigators found that the college held no classes, kept no student records, and promised to grant teaching credentials to those who paid for them. Teachers from across Los Angeles County had received their teaching credentials through St. Stephens. Among them were Superintendent Wade and Bernice Woods, a member of the Compton Unified board of trustees, with both high-ranking officials receiving so-called doctorates.[70] Kelvin Filer remembered his disgust: "I just didn't understand. How can you say that we are supposed to be examples for students and you have a purchased diploma?"[71]

The St. Stephens scandal also exposed the district's penchant for nepotism. While it was investigating the diploma mill, a state commission also examined the hiring of trustee Woods's daughter as a typing teacher in the district. The younger Woods had received her position based on a letter from an assistant superintendent of Compton Unified. The letter falsely claimed she had worked in the district for six years as a typist when in actuality she had only worked for three years as a typist and switchboard operator. On receiving her new position, the daughter's salary increased by more than $4,000.[72]

While nepotism existed in municipal politics across the country, no matter who was in charge, the cronyism in Compton added to the public scrutiny and perception of the town. In 1981, the *Los Angeles Times* ran an article about Compton Unified stating that "while nepotism is not illegal, the fact that at least 15 relatives of the trustees and superintendent have worked for the district in recent years has seriously undermined employee morale."[73] The article noted that residents avoided discussing favoritism, saying "fear silences the voice of many dissatisfied employees and parents" because "they, their friends or relatives work for Compton Unified, the city's largest employer." The *Times* went on to blame the district's nepotism, along with the town's poverty, for the students' "lackluster academic performance."[74] Compton Unified's troubles were multifaceted and the needs of adults had surpassed the needs of the children.

Along with poverty and corruption, family instability hindered school performance. Almost 40 percent of the children in Compton lived in poverty, and these families' precarious circumstances shaped their children's performance in the schools, molding the climate of the schools themselves. The poverty, coupled with demographic changes, political conflict, lack of economic development, and other factors, produced a community where children learned life's lessons on the streets instead of in the classroom. The official dropout rate in Compton Unified was almost 29 percent, about 40 percent higher than the statewide average.[75] All these factors took their toll on Compton's schools.

Standardized tests had become important indicators of success of local school programs, and by this measurement Compton Unified's teachers and students were among the worst in the nation. Test scores had sunk so low that in 1980, in an act of sheer desperation, unidentified district employees hand-altered answers from wrong to right on 1,800 state-mandated achievement tests. The district average leaped 53 percentile points, though test-developers, educators, and statisticians believed a 12–percentile increase was the largest possible in one year. When questioned about the meteoric jump, Wade replied the rise resulted from a district-wide program aimed at improving test taking and said the state's questioning of the improvement "clearly demonstrated to me that they felt that black students did not have the capacity to achieve as rapidly as we did."[76] State officials did not retreat in the face of racial allegations but rather, in an unprecedented action, invalidated the tests and required the district to retest its students. On the new exam the students scored substantially lower. The next year, Compton students scored at the very bottom of the scales. Third graders rated in the first (absolute lowest) percentile in reading, the third in writing, and the second in math. In addition, state officials' investigation found that altering test scores had not been the only violation. Superintendent Wade had also violated the state education code when he ordered low achievers and others who might bring down the district's average not to be tested.[77] Though Wade was subsequently fired, it was clear that the fiddling extended beyond him; changing the answers was time consuming because the tests were varied and therefore each question had to be read and changed individually. The district refused to cooperate with the investigation, however, and no one was ever connected directly to the tampering.

While these types of tests may not have been the most effective way of measuring success, they did remain significant markers to contemporaries and students' poor performances had repercussions. In 1981, the year after the test taking controversy, standardized tests became even more important when California implemented examinations to receive a high school diploma. As graduation requirements became stricter, the need for teachers simultaneously increased as the number of students enrolling in teacher education programs declined. To fill its teaching need, Compton, along with a couple of other Los Angeles County school districts, issued emergency one-year teaching credentials to applicants with non-education related bachelor degrees. In fall 1982, seventeen of the sixty-seven new teachers hired in Compton worked on emergency credentials.[78] These teachers did not need to have any background of working with students, which meant the district was putting the least experienced teachers in the worst situations. Fewer qualified people wished to work for the district as its academic and management failures became more public.

Many Compton teachers felt the "despair that [hung] over Compton schools," and this mood served as the focal point for a February 1980 front-page exposé in the *Wall Street Journal*. For this piece, the author, Laurel Leff, worked as a substitute teacher for seven days in the district, where she taught at three of the district's eleven secondary schools and found that "getting a good education in the Compton schools still isn't easy." Compton Unified schools lacked supplies. Leff detailed how Compton High canceled its shop class because the equipment had been stolen. In one of her classes students said the Pledge of Allegiance to a nonexistent flag because that too had disappeared. While she never felt threatened or saw violence beyond roughhousing, she stressed that the "mere expectation of violence" at the schools was "disquieting" and asserted that informal conversation as well as formal security measures revealed much about teachers' safety concerns. At Centennial

High, officials required all students to wear identification badges that teachers checked throughout the day. Without a badge, students were sent home. At Compton High, administrators implemented a policy forbidding teachers to stay after school in buildings far from the main building as a "preventive measure."[79] The potential for violence permeated every aspect of teachers' daily work experiences.

The district responded to this exposé in a letter to the editor signed by Aaron Wade, the district superintendent. Wade called the article a "cheap shot" and challenged the merit of the reporter's "eavesdropping at three of our 30 schools."[80] Wade asserted that Compton's struggles were "typical national problems, not only in the education arena, but in those problems in the general society as well."[81] Wade's critique spoke to faults in the larger public discourse that focused on "the worst" schools rather than on broader inequalities across the spectrum of public schooling.

Compton's school problems remained in the headlines, helping to define the town's public image. A 1981 *Los Angeles Times* article, "Compton's Schools: Sea of Troubles," described teachers paying for or machine-copying books for their classrooms, as well as teachers, students, and parents personally funding field trips. The article documented, however, that Compton Unified received proportionally more federal aid than any other district in the county other than the behemoth Los Angeles Unified. A couple of months later the *Times* reported that the U.S. Department of Education planned to investigate misuse of federal money by Compton Unified, concentrating on $6 million in Title I funds for the 1980–81 school year.[82] In the public eye, Compton Unified appeared bungled, at best.

Comptonites reacted to the public perception, academic failures, and financial mismanagement. Parents at Ralph Bunche Elementary School sought to pull their school out of Compton Unified and have it join Los Angeles Unified instead. In stating the reasons, the parents alleged that Compton schools were in an "intolerable condition," where security was inadequate, classrooms were poorly equipped, and buildings were unclean.[83] The fact that Los Angeles Unified spent more money per pupil also attracted the parents. Compton Unified board members opposed the departure, however, arguing that the district provided students with quality educations and that the district could not afford the loss of the state funds it received through average daily attendance.[84] Compton's economy could not compensate for the money that would be lost from the transfer of Bunche to Los Angeles. Despite parents' efforts Bunche remained in Compton Unified.

This type of parental protest continued. In November 1984, parents removed over 40 percent of the students at Carver Elementary School, demonstrating against the school's lack of heat. Other parents moved their children permanently out of the district. In 1985, it was estimated that approximately 2,500 Compton Unified students attended neighboring districts. According to Superintendent Kimbrough, the departure of these students meant sapping the district of some of its best students and their supportive parents as well as costing the district state money. The district did everything possible to block students from leaving.[85] Later that year, the Concerned Parents of the Compton Unified School District approached the school board about "our children's safety and educational growth." Among their concerns were the insufficient number of teachers, lack of materials and supplies, and dirty bathrooms. Parents also kept their children out of school in support of salary demands by teachers.[86]

When parents saw a functioning school, they willingly put aside other concerns to keep it going. A prime example was the case of Lawrence Freeman, principal of Willowbrook Middle School. Freeman was a highly praised leader, receiving credit for turning the junior high from a place of "chaos and anarchy" to a school that was overenrolled, because of its "excellence."[87] At the same time he was lauded for his accomplishments, however, Freeman came under the scrutiny of federal auditors for wasting more than $100,000 in federal education funds on "entertainment," including student trips to amusement parks and professional basketball games.[88] Some district administrators initially supported Freeman, but eventually relegated him to a non-leadership role in district headquarters. The decision caused an uproar. Willowbrook parents protested Freeman's removal, but the district administration stood firm and effectively pushed him from the district altogether.[89] The comparison between what happened at the Willowbrook and Bunche schools reveals the tension between the community's understanding of effective leadership on the one hand and what outside observers understood as objective signs of corruption on the other.

Other Compton officials caused concern with federal auditors. In 1982, at the same time as the Freeman controversy, federal agents also investigated $334,000 of other misused funds from across the district. They contended administrators misspent the money on travel, conferences, and entertainment. In the most egregious example, Compton officials used federal Title I money for a six-day conference in Honolulu that had no direct relationship to the Title I program. In 1983, as part of a multiyear investigation into misappropriation of federal funds, FBI agents seized records of the district's purchasing and maintenance and operations departments.⁹⁰ The blatant corruption and illicit use of funds earmarked for struggling students demonstrated district officials' devaluation of improving the schools.

Surely, Compton Unified's problems extended beyond normal school troubles, but many of its struggles came to light at the same time that the effectiveness of the American school system as a whole was being examined. Worried that the United States trailed Japan in the international economy, the federal government sponsored a study to see whether American schools prepared students for global competition. In April 1983, Terrel Bell, the U.S. secretary of education, and the National Commission on Excellence in Education released *A Nation at Risk*, a report that described the mediocrity of American schools. It stated: "Our society and its educational institutions seem to have lost sight of the basic purposes of schooling, and of the high expectations and disciplined effort needed to attain them." The report listed indicators of the nation's "risk," ranging from the startling number of functionally illiterate adults (23 million) to the dramatic increase in remedial mathematics courses in four-year colleges (72 percent in five years). To address the wide array of problems and what it dubbed "the rising tide of mediocrity," the commission outlined a series of recommendations, including strengthening high school graduation requirements, raising standards and expectations at the secondary and college levels, and improving the preparation of teachers.⁹¹

Independently, California sought to reform its public schools, beginning before *A Nation at Risk* to do so. By granting the state control over school expenditures, Proposition 13 had shifted the power over education from local control to Sacramento. Proponents of implementing large-scale changes to the state's system of K-12 education populated both the state legislature and Department of Education. California educators, parents, politicians, and students spearheaded a massive educational reform movement, demanding higher standards in education. Their efforts culminated in 1983 when the California legislature passed what became known as the Hughes-Hart Education Reform Act. Under this act, California made major overhauls to its public school system, including designing state curriculum frameworks and increasing admission requirements for its state colleges and universities. California also became the first state in the nation to establish statewide accountability standards by which to judge school performance.⁹²

Education reform on both the federal and state level had become all about changing the classroom and the school, not the larger social forces that influenced students' ability to learn. As a result, the shifts in policy did not necessarily mean changes for Compton's students.[93] While educators and legislatures sought to alter the state's public schools by focusing on academics, Compton Unified's problems continued both in and outside the classroom. Just being at school posed a danger to students and teachers because the schools were sites of numerous shootings. In April 1983, a campus guard was shot at Compton High during a gang-related incident at lunch. A few months later, another gang-related shooting rampage wounded five students at Dominguez High, despite school officials' claim that Dominguez was clean of any gangs. A month later two students were shot at Compton High.[94]

Gangs were certainly not responsible for all the unrest in Compton's schools, but violence was nonetheless both a ubiquitous threat and a too frequent reality. One event in particular, a gang-related fight among spectators at a Dominguez High School football game, brought attention and concern from outside the town's borders. After the incident, principals of the league's other schools voted six to one to relocate Dominguez's remaining home games because of concerns about the safety of their players and fans. League officials quickly overruled this policy, leaving individual principals the option of forfeiting their schools' games with Dominguez.

The choice over forfeiting a game and ensuring people's safety was not clear cut. Two schools immediately agreed to play their scheduled fall and winter competitions at Dominguez, the rest citing Dominguez's security plan as insufficient.[95] Even after the Downey school board allowed participation at Dominguez sporting events, some school board members remained outspoken opponents of doing so, calling Dominguez High's athletic events "armed camps." One Downey school board member, Robert Riley, expanded: "If we want to play in an armed camp, we might as well play in Saigon or Beirut." Another disgruntled Downey school board member, Donald LaPlante, asked: "if our people aren't safe to go there under normal circumstances, why should we send them in there under armed guard?"[96] Many parents did not want to risk sending their children to Compton, even for the duration of a sporting match. It would be next to impossible to shake such a stigma.

Compton Unified's negative reputation extended to academics. This image proved true, as the district's students on a whole functioned well below state average. In 1989, Centennial High School enrolled 1,489 students but graduated only 258 (219 African American and 37 Latino). Of those 258, only 43 earned an academic diploma (26 African American and 17 Latino).

Only 3 African American (and no Latino) students matriculated into the University of California system. The other two district high schools, Compton and Dominguez, had similarly bleak numbers.[97] The following year, Compton Unified ranked in the lowest quartile compared to schools with similar population characteristics statewide.[98]

In a letter to the editor of the *Los Angeles Times*, Fran Sifuentes, a resident of Compton for twenty-five years, explained that it was not just Latino students who suffered because of systemic exclusion; the district impaired all of its pupils. He stated, "black children are being equally denied a good future, even though blacks have held the key political and administrative positions for many years." He concluded woefully, "Compton is throwing away its youth and no one seems to be able to do anything about it."[99] The statistics on Compton schools' performances supported this opinion. In 1991, Compton High graduated 207 students, of whom less than 15 percent had completed the courses necessary for college entry. The percentages were higher for the other two comprehensive high schools in Compton Unified, but only fourteen students from the three schools combined matriculated into the University of California system.[100]

Working in Compton Unified

Working in Compton Unified was difficult. In the classroom, Compton's teachers faced violence, or the threat of violence, and routinely asked the district and administrators to help alleviate these perils as well as to compensate them adequately for their work. In 1983, as part of their demands during contract negotiations, teachers clamored for two-way communication systems between classroom and administration buildings on every campus so that teachers could alert security if necessary. The CEA—the teachers' union—also petitioned for a 10 percent pay raise for all teachers to equalize the district's pay scale with neighboring districts.[101]

Compton's lower pay scale also made it challenging to attract and retain substitute teachers. These tasks became more onerous in 1983, when the State of California required that all teachers pass the California Basic Educational Skills Test. As a result, the pool of replacement teachers shrank. Compton remained unable to compensate the teachers competitively. At the beginning of the school year, Compton Unified lost 80 percent of its substitute teaching pool, resorting to using administrative personnel to cover classes. By midyear, the dearth of substitutes forced the board of trustees to raise its pay scale, but even with the increases, the district still only retained half the necessary replacement teachers.[102]

Pay differences with neighboring districts continued to plague Compton Unified. Classroom and substitute teachers voiced disapproval of their pay during contract negotiations during the 1984–85 school year and asked for a 12 percent pay raise. When the district counter-offered with a 1 percent raise, the CEA requested a state arbitrator. The mediator recommended a 6 percent wage increase, which the district administrators rejected, claiming the raises would eat up reserve funds. Tensions mounted and after a strike threat, the teachers and the district settled on a 3 percent raise.[103]

Despite this modest victory, teaching in Compton remained less than ideal; Compton teachers continued to face "the worst job environment in Los Angeles County," according to a 1986 *Los Angeles Times* article. To support this assertion, the *Times* reporter pointed to the district's mounting cost for workers' compensation, which had doubled in the previous six years and greatly exceeded that of other county districts. The reporter noted that Compton employees requested an unusual amount based on stress. District officials used these claims against the teachers, however, as they cited the high workers' compensation payments as one cause for the district's strapped budget.[104]

Paying and fighting workers' compensation claims was only one area in which Compton Unified spent proportionately more money than other districts. Compton Unified devoted a smaller percentage of its budget to teacher salaries than other Los Angeles County districts, while spending more money for clerical, maintenance, and administrative salaries.[105] Kelvin Filer explained that many board members supported employing a large number of nonteaching personnel because "classified employees tend to be individuals from the community" and therefore are people who voted for the school board.[106] In classic machine-politics style, but more acutely than in other places, board members shored up their political power by allocating funds for employment rather than educational purposes. According to Superintendent Kimbrough, board members' misspending of funds had caused most of the district's ills; Compton Unified was "overemployed by 30 percent." Kimbrough explained that paying for so many staff members meant "you don't fix roofs or provide textbooks."[107] Compton Unified played a dual role in its community—as both employer and educator. Over the years the employer function came to take precedence.

While Compton Unified designated funds in ways most school districts did not, the allotments went to legal (though sometimes questionable) areas. Due to the manner in which Compton Unified's administrators divided funds, district schools lacked basics. Compton High's poor conditions forced one chemistry teacher to heat the classroom with open gas jets. Former Compton teacher Georgia Maryland said that teachers and staff members worked without decent supplies and in buildings in constant state of disrepair.[108] Parent Linda Allen recalled that Compton High did not have proper bathroom facilities. She said, "I remember the boys telling me that they didn't have any doors on the stalls in the bathrooms, and things like that. My kids, silly as they were, they would hold themselves all day, and then almost break the door down when they got home, trying to get into the bathroom."[109] The district also spent money to repair the buildings and replace equipment that arsonists or thieves had ruined or stolen. In 1980 the district adopted an arson prevention program and in 1981 it declared a war on vandalism, but neither program succeeded. During the 1984–85 school year, Compton Unified suffered $2 million worth of arson damage.[110]

District conditions threatened to deteriorate even more when, in July 1986, California governor George Deukmejian vetoed funding to so-called inner-city schools. This money had comprised 6 percent of Compton Unified's general fund and, because of the veto, district leaders needed "to find how to cut $3.8 million from our budget," according to Kimbrough.[111] In order to do this, members of Compton Unified's board of trustees attempted another solution, only to generate major backlash from their constituents. In 1986, the district discovered two bond issues—from 1962 and 1968—that had been initially approved but never issued. Issuing these bonds would open new sources of money for the schools but would also mean increasing taxes for Compton residents, something many could not afford with their already high rates. After much criticism, school district officials decided to rescind the bonds.[112] Despite its ultimate defeat, the reintroduction of the bonds indicated local schools' desperate need for more funds.

The lack of new funds and the misuse of existing monies reinvigorated questions and complaints about salaries. In fall 1986, Compton teachers once again sought a pay raise. At a meeting of the district board of trustees in September, a group of teachers led by their union expressed their grievances. Joyce Napier, a teacher at Wilson Riles Elementary School, explained, "I came to this district excited, enthusiastic with great ideas and goals and tonight I stand frustrated, tired and disappointed. My first year of teaching I met everything you could imagine, even my room was burned down last year but

I'm back because I'm dedicated and I want to be in this District. . . . This week I had almost 50 students." From the district she wanted "a salary that can give me—not extravagance but—the things I need—pay my house, pay my car payment. I'm just here tonight to just ask you to please think about us new teachers." She continued by saying that new teachers had to make a decision: "Are we going to stay in this District? Are things going to change for us to improve things so that we can go into that classroom and work with those children and provide an education for them or are we going to go knocking somewhere else? Maybe we'll get a little bit more money or maybe we will at least be able to walk on the campus and feel secure. Those are big things to a teacher in the classroom."[113]

The challenges created by poor conditions and low salaries reached beyond new teachers. At the same meeting, Marilyn Mayor, a veteran teacher of twelve years, explained, "I choose to stay here to offer my services, to offer my expertise and to be flexible and understand that money isn't everything, but it is something. It tells me that you care; that you want to keep qualified, dedicated, experienced teachers." This sentiment was echoed by Compton graduate, resident, and teacher, Tulaurny McLauen, who remarked: "I'm a teacher, I've dedicated seven years to this district and was a student here and survived and now I'm 42 and I'm very disappointed and I just wanted to let you know that I was in agreement with [CEA union president] Wiley Jones and the other guy that told you that we're considering leaving—leaving the District— and I really don't want to, but I need money."[114] An independent fact-finding commission revealed that Compton teachers were the lowest paid of Los Angeles County's forty-three public school districts.[115]

Teachers' concerns extended beyond higher pay to issues of better security and smaller classes. To ensure safety, according to Floyd Worsham, a teacher for twenty-one years in Compton Unified, "most schools do not have any security. Instead, the district mostly utilizes a police force." When trouble arose, school personnel called the police, erasing the possible deterrent and protection effects of maintaining full-time security on campus. As for class size, Wiley Jones, CEA president, noted: "Some Kindergarten classes have up to 36 students, and other elementary classes have 40." According to the union contract, class size should have been 30 students, plus or minus one. In many cases, several teachers said that 34–35 was the average number of students per class.[116]

During the 1986–87 school year, Compton teachers staged a series of job actions to demand that the district rectify these problems. Jones asserted they were no longer willing to tolerate "being third-class citizens."[117] Teachers walked out of the schools in November 1986, but their work stoppage did not force the district's hand, and the work actions continued. In January, police arrested twenty striking teachers after demonstrators refused to leave the school district offices. By mid-March, Compton educators had struck for a total of sixteen school days. The job actions became so crippling that a judge imposed a court injunction against the teachers.[118]

The atmosphere around the strike deteriorated. Board members had turkeys sent to their homes to taunt them. Compton Unified officials received angry calls at home and at work, day and night. Teachers picketed the residences and business of the trustees who opposed the pay raises. Superintendent Kimbrough felt threatened enough to begin carrying a gun for personal protection.[119]

The strike brought national attention to the plight of Compton Unified schools. In a speech about California's shortchanging its students, Mary Hatwood Futrell, president of the National Education Association, singled out Compton Unified School District for its "horrible" conditions. Futrell described her visit to three Compton schools, where she was "absolutely appalled" to find leaky ceilings, broken windows, "filthy" bathrooms, bird droppings on classroom floors, and no fire extinguishers. "I'm surprised that the Fire Department or the Health Department had not gone in and closed down those schools for being unsafe and unhealthy," she said. At one school, she added, teachers also served as janitors. "They have their own mops and their own brooms and they are cleaning their own buildings," she said.[120] Futrell promised to ask the state superintendent of schools to "intervene." Compton Unified officials dismissed her remarks as politically motivated.[121] They did not, however, dispute the veracity of her observations.

After seven bitter months, Compton Unified and its teachers reached an agreement. The teachers overwhelmingly ratified a three-year contract to gain a 7 percent salary increase for the first year. The next year they received a 5 percent increase and the following year's figure was to be tied to the cost of living. While a notable increase for its teachers, Compton Unified's pay fell below neighboring districts. In Compton Unified, a starting teacher made slightly more than $23,000 while in neighboring Los Angeles Unified starting pay was $27,000. The median salary for Compton teachers stood around $25,000, as compared to the statewide average of $29,000. Compton's maximum pay was $38,000, while in Los Angeles it was $49,000.[122]

As a result of the low pay and dismal conditions, many teachers left the district. Just three weeks before the fall 1989 semester, school officials scrambled to replace 154 teachers (almost 13 percent of the teaching force), the largest exodus Compton Unified had ever experienced. Compton Unified had a particularly difficult time recruiting bilingual teachers, who were in demand throughout the entire Southwest. To meet this growing need Compton Unified began to employ teachers from Spain. Their numbers, however, were insufficient to fill the district's bilingual positions. In the 1989–90 school year, Compton Unified employed only eleven teachers from Spain. The district's inability to retain teachers seemed so predictable that in the *Los Angeles Times*, the story became not about the teachers who left Compton Unified, but rather why teachers chose to stay.[123]

Remaining teachers continued to endure terrible teaching conditions. At an October 1989 school board meeting, teacher Chester Lampkin presented each board member with a ragged textbook from his classroom, pointing out that each book was missing a number of pages and complaining that these were the only books available to issue to students. In response, Kimbrough stated that the district had spent hundreds of thousands of dollars for textbooks and that he was well aware that some students were still without them. He assured all concerned that the district would address the textbook shortage. At the same meeting, another teacher, Ms. Bahato, complained that drugs were being sold on Compton High's campus and students were just "hanging out."[124] Throughout that school year, as they had in the past, parents and teachers continued to express similar grievances to the board of trustees. When their contract expired that school year, Compton teachers once again protested low pay, inadequate supplies, and unsafe schools. During March 1990, taking action on stalled labor negotiations, almost all the teachers at ten Compton Unified schools called in sick with the "blue flu."[125]

Teachers were not the only people walking out of Compton schools in protest. In March 1990, parents, under the leadership of the newly formed group Save Our Children, joined hundreds of students in a series of demonstrations, highlighting the urgent educational and physical conditions of the district's schools. Joy Turner founded the organization along with five other parents after she discovered her son had missed forty-two days his senior year without her being notified. The twenty-five members of the organization pressured the district to tackle problems such as fixing damaged restrooms and classrooms, getting hot water for the gymnasium showers, developing stronger academic programs, providing better security, and renovating the school auditorium and the stadium, both of which were closed because of disrepair.[126] In describing the future of Compton, Jacqueline Carter asserted: "We're going to be stuck with a bunch of teen-agers who cannot succeed."[127] The group blamed the district's inability to retain qualified—or even permanent—teachers and counselors, urging the district to increase the pay of its certificated employees.

The district insisted that it did not have the money to pay for both raises and repairs. But a state fact-finding report said Compton Unified, which claimed it was facing a $2.27 million budget shortfall, could actually afford to disburse over 12 percent more on teachers' salaries than it was allocating that year. The report also said district officials either engaged in "deliberate deceit," or were displaying incompetence by claiming that the district was facing a deficit, while showing no signs of trying to minimize expenditures. The financial data submitted by the district were "irreconcilable" with the district's spending habits, according to the report.[128]

Despite the report, Compton Unified's board members continued to plead poverty. In April 1990, Compton Unified board members announced that the district was $1.4 million short of the state- and county-recommended final balance limit, opening the potential of ending the school year in the red. By mid-May, the *Los Angeles Times* reported that the budget shortfall might be between $7 and $9 million and that district officials were looking to cut jobs, including security personnel and school nurses.[129]

Violence on campus continued to detract from the learning environment at Compton schools. A rival gang member shot a sixteen-year-old student at Centennial High in February 1991. A couple of months later, a gunshot intended for a security guard at Ralph Bunche Middle School killed eleven-year-old Alejandro Vargas. That year, along with these two shootings, an elementary school janitor was killed, a Compton High student was shot in the face, and another Centennial student was murdered, all on or near Compton campuses. "In Beverly Hills, [a school shooting] would be unusual," said John Swanson, a Compton police detective. "Here, it's not unusual."[130]

Gaining National Attention

Compton's problems gained national attention and as a result, Compton's place in the national consciousness came to far exceed its actual size. Portrayals of the town, such as the 1980 and 1981 exposés in the *Wall Street Journal* and *Los Angeles Times*, both created and reinforced its racialized identity.

National studies, television programs, music, and films introduced Compton to the American public in a way that earlier cultural productions had just begun to do. Unlike their predecessors, some of the newer pieces with broadest impact were created by Comptonites themselves. This public image would shape how outsiders related to Compton, which in turn affected the place itself.

Compton's notoriety caused it to become the subject of academic studies. In 1987, a study out of Roosevelt University in Chicago investigated the "geography of wealth and poverty in suburban America" from 1979 to 1985. The study showed that not all metropolitan areas fit the stereotype of the "impoverished, blackening central city and the affluent, white suburb."[131] According to its findings, the average income in suburban Los Angeles was lower than that in the city of Los Angeles and it identified Compton as the ninth poorest suburb in the entire country.[132] Being a suburb clearly did not ensure access to the middle class.

Compton as a violent place joined its image as impoverished. In 1987, city council members enacted an ordinance outlawing handguns. Council members unanimously passed the statute, citing the need for drastic measures in a place where the crime rate was higher than county and state averages. The local law caused quite a stir, and at the next council meeting concerned parties, both for and against the measure, packed the hall to standing-room capacity. The audience included four television camera crews and a lobbyist from the National Rifle Association. Under enormous pressure from this crowd, three council members reversed their decision, choosing to reject the ordinance on the basis that it stripped Comptonites of a means of self-defense.[133]

Admitting Compton's handgun problem reinforced the town's violent image, which began to appear in popular television shows. In 1990, the legal drama *L.A. Law* portrayed a judge determining what type of sentence she should pass on a Latino youth from Compton. The judge delivered a monologue about how psychiatrists viewed individuals as products of their environment and then compared children in fancy suburbs, who played hockey and whiffle ball, with children from Compton, who joined gangs and played with drugs. Compton came to represent a place where just being there posed danger to one's psyche. In response to the episode, members of the Compton Unified board of trustees demanded an apology from the show's producers. They had a similar reaction the next year when the television comedy *The Fresh Prince of Bel-Air* portrayed the town negatively. In that case, members of the board actually met with representatives from the show's production company to discuss the depiction.[134]

The representations of Compton existed as part of a larger onslaught of television and film images of urban crime, violence, and poverty. The 1988 film *Colors* chronicled two white Los Angeles police officers as they tried to control gang violence. The film and popular television shows like *America's Most Wanted*, which premiered that same year, featured imagery that was deeply racialized and helped build white fear, as blacks and Latinos were portrayed as violent criminals. They also helped define cities for many viewers. Cities were poor, black, and violent, and this definition helped link in popular discourse the image of Compton with the black ghetto.

Popular images helped shape the conversation around race in the 1980s, which in turn influenced the decade's political dialogue. The most explicit example of this was in the 1988 presidential campaign when the Republican Party tapped into anxieties around race and crime. In a commercial critiquing Democratic presidential nominee Michael Dukakis, the party employed an image of an African American Willie Horton to warn against Dukakis's lenient attitude toward crime.[135] The cultural representations of places like Compton helped create the climate in which the Horton advertisement became powerful.

Comptonites also created their town's image, particularly with the rise of gangsta rap. Previously the hip hop world centered in New York and in other East Coast cities but black residents of Compton and other Los Angeles area localities developed a new style, emphasizing the experiences of black youths in their West Coast neighborhoods. These new artists purposely centered their poetics on a place, grounding their lyrics in a specific locality. Scholar Eithne Quinn explains, "hard-core artists had found a niche precisely by projecting a sense of authentic and dangerous regional locality."[136] In the case of the extremely popular and influential group NWA the rhymes associated Compton with the worst features of urban blight.

Comptonite Eric "Eazy-E" Wright created NWA in 1986, and the group soon gained regional and then national fame. The original members included Ice Cube (O'Shea Jackson), MC Ren (Lorenzo Patterson), Dr. Dre (Andre Young), DJ Yella (Antoine Carraby), Arabian Prince (Mik Lezan), and the D.O.C. (Tracy Curry). Although Arabian Prince and the D.O.C were only members of NWA from 1986 to 1988, they remained involved as ghostwriters. Produced by Eazy E's independent label Ruthless Records, NWA's first track, "Boyz-n-the-Hood," hit the street in September 1987 and by the end of the year it was the most requested song on KDAY, a Los Angeles R&B and hip hop radio station. The beginning of "Boyz-n-the-Hood" marked Compton as the center of activity and the chorus put forward the "boyz" experience of "knowing nothing in life but to be legit." The original record sold thousands, but it took awhile for NWA to get signed to a record label. Once Priority Records signed NWA, the company sold over 300,000 copies of the single.[137]

NWA's *Straight Outta Compton* album gained significant attention from both the listening public and music critics. The album went gold in six weeks and eventually went double platinum, even though it received almost no initial radio play or support from the extremely influential MTV. Even so, middle-class whites comprised a large portion of the listeners. Eazy E explained why he thought NWA had such a large white audience: "They like listening to that 'I don't give a fuck' attitude, the Guns N' Roses attitude. They buy something like 70 per cent of our stuff. They wanna really learn what's going on in different parts of the neighborhoods, they wanna be down, just like I want to be down too."[138]

It was the album's second track, "Fuck Tha Police," that caused a firestorm. In a letter to NWA, FBI officials objected to lyrics such as: "Fuck the police, Comin' straight from the underground, Young nigga got it bad cuz I'm brown, And not the other color so police think, They have the authority to kill a minority."[139] Law enforcement officials believed the lyrics could increase violence. Along with the FBI condemnation, the Fraternal Order of Police, which at the time had more than 200,000 members, declared a boycott of the group. Some African American civic and political leaders also spoke out against the song, criticizing it as a distortion of the black community.[140]

The song caused an enormous uproar but also vaulted the album to the top of the charts. For many listeners the song "perfectly captured the zeitgeist of young Blacks and Latinos suffering under the twin oppressions of gangs and police, not just in L.A., but across the country," according to music business veteran and journalist Dan Charnas.[141] Verna Griffin, Dr. Dre's mother, reflected: "It made me remember a time when my boys were standing outside by my car, having a friendly conversation with other boys in the neighborhood, when all of a sudden I looked out the window and saw the police with all of them spread-eagle against the police car. This harassment was for no obvious reason except they saw black boys grouped together and automatically presumed they were up to no good." Remembering this story, Griffin realized that "the lyrics in the songs were just stories about things that were actually happening in their lives. Some people just had a hard time getting past the profanity to hear it."[142]

While NWA may have helped put Compton on the map, others helped cement it. Following NWA's success, artists such as Compton's Most Wanted and DJ Quik emerged quickly, also making claims about the West Coast suburb. Compton's Most Wanted declared: "If you're from Compton you know it's the 'hood where it's good" and DJ Quik described his hometown as, "home of the jackers and the crack."[143] Place was central to these groups' self-definition. In turn, the groups helped form Compton as a nationwide symbol of gangs and gang violence.

The television and film portrayals and the rap music had different origins, but they had a symbiotic relationship. Gangsta rappers consciously reacted to the images portrayed by the white media and they played off of those ideas in their own work.[144] For example, in 1990, Ice Cube, former member of NWA, titled his first solo album "AmeriKKKa's Most Wanted." Not only were the rappers answering back to those representations, but they were also incorporating them and using the fascination with racialized violence to sell albums. Filmmaker John Singleton used the title of the NWA song "Boyz-n-the-Hood" as the name of his 1991 acclaimed film, in which Ice Cube made his film debut. The local artists helped to create Compton as a commodity. Dr. Dre explained: "We came out with Compton, the NWA thing, so every time somebody sees Compton they gonna buy that shit just 'cause of the name, whether they from there or not. Compton exists in many ways in the music to sell records."[145] Compton, and other similar communities, was simultaneously a place of myth and reality.[146] The lyrics spoke to both the experiences of the rappers as well as the constructed image of their hometown.

While scholars have debated why place served as a central element to gangsta rap, few have considered its impact on the place.[147] Compton's negative image affected its business areas, its schools, and even its relationships to other towns. Adjacent cities worked to disassociate themselves from their infamous neighbor. This desire could be seen in border towns' renaming of Compton Boulevard, a major east-west artery that ran from the Pacific coast through the southern part of Los Angeles County. The first town to make this change was the adjoining Paramount to the east, which did so as a "marketing effort to attract middle-income families." One Paramount business owner wrote in a letter of support for the change: "The word 'Compton' does not paint a picture of a first-class residential community since the area is too well known for the slums and strife that existed there for the last 20 or so years."[148]

Paramount changed the street name to Marine Avenue, hoping to invoke a more serene image. After Paramount implemented the change, the neighboring cities of Hawthorne, Lawndale, and Gardena all considered doing the same. By 1990, all the towns west of Compton had renamed Compton Boulevard Marine Avenue. Later that year, the residents of the county area known as East Compton renamed their locality East Rancho Dominguez.[149] Simply having Compton in a name seemed enough to associate it with Compton's troubles and thereby threaten businesses and housing values.

Racial prejudices fed into this vitriolic association with the name Compton. According to social critic Alida Brill, the white residents of Lakewood used "Compton" as a synonym for "takeover": "The word *Compton* has come to mean absorption by another culture." Blacks had replaced Compton's white residents and Lakewood residents expressed trepidation that the same would happen in their community, causing their solid housing stock to decrease in value. Lakewood residents believed that in Compton the changing racial demographics caused the town's poverty, further increasing their fear of becoming another Compton. In the words of Larry Van Nostran, the former mayor of Lakewood, "I used to go to Compton years ago, to the Sears, it was so nice. They called it the 'model garden city' in those days. Now look at the place. It could happen here, to us. Lakewood could become another Compton if we are not careful."[150] What happened to Compton seemed frighteningly permanent.

The shifts in the Los Angeles economy made it more difficult for people of color to get high-paying jobs. Compton, already a center of poverty and home to mostly minority residents, was particularly hard hit by these changes in employment patterns. Town officials failed miserably at multiple attempts at redevelopment, which could have led to the creation of new jobs. As a result, they held tightly to control over jobs within Compton's municipal government and school district, excluding Latinos from many of the positions.

As such, the demographic shift did not translate into equal service for all of Compton's populace, particularly its students. By 1989, Latinos comprised the largest ethnic population in Compton Unified. Along with its already long list of educational challenges, the district now faced second-language learning issues, but the school district failed to provide enough bilingual staff. The school district was the largest employer in the town and, perhaps almost predictably, African Americans did not want to share jobs with Spanish speakers. Latinos' efforts to achieve integration despite the black political elite's resistance revealed much about the contest for power within the community. Similar contests revolved around control of city hall. The town's debilitating poverty shaped the choices that officials and administrators made.

Compton residents—both black and brown—protested the conditions of the school district and of the town. From the district they demanded safe schools that provided adequate education. From the town they looked for viable redevelopment plans and housing alternatives. Despite their protests, officials' fiscal mismanagement and the community's systemic poverty continued to plague Compton and its schools. Anger toward poverty and the school district's shortcomings would both come to a head in the next few years, with a racially charged court verdict and a state takeover of Compton Unified on the horizon.

Enter the State

In April 1992 Compton city councilperson Patricia Moore planned to bus a group of "concerned citizens" to Simi Valley to hear the closing arguments in the trial of four Los Angeles police officers charged with the beating of black motorist Rodney King. Moore told the *Compton Bulletin* she wanted African Americans to attend so that they could be "the last thing on [jury members] minds."[1] Not surprisingly, having lived in a racially charged area, many Compton residents took the trial personally, believing King's beating was racially motivated. Moore wanted to ensure the jury members saw that concern.

Nevertheless, on April 29 the jury of twelve acquitted the officers. The verdicts stunned many Americans, who for over a year had been bombarded by images from a bystander's amateur video of the abuse. Police and elected officials urged calm and order, but their pleas could not contain the brewing anger. The rage was most palpable in the southern part of Los Angeles, an area mostly inhabited by poor and working-class blacks and Latinos. Groups of discouraged Angelenos gathered on the streets and in front of the headquarters of the Los Angeles Police Department (LAPD). Soon the crowds turned into protests and the protests turned into violence. Within hours of the verdict, a white man lay on the asphalt in the middle of an intersection in South Central Los Angeles, beaten, kicked, and bashed with a fire extinguisher by irate African Americans. His name, Reginald Denny, became "almost as famous as King's," as people across the nation and around the globe watched Los Angeles and its surrounding areas go up in flames.[2]

The immediate response of local law enforcement officers failed to stop the disturbances. The LAPD reacted slowly: police officials had decided not to mobilize their officers during the trial, and when the verdicts came down that afternoon, most of the force's one thousand detectives had already gone home for the day. Within hours the situation turned dire. Shortly after nine that evening, California governor Pete Wilson requested two thousand soldiers from the California Army National Guard. These troops were, however, unprepared to intercede immediately because LAPD administrators had repeatedly assured military officials they would not be needed to quell any disturbances resulting from the verdict. Consequently, National Guard officers had lent a considerable amount of "control equipment" to other agencies.[3] These inadequate mobilizations allowed the riots to continue and to spread throughout the Los Angeles area, including Compton.

Compton had escaped damage during the 1965 uprisings, but time had changed that. In 1965 Compton was on the edge of being a suburb, but in 199, it was an "urban ghetto." At the time of the trial, Compton's 10.1 square miles were home to just over ninety thousand people, approximately 53 percent African American and 44 percent Latino.[4] In 1992 just over 25 percent of Compton residents lived below the official poverty line and their frustration with this bare existence manifested in the days after the verdict. Many rioters looted stores, using the opportunity not only to express their anger toward local businesses but also to fill their households with much needed items, including diapers and groceries. Compton's systemic poverty laid the groundwork for the frustration and desperation exhibited in 1992. The bleak economy also outraged many residents.

The verdicts in the King trial brought the enmity accrued over years of police brutality and poverty to a boiling point. As Compton residents started fires and looted stores, municipal officials could do little but look outward for assistance. In response, the members of Compton's city council placed the town under a state of emergency, enabling them to ask for state and federal aid. Outside help came quickly. Approximately 250 marines swept into Compton to rein in the outbreak of looting and arson.[5] With the blessing of local elected officials external forces occupied the town.

Compton's leaders would not always welcome outside intervention. During the same year as the King riots, local officials resisted a state takeover of Compton Unified. Defining it as "academically bankrupt," state assemblyman Willard Murray led the charge to have the state take control, but the initial attempts failed. In 1993, however, when school district officials requested, and the state granted, a $10.5 million emergency loan to keep the school district running, the state took charge of the beleaguered district. A few months later, in an unprecedented move, the state also seized control over academics.[6] It is important to note that while the state took on a double mandate it was only after it became financially invested that academics became a concern.

The presence of a state administrator in Compton prompted disagreement among some local residents. For Compton's elected officials, riots were the sort of emergency that warranted outside aid while fixing their failing school system was more of a local affair. With the uprisings, local officials willingly relinquished power for a limited time because of a situation they did not create. The school takeover, on the other hand, had no time limit and directly called into question how Compton residents managed their own community, thereby challenging local authority and competency.

The state takeover of Compton Unified illuminated the power struggle between state and local entities. Both opponents and proponents of the state takeover invoked racial ideologies and their relationship to citizenship rights as a way to argue for and against outside intervention in the district. Due to the history of decentralized school governance, many Americans have viewed public schools as the most local of institutions. But the postwar reality was a much different picture: state and federal powers have had much sway in educational institutions through, for example, such means as curriculum mandates and funding resources. This relationship between the local and the state became heightened during the state takeover.

The state, however, kept its focus narrow: Compton Unified's low test scores and high debt necessitated intervention. Just as in 1992, when the authorities overlooked the endemic problems that fueled the Rodney King riots, the state did not address Compton Unified's troubles as part of a larger web of problems. By focusing on the day-to-day financing of the district's basic needs, state officials, like local officials before them, neglected the larger, systemic economic problems that afflicted Compton's community. Ultimately the state takeover of Compton Unified inadequately addressed the needs of the students because it did not address the interrelation of the district and community's problems and their effects on the public schools.

A Crisis Worthy of Intervention

In a televised speech on May 1, 1992, the second day of the uprisings following the Rodney King trial, president George H. W. Bush called the riots "random terror and lawlessness," scoffing at the idea that they were in any way a form of protest. That same day, Governor Wilson, Los Angeles mayor Tom

Bradley, and officials in Washington decided the federal government should send armed forces to Los Angeles. President Bush ordered the Justice Department to dispatch one thousand federal riot-trained law-enforcement officials to help restore order in Los Angeles. These officials included Federal Bureau of Investigation SWAT teams, U.S. Marshal Service riot control units, the border patrol, and other federal law-enforcement agencies. He also committed 3,000 members of the Seventh Infantry Division and 1,500 marines. Included in these troops were two hundred members of the U.S. Marshal's special operations group, whose duties had included the 1990 mission to take Panamanian dictator Manuel Noriega into custody. President Bush federalized the National Guard, instructing General Colin Powell to centralize all forces under one command.[7] Stopping the events in South Los Angeles warranted the full weight of the federal government.

Over the next few days, federal involvement in the crisis deepened. Mayor Bradley sought an official federal disaster declaration and President Bush dispatched even more federal troops. The president also announced that a federal grand jury had issued subpoenas as part of an accelerated investigation by the Justice Department into whether the officers involved violated federal civil rights laws. Ironically, even as the federal government researched this contravention of rights, its own forces breached others. Before the riots, police and immigration authorities had worked separately. But during the uprisings, border patrol teams accompanied the National Guard. Officer from the U.S. Immigration and Naturalization Services (INS) guarded the areas with the LAPD and Los Angeles County Sheriff's Department (LASD). The official rationale for the joint patrols was that border patrol officers served as translators. However, the entangled presence of immigration authorities and police produced numerous abuses. Immigrants' rights groups reported that the LASD and LAPD stopped individuals who "looked Latino" and questioned them about their citizenship status. Individuals who could not prove citizenship status were sent to INS stations for further interrogation.[8]

Latino arrests illuminated the changed demographics of Los Angeles, as well as the strains that came with the shifts. The participants in the 1965 uprisings had almost all been black, which reflected the racial composition of Watts. In 1992, 51 percent of those arrested were Latino, which showed the changing face of the area and Los Angeles County at large.[9] As Latinos became a larger portion of the Los Angeles population, fear and resentment mounted. Even established Latino leaders in areas such as Boyle Heights and East Los Angeles separated themselves from these new Central American and Mexican immigrants, whom they viewed as threats to the established peace. Many Angelenos, especially African Americans who had remained on the lowest rungs of the economic ladder, saw these immigrants as competition for jobs. Locally, in Compton, residents played out this conflict on a daily basis.

In addition to raising ethnic strife among Los Angeles's multitude of ethnic populations, the riots took their toll on the economy, property, and human life. In total, 53 people died and property damage totaled approximately $1 billion. In Compton specifically, police reported 179 vandalized buildings and the fire department recorded 136 fires. Two people died and three police officers were shot. While rioters caused no damage to public facilities, destruction of private property reached an estimated $100 million. As a result of the widespread devastation, Compton citizens and business owners became eligible for disaster loans.[10]

Yet, even with recovery funds, Compton lost approximately $1.5 million in property tax revenue and an estimated $500,000 in sales tax revenue as a result of damages. Additionally, property damages to businesses hindered their reopening, strapped their owners for cash, and ultimately caused the loss of over five hundred jobs. In order to request additional financial assistance from the state, the members of the Compton city council unanimously adopted a resolution finding that the civil unrest had catastrophically disturbed economic development in the town.[11] The riot damage, coupled with Compton's already drained economy, made the municipal government incapable of fixing its own troubles.

Poverty had a long history in the Los Angeles region and played a central role in the 1992 riots—both in the origin of the uprisings and as a chief reason for outside intervention. Official reports and academic analyses would later identify the deeper roots of the riots. The trigger may have been the verdicts, but "the background [was] a long background of neglect," noted Margaret Weir, a social sciences professor. "It is very much a product of the neglect of the inner cities for the last 25 years," when the poverty rate rose dramatically.[12] A state committee investigating the 1992 riots concluded that the conditions that fueled the spring unrest were virtually the same as those that led to widespread urban disturbances in the 1960s. The panel argued that the level of poverty and despair in South Los Angeles matched that of the 1960s, becoming even more aggravated in the 1990s by an "increasing concentration of wealth at the top of the income scale and a decreasing federal and state commitment to urban problems."[13]

Poverty incited the Los Angeles riots and poverty created Compton's failing public school system. The reverse was also true. Poor schools helped create a population unprepared to hold well-paying jobs, helping reinforce an area of concentrated poverty. Compton Unified's problems had become so egregious that by 1992, just a few weeks after the riots, state assemblyman Willard Murray proposed legislation for a state takeover of the district. Previously the state had intervened in financially insolvent districts, such as the Richmond and Oakland Unified Districts, but had never intervened based on educational performance.[14]

By many state measures Compton Unified was failing. In 1992, the district served 28,240 students in three high schools, one special education center, eight junior high schools, and twenty-four elementary schools. The population came from a low socioeconomic status: 41 percent from families who received Aid for Dependent Children and 61 percent who qualified for free and reduced lunch.[15] Of California districts that enrolled 1,500 pupils or more, Compton Unified students scored the lowest in twelve of fourteen categories tested in the 1989–90 school year. The composite percentile rank for Compton students was 1.0, which meant that 99 percent of the students in the state scored higher than Compton students. In comparison, Los Angeles Unified had a composite percentile rank of 15.7; Pasadena Unified 19.5; and Long Beach Unified 24.5.[16]

Murray's bill passed the state senate and assembly only to be vetoed by Governor Wilson.[17] In his veto message, Wilson explained that, though "drastic corrective action is required in Compton," local control should be removed only as a last resort. He added that the district was "on probation" and that he would entertain similar legislation in the future "if there is not dramatic improvement in the performance of the schools."[18] According to Murray, racial prejudice, rather than concern for educational achievement, dictated the governor's stance. Providing adequate education, the key to embracing one's citizenship rights, was not the state's priority when it came to poor minority students. Murray explained: "I am utterly disgusted and disappointed with the veto because no one seems to care that 28,000 little, poor, black and Hispanic children are not receiving even a minimal education." He continued: "If these were Anglo kids, these educational conditions would not be tolerated."[19]

Officials on the county level also recognized Compton Unified's troubles, though their concerns centered on financial, not academic problems. In 1992, the Los Angeles County Office of Education (LACOE) billed the district for three years of special education costs it had never paid. Later that year, an audit found that the budget Compton Unified had submitted to the county office of education differed from the one actually adopted by the school district. In the county version, the budget reported a $4.1 million surplus when in actuality the district fell in the red. In response, LACOE gave Compton Unified an ultimatum—get your act together or face a budget review committee. If the latter found financial missteps, LACOE could seize control of Compton Unified.

Compton Unified extended its deceit and incompetence beyond the county. District superintendent J. L. Handy also reported the false balance to officials in Sacramento, who in turn became wary of the entire district's operation when they discovered the financial mismanagement and questionable bookkeeping practices. The misrepresentation was compounded by the fact that California state law required that school districts maintain a 3 percent reserve.[20] Discovered as fraudulent, Compton Unified came under close scrutiny.

Once under the county's eye, Compton officials had to make tough choices as to how to eliminate millions of dollars from the budget and lay off more than a hundred district employees. In December 1992, the county finally approved Compton Unified's revised plan, contingent on the district administration and board of trustees going through with the cuts. The district did not implement its own plan for personnel layoffs, however, and instead had an enormous increase in salaries and benefits.[21] At the same time the federal government informed the district that it owed $5 million in back taxes.

The divergent budgets, coupled with low test scores, employee dissatisfaction, and a $1.2 million tax penalty (eventually reduced to $700,000) led to the district's firing of Superintendant Handy. Despite its financial problems, the district willingly bought out the last year and a half of his contract. School trustee Kelvin Filer explained that Handy was "in over his head and [didn't] know what he's doing."[22] Deficient leadership had created and compounded the district's crises.

Desperate Times, Desperate Measures

Even though Compton Unified pulled through the 1992 state legislation and county audit, the district's financial problems remained undeniable. Compton's

debt became so overwhelming that, in March 1993, the district's board of trustees sought an emergency loan from the State of California to pay its teachers
for the last two months of the school year and to open the schools in the fall.
While officials in Sacramento debated the merits of giving the money, it remained unclear whether the district could afford to keep the schools open in
June. Compton administrators' misrepresentation of the district's financial
status had angered state commissioners, however, causing deeper distrust of
local officials' ability to govern the district effectively. By mid-April, the California Department of Education had officially posted a call for a state administrator, who would be responsible not only for bringing the district back to
financial solvency but for "work[ing] to develop a quality education program." The administrator would remain in the job until the state superintendent determined state involvement was no longer necessary. The appointed
administrator would assume all the legal rights, duties, and powers of the
elected board of trustees.[23]

State education officials did not believe that a mere loan would fix Compton Unified's problems, and, clearly, they had little faith that locally elected
officials would, if left alone, get to the roots of the district's problems. In 1992,
state lawmakers passed legislation to have LACOE provide educational and
managerial services to Compton Unified. As part of this process, LACOE
produced a corrective action report for the district. Issued on May 4, 1993,
the report identified problems in seven broad categories (governance; instruction; staff development; personnel; financial accountability; community; and safety, security, and environment), while offering priority corrective
actions for each. The finding in the governance section captured the overall
tenor of the report: the district's central focus lay "on the needs of adults, not
on the needs of students. Available resources are distributed on personal relationships, not on the District priorities."[24] Finding a wide range of problems,
from teacher-centered instruction to dilapidated facilities, the report also
created a blueprint for change, including teacher training, administrative reorganization, and hiring more bilingual teachers.

The report became part of the argument against state control. Opponents
of a state takeover argued that the district should have time to implement the
report's recommendations. The opposition also held that provisions in a 1992
law that allowed for individual school turnarounds better fit the issues outlined rather than a complete takeover of the district. The school district board
of trustees also sought to block the legislation on several other grounds: it
unfairly targeted Compton Unified when other districts also struggled; it

usurped local control for an indefinite amount of time; it established a dangerous precedent; and it was too costly.[25]

Despite his reluctance, in late spring of 1993, Governor Wilson signed the measure to allocate Compton Unified $10.5 million and to appoint a state administrator in order to prevent needless harm to "innocent children, good-faith small business vendors and district employees."[26] A few months after intervening for financial problems, the state extended its purview to academics. Implementing the report's recommendations became one of the requirements for the state administrator.[27] The district could not get back local control based solely on fiscal conditions.

The state superintendent of education appointed Stan Oswalt as the acting state administrator for Compton Unified. Oswalt had served as a superintendent for thirty years in other California districts before retiring. After his retirement, state officials tapped him as trustee for the West Covina Unified School District because of its financial problems. After almost five years at the post Oswalt brought solvency to the district, enabling it to repay its state loan in 1992. On July 7, 1993, Oswalt assumed the duties of Compton Unified's board of trustees. As a state administrator—rather than as state trustee—he expropriated all the power, authority, and responsibility of the elected board of trustees, personnel commission, and superintendent. In addition to losing their decision-making role in policy and personnel, board of trustee members no longer received compensation and health benefits from the district.[28] With the signing of one bill, Compton Unified's elected officials lost all their power over their school district.

State power, however, did not bring stability to Compton Unified. Rather, leadership remained in flux. In August 1993, the state appointed Oakland schools chief Richard "Pete" Mesa permanent state administrator of Compton's schools, but after the appointment became public, Mesa rejected the offer, leaving Oswalt at the helm.[29] Though only an "acting" superintendent, Oswalt aggressively moved to clean up the district, often ruffling feathers in the process. School district board of trustees president Kelvin Filer recalled: "[state officials] were rude, the way they came in basically and took over the offices and said 'Hand in your keys' . . . I thought it could have been handled in a much nicer and more efficient manner than to come in and basically claim to kick the board members out."[30] The board of trustees continued to hold monthly meetings, but the state superintendent could review and veto all its decisions.[31]

Oswalt's manner reflected his belief that he needed more control to fix the district. He wanted the authority to "rip up" union contracts, remove the current school board, and lay off employees with a sixty-day notice. In addition, he requested an additional $9.45 million in emergency funds to "run the district like a private business," one where efficiency and cost-effectiveness took precedence. His demands met with immediate criticism from board members who said they favored the additional funding but opposed giving Oswalt unprecedented powers. At the same time, community members severely criticized his proposed plan to sell off unused district property to fund the refurbishing of area schools, claiming that land-grabbing was his and the state's true motivation. Others, like Filer, believed that, although the law stated that the profits from the sales of surplus land should be used for capital improvements, the monies should go toward paying off the state debt and avoiding further cuts.[32] Losing control over finances meant losing real power to make decisions about the community. Furthermore, racial politics played into local black officials' hostility toward the takeover. Deep into a close race for Compton's mayoralty, council member Omar Bradley articulated this sentiment: "Ultimately, to take over the Compton Unified School District profusely suggests that African Americans can not administrate in an equitable, professional and effective manner. This of course, can be no further from the truth." He continued: "For given the same facilities, staff, equipment and environments as predominantly non-minority school districts, the administrators, staff, teachers and alike can produce as good or better students than any district in California."[33]

Black-Latino Interactions Under State Control

Even though the state controlled the schools Compton residents continued to struggle over the issues of language and race. According to former resident Juan Carillo, these conflicts manifested themselves "in schools, you know, turf wars, gang wars." He explained that in schools one could see the tensions through "the fights and the segregation among groups."[34]

Racial politics also played out in town politics. In 1993, Compton voters elected a new mayor, Omar Bradley (no relation to LA mayor Tom Bradley). Bradley, a lifelong Compton resident, Centennial High graduate, teacher in neighboring Lynwood, and city council member, took the town's reins after sitting mayor Walter Tucker, III, entered the U.S. Congress. Some voters held high hopes for Bradley because he seemed "a thing apart from a tired black political establishment."[35] Compton resident Frank Allen recalled, "when I first met [Bradley], he seemed a very intelligent man, and I was impressed, at first—that first blush."[36]

Bradley's unapologetically aggressive manner soon raised many eyebrows. In his first days as mayor, Bradley angered many Latino residents by failing to make good on his pledge to appoint Pedro Pallan, who had been the first Latino on the school district personnel board, to his vacated city council seat. Many Latinos had campaigned for Bradley because of this promise. In addition to this alienating move, once in office, Bradley championed black self-sufficiency.[37] For years Compton's black officials had been staking their political turf in opposition to Compton's growing Latino population, and Bradley was no exception. But Bradley antagonized Compton residents of all ethnicities. During his eight-year administration, he grew to be a looming figure in city hall with many residents of all ethnicities regarding him as "mercurial, controversial or potentially dangerous."[38] Bradley became one of the most outspoken opponents of the state's involvement in Compton Unified.

To find solutions for the ever-widening gap between Compton's black and Latino residents, Comptonites met at the town's first multicultural summit in April 1994, a day-long event sponsored by Compton College, the NAACP, and the Mexican American Legal Defense and Educational Fund (MALDEF).[39] This meeting was an important acknowledgment that there was indeed a problem, a new development for many of the black leaders.

The summit focused on sharing power, not shared poverty. Robert Almanzan, one of MALDEF's leaders, explained: "The African-Americans are empowered in Compton, and the Latinos feel left out. We are here to promote solutions in a nonviolent, less-confrontational way." Royce Esters, president of Compton's branch of the NAACP, suggested that Compton's African American and Latino residents "need to work on becoming a 'we.'"[40] School-district jobs—from teachers and administrators to cafeteria workers and custodians—appeared to be one of the major obstacles in establishing this unity. In 1992 the student population of Compton Unified was almost 57 percent Latino while only 19 percent of the classified staff and only 3 percent of the certificated staff identified themselves as Latino. African American staff representation was 70 percent as compared to the student enrollment of 42 percent.[41] Even under state control, the black-run political machine managed to hold on tightly to its jobs.

At the summit, the new state-appointed superintendent of Compton

Unified, Jerome Harris, spoke. Harris brought home some of the harsh realities of the district by comparing it to those of underdeveloped nations, asserting: "Our schools are befitting to any Third World country. If they were in South Africa some of them would be closed down." Harris charged that Compton residents had neglected district schools since the 1950s when Compton was a district run by whites and the town was considered an "all American City." He assured the audience that the district had enough money, insisting "It's not about money, it's about attitude."[42] What Harris failed to recognize was that while the schools themselves may have had funds, poverty deeply affected every aspect of the community.

Clearly, racial tensions and job competition went hand in hand. According to the 1993 LACOE corrective action report, the district had experienced "a phenomenal increase in the enrollment of minority students, especially Hispanics." The report identified many of the new students as "recent refugees and/or immigrants, with significant language and cultural needs in adapting to a new country," and it held that the district had not developed a plan or philosophy in dealing with the new students. The report outlined several steps the district must take immediately to accommodate the students, including training on the basic components of creating effective educational programs for English language learners.[43] But, at the 1994 summit, Harris recognized that even though the state had intervened, bilingual education remained a major problem, explaining: "We don't have enough bilingual teachers and we're reaching out."[44] In fact, for years district officials had looked beyond town borders, recruiting teachers in both Texas and Spain and contracting with Teach For America (TFA), a not-for-profit organization that since 1990 had placed emergency-credentialed teachers in under-resourced districts nationally.[45] Yet, even the "bilingual" teachers the district hired did not always have the minimum skills to fit state standards. TFA corps member Sarah Sentilles taught a bilingual first grade class in Compton Unified because, even though she "faked her way" through her college Spanish literature classes, her principal identified her as "the only first grade teacher who [spoke] Spanish."[46] Her level of Spanish failed to meet state expectations for its bilingual teachers.

Despite the Unity Summit's attempts to "heal racial rifts," tension between blacks and Latinos deepened. This conflict came to a head in July 1994, when a local television station broadcast an amateur videotape of a black Compton police officer beating and stomping a Latino teenager. The officer had responded to a call from a social worker, who was trying to enter the mobile home to investigate child abuse. The officer struck seventeen-year-old Felipe Soltero when he would not allow him and the social worker inside. Soltero suffered a concussion, a bruised forehead, and an injured left elbow. Immediately compared to the 1991 Rodney King case, the beating became a lightning rod for accumulated Latino grievances against Compton's black political elite. This incident was followed a few weeks later by the acquittal of African American Willie Dyer for the beating death of his Latino neighbor Jose Arellano. In response to the verdict, approximately sixty Latinos picketed outside the federal courthouse asking for a civil rights investigation.[47]

The politics of Compton Unified brought to the forefront tensions between blacks and Latinos. Just days after the start of the 1994–95 school year, almost a quarter of the student body at McKinley Elementary School did not show up for class. Latino organizers had asked parents to keep their children out of school to protest what they perceived as school administrators' inadequate response to Latino educational needs. Parents of approximately 100 of the school's 431 students heeded the call. Although one out of four was only slightly above the daily absentee rate for a normal school day, the nature of these absences forced district administrators to take notice. The rhetoric Latino activists employed when describing the management of Compton's public schools served as the most disquieting aspect of the walkout. Frank Madrid alleged that the district was "very racist" and run by African Americans who had "no concern whatsoever" for the needs of Latinos.[48] "The Compton Unified School District is like Mississippi," asserted John Ortega, lead counsel for the Union of Parents and Students of Compton United, the association that organized the attendance strikes. "In Mississippi, they didn't want to educate blacks in the '50s, and in the '90s, Compton doesn't want to educate Latinos."[49] As whites had done in various places across the country, African Americans in Compton employed racial ideologies as a means to maintain their economic and political power. Race once again became a defining factor of who attained economic opportunities but, in this case, blacks held power.

These tensions continued to build as the tight job market affected Compton, and California as a whole. By 1994, California was in the midst of the state's worst recession since the Great Depression. The strains over job competition materialized in the battle over California's 1994 Proposition 187, known as the Save Our State initiative. Proposition 187 diverted the blame for the soured economy and social disorder to immigrants, targeting the state's rapidly growing Latino population, as it proposed to bar undocumented immigrants from receiving state-funded human, health, social, and education resources and services. Political scientists R. Michael Alvarez and Tara L. Butterfield found that "voters who perceived the economy as poor, perceived themselves as threatened financially by illegal immigrants, or who lived closer to the immigrant source were more likely to support the measure."[50] Many black Compton residents fit this description as they experienced the influx of Central American and Mexican immigrants.

Leading up to the 1994 election, about 64 percent of California's black electorate expressed their support for the initiative. While fewer actually voted for the measure, blacks' muted opposition revealed a complicated relationship between blacks and Latinos in California.[51] Compton Democratic mayor Omar Bradley echoed this. In discussing Proposition 187, Bradley said, "illegal immigration has placed the African American in the position of having to compete for resources that are few and far between" and explained this was why "even though this is a Republican initiative, you're going to find a lot of blacks favoring it."[52] Exit polling found that 64 percent of Compton's non-Latino voters supported the proposition while less than 1 percent of Latino voters did so.[53] The proposition became another way African Americans could feel like they were protecting their jobs.

Bradley admitted that in Compton, blacks, who had spent thirty years gaining power from whites, felt politically threatened by immigrants from Mexico and Central America. He stated, "We've seen a lot of Latino groups come to us and say 'we want the power, we demand the power.'" Though he used the legacy of the civil rights struggles to bolster his arguments, he reframed the new conflict by claiming that, "the question is not black versus Latino, the question is American versus non-American."[54] The recent wave of immigration had redefined the debate as being "us versus them." In California in the 1990s, the boundaries for those who deserved access to services and opportunities were demarcated by who was perceived to be American. Despite Compton's history of having a Latino population, by 1994, being Latino had come to mean being un-American.

Latino immigrants affected everything in Compton, including religious, economic, political, and educational institutions. In one of Compton's Catholic parishes, Our Lady of Victory, church leaders reduced the number of English masses to one while increasing the number of Spanish services. Long-time black parishioner Frank Allen recalled "when I first started going to Our Lady of Victory there were four English speaking masses and there was one Spanish mass . . . in our church I feel like we're losing ground . . .

when people feel like they are losing ground, they go to higher ground."[55] His wife Linda added that she thought that this reduction was "why many of the older [black] people have left."[56] Katherine Nelson concurred that as an African American in the church "it seems like you are taking a back step, you are a second class citizen."[57] Compton resident and long-time Latina activist Lorraine Cervantes remembered shopping in a grocery store after it had recently hired its first Spanish-speaking clerk. One Latina customer stopped a little too long to speak with the cashier and Cervantes recalled the black patron behind her commenting "they are taking over."[58]

In Compton, black residents used racial prejudices to express tensions over jobs, as black political elites attempted to hang on to power. In a *New York Times* article discussing the growing Latino population in many cities, Dr. David Hayes-Bautista, director of the Center of Latino Health at the University of California, Los Angeles, stated that "some of the things black councilmen [in Compton] say about the Latino population sound like the kinds of things Southern whites would have said about blacks in the '50s: 'We were here first. We're being pushed out. These are our jobs; how dare you take them away?'"[59] In 1998, Californians endorsed the anti-immigrant feeling when, with 61 percent of the vote, they passed Proposition 227, which required instruction in California's public schools to be conducted in English only.

Racial tensions in the schools mirrored this statewide stance and the racial discrimination faced by Latinos in Compton as a whole. For years, Latino students and parents complained about the treatment from school staff on issues such as grades and discipline and, after a long campaign, they got officials in Washington to listen. In 1998, the U.S. Department of Education began what would become a two-year investigation, ending with the DOE instructing the state-run district to reduce racial discrimination and harassment. The district hired an ombudsman to report regularly on the number of racial complaints and their resolutions, as well as to keep records on how many students were disciplined and on their ethnic background.[60]

Combating Impoverishment

In response to the state's worst recession since the Great Depression, Comptonites entertained ever-more desperate measures to secure jobs and a more secure economic footing. State assemblyman Willard Murray, the same politician who spearheaded the state takeover of Compton Unified, saw a prison as a fix for Compton's problems. In 1994, he introduced a bill that proposed building a prison in "an unspecified location somewhere in Southern California."[61] This "unspecified" site was Compton. Murray argued in the bill that the new carceral institution would relieve California's correctional system of overcrowding, which at the time reportedly stood at 180.5 percent of its capacity.[62] While pushing the legislation, Murray not only focused on the benefits to the penal system, but also asserted that the facility would have a positive impact on Compton. In an opinion piece in the *Compton Bulletin*, Murray explained his proposal: "Having spoken with various community leaders, and having done much research, I have determined that because of Compton's high crime rate, and high unemployment, it is very difficult to attract businesses such as department stores, malls and membership clubs."[63] Murray reasoned that the new prison would fuel the local economy, by providing "recession-proof" jobs, and patronage for nearby businesses.

Most American prisons existed in rural, majority-white areas, bringing jobs to those communities, but Murray argued that Compton would benefit from the enterprise. According to Murray the prison would employ over 1,000 people after construction and would have an annual budget of $35 million.[64] In addition the prison would bring state and federal subventions that could pay for things such as parks, daycare centers, and after-school programs. He also implied that prisons would help lower Compton's high crime-rate by bringing more law enforcement personnel into the area. All this would improve the town's image, and, in turn, raise property values. Increased property values would then lead to better funded municipal services and public schools. In short, Murray contended: "prisons make good neighbors."[65]

Not all Comptonites backed Murray's plan. Some local officials resisted, saying that "a prison would add to Compton's reputation as a crime-ridden city."[66] U.S. representative and former Compton mayor Walter Tucker, III, surveyed residents asking if a state prison was the type of economic development they would want.[67] Tucker opposed the facility, asserting: "Compton has much too much to offer families and businesses to settle for being California's latest prison colony, a warehouse especially for our young black and brown males."[68] The War on Drugs had disproportionately affected blacks and Latinos and it was a symbolic insult to bring a prison into their backyard.

Murray proposed the Compton prison during the 1994 campaign around

Proposition 184, commonly known as the "Three Strikes and You're Out" law, which required state courts to impose twenty-five years to life sentences on persons previously convicted of two serious criminal offenses, regardless of the third crime's nature. If the proposition passed, the inmate population would balloon, making the new prisons even more necessary.

California voters overwhelming passed the proposition with 72 percent of the vote, further stretching the already overcrowded corrections system while heightening the racial disparities.[69] But this statewide problem did not sway many Comptonites to support Murray's idea. In the wake of the proposition, the city council passed a resolution adamantly opposing the construction of a prison in Compton, and then put it to the voters in a 1995 "advisory measure."[70] Comptonites overwhelmingly voted against the prison, and Murray dropped the cause.[71]

Even though the prison did not come to fruition, the rhetoric on either side of the debate is illustrative of the larger context. The mere fact that Murray proposed it illuminates how much Compton had changed from the dreams of the original Comptonites. Prisons were not the "good neighbors" for which residents had hoped. Rather, prisons were a direct contrast to their aspirations of advancing their social status by moving to a town marked by its residential character. Yet these dreams had long been disconnected from the town's reality. As early as the 1930s, the town's residential tax base proved insufficient to cover its needs. Without a retail, industrial, or corporate tax base, Compton officials continually raised taxes on residents, helping push the middle class out of the town, and worsening the town's economic base.[72] In proposing the prison, Murray took a pragmatic approach to bringing revenue to the beleaguered town.

Despite Murray's persuasive case, it is not surprising that some Comptonites had a visceral reaction against adding a prison to their town. Since 1970 prison populations across the United States had risen, with black men experiencing the highest rate of incarceration. Much of the increase in imprisonment had been since the mid-1980s, with enforcement of and longer sentencing for stronger drug laws, which disproportionately affected people of color. The criminalization of spaces and the large increase in prison populations helped shape the urban crisis, as imprisoned urbanites could neither contribute to their cities nor provide for dependents they left behind. Children also suffered from a variety of issues when their caregivers were imprisoned. Some of these stressors continued even when the family reunited because many ex-convicts struggled in finding a job to support themselves and their dependents.[73] Though Heather Thompson writes about the urban centers, her analysis can be extended to suburbs that also experienced "crisis, declines, and transformation in postwar American history."[74]

Compton's crisis took multiple forms, including few businesses, high taxes, joblessness, and crime. State and federal agencies, along with some private investments, tried to tackle these problems. Following the 1992 riots, Southern California Edison pledged to pay $35 million over five years to develop a job-skills training center in Compton. In 1992, the town was designated an enterprise zone, which gave companies state tax incentives for development aimed at revitalization.[75] Compton's small tax capacity had forced the town to overtax businesses in the community. Compton business owner and future city council member Fred Cressel explained that the town had the highest utility user tax at 10 percent and some of the highest property taxes in the entire county. He asked, "how can you attract a manufacturing company if their bills run $15,000 a month and they're going to have to pay a surcharge of 10 percent? How can you get them to locate? The bottom line is everyone talks about crime and graffiti, that's not what keeps businesses out of a community. What keeps businesses out of community is how much their profits is [sic] going to go down the tube."[76]

Local officials recognized that Compton's economy had severe problems, and as a result they willingly tried a variety of redevelopment plans. Previous projects, including the auto mall and giant hotel, had run into problems, which, according to the *Los Angeles Times* spoiled "city leaders' plans to make Compton a stopping point for consumers throughout the Los Angeles area."[77] In a move to increase revenues and provide new jobs, over the objections of many residents, the city council approved building a casino in Compton. In fall 1995 a private investment group broke ground on the edge of Compton near the 91 Freeway for the development of the Crystal Park Hotel and Casino complex. These investments fell short of what the town and its residents needed.[78]

Joblessness in Compton, as in other areas of concentrated poverty, was intimately connected to other social ills. In December 1994, the U.S. Departments of Education and Labor awarded a $536,000 grant for a school-to-work partnership program, but this was just a drop in the bucket of what Comptonites needed. Consistent high rates of unemployment triggered other problems in neighborhoods that adversely shaped social organization, ranging from crime, gang violence, and drug trafficking to family break-ups. Poverty also created incentives for inner-city residents to participate in the informal economy—all those economic activities, legal and illegal, that eluded the national income accounts. In particular, the drug business grew.[79] In turn, the high crime rate and gang activity that accompanied the drug trade made it more difficult to attract businesses. In 1993 Compton had 59 homicides, 85 rapes, 1,135 robberies, 1,115 aggravated assaults, 1,750 burglaries, and 1,486 auto thefts. The next year there were 81 murders, nearly double that of nearby Inglewood, and only ten fewer than San Francisco, a city whose population was seven times larger than Compton. Twenty-seven percent of the town's 91,400 residents lived below the official poverty line, twice the proportion in Los Angeles County as a whole.[80]

This instability resulted in high absenteeism and transience among Compton's students. Sentilles recalled that students left school, were transferred, or appeared at her classroom door in the middle of the year "without notice or for no clear reason."[81] Furthermore, once in the classroom, "the behavior of some students reminded me that they did not come from stable homes," Sentilles explained: "Some slept through school because the noise on their streets or in their living rooms had kept them awake the night before. Others came to school in tears, holding their stomachs because they were so hungry. Still others came to school dirty, hair uncombed, faces unwashed."[82] Poverty made its mark at home, on the streets, and at school, and helped define the workings of each individual Compton classroom.

Part of the Problem

In the midst of all these power struggles, two major political corruption scandals involving two elected officials shook Compton. In August 1994, U.S. Representative Walter Tucker, III, was indicted on ten federal charges of extortion and filing false income taxes while he served as Compton's mayor. The indictment contended that Tucker received $30,000 in bribes from a company that sought to build and operate an incinerator in the town. He was also charged with demanding an additional $250,000 to support the proposal and with signing income-tax forms for 1991 and 1992 that reflected less money than he had earned.[83]

Tucker denied wrongdoing but many residents felt betrayed and quickly convicted him in their minds. Even so, just a few months later, in November, area residents reelected Tucker to his house seat.[84] The scandal spilled into

1994 as Tucker was indicted again and eventually convicted of seven counts of extortion and two counts of failing to pay federal income taxes on the bribe payments. In doing so, "Compton's favorite son came to a crashing halt."[85]

Other Compton politicians came under criminal investigation. A two-year undercover FBI inquiry targeted both Tucker and former city council member Patricia Moore. In the investigation, FBI agents posed as businessmen and offered officials bribes to have items placed on city council agendas. Federal investigators videotaped many of the meetings and then probed Compton town records. In September 1995, Moore was indicted on twenty-three counts of extortion and accepting bribes, totaling approximately $62,000. According to the indictment, Moore extorted money from two companies.[86] Federal prosecutors used hundreds of hours of videotape and audiotape to support their case. After pleading guilty to extortion charges, Moore changed her pleas as she declared she had been "pressured" and "railroaded" into doing so and further alleged that her civil rights had been violated.[87] She made racial bias the center of her defense, filing a motion with the judge to dismiss the case against her, alleging a nationwide FBI plot to oust black leaders. Despite her allegations of discrimination, as well as her claims of being raped and sodomized by one of the prosecution's star witnesses, a jury convicted Moore on fifteen counts of extortion and two counts of failing to file income tax returns.[88]

Compton Unified was also plagued by corruption scandals. In September 1994 the *Compton Bulletin* ran a two-part series exposing fraud in the district's workers' compensation fund. According to sources, an audit of the program uncovered possible deceit in the benefits paid to people who no longer worked in the district, as well as the payout of close to a million dollars to physicians and clinics who had over-billed or double-billed the district. An investigation revealed that district officials had known about the discrepancies for a long time and that some may have been involved. Only a few months later, in a separate scandal, Compton Unified purchasing director Charles Monk was put on leave, and was then convicted of funneling sales to fake companies and submitting sham invoices. Monk's conviction was a rarity; though it was clear that corruption and mismanagement of funds infested Compton Unified, the district attorney never charged any of the district's high-level administrators or board members.[89]

Mismanagement occurred on the school site level as well. Sentilles described her everyday battle to get classroom supplies. At her first school, she had difficulty getting pencils and other necessities from the supply clerk until she noticed that other teachers were bringing him food. She too started to buy him candy and he started to give her supplies, but still, in her words, "not everything I needed, but more than the nothing he had given me before."[90] At her second school, she asked for Rigby readers, reading primers that came in sets, and was informed by numerous sources—the school principal, her grade-level chair, the supply clerk—that the school did not have such books. Later that year, however, she attended a district-wide in-service for teachers and discovered that the district had provided each elementary school with these sets. That day she rushed back to her school site, where she and the principal searched through the supply clerk's office, finding that "in the back corner of his office, were trays and trays of Rigby books, covered in a thin layer of dust."[91] Faced with an already limited pool of supplies district wide, Compton Unified teachers also had to battle negligence and malfeasance at their individual school sites. The state takeover had done little to ameliorate these endemic problems.

Struggling Under State Control

Despite the problems they created through their own mismanagement and corruption, local leaders fought state control. School trustee Basil Kimbrew announced that the district board of trustees was suing Delaine Eastin, Jerome Harris, and the State of California for "the unconstitutional take-over and running of the Compton Unified School District."[92] Some Compton residents, angry at the state's role in their district, argued that the school board relegation to an advisory position negated their right to vote for their representatives. Under the rules of the takeover, the state administrator, not their elected officials, was responsible for making policy decisions. Along these same lines, some residents opposed to the takeover argued that the state had violated their Fourteenth Amendment rights by singling out Compton for receivership even though California had other failing districts. Lawsuits demanding that the state relinquish authority proved unsuccessful, however. California's Department of Education won the support of the courts to keep control of the district because it appeared the most feasible way to raise dismal test scores, fix dilapidated school buildings, hire adequate teachers, purge corrupt administrators, and pay down the enormous debt.

Not all residents opposed the state takeover of the district, however.

Lorraine Cervantes believed that the state takeover was needed "because we couldn't make [Compton Unified's administrator] do right" because they were hiring and giving raises to friends and relatives based on fake degrees.[93] Linda Allen considered the state intervention "was long overdue" because, as her husband explained, "you'll hear the horror stories about the bathrooms and the books and the poor state of the classrooms and the buildings. And you know that just passes on to the teachers because any teacher that is worth his salt won't want to come here and teach in this type of devastation. . . . You knew [the state takeover] was going to happen and it should have happened a lot sooner."[94] For many Compton residents the problem was not who controlled their schools, it was how to improve their schools.

The state's own management of the district hurt the argument that it provided Compton's students with equal access to quality education. On taking the helm of the district, Harris fought to change the district's culture of teaching. He explained: "Teachers thought they were doing a great job. But there really was no connection between being a good teacher and student performance."[95] Harris created structures to make this link. First, he had students take a district-wide test every six weeks and, as a motivator for teachers, he published and distributed the ranked results of each class at each grade level. He also required that every teacher stand up while teaching, rather than teaching from behind a desk. Many of the teachers found his strategies insulting.[96]

In managing the district, the state did not retain its own appointed leaders. In March 1996, three years after the takeover, Compton Unified hired its third state administrator, Dhyan Lal. While many saw his predecessor Harris as insensitive, Lal had the reputation as having a more "humanistic" approach.[97] But not everyone saw Lal as an improvement. Compton Unified board member Saul Lankster remarked: "[State Superintendent of Instruction] Delaine Easton just doesn't get it that the whole problem is the dictatorial form of government that doesn't work. His replacement Dhyan Lal is an appointed overseer and I analogize that to slavery. We have a new overseer who may not hit as hard but does not change the institution."[98] After only four months, Lal resigned his position, leaving Compton Unified without a guide.

Along with constant turnover in leadership, the state also faced the everyday difficulties of running the school district. In May 1996, Eastin rated the district's performance as "D-Plus."[99] Even under her watch, Compton Unified was barely passing. Eastin also said that in addition to improving student performance, the district also needed to rebuild its aging facilities before she would release it from receivership. But these were not the only problems the district faced. The next month, 80 percent of Compton's teachers walked out. They had been working without a contract since June 1995, and their salaries had not changed since 1993, when they had taken a 3 percent pay cut to help the district remain solvent. The teachers and state settled after the one-day strike.[100]

Even with the new contract, teacher retention remained a major problem for the district, as many were dissatisfied with the shortage of supplies, lack of support, and low salaries. To fill the gap every year TFA placed dozens of emergency-credentialed teachers in Compton's classrooms, but many corps members left the district during or after their two-year commitment. At a Compton Unified meeting, Liam Garland, a second-year TFA corps member, addressed the issue of teachers' salaries, and asked why he should stay in the district with no pay increase. Lanskster replied that Garland should stay for the same reasons board members serve without compensation—because the children needed him.[101] Though Garland himself would stay for a third year, this argument did not hold much sway with many new teachers, as neighboring school districts, also with needy children, offered much more than Compton Unified—higher pay, more supplies, better facilities, and greater support.

Disillusioned, some Compton teachers left the profession entirely. Dan Olmos taught at Roosevelt Elementary School for two years before going to law school. Roosevelt had about 1,600 students in kindergarten through fifth grade. Olmos recalled, "When I was a teacher there, we had two functioning bathrooms, no nurse, five old computers, outdated books and supplies, more than half uncredentialed teachers, not one blade of grass." After his first year he knew he would leave teaching. He explained, "I was leaving Compton because I stopped believing in what I was telling their children: If they value their educations and worked hard everything would turn out fine."[102] Having worked with these children for one year, Olmos concluded that their problems ran deeper than what could be fixed in the classroom.

Journalists and parents corroborated Compton's teachers' complaints and pressures on the district. In January 1997, the *Los Angeles Times* reported that since the state takeover three and a half years earlier, many school buildings had fallen into deeper disrepair. The article cited records showing a backlog of 2,400 work orders to fix everything from broken water pipes to exposed electrical wires. An educational adviser to Governor Pete Wilson was quoted as saying, "If these schools were prisons, they would be shut down." Eastin conceded that the conditions of Compton Unified schools ranked at the very bottom of all the public schools in the state, but argued that the state-controlled district prioritized putting money into fixing accounting practices and raising test scores.[103] Even though the school buildings had suffered years of deterioration, Compton residents believed state administration should have made *some* movement toward fixing the problems. While no one expected overnight change, residents could not accept this state-sanctioned dereliction.

This neglect compounded the resentment toward the state administration. Tensions had been high from the beginning, with someone reportedly firing a gun at the first state-appointed superintendent, and with California highway patrolmen serving as bodyguards for subsequent superintendents. The turnover rate of superintendents heightened Comptonites' skepticism that the state had a plan in place for the district.[104] In 1996, after learning that Randolph Ward would be the fifth state administrator in three years, Compton school board member Toi Jackson warned that Ward would be "Stepping into a lion's den." An editorial in the *Long Beach Press Telegram* explained why the lion's den was an apt analogy for Compton Unified. School board members had been "roaring" ever since the state took over the district, and, despite all the district's glaring troubles, the lions had run out every administrator appointed by the state. Within two years, four had resigned in "the face of opposition and the lack of cooperation from board members, some parents and teachers." The editorial went on to claim boldly that this stubbornness to proceed with inferior resources showed that the "lions in Compton are devouring their own young."[105] The state takeover did not go over smoothly—even though Compton Unified had conspicuous problems, many residents remained or had become wary of outside intervention.

Calling for Local Control

Much of this suspicion came from the state's handling of the district. In July 1997, a group of Compton parents together with the American Civil Liberties Union (ACLU) filed a class-action lawsuit against the state alleging its control of the school district had failed to provide students with basic educational opportunities available to children elsewhere in California. The district's students still had the worst test scores in the state and 70 percent of the students

going from eighth to ninth grades did not meet minimum high school qualifications. The lawsuit also alleged that the schools had filthy bathrooms without lights, toilet paper, and soap; leaky roofs; classrooms without air
conditioning and heating; exposed wiring; and not enough textbooks. Mark
Rosenbaum, the legal director for the Southern California ACLU, labeled the
treatment of students in Compton Unified "state-sponsored child abuse."[106]
Once again, state officials responded that they had taken steps to address the
problems, but it was difficult to fix a district that local officials had neglected
for thirty years. The state and district reached a settlement with the ACLU,
requiring basic things: all broken wires and loose electrical wiring and fix-
tures must be replaced, bathrooms must be cleaned and repaired, and drink-
ing water must be clean. The agreement also mandated that the district get
more certified teachers and buy more textbooks.[107]

At its core, the takeover of the district uncovered tensions in citizenship
rights that arose from Compton's status as a minority-run town. How should
the state deal with a district that was clearly not serving its students? At the
same time all voters were entitled to their right to full political power over
their communities via the ballot box. The right to vote for one's policymakers remained a strong arguing point for the departure of the state from
Compton Unified. In 1997, as school trustees sued the state for control of
the district, officials at the Justice Department confirmed that they were investigating whether California had violated the federal voting-rights act
when it took over Compton Unified, limiting the voting rights of the town's
racial minorities by reducing the elected school board to an advisory
position.[108]

The issues of funding and voting rights converged when the state proposed that the school district assume a $107 million bond to pay for the ren-
ovation of Compton's schools. Compton residents had built the majority of
their schools between the 1930s and 1950s and the facilities desperately
needed repair. While the funds were important, the discussions around the
funds were equally important. Opponents of the proposal claimed that the
bond would cause the citizens of Compton to be taxed without representation because the state superintendent would have decision-making power
over the funds.[109] Some Comptonites also worried that the bond would cause
taxes to rise in a town with an already disproportionately high tax rate. While
Compton's schools needed repair, taxpayers simply could not afford to renovate them.

Not all residents, however, opposed the bond measure. In an opinion article in the *Compton Bulletin*, Compton Chamber of Commerce president Shirley Allen explained that only through authorization of the bond measure would Compton's students get the schools they deserved. In addition, Allen argued that only through making these types of decisions for their students would Compton leaders exhibit the leadership necessary to regain local control of their school district.[110] Passing the measure meant more than simply getting the money to renovate the schools.

Though able to decide on the bond measure, some Comptonites held that their voting rights remained violated. In January 1998, Ward, the state superintendent, moved to appoint a new school trustee. Ward felt a new election would cost too much money and instead sought to appoint to the board's empty seat the runner-up in the last election. Some residents, particularly the members of the city council, disagreed with this decision, asking the city attorney to investigate its legality.[111] Mayor Bradley also attended a meeting of the Compton Unified's advisory board of trustees to address this very issue, announcing that the town had filed an injunction against the State of California to block the appointment of an additional school board member. He argued that the right to vote was one for which blacks had suffered greatly and, after imploring the community to *"wake up,"* he stated, *"this is our School District, these are our children, and we will decide what is best and what will happen to them."* He concluded, *"This is not a personal battle; this isn't even political; this is human."*[112]

The battle went on for a few more months, with Ward eventually swearing in the new board member on March 10, 1998. Even in defeat over the appointment, Compton residents did not retreat quietly. At the new board member's first meeting, school trustee and sister of the mayor, Carol Bradley-Jordan, was arrested for allegedly disrupting the proceedings while attempting to block the swearing in.[113] While both sides staked out their political turf on the language of citizenship rights, the fight over the new board members was a distraction from the real troubles that plagued the district.

Compton Unified's financial debt was the emergency that spurred state officials to intervene in the district. Poverty had long plagued Compton and its surrounding areas—creating the environment for the Rodney King riots and producing Compton's failing school district. The state, however, only interceded in the poverty-stricken areas in these times of crisis. In doing so, the state remained narrowly focused on its mandate: during the riots, outside law enforcement aimed to stop lawlessness and to protect communities; in

Compton Unified, the state officials sought only to return state money and to raise test scores.

The state takeover of Compton Unified was short-sighted, failing to recognize that the problems in Compton's public school system were symptomatic of broader, endemic community troubles. During the time of the state's intervention in Compton Unified, relations between black and Latino Comptonites worsened, violence erupted, two of Compton's elected officials were indicted on felony charges, political battles in city hall raged, and adequate jobs and housing remained unattainable for many residents. Fixing Compton's educational system meant more than ridding the school system of corruption, fixing its buildings, and repaying its debts. A solution required addressing the community's systemic failing: overcrowded houses, gang violence, and joblessness. While the state intervention marginally improved Compton students' test scores, it left intact a system that continued to fail its young people, black and Latino.

Epilogue

Out from Compton's Past

In December 2001, after eight tumultuous years of state control, Compton's elected officials regained decision-making power over their school district. No ceremonies, not even a press conference, marked the event. Instead, business continued as usual. New superintendent Jesse Gonzales commented: "It's just another day at the office. We're just going to continue to improve the district and keep moving forward."[1]

As Gonzales's statement implied, the fact that Compton regained local control over its school district did not mean the district's problems disappeared. Poverty, violence, and corruption continued to plague the town and its school system. Despite court, state, and federal mandates, over 20 percent of the district teachers still worked on emergency teaching credentials. The district also continued to have a high rate of teacher turnover, lack of teaching materials, and poor facilities.[2] During the takeover of the beleaguered district, state administrators had focused on students' dismal test scores and the district's massive financial debt, but they left unaddressed the vicious cycle that had created these problems. As a result, the perpetual series of educational, economic, and social crises persisted unabated. And so the cycle continues.

The state takeover of Compton Unified exemplifies how the schools' crisis paralleled the suburban crisis. White flight and divestment devastated Compton and exposed the town and communities like it to potentially harmful, or at best dubiously helpful, external interventions in their schools. But the takeover was just one type of educational reform that happened in Compton. Its schools became experimenting grounds for nearly every other variety of reform: private contracts, alternatively certified teachers, increased standardized testing, and charter schools. It was no surprise that Compton was part of these reforms. Compton, like many communities in similar positions, became a guinea pig for experiments in school reform. We can learn valuable, and cautionary, lessons from its experience.

Regaining, and Relinquishing, Local Control

In December 1996, state assemblyman Carl Washington, who represented parts of South Los Angeles, including Compton and Willowbrook, proposed a bill (AB 52) to have the state gradually relinquish control of Compton Unified. State superintendent Delaine Eastin objected, calling the district a "corrupt organization" and arguing that current board members would "rehire their relatives and friends and continue running their scams." Over her objections, the state legislature passed the bill and the governor signed it.[3]

Enacted in September 1997, the law did not return local control immediately. Instead, Compton Unified first had to show significant progress in five areas—pupil achievement, financial management, facilities management, personnel management, and community relations. Los Angeles County's Fiscal Crisis and Management Assistance Team (FCMAT) would assess the progress and report back to the legislature.[4] Comptonites would gain local control, but on the state's terms and timetable.

In the meantime, the district took atypical measures to educate its students. In December 1997, the district, still under state control, contracted Sylvan Learning Center, a private corporation, to provide tutoring and supplemental services for 150 students in four Compton schools.[5] In 1998, the arrangement expanded into a multi-million-dollar contract after the district implemented a policy that linked reading proficiency (as measured by the state test) to promotion. Test results had indicated that as many as one in three students might be retained. To avoid this situation, the district required summer school for many students and added more school-based tutoring in math and reading, to be provided by Sylvan.[6] State-appointed administrator of Compton Unified Randolph Ward warned that Compton did not have the capacity to bump the scores more than it was already doing, and that to raise the scores substantially, the district would have to outsource some of its teaching. The Compton Unified contract marked Sylvan's first major entry into a California public school system, and its largest initial contract ever, covering 1,200 students. Perhaps more than the size of the contract, the very arrangement had broad policy implications, as state education officials sought private sector help in the one district the state controlled.[7]

Such outsourcing at the behest of the state went against years of fighting to control jobs and keep the districts' resources within the community. The school district had been the town's largest employer for years, as it provided both blue-collar and white-collar employment opportunities. White Comptonites resisted sharing jobs with African Americans when blacks moved into the town. African Americans later resisted employing Latinos when the Latino population grew. The district also was "top heavy," employing a large proportion of administrators and nonteaching staff. Board members allowed this to happen, as these jobseekers were constituents. Outsourcing jobs went against this historical grain.

While school districts have for many years contracted private organizations to provide operational functions such as food services or testing materials, Compton Unified was on the early end of districts' hiring for-profit organizations to provide core educational services within the school day. State control allowed for this privatization and other experimentation to occur more easily. In addition to privatization, Compton schools implemented frequent and high stakes standardized exams, testing all its students quarterly in English and math. The district also employed curriculum guides to standardize instruction to the state frameworks.[8] And, over time, much of what happened under the state receivership of Compton became statewide policy.

In 1999 California passed the Public School Accountability Act, a set of regulations that imposed a set of rewards, sanctions, and support for schools' reaching achievement goals. The Academic Performance Index (API) became the cornerstone of the act, as it used a variety of measures to rate a school's academic performance and growth.[9] With this new statewide accountability system Compton and Sylvan's type of contractual relationship became more common in California. More specifically, written into the code were provisions for using third-party contractors. Such policies encouraged the development of a "hidden market," in which private contractors could profit handsomely from public money made available. The arrangement would become sanctioned nationally under the 2002 federal No Child Left Behind (NCLB) law.[10] Using Compton as a base for experiments on how best to fulfill such accountability measures, and drawing on the lessons he learned there, former state-appointed administrator Ward penned a book for school leaders on how to improve achievement in low-performing schools.[11] Compton Unified had literally become the improvement model.

Outsourcing to Sylvan was expensive and it did not indicate improvements in Compton's economic situation. Just a few years later, in 2002, Compton's unemployment rate was three times the national average and the State of California declared the suburb an "enterprise zone," an economically distressed area that received special incentives to encourage business investment and promote creation of new jobs.[12] The next year, the state gave Compton a $500,000 grant for job training and employment and the federal Department of Housing and Urban Development allocated $4 million for a variety of programs, including business development, job growth, and affordable housing.[13]

Outsourcing to Sylvan also did not mean that Comptonites had given up on fighting for local control. As the Public School Accountability Act gave more oversight of districts to the state, local control became somewhat more of a reality for Compton Unified. In 2000, after two and a half years, the ACLU settled its class-action lawsuit, *Serna v. Eastin*, with California's Department of Education. The case's consent decree mandated improvement in school facilities, sites, and classrooms. Already monitoring Compton Unified, FCMAT added to its duties overseeing compliance with the consent decree.[14] That same year, following the criteria laid out through AB 52, Compton Unified reclaimed two of its five powers, with the other three remaining in the hands of the state administrator.[15] Yet, even when the state relinquished direct control over the district, FCMAT oversight would remain under the consent decree.

Despite this half-hearted vote of confidence from the state, Compton Unified rated among the lowest performing schools in California. In addition to academic concerns, the physical plants remained problematic. Just a few weeks after regaining some of its power, Compton Unified failed a state inspection for safety and sanitation.[16] Compton also continued to lack adequate resources. In an attempt to help, and despite its own financial woes, the city council gave the school district $500,000 for the purchase of textbooks.[17]

Even with these persistent problems, FCMAT found that the district had made progress in all of the major operation areas.[18] As a result, it permitted the board to begin a search for a superintendent to replace the state administrator. The state vied to pull out of Compton Unified claiming progress had been made, a disingenuous move at best.

In August that year, after a national search, Compton's board of trustees introduced as the new superintendent Jesse Gonzales, an administrator from New Mexico. The state relinquished power over the next few months and on December 11, 2001, Gonzalez, not the state administrator, called the board of trustees meeting to order. The administrator, Randy Ward, stayed with the district to oversee test scores and finances, but the final decision-power now lay with the board of trustees. Local officials gained complete control in June 2003.[19] Even so, FCMAT oversight would remain under the *Serna v. Eastin* consent decree until 2008.[20] Yet the appointment of a Latino administrator signaled clearly that some things had changed in Compton.

Still in Distress

The story of reforms and changes in Compton Unified continued after Comptonites regained local control. Unfortunately, the state takeover had not fundamentally changed the everyday workings of the schools, as shown in the case of Centennial High School, one of Compton Unified's three comprehensive high schools. In spring 2003, Centennial lost its accreditation from the Western Association of Schools and Colleges because of both facility and instructional inadequacies. Losing accreditation was extremely rare and indicated to colleges and universities that a school failed to meet a minimum standard of competency.[21] Given that the state had just relinquished control, many of these failures had occurred under the state's watch.

The loss of accreditation had practical implications. While the school remained open, its students were given the option to transfer. As a result, approximately two hundred students from Centennial moved to Compton High School, overcrowding the school and mixing students from different gang territories.[22] According to Father Stan Bosch, priest at Compton's Our Lady of Victory Church, racial tension flared on campus, and school officials called him over "almost weekly" to help quell the conflicts.[23] These battles reflected the town's ongoing gang warfare, which shifted from intra-ethnic fighting (black and Latino) to a free-for-all, with everyone fighting everyone else regardless of ethnic background.[24] Here was yet another set of problems that the state takeover failed to address.

Despite their evident failures, these narrowly focused takeovers remained popular across the nation, to the point of being enshrined in law as an option in NCLB. A reauthorization of the Elementary and Secondary Education Act (ESEA), NCLB revamped federal education policy, putting into national law a set of ideas that had been percolating for several decades and implemented in many states. In accordance with these beliefs, reformers valued competitive markets and individual freedom, and as a result, their approach discounted the larger economic, political, and social contexts in which the schools developed, as well as the historical legacies of oppression and economic structure in which the schools remained.[25] Denying the relevance of such factors, neoliberals redefined educational reform as entrepreneurial and market driven.

This legislation was a high priority for newly elected president George W. Bush, and he revealed it just three days after his 2001 inauguration. Four central principles undergirded the plan: high standards for all students; accountability for reaching those standards through measurable outcomes; sanctions for those not meeting the standards; and choice for students in persistently low-performing schools.[26] Politicians from both sides of the aisle enthusiastically supported these goals, under the mantle of representing distressed communities like Compton. Compton Unified was the type of district that exemplified those patterns of failure NCLB was supposed to alleviate. With its broad base of nonpartisan support, NCLB came to contain many disparate programs, including required after-school tutoring at struggling schools, despite the dubious results from experiments like that of Compton Unified's with Sylvan.[27] NCLB also identified individual school takeovers as an option for states. This latter option would soon play out in Compton, once again putting it in the national spotlight.

NCLB affected Compton's schools in a variety of ways. The newly redefined ESEA required all states to implement statewide accountability systems, which in practice meant increasing annual standardized testing of students. Under state receivership, Compton Unified tested all its students, but now the test scores helped rank Compton Unified against other California districts. Under NCLB, California's districts now had to meet two sets of accountability targets: the state API scoring system and the new federal Adequate Yearly Progress (AYP) goals. This focus on test scores eventually led many teachers to engage in a kind of "educational triage"—schools began rationing instructional resources to the students most likely to improve the school's test scores (and ratings) and away from students who seemed to be hopeless cases.[28] In a short time, multiple studies revealed how these federal accountability policies not only failed to meet the needs of minority students and English learners, but instead had the reverse effects on schools by exacerbating historic inequities.[29] Black and Latino youth comprised the near total of the student population of Compton Unified.

Accountability pressures mounted in Compton as they did elsewhere, but there were occasional, isolated success cases. In 2006 one of Compton's elementary schools, Bunche Elementary, was one of the 377 public elementary schools designated a California Distinguished School for improving its API scores. It was the first time in the twenty-one years since the beginning of the distinguished school program that a Compton school earned that ranking.[30] In 2008 Charles W. Bursch Elementary became Compton Unified's second school to receive this designation, but that same year the California Department of Education placed the district as a whole in "Program Improvement" for consistently failing to meet its Adequate Yearly Progress targets.[31] Of course, this designation came along with a whole new set of requirements, and outside monitoring.

Turning Around a School While Racing to the Top

The national climate around education reform had indeed changed as both Republicans and Democrats embraced reform efforts. Like his Republican predecessor, Democratic president Barack Obama made education reform central, including education in the 2009 American Recovery and Reinvestment Act. As part of the over $800 billion stimulus, Congress authorized $100 billion for education, with $4.3 billion allotted to a new program, Race to the Top. As its name implied, it was a competitive program that offered monetary incentives for states to create educational reforms. The administration defined the parameters by requiring states to commit to approaches supported by the administration before applying. In order to qualify for funds, states were required to expand high-stakes accountability policies including charter school conversions, and test-based accountability. Both Race to the Top and No Child Left Behind grew out of earlier reforms for which Compton was a test case. Such policies had failed to remedy the situation in Compton, but no one seemed to be listening.

The new federal Race to the Top funds appealed to California policymakers because in 2009 its schools faced the worst financial crisis in years: $12 billion in cuts, class size increases, and elimination of programs and jobs.[32] At the last minute, lawmakers in Sacramento attempted to qualify the state for the first round of stimulus money, quickly writing, and narrowly passing by a single vote, the "parent trigger" law, which gave parents a way to require school districts to turn around a troubled school.[33] The 2010 law showed that the state used results from high-stakes tests to expand the number of charter schools within its borders. California did not receive the money, but the trigger law stood.

Once again, Compton Unified served a test case for reform, as it had for high-stakes testing, privatized outsourcing, and state controlled curriculum. Parents at McKinley Elementary School became the first in the country to enact the law. By a variety of measures, McKinley was failing. Using California's accountability ranking, it had a low API number and ranked the worst among "similar schools" in the state.[34] And it was not just the numbers that spoke, it was the parents. Shemika Murphy's seven-year-old daughter struggled in reading and Valarie McMillan's son did too. Ismenia Guzman wanted to see real and immediate changes in the school, and began to organize alongside the not-for-profit organization Parent Revolution.[35]

Parent Revolution spearheaded both the passing of the trigger law in California and the campaign at McKinley. Though named as if run by parents, the group was a project of the Los Angeles Parents Union and was closely connected to the Green Dot Charter school group. Unlike real community-based organizations, Parent Revolution worked with a $1 million budget that was primarily funded by venture philanthropists, including the Bill and Melinda Gates Foundation and the Walton Family Foundation.[36] Its employees drew up the petitions, led the petition drive, and designated Celerity Educational Group, which ran several charter schools in the Los Angeles region, as the preferred school operator.[37]

Parent Revolution purposefully targeted McKinley as a test case for the new law because it was a struggling school in a floundering district, even though both the state and FCMAT had pronounced it healthy enough to return local control. In August 2010 the state released an audit stating it had "grave concern" about the district's ability to advance students academically. Fewer than half of Compton's students graduated from high school and just 2 percent went to college. McKinley ranked in the bottom 10 percent of similar schools in California with similar racial and economic backgrounds.[38] McKinley's students chronically underperformed with less than a quarter of all students meeting state standards in math and reading.[39]

Though under the trigger law parents would have four options for their school's turnover, Parent Revolution advocated for one solution: a charter takeover of McKinley. Nationally, charter schools had grown out of the choice movement, which previously focused on voucher programs, and they had become the favored way of implementing choice. By definition, charter schools were created when an organization or association of parents and teachers obtains a charter from a state-authorized agency. In exchange for autonomy, the founding organization promised to achieve a self-selected set of performance goals within a certain time period. Though charters could theoretically be run by a nonprofit or for-profit group, a national organization, or a local community group, more and more, California and the country saw control of charter schools by private management organizations rather than grassroots organizations.[40]

Electing to go charter did not solve McKinley's issues. Instead, Compton became a forum in which the national debate around charter schools played out. Would the charter school perform better than the regular public school? How, if at all, would it deal with students with special needs? What were the ramifications of underperformance? Some charter school proponents believed that the takeover of a regular school was a failure waiting to happen, as they believed charters work best when started from scratch. In fact, one of the original arguments for charter schools was that they help foster innovation, a questionable proposition if the charter operator just took over an existing school. Finally, would a charter school be considered successful if the students and their families weren't opting into it?

Given Comptonites' history of struggles to control their school district, it perhaps is not surprising that prior to the trigger law the district had never even accepted an application from a charter hopeful.[41] Another common argument in support of charter schools was that they "liberate educators from bureaucratic regulations and union contracts that stifle creative educational improvements."[42] Charter school directors, rather than central office administrators, had the ability to hire and fire. Because Compton officials had long recognized the role the school district played in employing people from the community, many bristled at the idea of outsider authority over jobs, just as they had in the case of state control.

Local issues also influenced the conversation around McKinley, renewing the debate over local control. While superficially putting the fate of the school into the parents' hands, the shifting of governance from the district to a private charter management organization did not necessarily empower the parents, since the law did not address or require sustained community involvement.[43] Indeed, anti-trigger law sentiments became an expression of hometown pride.[44] At a school district board meeting, opponents of the takeover chanted "Compton! Compton!"[45] Their worries that they would not have access to power were supported by the fact that money and support came from outside. The pro-charter group in Compton aligned itself with national figures. When the opponents of the trigger law protested at the board meeting, supporters did not attend, instead meeting with Michelle Rhee, former chancellor of the Washington, D.C., public school system, who was known for her aggressive style of reform, including supporting private charter schools and busting collective bargaining agreements.[46]

Some Comptonites also questioned the process by which decisions about Compton schools were made. Opponents of Parent Revolution (and groups like it) called them "Astroturf," because they represented fake grassroots sentiments.[47] Parent Revolution's own website admitted its organizing at McKinley was "not a perfect campaign," noting that it had presented a pre-packaged plan to parents rather than helping them devise their own solution. The organization also acknowledged that its organizers, not parents, gathered the majority of signatures on the petitions.[48] Some parents claimed signature gatherers lied to them as to the purpose of the petition. Parents who ran McKinley's Parent-Teacher Association opposed the takeover and claimed to have gathered signatures of those who wished to rescind theirs from the original petition.[49]

Compton Unified rejected the parent petition, judging that, for several reasons, it was not properly drawn up: inadequate number of valid signatures; no evidence that parents were given a formal description of the change that would happen; each signature page did not contain a date and a complete heading; no evidence of a rigorous review process of the proposed charter school; and the inability to verify certain signatures.[50] Ultimately a court found the parents' petition lacking on technical grounds and McKinley remained as it was.[51] In the meantime, Los Angeles County approved a charter school run by Celerity at a neighborhood church just a few blocks from McKinley. While the school quickly filled after its opening in September 2011, only about a fifth of the children would have gone to McKinley, bringing into question the true depth of parental support for triggering the school takeover.[52]

The case of McKinley embodied the approach that had come to define education reform at the beginning of the twenty-first century. Funded by private money, such reforms emphasized choice and accountability, as well as the benefits of deregulation, which would help move schooling from under the bureaucracy and toward meaningful improvement.[53] Boosters emphasized that charters gave parents a choice in schools and that the alternative schools had fewer restrictions than traditional public schools.[54] The empirical data as to whether these schools work remained contested.[55]

McKinley was more than representative—it was also a catalyst. By August 2012, seven states had enacted some version of trigger laws.[56] It also inspired the 2012 Hollywood film *Won't Back Down*, produced by Walden Media, the same company that financed the 2010 pro-charter documentary *Waiting for Superman*.[57] While the movie was set in Pittsburgh, Pennsylvania, it played out the drama that had only just happened in Compton. Like many Compton schools, the school portrayed in the film had been "failing" for years. The film protagonist, a mother of a struggling student, teamed with a downtrodden teacher to use the newly passed parent trigger law to bring about a school turnaround. Together they overcame a series of obstacles to change, including the largest: the teachers' union. In framing the teachers' union as the villain the film played on simplistic narratives of educational crisis that had become popular across the country. As a result, the film obfuscated the much deeper roots of the problems and effectively blocked avenues to change. From its founding as a suburb, through a devastating earthquake, to its residents' holding onto their suburban dreams even when they weren't in their best interests, Compton and its schools had a long history of struggle, one that would not easily be ameliorated.

Reforming with Too Narrow a View

The reform debate is one we need to view historically and with a critical eye to the politics involved. The focus of reform remains too narrowly on schools, teachers, administration, and testing, which means that it fails to account for the many other disruptions present in the lives of Compton Unified's students. One such paramount disruption included frequent violence. In 2003, Compton again made headlines when the older sister of tennis stars Venus and Serena Williams was killed in a drive-by shooting in town.[58] In 2005, Compton's murder rate soared to seventy-two, a drastic increase of 70 percent from the previous year.[59] The devastating violence returned the town to the national and international consciousness. In March 2006, both National Public Radio (NPR) and the British Broadcasting Company (BBC) ran feature stories about the violence in Compton.[60] According to NPR reporter Luke Burbank, "Nobody claims to know definitively why the murder rate spiked last year, but a few things stick out. For one, a large number of O.G.'s, original hardcore gang members, have been getting out of prison after serving 10 to 15 year sentences. There's also more racial tension between Compton's black and Latino gangs than ever before."[61]

Local politics compounded the problem of violence, as can be seen in wrangling over the fate of Compton's police department. In 2000, Mayor Bradley began to discuss dissolving the police and fire departments and out-sourcing municipal services to the Los Angeles County Sheriff's Depart-ment.[62] The fire department withstood the frontal attack, but the fate of the police department became a heated battle. According to Father Bosch, "there were many, many voices that were saying to exit our police department is to exit a piece of the identity of the city."[63] Hundreds of Compton residents marched to city hall to protest the increased hostility the mayor seemed to be directing toward the department and his unwillingness to put it to a public vote in a referendum.[64] After much public outcry, Bradley dissolved Comp-ton's police department, forcing the town to rely on the county for the neces-sary services.[65]

Even after the fact, Bradley's decision to disband the local police depart-ment and bring in the county sheriff continued to raise doubts; according to Burbank, "some people are wondering if the LA County Sheriff's Depart-ment is doing its job policing the city."[66] Unlike the local police who remained in Compton throughout their tenure, county sheriffs rotated all over the county and, in Burbank's words, "don't know enough about the gang scene in Compton."[67]

Many Compton residents and officials believed that while the sheriffs proved ineffective in preventing violence, stopping it completely went be-yond the ability of any law enforcement agency. Compton city manager Bar-bara Kilroy told the BBC that while town officials were hoping to free up money to hire more police officers, she believed local politicians could do little to stop the gangs, because "crime and gang problems are essentially sociological—they go to the society as a whole."[68] Truly changing Compton's community would mean addressing a whole host of issues, not least of which was overcoming the ethnic divisions that often fueled gang tensions. Bosch explained to the same reporter that Compton suffered from an absence of "any real coordination between the disparate, often ethnically divided, re-form groups, which are working almost at cross-purposes it seems."[69] Even in attempting to fix Compton's ills, broader social issues, such as racial and eth-nic conflicts, blocked the way.

Popular accounts, both in film and in writing, highlighted how these so-cioeconomic problems affected Compton and its schools. In the 2003 docu-mentary *OT: Our Town*, filmmaker Scott Hamilton Kennedy recorded the story of one high school English teacher, Catherine Borek, as she and her students put together the first play in over twenty years at Compton Unified's Dominguez High School. The film followed the honors students as they wrestled with all the components of producing a play, from understanding and relating to the text to memorizing lines and performing in front of their community. Throughout the film, the viewer glimpses life in Compton and at Dominguez High. While ultimately a story of success, the documentary also revealed many of the daily challenges faced by school-age Comptonites.[70] In some ways, *OT* was a positive but realistic expression of the reform impulse.

Not all popular accounts of Compton and its schools represented such successes. In 2005 Sarah Sentilles, a former Teach For America teacher in Compton Unified, published a memoir of her two years teaching elementary school students in the district. In contrast to the success and perseverance of the teacher in *OT*, Sentilles's book, *Taught by America*, put the reform enterprise in a more ambivalent light, as it highlighted, through a series of vignettes, the despair and anger she experienced as a novice teacher in the troubled district: "In Compton . . . I witnessed suffering, resilience, survival, joy, violence, love, and deep pain. I witnessed the workings of systemic oppression—oppression that had served my interests even as it remained invisible to me."[71] Her story and her experiences, in her own assessment, were not triumphant and point to the frustrations of working in stressful conditions without adequate resources. In her own words, "I struggled while I was teaching in Compton. When I stopped teaching, I struggled harder still. I didn't know what to do with what I had experienced."[72] In the end, Sentilles knew her work had not altered the harsh realities of Compton and remained skeptical that her experiences had a positive impact on the lives of her students.

Participation in sports has had a long tradition as a "way out" of places like Compton. In December 2011, *Sports Illustrated* and CBS News together produced a "special report" about gangs and schools. The report used Compton to illustrate how students use sports "to survive in gang-infested communities," even employing NWA's "Straight Outta Compton" as the report's title.[73] Ironically, the article failed to reflect on the priorities that enabled the district to maintain basketball and football programs at the high schools at the expense of the academic budget.

The interest in employing sports as a means out of gang life also came from outsiders. In 1996 British film producer Katy Haber and Los Angeles activist Ted Hayes founded the Compton Cricket Club, also dubbed the "Homies and the POPz." The team actively recruited in Compton schools as an explicit anti-gang measure, offering an activity and membership alternative to gangs. The team went beyond that measure, touring as the only all American-born team.[74]

Major League Baseball (MLB) also established a presence in Compton. In February 2006, MLB opened its first "Urban Youth Academy" in Compton with the goal of increasing interest in baseball among inner-city youth, especially African Americans.[75] Since the 1980s, interest and participation in baseball among African Americans had been declining. At the same time, the sport drew new levels of interest in Latin American countries and among Latinos in the United States. The new clinic aimed at revitalizing interest in the sport among inner-city youth, valued as both potential consumers and players. It also promised to help the community's youth by providing an alternative to the streets. It is telling that baseball commissioner Bud Selig wished to place the clinic in Compton to reach more African American players, not realizing that Compton had become majority Latino.

Part of Compton's reputation as a black town stemmed from the fact that African Americans continued to control it. After Mayor Bradley unilaterally dissolved the police department, several religious leaders formed an interracial and ecumenical coalition, Pastors of Compton. The group was instrumental in defeating Bradley in his try for a third term as mayor, and electing mayor Eric Perrodin, an African American, who was a deputy district attorney, former Compton police officer, and brother of deposed police captain Percy Perrodin.[76]

While Compton's image as the black inner city is compelling, the story of the town it symbolizes is more complex than this limited impression allows. By 2011 Latinos comprised two-thirds of Compton's population, but no Latino held elected city office. City council members represented specific geographic areas, but they were elected in citywide elections, unlike in neighboring Los Angeles, where council members were elected by the area that they represented. Despite their numbers, two factors in particular diluted Latino voting power: some residents were not U.S. citizens and many were too young to vote. In 2011, Latinos sued the town for violating the California Voting Rights Act of 2001, alleging that Compton's commitment to at-large voting manifested in "a particularly noxious brand of racial politics that plays out in schools, elections and even civic events."[77] The three Latino plaintiffs in the suit sought district-by-district ballots, hoping to get a majority of voting-age Latinos in at least one, and a settlement in the case brought about this change in voting from at-large to district voting.

Along with political strife, the recession during the first decade of the 2000s hit California fiercely and struck Compton even more intensely. Unemployment rose to 20 percent, and the town compounded these problems by laying off 15 percent of its workforce. In 2009 Mayor Perrodin and council members pursued a plan to reopen the police department, spending over $1 million on equipment before killing the idea in 2011 as cost-prohibitive. The town could not pay its policing contract and amassed $369,000 in late fees in a year. Due to the rise in home foreclosures the town collected fewer property taxes, its major source of income. In 2011, the deficit of about 80 percent of general funds caused the rating firm Standard & Poor's to downgrade Compton's bonds to just above junk status.[78] By summer 2012, the town was on the brink of bankruptcy, with $3 million in the bank but $5 million worth of bills. Furthermore, it faced a $43 million deficit, the result of years of misusing money from water, sewer, and retirement funds to balance its general fund.[79] The school district was also running on a deficit, with an estimated $17 million shortfall in March 2013. In order to balance the budget, Compton Unified's board of trustees recommended reduction of the work year for employees as well as trimming "overstaffing."[80] With its credit shattered, Compton's financial hole had become even deeper, and even harder to escape.

Instead of taking the popular culture's depiction of educational problems and solutions at face value, we need to understand the historical production of unequal schooling in order to disrupt it. The roots of discontent over low performing schools, as well as the inadequacy of many current reforms, lie in the deeper social and economic roots of school failure.

The long history of fiscal instability in a quintessential southern California bedroom suburb illustrates a basic contradiction between suburban dreams and fiscal realities that was common across the United States. Supporters once heralded Compton as the home of the suburban dream, but the story of its educational system both reflected and dissolved that ambition. Compton was always swimming upstream as a predominantly blue-collar, inner-ring suburb in an era of metropolitan expansion and differentiation. Over the twentieth century, through a series of specific events, individual decisions, and broader circumstances, Compton became a concentrated area of poverty. In this regard, it hardly represented the promise of the "suburban dream."[81]

Compton's experience illustrates how, regardless who was in control, the suburban dream of exclusion and local control of resources could turn into a nightmare when resources evaporated and towns became majority-minority.

Massive black migration into greater Los Angeles made Compton vulnerable to the changes that occurred in the 1950s and '60s. Once racial change occurred, the community's problems became more pronounced. The period of sharp racial divisions in its history represented a holding pattern, a standoff of sorts, but eventually the transition was complete and a new era in the community's history began. While some residents remained in Compton, many moved to other suburbs when they could afford to do so. Compton, as in other majority-minority communities, became a desert island of sorts, attracting relatively poor residents and little economic development. As a result, remaining in Compton often meant experiencing tensions and conflicts over the town's small pool of resources. Parents battled for better educational circumstances for their children and newcomers fought for access to employment possibilities.

An examination of these local battles raises questions about American public education as a whole and challenges the validity of the prevailing system for funding public schools. Designed as a residential community, Compton's middle-class residents wished to keep it a bedroom community, discouraging business development. When the economic base proved too small for the financial obligations of its rapidly growing population, town leaders searched for ways to attract industry and to redevelop commerce, but by then it was too late. Compton had already become viewed as a black town, one notorious for its violence, and businesses were scared away. The national projection of the town's image in the late 1980s, with gangster rap and *Boyz n the Hood*, was the icing on the cake, making the prospects of serious investment in the community dim at best.

Compton represented one such story of how schools struggled to provide students with basic educational skills. Like many other American school systems, such as Bridgeport, Connecticut, Emeryville, California, and Roosevelt, New York, Compton was caught in a vicious cycle. It had never had local wealth on which to draw, and when state funding got slashed Compton's property taxes soared to provide the minimum necessary services in the town and the schools. With such a disproportionately high tax rate, it became an even less attractive place for people to settle. Compton and its school district had insufficient funds to provide educational services to the increasingly needy population, and the disparity between districts like Compton and wealthier districts grew. In 2011, Beverly Hills, for example, could afford to spend $3,000 more per pupil than Compton, which enabled it to have smaller class sizes, more counselors, and other academic support.[82] If American school districts continue to rely on property taxes for the majority of their revenue, this disparity will continue—some will succeed, while others will fail.

Schools and communities operate in the society at large. While Compton offers a compelling story of corruption, incompetence, and malfeasance, these were complicating factors to Compton's situation, not its structural roots. Social, economic, and political transformations overtook Compton. In examining the transformations, the relationship between economic and educational opportunities shows a clear correlation between the plight of students and the community. Poverty and its close relative racial segregation shaped public education and in turn, the failures of the schools shaped the community. Thus, equalizing opportunities necessitates reducing both poverty and segregation while working to reform the schools.

As the nexus of race, place, and poverty comes to the forefront in the discussion about public education, it forces the debate to include fundamental questions: who is responsible for teaching the nation's large populations of disadvantaged students? How can all public schools come to provide a suitable and safe environment for education?

Historical insight matters to policy debates and exploring the roots of these problems, as well as failed attempts at remedying them, serves as a first step toward unmaking the American public school crisis. Historical modes of analysis force us to consider how multiple causes shaped events and circumstances. Taking this contingency into account undercuts the too often pat answers that present-minded reformers and politician rely on to craft policy.[83] It also reveals that the ways they frame the problems often do not accurately reflect the complicated dynamics in which schools operate. In the case of Compton and its schools, the problem is one of broader inequalities and as a result, fixing the school district's problems must address what separates that community from prosperity. The causes are complex: relying on reforms that introduce competition and entrepreneurialism into local schools without addressing the gulf in resources is not enough. Instead, we must take on the broader, and intertwined, issues of race, place, and schools. Caring for children is one of society's most fundamental purposes and, however difficult, we must strive to meet this obligation. In the meantime, our children are waiting, not for the strong-arm tactics of would-be Supermen, but for policymakers willing to address the complex problems that threaten students from inside and outside the school walls.

Abbreviations

Collections and Archives

BCP   Bert N. Corona Papers, 1923–1984 collection, Stanford University
CCH   Office of the City Clerk, Compton City Hall, Compton, California
CPL   Compton Public Library, Compton, California
CSA   California State Archives, Sacramento, California
CSUDH   California State University, Dominguez Hills
CUSD   Compton Unified School District, Compton, California
EC   *Los Angeles Examiner* clippings, Regional History Center, Special Collections, University of Southern California
Gutman   Gutman Library Special Collections, Harvard School of Education, Cambridge, Massachusetts
LACOE   Los Angeles County Commission of School District Organization Papers, Los Angeles County Office of Education, Downey, California
LAPL   Los Angeles Public Library
NAACP   National Association for the Advancement of Colored People, Region 1, Records 1942–1986, Bancroft Library, University of California Berkeley
SCLSSR   Southern California Library for Social Studies and Research
UCLA   University of California, Los Angeles, Special Collections
UCLA-OH   University of California, Los Angeles, Oral History Program, for the California State Archives State Government Oral History Program

Newspapers

BS   *Baltimore Sun*
CB   *Compton Bulletin*
CDD   *Chicago Daily Defender*
CE   *California Eagle*
CH   *Compton Herald*
CHA   *Compton Herald American*
CJ   *Compton Journal*
CJI   *Compton Journal and Independent*

CW	*Compton Windows*
HACH	*Herald American and Compton Herald*
LAE	*Los Angeles Examiner*
LAS	*Los Angeles Sentinel*
LAT	*Los Angeles Times*
LAW	*LA Weekly*
LBPT	*Long Beach Press-Telegram*
NYT	*New York Times*
TB	*The Bulletin*
WSJ	*Wall Street Journal*

Notes

Introduction

1. Jennifer Medina, "In Compton, Calif., Parents Force an Overhaul," *NYT*, December 7, 2010, A16.

2. Ibid.; Jim Newton, "Compton Parents Trigger Reform," *LAT*, February 15, 2011.

3. Jim Newton, "Education Battle at Compton Unified School," *LAT*, April 18, 2011.

4. "Compton Board Targets Cuts for Budget Crunch," *Wave*, March 1990; "Wells Says Murray Is All Wrong About Compton," *CB*, April 15, 1992, A-2.

5. State of California: Assembly Bill Number: AB 33; Howard Blume, "School District Requests Bailout of $18.4 Million," *LAT*, March 25, 1993; "Compton Schools in Trouble Again," *LAS*, March 25, 1993, A1; Psyche Pascual, "State Appointee Takes Over Compton Schools," *LAT*, July 10, 1993. For discussion on state takeovers, see David R. Berman, "Takeovers of Local Governments: An Overview and Evaluation of State Policies," *Publius* 25 (1995): 55–71; Liam J. Garland, *Navigating Treacherous Waters: A State Takeover Handbook* (Lanham, Md.: Scarecrow Press. 2003); Nicolas Lemann, "'Ready, Read!' A New Solution to the Problem of Failing Public Schools Is Emerging: Takeover by Outside Authorities, Who Prescribe a Standardized, Field-Tested Curriculum," *Atlantic Monthly* 282 (November 1998): 92–104; Richard C. Hunter and Jeff Swann, "School Takeovers and Enhanced Answerability," *Education and Urban Society* 31 (1999): 238–54.

6. "Minutes of a Regular Meeting, Board of Trustees, December 11, 2001," CUSD; "Control of Schools Returned to Compton; New Board Seated," *LAS*, December 20, 2001, A4.

7. For the new suburban history that explores diversity, see Matthew D. Lassiter and Christopher Niedt, "Suburban Diversity in Postwar America," *Journal of Urban History* 39 (2013): 3–14; Kevin M. Kruse and Thomas J. Sugrue, eds., *The New Suburban History* (Chicago: University of Chicago Press, 2006); Becky M. Nicolaides, *My Blue Heaven: Life and Politics in the Working-Class Suburbs of Los Angeles, 1920–1965* (Chicago: University of Chicago Press, 2002); Andrew Wiese, *Places of Their Own: African American Suburbanization in the Twentieth Century* (Chicago: University of Chicago Press, 2004); Adam Rome, *The Bulldozer in the Countryside: Suburban Sprawl and the Rise of*

American Environmentalism (New York: Cambridge University Press, 2001). These works build on an established historiography on suburbia. Some seminal early works are Kenneth T. Jackson, *Crabgrass Frontier: The Suburbanization of the United States* (New York: Oxford University Press, 1984); Zane Miller, *Suburb* (Knoxville: University of Tennessee Press, 1982); Sam Bass Warner, *Streetcar Suburbs: The Process of Growth in Boston, 1870–1900* (Cambridge, Mass.: Harvard University Press, 1962); Robert Fishman, *Bourgeois Utopias: The Rise and Fall of Suburbia* (New York: Basic Books, 1987). For discussion of schooling, see Matthew D. Lassiter, *The Silent Majority: Suburban Politics in the Sunbelt South* (Princeton, N.J.: Princeton University Press, 2006); Kevin M. Kruse, *White Flight: Atlanta and the Making of Modern Conservatism* (Princeton, N.J.: Princeton University Press, 2005); Ansley Erickson, "Schooling the Metropolis: Educational Inequality Made and Remade Nashville, Tennessee, 1945–1985" (Ph.D. dissertation, Columbia University, 2010); Andrew Highsmith, "Demolition Means Progress: Race, Class, and the Deconstruction of the American Dream in Flint, Michigan" (Ph.D. dissertation, University of Michigan, 2009).

8. For a discussion of racialization of space, see Wiese, *Places of Their Own*. Recent works, such as Eric Avila, *Popular Culture in the Age of White Flight: Fear and Fantasy in Suburban Los Angeles* (Berkeley: University of California Press: 2004) and Robert O. Self, *American Babylon: Race and the Struggle for Postwar Oakland* (Princeton, N.J.: Princeton University Press, 2003), have reinforced many of these assumptions about the history of racial and class divisions that occurred between city and suburbs.

9. Les W. Arnold, "A Promise for the Future," *Compton Journal Pictorial Review & 1945 Annual* (1945).

10. Bernadette Hanlon, *Once the American Dream: Inner-Ring Suburbs of the Metropolitan United States* (Philadelphia: Temple University Press, 2010), 30.

11. Robert M. Fogelson, *Bourgeois Nightmares: Suburbia, 1870–1930* (New Haven, Conn.: Yale University Press, 2007).

12. Alberto M. Camarillo, "Chicano Urban History: A Study of Compton's Barrio, 1936–1970," *Aztlan* 2 (1971): 81. Scholars do not agree on classifying Latinos as a race. Furthermore, in the U.S. census Hispanic is not a race but an ethnicity. I am using the term race as the point of conflict. Part of this conflict includes the historical disinclination and construction of Latinos as "white."

13. David Tyack, *The One Best System: A History of Urban American Education* (Cambridge, Mass.: Harvard University Press, 1974).

14. Jack Schneider, "Escape from Los Angeles: White Flight from Los Angeles and Its Schools," *Journal of Urban History* 34 (2008): 995–1012.

15. Myron Orfield, *Metropolitics: A Regional Agenda for Community and Stability* (Washington, D.C.: Brookings Institution Press, 1997).

16. Orfield, *Metropolitics*; William H. Hudnut, III, *Halfway to Everywhere: A Portrait of America's First-Tier Suburbs* (Washington, D.C.: Urban Land Institute, 2003); Henry C. Binford, *The First Suburb: Residential Communities on the Boston Periphery, 1815–1860* (Chicago: University of Chicago Press, 1985).

17. *Shelley v. Kraemer*, 334 U.S. 1 (1948).

18. U.S. Census Bureau, Census 2000.

19. Sheryll D. Cashin, *The Failures of Integration: How Race and Class Are Undermining the American Dream* (New York: Public Affairs, 2005); Karyn R. Lacy, *Blue-Chip Black: Race, Class, and Status in the New Black Middle Class* (Berkeley: University of California Press, 2007).

20. Avila, *Popular Culture in the Age of White Flight*; Lassiter, *The Silent Majority*; Nicolaides, *My Blue Heaven*; Wiese, *Places of Their Own*.

21. Dorothy Townsend, "Compton to Elect First Negro Mayor Tuesday," *LAT*, June 1, 1969, C1; "Elect Black Councilman Mayor of L.A. Suburb," *CDD*, June 21, 1969, 9; Steven R. Roberts, "Compton, Calif., 65% Negro, Believes in Integration and in Peaceful Change," *NYT*, June 8, 1969, 65. In the late 1960s, African Americans began to be elected mayors in major American cities. For in-depth analysis of this political transformation, see David R. Colburn and Jeffrey S. Adler, eds., *African-American Mayors: Race, Politics, and the American City* (Urbana: University of Illinois Press, 2001).

22. NWA, *Straight Outta Compton* (Priority Records, 1988).

23. NWA, *Straight Outta Compton*; John Singleton, *Boyz n the Hood*, dir. John Singleton (Columbia/Tristar Studios, 1991).

24. Oral histories also presented methodological challenges. When using the interviews as evidence I needed to be aware of the interviewee's position in society when examining how she or he remembered and reflected on a particular event or moment. Furthermore, I wanted to use the oral histories not to fill holes or create textures, but as an equal form of evidence that lay side-by-side with others. Interweaving the variety of sources created a mosaic, a more complete picture of Compton.

25. Mark Brilliant, *The Color of America Has Changed: How Racial Diversity Shaped Civil Rights Reform in California, 1941–1978* (New York: Oxford University Press, 2010); Shana Bernstein, *Bridges of Reform: Interracial Civil Rights Activism in Twentieth-Century Los Angeles* (New York: Oxford University Press, 2011); Scott Kurashige, *The Shifting Grounds of Race: Black and Japanese Americans in the Making of Multiethnic Los Angeles* (Princeton, N.J.: Princeton University Press, 2008); Allison Varzally, *Making a Non-White America: Californians Coloring Outside Ethnic Lines, 1925–1955* (Berkeley: University of California Press, 2008).

26. Historians have segregated the experiences of each of these groups into separate scholarly literatures. See Raymond A. Mohl, "Blacks and Hispanics in Multicultural America: A Miami Case Study," in *The Making of Urban America*, ed. Raymond A. Mohl (Wilmington, Del.: Scholarly Resources, 1997); Nicolás C. Vaca, *The Presumed Alliance: The Unspoken Conflict Between Latinos and Blacks and What it Means for America* (New York: Rayo, 2004); Neil Foley, *Quest for Equality: The Failed Promise of Black-Brown Solidarity* (Cambridge, Mass.: Harvard University Press, 2010); Brian D. Behnken, *Fighting Their Own Battles: Mexican Americans, African Americans, and the Struggle for Civil Rights in Texas* (Chapel Hill: University of North Carolina Press, 2011); Brian D. Behnken, ed., *The Struggle in Black and Brown: African American and Mexican*

American Relations During the Civil Rights Era (Lincoln: University of Nebraska Press, 2011). For Compton, see Albert M. Camarillo, "Black and Brown in Compton: Demographic Change, Suburban Decline, and Intergroup Relations in a South Central Los Angeles Community, 1950 to 2000," in *Not Just Black and White: Historical and Contemporary Perspectives on Immigration, Race, and Ethnicity in the United States*, ed. Nancy Foner and George M. Fredrickson (New York: Russell Sage, 2004); Albert M. Camarillo, "Cities of Color: The New Racial Frontier in California's Minority-Majority Cities," *Pacific Historical Review* 76 (2007): 1–28. Scholars have examined whites' resistance to black education and Latinos' battles for educational access and for bilingual education. See Ruben Donato, *The Other Struggle for Equal Schools: Mexican Americans During the Civil Rights Era* (Albany, N.Y.: SUNY Press, 1997); Guadalupe San Miguel, *Brown, Not White: School Integration and the Chicano Movement in Houston* (College Station: Texas A&M University Press, 2001).

27. For works about disadvantaged groups in multi-ethnic communities struggling over limited resources, see Joel Perlmann, *Ethnic Differences: Schooling and Social Structure Among the Irish, Italians, Jews, and Blacks in an American City, 1880–1935* (New York: Cambridge University Press, 1988); Ronald D. Cohen and Raymond A. Mohl, *The Paradox of Progressive Education: The Gary Plan and Urban Schooling* (Port Washington, N.Y.: Kennikat Press, 1979); Daniel Perlstein, *Justice, Justice: School Politics and the Eclipse of Liberalism* (New York: Peter Lang, 2004); Sieglinde Lim de Sanchez, "Crafting a Delta Chinese Community: Education and Acculturation in Twentieth-Century Southern Baptist Mission Schools," *History of Education Quarterly* 43 (March 2003): 74–90.

28. As cited in Jennifer Medina, "In Compton, Calif., Parents Force an Overhaul," *NYT*, December 7, 2010, A16.

29. Thomas J. Sugrue, *Sweet Land of Liberty: The Forgotten Struggle for Civil Rights in the North* (New York: Random House, 2008); Martha Biondi, *To Stand and Fight: The Struggle for Civil Rights in Postwar New York City* (Cambridge, Mass.: Harvard University Press, 2006); Jeanne F. Theoharis and Komozi Woodard, *Freedom North: Black Freedom Struggles Outside the South, 1940–1980* (New York: Palgrave Macmillan, 2003); Thomas J. Sugrue, *Origins of the Urban Crisis: Race and Inequality in Postwar Detroit* (Princeton, N.J.: Princeton University Press, 1996); Arnold Hirsch, *Making of the Second Ghetto: Race and Housing in Chicago, 1940–1960* (New York: Cambridge University Press, 1983); Self, *American Babylon*; Jack Dougherty, *More Than One Struggle: The Evolution of Black School Reform in Milwaukee* (Chapel Hill: University of North Carolina Press, 2004).

30. Myron Orfield, *American Metropolitics: The New Suburban Reality* (Washington, D.C.: Brookings Institution Press, 2002), 9.

31. Elizabeth Kneebone and Emily Garr, "The Suburbanization of Poverty: Trends in Metropolitan America, 2000 to 2008," Metropolitan Opportunities Series 2 (Washington, D.C.: Brookings Institution, 2010); Roberto Suro, Jill H. Wilson, and Audrey Singer, "Immigration and Poverty in America's Suburbs," Metropolitan Opportunities

Series 18, 2011; Scott W. Allard and Benjamin Roth, "Strained Suburbs: The Social Service Challenges of Rising Suburban Poverty," Brookings Institution Report, 2010.

Chapter 1. On Shaky Ground

1. Interview with Ruth Ashton Taylor by Shirley Biagi, "Women in Journalism" oral history project of the Washington Press Club Foundation, November 16, 1990, 24, in the Oral History Collection of Columbia University and other repositories.

2. "Compton," *LAT*, March 12, 1933, 2; LaRee Caughey, "The Long Beach Earthquake," in *Los Angeles: Biography of a City*, ed. John Caughey and LaRee Caughey (Berkeley: University of California Press, 1976), 303.

3. There are conflicting estimates on exactly how much the property damage cost. Calculations range from $30 million to over $60 million, but most approximations fall between $40 and $50 million. See E. A. Thomas, H. C. Grant, and E. A. Romer, "General Report on Damage Resulting from the Earthquake of March 10, 1933," Shell Oil Company, Wilmington Refinery Division, Engineering Department, 1933, 6; Environmental Research Laboratories, "A Study of Earthquake Losses in the Los Angeles, California Area: A Report Prepared for the Federal Disaster Assistance Administration, Department of Housing and Urban Development," 1973, 50.

4. "Compton," *LAT*, March 12, 1933, 2; R. W. Binder, "Engineering Aspects of the 1933 Long Beach Earthquake," in *Proceedings of the Symposium on Earthquake and Blast Effects on Structures*, ed. C. Martin Duke and Morris Feigen (Los Angeles: Earthquake Engineering Research Institute, 1952), 187.

5. "Compton," *LAT*, March 12, 1933, 2.

6. "Fine New City, That's Compton," *LAT*, March 11, 1934, 26; "Most of the City's Schools Will Open Tomorrow," *LAT*, March 19, 1933, 1.

7. *Pacific Director Company's Compton City Directory 1946–1947*. For Los Angeles in this period, see Richard Griswold del Catillo, *The Los Angeles Barrio, 1850–1890: A Social History* (Berkeley: University of California Press, 1979).

8. "Compton," *LAT*, January 1, 1897, 33; Richard Bigger and James D. Kitchen, *Metropolitan Los Angeles: A Study in Integration*, vol. 2, *How the Cities Grew* (Los Angeles: John Randolph Haynes and Dora Haynes Foundation, 1952), 16.

9. "More Towns," *LAT*, January 1, 1887, 4.

10. "The World's Fair," *LAT*, January 15, 1893, 8.

11. Savannah Chalifoux, phone interview with author, August 16, 2007, interview in possession of author.

12. "Compton," *LAT*, January 1, 1897, 33; Secretary Improvement Association, "Compton, California: Facts, Figures and Illustrations of Interest to the Farmer, the Dairyman, the Gardener, and the Investor" (1905) in Local History Collection, "Compton, History—'Facts About Compton'; Info Booklets, 1905–1907," Folder, CSUDH.

13. John D. Weaver, "1909," *Westways* 71 (1979): 22.

14. Bigger and Kitchen, *How the Cities Grew*, 2.

15. Ibid., 5.

16. Compton by Methodists and Pasadena by a group from Indiana, ibid., 16.

17. Ann Scheid Lund, *Historic Pasadena: An Illustrated History* (San Antonio: Lammert Publications, 1999), 31.

18. Robert Winter, "Pasadena, 1900–1910: The Birth of Its Culture," *Southern California Quarterly* (Fall 2009): 295–317.

19. Michael E. James, *The Conspiracy of the Good: Civil Rights and the Struggle for Community in Two American Cities, 1875–2000* (New York: Peter Lang, 2005), 31.

20. Geoffrey Gilbert, "Our Neighbors," *LAT*, July 18, 1887, 7.

21. R. C. Gillingham, "Early Beginnings," in *Commemorative Souvenir of the Celebration of Compton's 75 Years as a City*, ed. F. C. Hemphill (Compton: Diamond Jubilee Committee of the City of Compton and Compton Chamber of Commerce, 1963), n.p.

22. Becky M. Nicolaides, "The Quest for Independence: Workers in the Suburbs," in *Metropolis in the Making: Los Angeles in the 1920s*, ed. Tom Sitton and William Francis Deverell (Berkeley: University of California Press, 2001), 80.

23. Greg Hise, "Industry and Imaginative Geographies," in *Metropolis in the Making*, ed. Sitton and Deverell, 18.

24. Clark Davis, *Company Men: White-Collar Life and Corporate Cultures in Los Angeles, 1892–1941* (Baltimore: Johns Hopkins University Press, 2000), 2.

25. Kevin Starr, *The Dream Endures: California Enters the 1940s* (New York: Oxford University Press, 1997), 12.

26. Louise H. Ivers, "The Evolution of Modernistic Architecture in Long Beach, California, 1928–1937," *Southern California Quarterly* 68 (1986): 257–91.

27. "A Thriving Farm Community," Compton's Centennial, 16.

28. Gillingham, "Early Beginnings."

29. "Trouble at Compton," *LAT*, September 20, 1893, 7.

30. Ibid., 7.

31. Gillingham, "Early Beginnings."

32. "Tail Wags the Canine," *LAT*, March 3, 1906, I11.

33. "Is Compton Still a City?" *LAT*, December 19, 1905, I16; "Curious Case Is Compton's," *LAT*, October 4, 1906, I12; Bigger and Kitchen, *How the Cities Grew*, 125–26.

34. "Is Compton Still a City?"; "Curious Case Is Compton's."

35. Walter Hodgin Case, *History of Long Beach and Vicinity* (New York: Arno Press, 1974), 129–42.

36. "City Council Minutes, November 23, 1906," CCH; "Is Compton Still a City?"

37. "City Council Minutes, April 7, 1907," CCH; "Compton Votes Bonds," *LAT*, July 10, 1907, I110; "City Council Minutes, July 20, 1907," CCH; "Compton Enjoys Rapid Growth," *LAT*, July 30, 1908, I18; "In Carnival Color Glows," *LAT*, May 13, 1916, I18.

38. Gerald E. Frug, *City Making: Building Communities Without Building Walls* (Princeton, N.J.: Princeton University Press, 1999), 50; Michan Connor, "Creating Cities and Citizens: Municipal Boundaries, Place Entrepreneurs, and the Production of Race in Los Angeles County, 1926–1978" (Ph.D. dissertation, University of Southern California, 2008).

39. Judith Rosenberg Raftery, *Land of Fair Promise: Politics and Reform in Los Angeles, 1885–1941* (Stanford, Calif.: Stanford University Press, 1992).

40. Constitution of the State of California, 1879, Article 9, Section 1.

41. Lawrence O. Picus, "Cadillacs or Chevrolets? The Effects of State Control on School Finance in California," *Journal of Education Finance* 17, 1 (March 1991): 3.

42. Case, *History of Long Beach and Vicinity*, 378.

43. Picus, "Cadillacs or Chevrolets?" 3–4.

44. Compton Junior College, "Compton Union District Secondary Schools Circular of Information and Announcement of Course, 1932–1933" (Compton, Calif., 1932), 13, Gutman.

45. "School Merger Planned," *LAT*, February 10, 1931, A2.

46. "City Council Minutes, January 27, 1931," CCH; "City Council Minutes, February 3, 1931," CCH.

47. Bigger and Kitchen, *How the Cities Grew*, 38–39.

48. Judith Raftery, "Implementing Public Education: City Schools," in *The Development of Los Angeles City Government: An Institutional History*, vol. 2, ed. Hyndra L. Rudd et al. (Los Angeles: Los Angeles City Historical Society, 2007), 565.

49. The district experimented with the plan beginning in 1930 and adopted it completely for the 1932–33 school year. Compton Junior College, "Compton Union District Secondary Schools Circular of Information and Announcement of Course, 1930–1931" (Compton, Calif., 1930), 7, Gutman; Compton Junior College, "Compton Union District Secondary Schools Circular of Information and Announcement of Course, 1932–1933" (Compton, Calif., 1932), 7, Gutman.

50. James, *The Conspiracy of the Good*, 127.

51. Raftery, "Implementing Public Education," 566.

52. Walter E. Mellinger, "Compton Is Growing at Fast Pace," *LAT*, August 12, 1923, V5; "Compton Sets Building Mark," *LAT*, January 10, 1926, E3.

53. "Compton Will Tell Its Story in Newspapers," *LAT*, February 3, 1924, E12; "Compton Puts Over Plan to Advertise City," December 14, 1925, A10; Helen Starr, "Figures Show Thriving Southwest Area of Compton and Lynwood Is Moving Ahead at Unprecedented Rate," *LAT*, June 7, 1925, G12.

54. Mellinger, "Compton Is Growing at Fast Pace."

55. "Another Industry," *LAT*, September 28, 1913, VI1; "Tire Factory to Open," *LAT*, November 6, 1913, II13.

56. "Tire Factory to Open."

57. "Compton Concern's Troubles," *LAT*, December 29, 1915, II5; "Tire Firm to Open Compton Plant Soon," *LAT*, February 17, 1916, III4; "Tire Company Will Expand," *LAT*, November 23, 1924, E12; "Southland Tire Will Step Out," *LAT*, December 7, 1924, G7; "Tire Firm Announces Expansion," *LAT*, May 10, 1925, F13.

58. For the automobile and the shaping of Los Angeles, see Scott L. Bottles, *Los Angeles and the Automobile: The Making of the Modern City* (Berkeley: University of California Press, 1987).

59. "Production of Industries at Compton Large," *LAT*, February 14, 1926, E2.

60. Mellinger, "Compton Is Growing at Fast Pace"; Becky M. Nicolaides, *My Blue Heaven: Life and Politics in the Working-Class Suburbs of Los Angeles, 1920–1965* (Chicago: University of Chicago Press, 2002).

61. "Population of Compton Shows Big Increase," *LAT*, February 14, 1926.

62. Nicolaides, *My Blue Heaven*, 41, 55.

63. Ibid., 8.

64. Josh Sides, "Straight into Compton: American Dreams, Urban Nightmares, and the Metamorphosis of a Black Suburb," *American Quarterly* 56 (September 2004): 585.

65. As cited in Douglas Flamming, *Bound for Freedom: Black Los Angeles in Jim Crow America* (Berkeley: University of California Press, 2006), 220.

66. Albert M. Camarillo, "Black and Brown in Compton: Demographic Change, Suburban Decline, and Intergroup Relations in a South Central Los Angeles Community, 1950 to 2000," in *Not Just Black and White: Historical and Contemporary Perspectives on Immigration, Race, and Ethnicity in the United States*, ed. Nancy Foner and George M. Fredrickson (New York: Russell Sage, 2004), 364.

67. Connor, "Creating Cities and Citizens," 168–69; Amy E. Hillier, "Residential Security Maps and Neighborhood Appraisals: The Home Owners' Loan Corporation and the Case of Philadelphia," *Social Science History* 29 (2005): 207–33.

68. "Willowbrook Seeks to Expel Negroes from School District," *LAS*, November 2, 1939, 1.

69. Ibid.

70. "School Transfer Halted," *LAS*, November 16, 1939, 1.

71. "Transfer of Pupils Hit," *LAS*, January 25, 1940, 1.

72. Alice Koons, "Back to First Principles," *LAT* September 25, 1932, G3; Clark Kerr, "Productive Enterprises of the Unemployed, 1931–1938" (Ph.D. dissertation, University of California, Berkeley, 1938), 83–84.

73. Koons, "Back to First Principles."

74. Kerr, 86.

75. "City Council Minutes, March 9, 1933," CCH; "City Council Minutes, March 28, 1933," CCH.

76. "Governor Holds Guard Ready," *LAT*, March 11, 1933; "Quake Centers at Long Beach," *LAT*, March 11, 1933; "Southland Starts Rebuilding After Survey Fixes Losses," *LAT*, March 12, 1933; "School Damage Surveyed," *LAT*, March 15, 1933.

77. "City Council Minutes, May 9, 1933," CCH; "City Council Minutes, July 11, 1933," CCH.

78. "560,000 Pupils in L.A. County Schools," *LAE*, September 10, 1933, EC.

79. Lloyd N. Morrisett and John A. Sexson, "A Report of a Survey of the Public Schools of the Compton Union High School and Junior College Districts" (Los Angeles County, 1949), 10.

80. Ibid.

81. "California's Disaster," *NYT*, March 12, 1933, E4.

82. "Salvation Army Dispenses with Red Tape in Relief," *LAT*, March 16, 1933, 7.

83. "Appeal to R.F.C.," *NYT*, March 16, 1933, 10.

84. "Dentists to Help Temblor Sufferers," *LAT*, March 15, 1933, A5.

85. "Throng Attends Town Fair," *LAT*, March 19, 1933, 17.

86. "Relief Is Speeded by Federal Forces," *NYT*, March 12, 1933, 1.

87. Ibid., 1, 24.

88. "Quake-Damage Aid Authorized," *LAT*, March 24, 1933, A1.

89. For example, all levels of government aided in rebuilding San Francisco after the 1906 earthquake and fire. See Dan Kurzman, *Disaster! The Great San Francisco Earthquake and Fire of 1906* (New York: W. Morrow, 2001).

90. "Minutes of an Adjourned Meeting, Enterprise Elementary School District Board of Trustees, November 16, 1933," Ed-P.S.R.-85–87, box 4, CUSD Board Minute Files, CSA.

91. "Earthquake Relief Quickly Mobilized," *NYT*, March 12, 1933, F23.

92. "Compton Fetes Recovery," *LAT*, September 15, 1933, D6; "Neptune to Rule," *LAT*, May 6, 1933.

93. "Compton City Hall Formal Reopening Program," in Local History Collection, Compton Folder, CSUDH.

94. Vierling Kersey, "Shall Public Schools in California Be Closed?" *California Schools* 4 (March 1933): 119–21.

95. Caughey, "The Long Beach Earthquake," 302.

96. As cited in ibid., 303.

97. Environmental Research Laboratories, "A Study of Earthquake Losses in the Los Angeles, California Area," 56. The Field and Riley Acts were Assembly Bills 2342 and 2391. For further discussion on the Field Act, see Harry W. Bolin, "The Field Act of the State of California," in *Proceedings of the Symposium on Earthquake*, ed. Duke and Feigen.

98. Binder, "Engineering Aspects of the 1933 Long Beach Earthquake," 189. See "Keep Buildings Safe," *LAT*, September 2, 1936, A4; "Law Upheld by Builders," *LAT*, August 26, 1936, A20.

99. "Adjusted Attendance Given to Compton City Schools," *CH*, August 10, 1934, 1; "Minutes of Regular Meeting, Compton City Elementary School District Board of Trustees, 21 June 1934," Ed-P.S.R.-85–87, box 1, CUSD Board Minutes Files, CSA.

100. "Minutes of Regular Meeting, Enterprise Elementary School District Board of Trustees, June 21, 1934," Ed-P.S.R.-85–87, box 4, CUSD Board Minute Files, CSA; "Minutes of Special Meeting, Enterprise Elementary School District Board of Trustees, June 30, 1934," Ed-P.S.R.-85–87, box 4, CUSD Board Minute Files, CSA; Elsey Hurt, *California State Government: An Outline of Its Administrative Organization, the Independent Agencies, 1850 to 1939*, vol. 2 (Sacramento: State Printing Office, 1936–1939), 58.

101. "$30,000 for Beautification Work at Schools," *CH*, September 18, 1936, 1.

102. "Minutes of Regular Meeting, Enterprise Elementary School District Board of Trustees, November 28, 1933," Ed-P.S.R.-85–87, box 4, CUSD Board Minute Files, CSA.

103. "New Deal President Gets Honor in Local School Name," *CH*, April 23, 1937, 1.

104. *Dar U Gar 1934*, Compton Junior College, 77, 86.

105. Ibid., n.p.

106. Ibid., 34.

107. Ibid., n.p.

108. Ibid., 66.

109. "Rebuilding Fete Near," *LAT*, March 26, 1936, A5.

110. Lee Shippey, "The Lee Side o' L.A.," *LAT*, September 25, 1935, A4.

111. "Billings Address Opens Campaign to Cut School Debts," *CH*, November 12, 1937, 1, 12. For outside funding being insufficient, see, for example, "Minutes of Regular Meeting, Enterprise Elementary School District Board of Trustees, November 29, 1938," Ed-P.S.R.-85–87, box 4, CUSD Board Minute Files, CSA.

112. "School Bond Ballot Called," *LAT*, June 2, 1938, 9; "Inglewood Bond Loses," *LAT*, June 4, 1938, A6.

113. "More About Future Growth of Compton Business District," *CH*, November 26, 1937, 2.

114. "Tax Is Highest of 10 Largest School Districts," *CH*, November 10, 1939, 2; "Taxes Attacked at Realty Meet Height of School," *CH*, November 17, 1939, 3; "Total Local Tax Rates Reach New High Levels," *CH* September 1, 1939, 1, 16.

115. "Total City Tax Rate Highest in LA County," *CH*, January 12, 1940, 2.

116. "5 New Schools for Compton," *LAE*, March 3, 1952, *EC*.

Chapter 2. The Fastest Growing Town

1. Ron Finger, phone interview with author, July 27, 2007, interview in possession of author.

2. Pamela Grimm, interview with author, July 13, 2007, Santa Monica, California, interview in possession of author.

3. Shirley Knopf, interview with author, July 10, 2007, Downey, California, interview in possession of author.

4. For studies on the economic and political impact of World War II on California and the West, see Roger W. Lotchin, ed., *The Way We Really Were: The Golden State in the Second World War* (Urbana: University of Illinois Press, 2000); Gerald D. Nash, *World War II and the West: Reshaping the Economy* (Lincoln: University of Nebraska Press, 1990); Harold G. Vatter, *The U.S Economy in World War II* (New York: Columbia University Press, 1985); Arthur C. Verge, "The Impact of the Second World War on Los Angeles," *Pacific Historical Review* 63 (1994): 289–314.

5. "Compton Leads Southland in Increase of Population," *LAT*, March 2, 1949, 1.

6. The call for local control was common among Southern California suburbanites, who used it to retain homogeneous communities and stable property values. See Eric Avila, *Popular Culture in the Age of White Flight* (Berkeley: University of California Press, 2004), 44; Gary Miller, *Cities by Contract: The Politics of Municipal Incorporation* (Cambridge, Mass.: MIT Press, 1981).

7. Arthur Verge, *Paradise Transformed: Los Angeles During the Second World War* (Dubuque, Iowa: Kendall/Hunt, 1993), 5.

8. Becky M. Nicolaides, *My Blue Heaven: Life and Politics in the Working-Class Suburbs of Los Angeles, 1920–1965* (Chicago: University of Chicago, Press, 2002) 187. Historians debate whether World War II transformed Southern California or the changes were a culmination of long-term developments. For proponents of the transformation idea, see Gerald D. Nash, *The American West Transformed: The Impact of the Second World War* (Bloomington: Indiana University Press, 1985); Nash, *World War II and the West*. For proponents of the continual processes idea, see Roger W. Lotchin, *Fortress California, 1910–1961: From Warfare to Welfare* (New York: Oxford University Press, 1992); Paul Rhode, "The Nash Thesis Revisited: An Economic Historian's View," *Pacific Historical Review* 63 (1994): 363–92; Abraham Shragge, "'A New Federal City': San Diego During World War II," *Pacific Historical Review* 63 (1994): 333–61.

9. Verge, *Paradise Transformed*, 6. Also see Carl Abbot, *The Metropolitan Frontier: Cities in the Modern American West* (Tucson: University of Arizona Press, 1993), 12–29; Henry S. Shryock, Jr., and Hope Tisdale Eldridge, "Internal Migration in Peace and War," *American Sociological Review* 12 (1947): 27–39; Josh Sides, *L.A. City Limits : African American Los Angeles from the Great Depression to the Present* (Berkeley: University of California Press, 2003).

10. Los Angeles Chamber of Commerce, "Collection of Eight Studies on the Industrial Development of Los Angeles County" (Los Angeles: Chamber of Commerce, n.d.); Nash, *The American West Transformed*, 213. For further discussion, see Philip Neff, Lisette Baum, and Grace E. Heilman, "Favored Industries in Los Angeles: An Analysis of Production Costs" (Los Angeles: Haynes Foundation, 1948); Douglas G. Monroy, "Mexicanos in Los Angeles, 1930–1941" (Ph.D. dissertation, University of California, Los Angeles, 1978), 71.

11. Greg Hise, "Home Building and Industrial Decentralization in Los Angeles: The Roots of the Postwar Urban Region," *Journal of Urban History* 19 (1993): 107–8.

12. Robert O. Self and Thomas J. Sugrue, "The Power of Place: Race, Political Economy, and Identity in the Postwar Metropolis," in *A Companion to Post-1945 America*, ed. Jean-Christophe Agnew and Roy Rosenzweig (Malden, Mass: Blackwell, 2006): 22; David M. P. Freund, *Colored Property: State Policy and White Racial Politics in Suburban America* (Chicago: University Of Chicago Press, 2007).

13. Nicolaides *My Blue Heaven*, 188; Sides, *L.A. City Limits*, 58.

14. Nicolaides, *My Blue Heaven*, 187; Shana Beth Bernstein, "Building Bridges at Home in a Time of Global Conflict: Interracial Cooperation and the Fight for Civil Rights in Los Angeles, 1933–1954," (Ph.D. dissertation, Stanford University, 2003), 170; *Compton Journal Pictorial Review & 1945 Annual* (1945).

15. Charles C. Cohan, "Los Angeles Development Reaches New Heights," *LAT*, January 2, 1948, E3.

16. Robert T. Hartmann, "City Home Building Lag Shown in Times Survey," *LAT*, April 13, 1948, 1.

17. Sides, *L.A. City Limits*, 59; Mark D. Van Ells, *To Hear Only Thunder Again: America's World War II Veterans Come Home* (Lanham, Md.: Lexington Books, 2001), 233; Freund, *Colored Property*.

18. Amy Elizabeth Hillier, "Redlining and the Home Owners' Loan Corporation" (Ph.D. dissertation, University of Pennsylvania, 2001). Hillier also questions to extent to which the HOCL maps mattered in redlining.

19. Bernstein, "Building Bridges at Home in a Time of Global Conflict," 172; Sides, *L.A. City Limits*, 98.

20. Deena R. Sosson, "History and Evaluation of the Compton-UCLA Urban Research and Development Project," in *Report on the Compton-UCLA Urban Research and Development Project, September 1968 to June 1969*, ed. Deena R. Sosson (Los Angeles: Institute of Government and Public Affairs, 1970), 12; Michael K. Brown, John O'Donnell, Averill Strasser, and Walter Szczepanek, "Social and Economic Problems of the City of Compton," in *Report on the Compton-UCLA Urban Research and Development Project*, ed. Sosson, b-3; Sides, *L.A. City Limits*, 125.

21. Compton Chamber of Commerce, "Pertinent Statistics, Compton, California, 1949," Compton Folder, Local History Collection, CSUDH.

22. "Parallel Parking Together with Municipal Parking Lost Is a Wise Solution's Traffic Problems," *CJ*, April 17, 1942, 4.

23. 1940 Census.

24. 1950 Census.

25. Lloyd N. Morrisett and John A. Sexson, "A Report of a Survey of the Public Schools of the Compton Union High School and Junior College Districts" (Los Angeles County, 1949)," 41.

26. Lawrence O. Picus, "Cadillacs or Chevrolets? The Effects of State Control on School Finance in California," *Journal of Education Finance* 17, 1 (March 1991), 4; "Compton Facing Test on New Tax," *LAT*, June 21, 1947, A3; "City Council Minutes, December 18, 1945," CCH; "City Council Minutes, September 2, 1947," CCH; "Census of Compton Starts Tomorrow," *CJI*, October 2, 1947, 1.

27. "Annual Report, City of Compton, For the Fiscal Year Ending June 30, 1949," 1, Local History Collection, Heritage House, City of Compton History, Box 5, Annual Reports folder, CSUDH.

28. "Annual Report, City of Compton, 1949," 31; "Annual Report, City of Compton, For the Fiscal Year Ending June 30, 1950," 27; "Report of the 1950–1951 Governmental Affairs, City of Compton, For the Fiscal Year Ending June 30, 1951," 23; "Annual Report, City of Compton, For the Fiscal Year Ending June 30, 1952," 27; Local History Collection, Heritage House, City of Compton History, box 5, Annual Reports folder, CSUDH.

29. 1940 Census; 1950 Census. In 1940 only 7.5 percent of Compton residents in the work force held professional jobs and this rose to only 8.6 percent in 1950.

30. It was 57.3 percent. Nicolaides, *My Blue Heaven*, 41.

31. 1940 Census; 1950 Census.

32. Morrisett and Sexson, "A Report of a Survey," 17, 21–26.

33. "City Council Minutes, January 13, 1942," CCH.

34. "City Council Minutes, February 18, 1942"; "City Council Minutes, March 10, 1942," CCH.

35. "City Council Minutes, March 24, 1942," CCH.

36. "Largest Permit in City's History for Victory Park," *CJ*, June 4, 1942, 1; "To Dedicate Victory Park," *CJI*, March 9, 1944, 1. The project ended up costing $1,728,000.

37. "Minutes of Regular Meeting, Compton City School District Board of Trustees, December 14, 1942," Official Minutes, Ed-P.S.R.-85–87, box 1, CUSD Board Minute Files, CSA.

38. "Big Housing Job Mapped as Vetter Tract Is Sold; Plan $750,000 Project," *CJ*, October 14, 1943, 1; "FHA Approves New Homes," *CJ*, October 21, 1943; "New Willowbrook Housing Project Work Started," *CJ*, December 9, 1943, 1; Connor, "Creating Cities and Citizens," 197.

39. Hal Draper, *Jim Crow in Los Angeles* (Los Angeles: Workers Party, 1946), 4.

40. Bernstein, "Building Bridges at Home in a Time of Global Conflict," 9.

41. R. J. Smith, *The Great Black Way: LA in the 1940s and the Lost African-American Renaissance* (New York: Public Affairs, 2006), 31. Historian Eduardo Pagán also put the Sleepy Lagoon trial and the Zoot Suit riots in this larger context: "the trial and riot were two episodes in a larger struggle over the structures of power and privilege in America, played out through contests over culture and social propriety." Eduardo Pagán, *Murder at the Sleepy Lagoon: Zoot Suits, Race, and Riot in Wartime L.A.* (Chapel Hill: University of North Carolina Press, 2003), 10; *People v. Zamora*, 66 Cal.App.2d 166 (1944).

42. Dominic J. Capeci, Jr., and Martha Wilkerson, *Layered Violence: The Detroit Rioters of 1943* (Jackson: University Press of Mississippi, 1991).

43. "City Council Minutes, January 18, 1944," CCH.

44. "City Council Minutes, January 25, 1944"; "City Council Minutes, February 1, 1944," CCH.

45. Morrisett and Sexson, "A Report of a Survey," 49.

46. "Federal Housing Agency to Build Project Near Compton," *CJI*, January 4, 1945, 1.

47. Ibid.

48. Lonnie G. Bunch, "Past Not Necessarily Prologue: The Afro-American in Los Angeles," in *20th Century Los Angeles: Power, Promotion, and Social Conflict*, ed. Norman M. Klein and Martin J. Schiesl (Claremont, Calif.: Regina Books, 1990), 117.

49. Sides, *L.A. City Limits*, 19. For more information on Watts, see Patricia Rea Adler, "Watts, from Suburb to Black Ghetto" (Ph.D. dissertation, University of Southern California, 1976); Norma Levinia Schneider, "And Night Becomes the Morning: A Story of the People of Watts" (MA thesis, California State University, Northridge, 1975).

50. Bureau of the Census, "Special Census of Compton, California, April 21, 1944" (Washington, D.C.: Government Printing Office, 1946). Many white Compton residents welcomed the Japanese internment, initiated by President Roosevelt's Executive Order 9066 on February 19, 1942. The order forced an estimated sixty thousand Japanese

American Angelenos out of their homes and businesses. In 1943, members of the Compton city council passed a resolution opposing the release of the interned from war relocation centers and sent a letter to Governor Earl Warren and Representative Ward Johnson to that effect. Executive Order 9066: Japanese Relocation Order, February 19, 1942, http://www.ourdocuments.gov/doc.php?flash=old&doc=74&page=transcript, accessed May 11, 2004; "City Council Minutes, July 1, 1943"; "City Council Minutes, July 20, 1943," CCH; "City's Resolution of Japs Received," *CJ*, July 22, 1943, 1.

51. In 1940, 57.3 percent of Compton residents held working-class jobs. Nicolaides, *My Blue Heaven*, 41, 55; Connor, "Creating Cities and Citizens," 171.

52. Douglass Flamming, *Bound for Freedom: Black Los Angeles in Jim Crow America* (Berkeley: University of California Press, 2005), 220.

53. Alberto M. Camarillo, "Chicano Urban History: A Study of Compton's Barrio, 1936–1970," *Aztlan* 2 (1971): 80–83.

54. "Entire Area Mobilizes to Fight War Housing Project," *CJI*, January 11, 1945, 1, 3.

55. "Compromise Boundary Limit Set on War Housing Project," *CJI*, January 18, 1945, 1, 2.

56. "Watts Situation Is Queer," *LAS*, March 13, 1947, 9.

57. "NAACP Challenging 'Ghetto' Plan of Compton Realtors," *LAS*, April 10, 1947, 1, 4; "Comptonites Use Veterans, F.H.A. to Cloak Race Drive," *LAS*, June 12, 1947, 4; "Unionists to Fight Compton Covenants," *LAS*, April 24, 1947, 19.

58. "Anti-Negro Signs in Compton," *LAS*, September 2, 1948, 1.

59. "New Paint Bomb Outrage Alarms Compton; White Woman Accused," *LAS*, October 7, 1948, 1, 4; "New Terrorism in Compton Unchecked," *LAS*, October 28, 1948, 1; "Lilly-Whites Terrorize Compton; Try 'Legal' Pressure in San Gabriel Area," *LAS*, September 30, 1948, A9; "Ku Klux Kompton," *LAS*, October 14, 1948, 23; "Negro Home Attacks Renewed," *LAS*, February 10, 1949, A1, A2.

60. "Serious Bulge in Enrollments Is Worry for Board," *CH*, August 9, 1940, 1, 9. For discussion of other cities that found their public resources stretched, see Abbot, *The Metropolitan Frontier*, 12–21; Richard White, *"It's Your Misfortune and None of My Own": A History of the American West* (Norman: University of Oklahoma Press, 1991), 507–8.

61. "Minutes of Regular Meeting, Enterprise Elementary School District Board of Trustees, December 15, 1941," Official Minutes, Ed-P.S.R.-85–87, box 4, CUSD Board Minute Files, CSA.

62. "Many Schools Crowded, Spare Space Used," *CJ*, November 18, 1943, 1.

63. Morrisett and Sexson, "A Report of a Survey," 128.

64. "Minutes of Regular Meeting, Enterprise Elementary School District Board of Trustees, September 21, 1942," Official Minutes, Ed-P.S.R.-85–87, box 4, CUSD Board Minute Files, CSA.

65. "38,000 in Funds Granted Schools," *CJ*, August 12, 1943, 1.

66. "Minutes of Regular Meeting, Compton City School District Board of Trustees,

November 8, 1943," Official Minutes, Ed-P.S.R.-85–87, box 1, CUSD Board Minute Files, CSA; "Approve School Lunch Subsidy in District Here," *HACH*, November 11, 1943, 1.

67. "Grant $68,597, to Local School," *CJI*, August 24, 1944, 1, 2.

68. "New Election Forecast on School Issue," *CJI*, May 24, 1945, 1.

69. "High Schools and College Need Million," *CJI*, March 8, 1945, 1, 6.

70. "$806,355 for School Extensions Is Sought," *CJI*, July 12, 1945, 1.

71. "Minutes of Regular Meeting, Compton City School District Board of Trustees, April 26, 1943," Official Minutes, Ed-P.S.R.-85–87, box 1, CUSD Board Minute Files, CSA; "Minutes of Regular Meeting, Compton City School District Board of Trustees, June 22, 1943," Official Minutes, Ed-P.S.R.-85–87, box 1, CUSD Board Minute Files, CSA.

72. "Lynwood Votes School Bonds by Substantial Majority," *CJI*, October 5, 1944, 1.

73. "School Pupil Cost Low Again," *CJI*, February 3, 1944, 2; "Minutes of Regular Meeting, Compton City School District Board of Trustees, January 12, 1942," Official Minutes, Ed-P.S.R.-85–87, box 1, CUSD Board Minute Files, CSA.

74. O. Scott Thompson, "Compton Junior College Play Big Part in War and Peace," *Compton Journal Pictorial Review & 1945 Annual* (1945).

75. Ibid.

76. "Minutes of Regular Meeting, Compton Union High School District Board of Trustees, August 2, 1943," Official Minutes, Ed-P.S.R.-81–94, box 1, CUSD Board Minute Files, CSA.

77. "High Schools Planning for Participation," *CJ*, April 1, 1943, 1; "Students Buy Bonds Here," *CJ*, May 6, 1943, 1; "Enterprise Sells $1900 in Bond Drive," *CJ*, April 22, 1943, 1; "Schools Here Make 100% Bond Sales," *CJ*, June 3, 1943, 1; "Two More Compton Schools Win Minute Men Flags," *CJ*, May 27, 1943, 1.

78. Thompson, "Compton Junior College Play Big Part in War and Peace"; "J.C. Student Drop Near 400," *HACH*, February 11, 1943, 1.

79. "Minutes of Regular Meeting, Enterprise School District Board of Trustees, July 20, 1942," Official Minutes, Ed-P.S.R.-85–87, box 4, CUSD Board Minute Files, CSA.

80. "Minutes of Regular Meeting, Enterprise School District Board of Trustees, September 21, 1942; December 21, 1942," Official Minutes, Ed-P.S.R.-85–87, box 4, CUSD Board Minute Files, CSA.

81. "Minutes of Regular Meeting, Compton City School District Board of Trustees, December 14, 1942," Official Minutes, Ed-P.S.R.-85–87, box 1, CUSD Board Minute Files, CSA.

82. "Minutes of Regular Meeting, Compton City School District Board of Trustees, January 24, 1944," Official Minutes, Ed-P.S.R.-85–87, box 1, CUSD Board Minute Files, CSA.

83. "Compton Third in School Area," *LAE*, April 10, 1949, EC; Los Angeles County Survey Committee, "Data Basic to the Study of the General Area Comprising the Compton Union High School District, April 1950," Compton Unified Reports Folder, Los Angeles County Commission of School District Organization Papers, LACOE, 2.

84. Morrisett and Sexson, "A Report of a Survey," 11.

85. Ibid., 45. Compton's need for double sessions was not unique in the California schools. See Charles Dorn, "'I Had All Kinds of Kids in My Classes, and It Was Fine': Public Schooling in Richmond, California, During World War II," *History of Education Quarterly* 45 (2005): 538–64.

86. "'Desperate' Classroom Need Told to State Senate Group," *LAT*, October 19, 1949, A1. The problems associated with overcrowding—not enough classrooms and not enough teachers—were not unique to Compton and its component districts. In the immediate postwar era, California as a whole was experiencing an "education boom," on all levels of schooling, from elementary through the university. See Kevin Starr, *Embattled Dreams: California in War and Peace, 1940–1950* (New York: Oxford University Press, 2002): 193.

87. "Rationing of Education for 500,000 Southland Children by 1951 Feared," *LAT*, October 20, 1949, A2.

88. "New Schools Will Rise in Compton," *LAT*, October 21, 1951, E1.

89. "U.S. Gives School $750,000 in Units," *CJI*, March 13, 1947, 1, 2; "State Aid for Local Schools," *CJI*, March 20, 1947, 1, 2; "School Bonds Get 9–1 Vote," *CJI*, December 15, 1949, 1; "Compton School Bonds Carry," *LAT*, October 16, 1948, 10; "Minutes of Special Meeting, Compton City School District Board of Trustees, December 16, 1949," Ed-P.S.R.-85–87, box 1, CUSD Board Minute Files, CSA.

90. For example, see "Minutes of Regular Meeting, Compton City School District Board of Trustees, September 13, 1948," Ed-P.S.R.-85–87, box 1, CUSD Board Minute Files, CSA; "Minutes of Regular Meeting, Compton City School District Board of Trustees, April 25, 1949," Ed-P.S.R.-85–87 CUSD Minute Files, box 1, CSA; "Minutes of Regular Meeting, Compton City School District Board of Trustees, May 9, 1949," Ed-P.S.R. 85–87, box 1, CUSD Board Minute Files 1, CSA; "$1,000,000 Program," *CJI*, May 25, 1947, 1, 6.

91. Diane Ravitch, *The Troubled Crusade: American Education, 1945–1980* (New York: Basic Books, 1983), 5.

92. 1940 Census; 1950 Census; Morrisett, "A Report of a Survey," 45.

93. For the enforcement of racial covenants, see, e.g., "City Council Minutes, September 7, 1948," CCH.

94. *Mendez v. Westminster School District of Orange County et al.* 64 F. Supp. 544 (C.D. Cal. 1946); *Westminster School District of Orange County v. Mendez*, 161 F.2d 774 (9th Cir. 1947); Morrisett and Sexson, "A Report of a Survey," 41. Also see, Camarillo, "Chicano Urban History."

95. Morrisett and Sexson, "A Report of a Survey," 8.

96. Ibid., 6.

97. Ibid., 16, 45.

98. James P. Allen and Eugene Turner, *The Ethnic Quilt: Population Diversity in Southern California* (Northridge, Calif.: Center for Geographic Studies, 1997), 80.

99. Morrisett and Sexson, "A Report of a Survey," 48.

100. "Opportunity Open to Schools to Ease Tension," *LAS*, January 16, 1947, 7.

101. "Trustees, Watchers Clash at Willowbrook Vote Count," *LAS*, May 30, 1946, 9.

102. "Students Walk Out on Insult at Compton," *LAS*, February 20, 1947, 9.

103. Morrisett and Sexson, "A Report of a Survey," 45.

104. Ibid., 23, 49. For information on the migration of blacks from the South to the Los Angeles region, see Sides, *L.A. City Limits*.

105. As cited in Morrisett and Sexson, "A Report of a Survey," 45.

106. James Jack Willard, *J. Jack Willard Recalls Lynwood: All American City, 50th Year* (Lynwood, Calif., 1971), 146.

107. Lourdes Castro Ramirez, "The Story of United Parents of Lynwood: Parents Organizing for Better Schools and Community" (M.A. thesis, University of California, Los Angeles, 2003), 12–13.

108. Willard, *J. Jack Willard Recalls Lynwood*, 147; "School District Separation on Ballot Today," *LAT*, November 18, 1949, 22; "No Muzzle for School Principal," *CJI*, October 27, 1949, 1. For demographic information on Lynwood and for parents' opinions on the elementary schools under their newly established unified school district, see Carlos Morrison Montandon, "An Inventory of Parent Opinion of the Public Schools of Lynwood, California, Pertaining to Certain Aspects of the Elementary School Program" (Ed.D. dissertation, Colorado State College of Education, 1952).

109. Willard, *J. Jack Willard Recalls Lynwood*, 148.

110. "Minutes of Regular Meeting, Compton Union High School District Board of Trustees, December 13, 1949," Ed-P.S.R.- 81–94, box 2, CUSD Board Minute Files, CSA.

111. Willard, *J. Jack Willard Recalls Lynwood*, 147.

112. "Jaysee Board Void," *CHA*, March 12, 1950, 1; "Void 4 Year Jaysee," *CHA*, January 26, 1950, 1; California Taxpayers' Association, "Organization and Fiscal Problems Involved in Unification of Compton Union High School District and Component Elementary Districts Compton City, Enterprise, Willowbrook," January 1956, Compton Unified Reports Folder, Los Angeles County Commission of School District Organization Papers, LACOE.

113. "Crisis in Schools," *CHA*, February 19, 1950, 1, 7; "School Plans Hotly Debated," *CHA*, February 16, 1950, 1; "Void 4 Year Jaysee."

114. Morrisett and Sexson, "A Report of a Survey," 93.

115. "Crisis in Schools"; "City Council Minutes, February 28, 1950," CCH; "School Unification Sought," *CHA*, February 23, 1950, 1.

116. Raftery, *Land of Fair Promise*; David A. Gamson, "District Progressivism: Rethinking Reform in Urban School Systems, 1900–1928," *Paedagogica Historica* 39 (2003): 417–34.

117. All quotations from, "Education Here Given High Praise," *CJI*, March 1, 1949, 2.

118. "Minutes of Regular Meeting, Willowbrook School District Board of Trustees, April 15, 1953," Ed-P.S.R. 85–87, box 3, CUSD Board Minute Files, CSA; "Minutes of Regular Meeting, Willowbrook School District Board of Trustees, March 25, 1953," Ed--P.S.R. 85–87, box 3, CUSD Board Minute Files, CSA.

119. Morrisett and Sexson, "A Report of a Survey," 2.

120. "All-America Cities," *Look*, February 10, 1953, 44.

121. Stated by William Holland in "All-America Cities," 44.

122. "Compton Group Gets Look Award," *LAS*, January 29, 1953, A4.

123. "New Schools Will Rise in Compton," *LAT*, October 21, 1951, E1; "To Open Bids for Jr. High," *CHA and the Compton Herald*, September 20, 1951, 1; "5 New Schools for Compton," *LAE*, March 3, 1952, EC; "Compton: Industrial Heart of the California Southland," 15, Local History Collection, box 3, History Business Directories folder, CSUDH; California Taxpayers' Association, "Organizational and Fiscal Problems Involved in Unification of Compton Union High School District and Component Elementary Districts Compton City, Enterprise, Willowbrook"; Sides, *L.A. City Limits*, 125. Overcrowding continued to produce the need for new buildings (and for more outside aid). See, for example, "Minutes of Regular Meeting, Compton Union High School District Board of Trustees, October 12, 1954," Ed-P.S.R.-81–94, box 3, CUSD Board Minute Files, CSA.

124. "Minutes of Regular Meeting, Enterprise School District Board of Trustees, March 10, 1954," Ed-P.S.R. 85–87, box 4, CUSD Board Minute Files, CSA.

125. "Minutes of Regular Meeting, Willowbrook School District Board of Trustees, February 7, 1951," Ed-P.S.R., box 3, CUSD Board Minute Files, CSA.

126. John L. Rury, "Who Became Teachers? The Social Characteristics of Teachers in American History," in *American Teachers: Histories of a Profession at Work*, ed. Donald Warren (New York: American Educational Research Association, 1989), 36. For discussion on the earlier feminization of teaching see, Geraldine Jonçich Clifford, "Man/Woman/Teacher: Gender, Family and Career in American Educational History," in *American Teachers*, ed. Donald Warren; Myra H. Strober and Audri Gordon Lanford, "The Feminization of Public School Teaching: Cross-Sectional Analysis, 1850–1880," *Signs* 11 (1986): 212–35.

127. "Bonds Issue Voted," *CHA*, October 22, 1950, 1; "Bonds Advance School Plans," *LAT*, October 22, 1950, 44; "Compton Approves Bonds, 2020 to 39," *LAT*, January 6, 1951, 6; "Minutes of Special Meeting, CUSD Board of Trustees, October 26, 1950," Ed-P.S.R. 81–94, box 2, CUSD Board Minute Files, CSA.

128. "10 School Districts Get $18,000,000 Building Aid," *LAT*, November 22, 1950, A6; "Clear Last Project in School Bldg. Program," *CHA*, August 17, 1952, 1; "School Aid Due for Compton," *LAE*, August 24, 1952, EC; "Schools to Get $127,942 U.S. Funds," *CHA*, August 17, 1952, 1; "School District Repayments Due This Year," *LAT*, May 15, 1952, 13; "Clear last Project in School Bldg. Program," *CHA*, November 20, 1952, 1; Public Law 874, 81st Congress (20 September 1950); "Minutes of Regular Meeting, Compton City School District Board of Trustees, February 25, 1957," Ed-P.S.R. 85–87, box 1, CUSD Board Minute Files, CSA.

129. Ibid.; California Taxpayers' Association, "Organizational and Fiscal Problems Involved in Unification of Compton Union High School District and Component Elementary Districts Compton City, Enterprise, Willowbrook"; "School Unification Sought"; "City Council Minutes, February 28, 1950," CCH; "District Moves for Unifica-

tion of All Schools," *LAT*, January 5, 1953, B7; "Minutes of Regular Meeting, Willowbrook School District Board of Trustees, October 13, 1953," Ed-P.S.R. 85–87, box 3, CUSD Board Minute Files, CSA.

130. "Minutes of Regular Meeting, Willowbrook School District Board of Trustees, December 12, 1961," Ed-P.S.R. 85–87, box. 3, CUSD Board Minute Files, CSA.

131. "Ask Big School Tax Boost," *CHA*, March 11, 1954, 1, 2; "High School Trustees Ask 60 Cents Hike in Taxes," *CHA*, May 13, 1954, 2.

132. Ibid.

133. "Minutes of Regular Meeting, Compton Union High School District Board of Trustees, February 25, 1957," Ed-P.S.R. 81–94, box 2, CUSD Board Minute Files, CSA.

134. "School Tax Raise Voted," *LAE*, May 30, 1954, EC. Voters in all of the districts were asked to raise the tax rates numerous times. See, for example, "Minutes of Regular Meeting, Compton City School District Board of Trustees, February 25, 1957," Ed-P.S.R. 85–87, box 1, CUSD Board Minute Files, CSA.

135. California Taxpayers' Association, "Organization and Fiscal Problems Involved in Unification of Compton Union High School District and Component Elementary Districts Compton City, Enterprise, Willowbrook," 4.

136. Frank P. Sherwood, "Some Major Problems of Metropolitan Areas," in *Metropolitan California*, ed. Ernest A. Engelbert (Sacramento: Governor's Commission on Metropolitan Area Problems), 16; John L. Rury and Shirley A. Hill, *The African American Struggle for Secondary Schooling 1940–1980: Closing the Graduation Gap* (New York: Teachers College Press, 2012), 99.

137. Hilary J. Moss, *The Struggle for African American Education in Antebellum America* (Chicago: University of Chicago Press, 2009); James Brewer Stewart, "The New Haven Negro College and the Meanings of Race in New England, 1776–1870," *New England Quarterly* 76 (2003): 323–77; James D. Anderson, *The Education of Blacks in the South, 1860–1935* (Chapel Hill: University of North Carolina Press, 1988); Adam Fairclough, *A Class of Their Own: Black Teachers in the Segregated South* (Cambridge, Mass.: Harvard University Press, 2007).

138. Rury and Hill, *The African American Struggle*; Perlstein, *Justice, Justice*; Jerald E. Podair, *The Strike that Changed New York: Blacks, Whites, and the Ocean Hill-Brownsville Crisis* (New Haven, Conn.: Yale University Press, 2002).

139. The per pupil costs for 1955–56 were budgeted at $245 for the Willowbrook Elementary District, $246 for the Compton City School District, and $279 for the Enterprise Elementary District. State Department of Education, Office of the Superintendent of Schools of Los Angeles County and the Bureau of School District Organization, "Report of the Los Angeles County Committee on School District Organization as Augmented for the Study of the Compton Union High School District, December 1953," Compton Unified Reports File, Los Angeles Commission on School District Organization, LACOE; Compton Union High School District Board of Trustees, "Statement in Support of Unification, April 24, 1962," Compton Unified Reports File, Los Angeles Commission on School District Organization, LACOE.

140. California Taxpayers' Association, "Organization and Fiscal Problems Involved in Unification of Compton Union High School District and Component Elementary Districts Compton City, Enterprise, Willowbrook," 10–12.

141. See, for example, "Minutes of Regular Meeting, Compton City School District Board of Trustees, September 28, 1959," Ed-P.S.R. 85–87, box 1, CUSD Board Minute Files, CSA.

142. "Minutes of Regular Meeting, Enterprise School District Board of Trustees, December 13, 1955," Ed-P.S.R. 85–87, box 4, CUSD Board Minute Files, CSA; "Minutes of Regular Meeting, Enterprise School District Board of Trustees, February 22, 1956," Ed-P.S.R. 85–87, box 4, CUSD Board Minute Files, CSA.

143. "150 Attend New Bunche School Rites," *LAE*, March 2, 1956, EC.

144. "Minutes of Regular Meeting, Enterprise School District Board of Trustees, October 11, 1961," Ed-P.S.R. 85–87, box 4, CUSD Board Minute Files, CSA.

Chapter 3. Separate and Unequal

1. As cited in Bob Ellis, "The Story of Reeve Street in Compton," *CE*, May 14, 1953, 8.

2. As cited in Bob Ellis, "Frightened Family Hides After Sale of Home to Negro," *CE*, May 21, 1953, 8.

3. "Compton Tract Will Be Open," *LAT*, July 23, 1950, F1; Ellis, "The Story of Reeve Street in Compton," 1. For the advertisements, see, for example, Classified Ad, No Title, *LAT*, July 14, 1950, B11; Classified Ad, No Title, *LAT*, July 19, 1950, B14.

4. Camarillo, "Black and Brown in Compton"; Josh Sides, *L.A. City Limits: African American Los Angeles from the Great Depression to the Present* (Berkeley: University of California Press, 2003), 125–29; Josh Sides, "Straight into Compton: American Dreams, Urban Nightmares, and the Metamorphosis of a Black Suburb," *American Quarterly* 56 (September 2004): 583–605.

5. *Barrows v. Jackson* 17 346 U.S. 249 (1953); *Shelley v. Kraemer* 334 U.S. 1 (1948). Change was not immediate. It was not until two years after the *Shelley* decision that the Federal Housing Administration stopped issuing mortgages to real estate that had covenants. Even then real estate agents found ways of discriminating. See Kenneth T. Jackson, *Crabgrass Frontier: the Suburbanization of the United States* (New York: Oxford University Press, 1985), 208. For Los Angeles in particular, see Susan Anderson, "A City Called Heaven: Black Enchantment and Despair in Los Angeles," in *The City: Los Angeles and Urban Theory at the End of the Twentieth Century*, ed. Allen J. Scott and Edward W. Soja (Berkeley: University of California Press, 1998), 344–46.

6. Otis Skinner, interview with author, October 19, 2004, Compton, California, interview in possession of author. Sides, "Straight into Compton," 585–86; Camarillo, "Black and Brown in Compton," 363–65. For a more general discussion on race and housing in all Los Angeles during the postwar, see Sides, *L.A. City Limits*, 95–130.

7. Winston W. Crouch and Beatrice Binerman, *Southern California Metropolis: A Study in Development of Government for a Metropolitan Area* (Berkeley: University of California Press, 1964), 231.

8. Sides, *L.A. City Limits*, 126.

9. Ibid., 159.

10. Omar Bradley, *The King of Compton! The Assassination of a Dream* (Los Angeles: Milligan Books, 2007), 16; David Franklin, "Compton: A Community in Transition" (Los Angeles: Welfare Planning Council, 1962), 1–3. For an overview of African American suburbs, see Wiese, *Places of Their Own*.

11. Bradley, *The King of Compton!*, 17.

12. As cited in Sides, *L.A. City Limits*, 126.

13. Maxcy Filer, interview with author, June 23, 2005, Compton, California, interview in possession of author.

14. Linda Allen, interview with author, October 18, 2004, Compton California, interview in possession of author.

15. Fred Cressel, interview with author, October 19, 2004, Compton, California, interview in possession of author.

16. Interview with Sylvester Gibbs, conducted by Josh Sides, June 2, 1998, transcripts donated to SCLSSR.

17. Lorraine Cervantes, interview with author, October 20, 2004, Compton, California, interview in possession of author.

18. Thomas J. Sugrue, *Sweet Land of Liberty: The Forgotten Struggle for Civil Rights in the North* (New York: Random House, 2009), 204.

19. Grimm, interview with author.

20. "Compton: Industrial Heart of the California Southland," 10, Local History Collection, box 3, History Business Directories folder, CSUDH.

21. Wendell Green, "Vigilantes Brutally Beat Man over Sale to Negroes," *CE*, February 19, 1953, 1.

22. Ibid., 2.

23. Grace E. Simons, "Brokers Arrested," *CE*, March 5, 1953, 1.

24. "Compton and the Constitution," *CE*, March 5, 1953, 4.

25. "Brokers Lay Plans for Compton Battle," *CE*, April 16, 1953, 3.

26. "Compton Acquits All 5 Realty Board Brokers," *CE*, May 7, 1953, 1.

27. "Compton Vandals Stage Sneak Attack," *CE*, April 16, 1953, 1.

28. "Guard Homes as Pickets March," *CE*, May 14, 1953, 1.

29. Ellis, "The Story of Reeve Street in Compton," 1.

30. "Auto Worker Condemned for Aiding Pickets," *CE*, May 21, 1953, 1; "UAW Censures Member for Compton Action," *CE* July 23, 1953, 1.

31. For discussion of homeowners' associations as the arbiters of the middle class in Los Angeles, see Mike Davis, *City of Quartz: Excavating the Future in Los Angeles* (New York: Verso, 1990), 160–64. For discussion of white homeowners' protection of their neighborhoods as protection of their class status, see Becky M. Nicolaides, *My Blue Heaven: Life and Politics in the Working-Class Suburbs of Los Angeles, 1920–1965* (Chicago: University of Chicago, Press, 2002); Thomas J. Sugrue, *Origins of the Urban Crisis: Race and Inequality in Postwar Detroit* (Princeton, N.J.: Princeton University Press, 1996).

32. "Plans Laid to Fight Against Compton Bias," *CE*, April 9, 1953, 2.

33. Ellis, "The Story of Reeve Street in Compton," 8.

34. "Compton Housing Row Flares," *CE*, May 14, 1953, 1.

35. "Invitation to Disaster," *CE*, April 23, 1953, 4.

36. All quotations in paragraph from "Full Compton Story Told in Eagle Series," *CE*, May 14, 1953, 8.

37. Ibid.

38. As cited in Franklin, "Compton," 83.

39. Eric Avila, *Popular Culture in the Age of White Flight* (Berkeley: University of California Press, 2004), 49; Sides, *L.A. City Limits*, 97.

40. Avila, *Popular Culture in the Age of White Flight*, 50.

41. Sides, *L.A. City Limits*, 127.

42. Gisele Hudson, "Compton Boosters Claim Affordable Homes, City Location Are Big Assets," March 1990, Compton Unified School District Folder, Compton File, CPL.

43. Sugrue, *Sweet Land of Liberty*, 205.

44. "Compton Home Attacked," *CE*, June 25, 1953, 2.

45. Ibid.

46. *CE*, June 25, 1953

47. "Why No Action, Compton Police?" *CE*, June 25, 1953, 2.

48. Grace E. Simons, "Compton Vandals in Sneak Attacks," *CE*, July 2, 1953, 1.

49. "Curb These Hudlums Now," *CE*, July 9, 1953, 4; Simons, "Compton Vandals in Sneak Attacks," 1–2.

50. Grace E. Simons, "Teenagers Sentenced," *CE*, February 26, 1953, 1.

51. "Compton Lads Get Suspended Terms," *CE*, March 5, 1953, 1.

52. Ellis, "Frightened Family Hides After Sale of Home to Negro," 1, 8.

53. *Barrows v. Jackson*; Patricia Rea Adler, "Watts, from Suburb to Black Ghetto" (PhD diss., University of Southern California, 1976), 301; Sides, *L.A. City Limits*, 121.

54. Bureau of the Census, U.S. Department of Commerce, "Special Census of Compton, California, April 30, 1952" (Washington, D.C.: Government Printing Office, 1952); Bureau of the Census, U.S. Department of Commerce, "Special Census of Compton, California, March 7, 1955" (Washington, D.C.: Government Printing Office, 1955). White residents' desire to resist the *Shelley* and *Barrows* decisions was not unique to Compton and existed in other Los Angeles suburbs. See, for example, Nicolaides, *My Blue Heaven*, 211.

55. Interview with Mary Cutherbertson, conducted by Josh Sides, June 20, 1998, transcripts donated to SCLSSR. Emphasis is in the original transcript.

56. Bradley, *The King of Compton!*, 4.

57. Grimm, interview with author.

58. Knopf, interview with author.

59. Letter to Everett P. Brandon, Field Secretary, NAACP, from Vannoy Thomspon, folder 37, Compton Ca, Undated 1955–1981, box 78, NAACP.

60. Knopf, interview with author.

61. Brad Pye, Jr., "Compton 'Queen' Causes Row," *LAS*, October 30, 1958, A1.

62. Finger, interview with author.

63. Sides, *L.A. City Limits*, 159. These problems of segregation and unequal education opportunities and facilities became the basis for the 1963 lawsuit *Crawford v. Board of Education of the City of Los Angeles*. The suit concerned Watts Jordan High school and nearby South Gate High. Separated by only a mile, their racial compositions were polar opposites. Jordan was 99 percent black while South Gate was 97 percent white. It took the judge seven years to rule on the case, but when he did in 1970, he ordered the school district to desegregate its nearly 700,000 students. Schneider, "Escape from Los Angeles," 999.

64. Charles Wollenberg, *All Deliberate Speed: Segregation and Exclusion in California Schools, 1855–1975* (Berkeley: University of California Press, 1976), 139.

65. Julie Salley Gray, "'To Fight the Good Fight': The Battle over Control of the Pasadena City Schools, 1969–1979," *Essays in History* 37 (1995).

66. Ann Scheid Lund, *Historic Pasadena: An Illustrated History* (San Antonio: Lammert Publications, 1999), 90.

67. Michael E. James, *The Conspiracy of the Good: Civil Rights and the Struggle for Community in Two American Cities, 1875–2000* (New York: Peter Lang, 2005), 275. *Brown* was not the only event to push the federal government into the arena of public education. When the Soviet Union launched Sputnik, the first satellite to orbit the earth, in October 1957, Americans panicked that they had lost their edge in the Cold War. Americans examined their own country in relation to the Soviet's success and concluded that American children needed to learn more mathematics and science to be competitive in the Cold War world. The federal government followed this lead, passing the National Defense Education Act the next year. The act granted over $1 billion in aid to public schools originally for a four year period beginning with the 1958–59 school year. This was the first comprehensive education legislation on the federal level. Along with this federal aid came a push for curricula revision, which came to fruition in the late 1950s and 1960s. Disciplinary scholars in the sciences and in mathematics developed new courses for K-12 students. Changes in history and social science course curricula soon followed. Yet, the renovations resulted in mixed outcomes because the authors lacked knowledge of the ins-and-outs of schooling and the teachers who implemented the new curriculum often lacked the nuanced knowledge of the discipline. Wayne J. Urban and Jennings L. Wagoner, Jr., *American Education: A History*, 3rd ed. (Boston: McGraw Hill, 2004), 296–97.

68. Gray, "'To Fight the Good Fight.'"

69. Grace E. Simons, "Pasadena Board Okehs Jim Crow School," *CE*, September 17, 1953, 1; "Push Fight Against Pasadena Schools," *CE*, November 19, 1953, 1.

70. Lund, *Historic Pasadena*, 90.

71. *Jay R. Jackson Jr. v. Pasadena City School District et al.*, 59 California 2d 876.

72. Wollenberg, *All Deliberate Speed*, 143.

73. James, *The Conspiracy of the Good*, 280.

74. "Minutes of Regular Meeting, Compton Union High School District Board of Trustees, August 5, 1958," Ed-P.S.R.- 81–94, box 3, CU.S.D Board Minute Files, CSA.

75. "Minutes of Regular Meeting, Compton Union High School District Board of Trustees, August 26, 1958," Ed-P.S.R.- 81–94, box 3, CU.S.D Board Minute Files, CSA.

76. "Dedication of Bunche Junior High school, Compton Union High School District, Speech 1958 April 10," Collection 2051, box 372, UCLA.

77. Ibid.

78. Grimm, interview with author.

79. Franklin, "Compton," 68–69.

80. Bradley, *The King of Compton!*, 18–19.

81. National Advisory Commission of Civil Disorders, *Report of the National Advisory Commission on Civil Disorders*, 2 vols. (Washington, D.C.: Government Printing Office, 1968).

82. Lassiter and Niedt, "Suburban Diversity in Postwar America," 4.

83. M. Filer, interview with author.

84. "Minutes of Regular Meeting, Compton Union High School District Board of Trustees, June 25, 1963," Ed-P.S.R.- 81–94, box 3, CU.S.D Board Minute Files, CSA.

85. Ibid.

86. Franklin, "Compton," 71.

87. As cited in ibid., 70.

88. Ibid., 70.

89. Bradley, *The King of Compton!* 20–21.

90. Kelvin Filer, interview with author, June 23, 2005, Compton, California, interview in possession of author.

91. Pamela Samuels-Young, interview with author, June 20, 2005, Compton, California, interview in possession of author.

92. *The Challenge*, Compton NAACP newsletter, March 1958, folder 39, Compton Ca, newsletters 1958, 1970–1972, box 78, NAACP; Letter to Hadessah Snider, from Tarea Hall Pittman, folder 37, Compton Ca, Undated 1955–1981, box 78, NAACP.

93. *The Challenge*, March 1958, ellipses in original.

94. M. Filer, interview with author.

95. *The Challenge*, February 1958.

96. Sides, *L.A. City Limits*, 165–67.

97. NAACP Flier, undated, folder 37, Compton CA, Undated 1955–1981, box 78, NAACP.

98. M. Filer, interview with author; "Compton NAACP Claims Bias in Bank Hiring," *LAS*, July 10, 1958, A2; "Compton NAACP Vows to Picket Bank Until Negroes Hired," *LAS*, September 4, 1958, A2; "Compton NAACP's Bank Picket Enters 3rd Month," *LAS*, October 30, 1958, A3.

99. *The Challenge*, March 1958, folder 39, Compton Ca, newsletters 1958, 1970–1972, box 78, NAACP.

100. Brad Pye, Jr., "Will Centennial High Become Another Little Rock?" *LAS*, April 16, 1959, C1; Brad Pye, Jr., "Librarian Case Held 'Explosive'" *LAS*, April 30, 1959, A1; Brad Pye, Jr., "Centennial Librarian Stays" *LAS*, May 14, 1959, A1, A2.

101. Letter to unnamed Field Secretary of the NAACP, from Odessa Ausbrooks, folder 37, Compton Ca, Undated 1955–1981, box 78, NAACP.

102. "Compton NAACP Told 'Get Hell Out of Town,'" *LAS*, October 13, 1960, A1.

103. "Bigots Hit NAACP Office in Compton," *LAS*, November 10, 1960, A4.

104. Franklin, "Compton," 51–52, 83; "Human Relations Council Begins Membership Drive," *LAS*, June 27, 1963, B3.

105. For the debate over the establishment of the Human Relations Committee, see "City Council Minutes, February 18, 1964" and "City Council Minutes, September 1, 1964," CCH. For the resolution, see "City Council Minutes, September 14, 1965," CCH.

106. "NAACP Offices Hit by 13 Shots," *LAS*, December 14, 1961, A1.

107. Ibid., 1, 2; "Teen Violence Plagues Police at High School," *CHA*, February 9, 1962, 1, 2. These were not the first set of brawls. Similar incidents had occurred in 1959 and 1960. See "Police Quell Post-Game Teen Brawl," *LAS*, October 8, 1959, A1; Clarice Gray, "PTA Council Probes Rioters," *LAS*, October 13, 1960, B12.

108. "Fourteen More Arrested in High School Violence," *CHA*, February 15, 1962, 1.

109. Alberto M. Camarillo, "Chicano Urban History: A Study of Compton's Barrio, 1936–1970," *Aztlan* 2 (1971): 81.

110. Ibid., 90.

111. Franklin, "Compton," 25.

112. Sugrue, *Sweet Land of Liberty*, 205.

113. Kevin M. Kruse, *White Flight: Atlanta and the Making of Modern Conservatism* (Princeton, N.J.: Princeton University Press, 2005), 5.

114. Finger, interview with author.

115. Franklin, "Compton," 28.

116. Interview with Sylvester Gibbs, conducted by Josh Sides, June 2, 1998, transcripts donated to the SCLSSR.

117. Katherine P. Nelson, interview with author, October 21, 2004, Compton, California, interview in possession of author.

118. Grimm, interview with author.

119. Gary Miller, *Cities by Contract: The Politics of Municipal Incorporation* (Cambridge, Mass: MIT Press, 1981), 17.

120. Alida Brill, "Lakewood, California: 'Tomorrowland' at 40," in *Rethinking Los Angeles*, ed. Michael J. Dear et al. (Thousand Oaks, Calif.: Sage, 1996), 99.

121. Avila, *Popular Culture in the Age of White Flight*, 42–43.

122. As cited in Daniel HoSang, *Racial Propositions: Ballot Initiatives and the Making of Postwar California* (Berkeley: University of California Press, 2010), 58.

123. 1960 Census.

124. Davis, *City of Quartz*, 165; Miller, *Cities by Contract*, 20; Michan Andrew

Connor, "'Public Benefits from Public Choice': Producing Decentralization in Los Angeles, 1954–1973," *Journal of Urban History* 39 (2013): 79–100.

125. Connor, "Public Benefits," 80.

126. Crouch and Binerman, *Southern California Metropolis*, 220–21.

127. Miller, *Cities by Contract*, 177.

128. Michael K. Brown, John O'Donnell, Averill Strasser, and Walter Szczepanek, "Social and Economic Problems of the City of Compton," in *Report on the Compton-UCLA Urban Research and Development Project, September 1968 to June 1969*, ed. Deena R. Sosson (Los Angeles: Institute of Government and Public Affairs, 1970), b-3.

129. Miller, *Cities by Contract*, 17.

130. Avila, *Popular Culture in the Age of White Flight*, 46.

131. Brown, O'Donnell, Strasser, and Szczepanek, "Social and Economic Problems of the City of Compton," b-3; Ahmed Mohammed Widaatalla, "Effect of Racial Change on the Tax Base of the City of Compton" (Ph.D. dissertation, University of California, Los Angeles, 1970), 158, 122, 126, 11–12.

132. Regional Planning Commission, "Willowbrook School District Study, Phase No. 1," 15.

133. Davis, *City of Quartz*, 169.

134. Michan Connor, "Creating Cities and Citizens: Municipal Boundaries, Place Entrepreneurs, and the Production of Race in Los Angeles County, 1926–1978" (Ph.D. dissertation, University of Southern California, 2008), 301.

135. Connor, "Public Benefits," 81.

136. Widaatalla, "Effect of Racial Change on the Tax Base of the City of Compton," 98.

137. HoSang, *Racial Propositions*, 58.

138. Sides, *L.A. City Limits*, 86–87.

139. Connor, "Creating Cities and Citizens," 202.

140. HoSang, *Racial Propositions*, 58.

141. Avila, *Popular Culture in the Age of White Flight*, 47.

142. Ibid.

143. Ernest A. Engelbert, ed., *Metropolitan California* (Sacramento: Governor's Commission on Metropolitan Area Problems), 3.

144. For discussion on the passage of California's Fair Employment Practices Commission, see Ethan Rarick, *California Rising: The Life and Times of Pat Brown* (Berkeley: University of California Press, 2005): 123–34; Mark Brilliant, *The Color of America Has Changed: How Racial Diversity Shaped Civil Rights Reform in California, 1941–1978* (New York: Oxford University Press, 2010), 159–61.

145. Compton City Manager, "Planning Grant Application: Model Neighborhood Demonstration Program" (Compton, 1967): Part 1A, 2; Part 1B, 1.

146. Ibid., 112–14; Regional Planning Commission, "Willowbrook School District Study, Phase No. 1," 9.

147. In discussing San Leandro, a northern California East Bay suburb, Robert Self

showed the benefits of a town not holding any bonded debt. See Robert O. Self, *American Babylon: Race and the Struggle for Postwar Oakland* (Princeton, N.J.: Princeton University Press, 2003), 108.

148. Morrisett and Sexson, "A Report of a Survey," 193.

149. Tai Jun Cho, "Commercial Structures in Three Ethnically Different Areas: Compton, East Los Angeles, and Riverside" (Ph.D. dissertation, University of California, Riverside, 1975), 128.

150. Brown "Social and Economic Problems of the City of Compton," b–5.

151. "Compton: Industrial Heart of the California Southland," 44, Local History Collection, box 3, History Business Directories folder, CSUDH.

152. Ibid., 43.

153. Ibid., 75.

154. For example, see "Willowbrook School Bonds Approved," *LAT*, January 30, 1957, 7; "Compton Plans to Build Schools," *LAT*, March 8, 1959, SC3; "Minutes of Regular Meeting, Compton City School District Board of Trustees, October 22, 1962," Ed--P.S.R. 85–87, box 1, CU.S.D Board Minute Files, CSA. Not all their attempts to pass bonds succeeded, though. For an example of a failed attempt, see "Minutes of Regular Meeting, Compton Union High School District Board of Trustees, April 23, 1963," Ed--P.S.R. 81–94, box 5, CU.S.D Board Minute Files, CSA.

155. "Minutes of Regular Meeting, Compton Union High School District Board of Trustees, October 22, 1963," Ed-P.S.R. 81–94, box 5, CU.S.D Board Minute Files, CSA; "Minutes of Regular Meeting, Compton Union High School District Board of Trustees, October 27, 1964," Ed-P.S.R. 81–94, box 6, CU.S.D Board Minute Files, CSA.

156. "Minutes of Regular Meeting, Compton Union High School District Board of Trustees, January 26, 1965," Ed-P.S.R. 81–94, box 6, CU.S.D Board Minute Files, CSA.

157. "Dollarhide Wins Council Seat: Victory Sets a Precedent," *LAS*, June 6, 1963, A1.

158. "Dollarhide Stuns Compton, Winds in City Council Race," *LAS*, May 9, 1963, A2.

159. A.S. "Doc" Young, "Appoint Negro to Compton School Board," *LAS*, July 18, 1963, B1.

160. "Name Negro to Compton City Planning Commission," *LAS*, August 29, 1963, C3.

161. "Burning Cross on Lawn Greets Doctor on All-White Block," *LAS*, November 21, 1963, A1, A4.

162. "Clawson Survey Finds 'Deep Racial Prejudice,'" *LAT*, October 12, 1963, 12. Clawson's district encompassed the suburbs of South Gate, Huntington Park, Bell Maywood, Vernon, Bell Gardens, Cudahy, Lynwood, Compton, Paramount, Bellflower, and Downey.

163. "Clawson Votes Against Rights Bill," *LAS*, February 13, 1964, B1.

164. *Burks v. Poppy Construction Company*, 20 Cal. Rptr. 618 (1962); *Lee v. O'Hara*, 20 Cal. Rptr. 617 (1962); *Vargas v. Hampson*, 20 Cal. Rptr. 618 (1962).

165. HoSang, *Racial Propositions*, 61–62.

166. For discussion on the passage of the Rumford Act, see Rarick, *California Rising*, 261–67; Brilliant, *The Color of America Has Changed*, 176–92; HoSang, *Racial Propositions*, 53–90.

167. Thomas W. Casstevens, *Politics, Housing and Race Relations: California's Rumford Act and Proposition 14* (Berkeley, Calif.: Institute of Governmental Studies, 1967); Raymond Wolfinger and Fred Greenstein, "The Repeal of Fair Housing in California: An Analysis of Referendum Voting," *American Political Science Review* 62 (September 1968): 753; Nicolaides, *My Blue Heaven*, 308; Rarick, *California Rising*, 273–75, 288–89.

168. "Rumford Housing Act Discussed at Human Relations Council Meeting," *LAS*, October 31, 1963, C3; "Negroes Unite to Save Fair Housing Bill," *LAS*, December 5, 1963, B1; "No Vote on 14 Group Open in Compton Sat," *LAS*, July 16, 1964, D1.

169. Nicolaides, *My Blue Heaven*, 308.

170. As cited in Self, *American Babylon*, 264. For discussion of the movement in support of Proposition 14 using rights-based language, see Self, *American Babylon*, 260–68; Brilliant, *The Color of America Has Changed*, 194.

171. *Understanding the Riots: Los Angeles Before and After the Rodney King Case* (Los Angeles: Los Angeles Times, 1992), 21.

172. David O. Sears, "Black-White Conflict: A Model for the Future of Ethnic Politics in Los Angeles?" in *New York and Los Angeles: Politics, Society, and Culture, a Comparative View*, ed. David Halle (Chicago: University of Chicago Press, 2003), 369.

173. "Compton City Council Nixes Proposition 14," *LAS*, August 13, 1964, D2.

174. Frank M. Jordan, California Secretary of State, *Supplement to Statement of Vote, November 3, 1964* (Sacramento: California Secretary of State, 1964), 68; 1960 Census.

175. Governor's Commission on the Los Angeles Riots, *Violence in the City—An End or a Beginning? A Report* (Los Angeles, 1965), 3.

176. Rarick, *California Rising*, 320.

177. Kevin Starr discusses in depth the "California Dream" in his book series Americans and the California Dream (New York: Oxford University Press) For the rise and fall of the "California Dream," also see Peter Schrag, *Paradise Lost: California's Experience, America's Future*, (Berkeley: University of California Press, 1998), 27–62.

Chapter 4. Becoming Urban

1. M. Filer, interview with author.

2. Ibid.

3. Josh Sides, "Straight into Compton: American Dreams, Urban Nightmares, and the Metamorphosis of a Black Suburb," *American Quarterly* 56 (September 2004): 591, 593.

4. Earl Caldwell, "City in California, 72% Black, Looks to Future Despite Woes," *NYT*, January 19, 1973, 18.

5. James P. Allen and Eugene Turner, *The Ethnic Quilt: Population Diversity in Southern California* (Northridge, Calif.: Center for Geographic Studies, 1997), 78; Governor's Commission on the Los Angeles Riots, *Violence in the City—An End or a Beginning? A Report* (Los Angeles, 1965), 1; Fair Employment Practices Commission, "Negroes and Mexican Americans in South and East Los Angeles: Changes Between 1960 and 1965 in Population, Employment, Income, and Family Status" (San Francisco, 1966), 5, 17, 19.

6. Brian Cross, *It's Not About a Salary: Rap, Race and Resistance in Los Angeles* (London: Verso, 1993), 9

7. For detailed accounts of the riots see Governor's Commission, *Violence in the City*; Paul Bullock, ed., *Watts: The Aftermath—An Inside View of the Ghetto by the People of Watts* (New York: Grove Press, 1969); Jerry Cohen and William S. Murphy, *Burn, Baby, Burn: The Los Angeles Race Riot, August 1965* (New York: Dutton, 1966); Robert Conot, *Rivers of Blood, Years of Darkness: The Unforgettable Classic Account of the Watts Riot* (New York: W. Morrow, 1967); Gerald Horne, *The Fire This Time: The Watts Uprising and the 1960s* (New York: De Capo, 1997); and David O. Sears and John B. McConahay, *The Politics of Violence: The New Urban Blacks and the Watts Riots* (Boston: Houghton Mifflin, 1973).

8. Alonzo A. Crim, "Educating All God's Children," in *Reflections: Personal Essays by 33 Distinguished Educators*, ed. Derek L. Burleson (Bloomington, Ind.: Phi Delta Kappa Educational Foundation, 1991), 92; Sides, "Straight into Compton," 591, 589.

9. M. Filer, interview with author.

10. Governor's Commission, *Violence in the City*. The McCone commission had its skeptics because of its composition. The panel chair was the former head of the CIA and a political conservative who lacked credibility with the black community in Watts. The two black members were a judge and a minister and their class status also made them circumspect to the residents of Watts. The report confirmed some of the skepticism as it neither dealt in depth with racism nor criticized police leadership. See Ethan Rarick, *California Rising: The Life and Times of Pat Brown* (Berkeley: University of California Press, 2005), 336–37. The two state representatives for the affected districts did not sit on the commission. See Mervyn M. Dymally, Oral History Interview, Conducted 1996 and 1997 by Elston L. Carr, UCLA-OH, vol. 1, 147, 184.

11. "Minutes of Regular Meeting, Willowbrook School District Board of Trustees, March 23, 1966," Ed-P.S.R. 85–87, box 3, CUSD Board Minute Files, CSA. For the McCone Report discussion of education, see Governor's Commission, *Violence in the City*, 49–61.

12. Sanford R. Goodkin Research Corporation, "Los Angeles County Model Neighborhood (Florence, Firestone & Willowbrook) Economic Study" (Los Angeles: Goodkin Corporation, 1970). 1–7.

13. Enterprise School District was comprised of unincorporated territory in the most westerly portion of the union high school district. Approximately 4.2 square miles, it contained four elementary schools. See Regional Planning Commission, "Enterprise

City School District Study, Phase No. 1" (County of Los Angeles: Regional Planning Commission, 1967).

14. David Halle, Robert Gedeon, and Andrew A. Beveridge, "Residential Separation and Segregation, Racial and Latino Identity, and the Racial Composition of Each City," in *New York and Los Angeles: Politics, Society, and Culture, a Comparative View*, ed. David Halle (Chicago: University of Chicago Press, 2003), 173–74.

15. 1970 Census.

16. Catholic University Law School Center for National Policy Review, *Trends in Black School Segregation, 1970–1974*, vol. 1 (Washington, D.C.: National Institute of Education, 1977), 130.

17. Gary Miller, *Cities by Contract: The Politics of Municipal Incorporation* (Cambridge, Mass.: MIT Press, 1981), 135.

18. Ibid.

19. Jack Schneider, "Escape from Los Angeles: White Flight from Los Angeles and Its Schools," *Journal of Urban History* 34 (2008): 1005.

20. Ibid., 1004.

21. Josh Sides, *L.A. City Limits : African American Los Angeles from the Great Depression to the Present* (Berkeley: University of California Press, 2003), 193; Miller, *Cities by Contract*, 177; Connor, "Creating Cities and Citizens," 200; Lawrence B. De Graaf, "African American Suburbanization in California, 1960 Through 1990," in *Seeking El Dorado: African Americans in California*, ed. Lawrence B. De Graaf et al. (Los Angeles: Autry Museum of Western Heritage, 2001), 430; Jack E. Jerrils, *The History of a City . . . Carson, California* (Carson, Calif.: Jerrils, 1972).

22. Miller, *Cities by Contract*, 136.

23. "'Gang War' Erupts in Compton!" *CHA*, December 9, 1965, 1, 2. For explanation of the development of gangs in Los Angeles, see James Diego Vigil, *A Rainbow of Gangs: Street Cultures in the Mega-City* (Austin: University of Texas Press, 2002).

24. "Compton Is Third in Major Crimes," *CHA*, December 12, 1965, 1, 2.

25. For criminalization of space, see Heather Ann Thompson, "Why Mass Incarceration Matters: Rethinking Crisis, Decline, and Transformation in Postwar American History," *Journal of American History* 97 (2010): 707.

26. Wilsey, Ham & Blair, "Compton Central Business District Study: Technical Supplement Report" (San Mateo, Calif.: Wilsey, Ham, & Blair, 1966), 6

27. James Bryant Conant, *Slums and Suburbs: A Commentary on Schools in Metropolitan Areas* (New York: McGraw-Hill, 1961); Michael Harrington, *The Other America: Poverty in the United States* (New York: Macmillan, 1962).

28. Stephen K. Bailey and Edith K. Mosher, *ESEA: The Office of Education Administers a Law* (Syracuse, N.Y.: Syracuse University Press, 1968), 49; For an in-depth discussion of the ESEA, its historical context, enactment, and results, also see Harvey Kantor, "Education, Social Reform, and the State: ESEA and Federal Education Policy in the 1960s," *American Journal of Education* 100 (November 1991): 47–83.

29. For examples of Compton area schools receiving these funds, see "Minutes of

Regular Meeting, Compton City School District Board of Trustees, February 7, 1966," Ed-P.S.R. 85–87, box 2, CUSD Board Minute Files, CSA; "Minutes of Regular Meeting, Compton Union High School District Board of Trustees, February 7, 1966," Ed-P.S.R. 81–94, box 6, CUSD Board Minute Files, CSA; "Education Proposal Approval for Compton School District," *LAS*, March 3, 1966, A2.

30. James Coleman et al., *Equality of Educational Opportunity* (Washington, D.C.: Dept. of Health, Education, and Welfare, Office of Education, 1966), 21.

31. For a detailed accounts of Ronald Reagan's 1966 gubernatorial election, see Lisa McGirr, *Suburban Warriors: The Origins of the New American Right* (Princeton, N.J.: Princeton University Press, 2001), 185–210; Rarick, *California Rising*, 355–66.

32. Elizabeth Brown, "Race, Urban Governance, and Crime Control: Creating Model Cities," *Law and Society Review* 44 (2010): 773; June Manning Thomas, *Redevelopment and Race: Planning a Finer City in Postwar Detroit* (Baltimore: Johns Hopkins University Press, 1997), 134–40; Marshall Kaplan, Gans, and Kahn, *The Model Cities Program: The Planning Process in Atlanta, Seattle, and Dayton* (New York: Praeger, 1970), 7–8; Mike Davis, *Dead Cities and Other Tales* (New York: New Press, 2002), 242. For Willowbrook's model neighborhood, see Goodkin Research Corporation, "Los Angeles County Model Neighborhood."

33. Letter to Los Angeles Federal Executive Board Steering Committee on Critical Urban Problems re: Presentation Made on April 24, 1969, Model Cities-Compton, box 1, CSA.

34. Michael K. Brown, John O'Donnell, Averill Strasser, and Walter Szczepanek, "Social and Economic Problems of the City of Compton," in *Report on the Compton-UCLA Urban Research and Development Project, September 1968 to June 1969*, ed. Deena R. Sosson (Los Angeles: Institute of Government and Public Affairs, 1970), b-9; Deena R. Sosson, ed., *History and Evaluation of the Compton-UCLA Urban Research and Development Project* (Los Angeles: Institute of Government and Public Affairs, 1970), 16.

35. Brown et al., "Social and Economic Problems of the City of Compton," b-27; City of Compton, "Special Census Summary-City of Compton" (1969). Compton's unemployment rate was 5.4 percent compared to 4.1 percent for the entire area.

36. Brown et al., "Social and Economic Problems of the City of Compton," b-5; City of Compton, "Special Census Summary-City of Compton."

37. "Minutes of Regular Meeting, Compton Union High School District Board of Trustees, July 9, 1968," Ed-P.S.R.- 81–94, box 7, CUSD Board Minute Files, CSA.

38. "Minutes of Regular Meeting, Compton Union High School District Board of Trustees, March 11, 1969," Ed-P.S.R.- 81–94, box 8, CUSD Board Minute Files, CSA.

39. "Rally to Probe What's Wrong with Compton Schools?" *LAS*, August 20, 1964, D1.

40. "Hiring of Non Credentialed Teachers OK," *CHA*, August 18, 1966, 1.

41. "Compton Union Hi Dist. to Participate in Teacher Corps Prog.," *CHA*, September 17, 1967, 2; "Minutes of Regular Meeting, Willowbrook School District Board of

Trustees, October 8, 1969," Ed-P.S.R. 85–87, box 3, CUSD Board Minute Files, CSA; "Minutes of Regular Meeting, Willowbrook School District Board of Trustees, March 13, 1968," Ed-P.S.R. 85–87, box 3, CUSD Board Minute Files, CSA; "Minutes of Regular Meeting, Willowbrook School District Board of Trustees, November 8, 1967," Ed-P.S.R. 85–87, box 3, CUSD Board Minute Files, CSA. For an in-depth discussion of the National Teacher Corps, see Rogers, "Social Policy, Teaching, and Youth Activism in the 1960s."

42. Letter to Burton W. Chace re: Transfer of Territory from Compton Unified School District to Lynwood Unified School District, Compton Unified Reports Folder, Los Angeles County Commission of School District Organization Papers, LACOE; "Caucasians Seek to Remove Children from Compton Schools," *LAS*, September 22, 1966, A1.

43. Letter to Fred Bewley re: Transfer of Territory from Compton Unified School District to Lynwood Unified School District, Compton Unified Reports Folder, Los Angeles County Commission of School District Organization Papers, LACOE.

44. "Rally to Probe What's Wrong with Compton Schools?" *LAS*, August 20, 1964, D1.

45. Lund, *Historic Pasadena*, 91.

46. Brilliant, *The Color of America Has Changed*, 236–37; Raftery, "Implementing Public Education," 578. For resistance to busing, see J. Anthony Lukas, *Common Ground: A Turbulent Decade in the Lives of Three American Families* (New York: Vintage, 1985); Ronald P. Formisano, *Boston Against Busing: Race, Class, and Ethnicity in the 1960s and 1970s* (Chapel Hill: University of North Carolina Press, 1991).

47. "The Challenge," Compton Branch NAACP Newsletter, October 15, 1970, Compton Ca Newsletters 1958, 1970–1972 folder 39, box 78, NAACP.

48. Letter to Stan Pottinger, Office for Civil Rights from Conrad Smith, Alvin Leonard, Clarence Reed, and Truman Jaques, Compton Ca, Undated 1955–1981 folder 38, box 78, NAACP.

49. L. Allen, interview with author. For rapid increase of African American school-age population, see Los Angeles County Regional Planning Commission, "Compton Union High School District Enrollment Projections and Analysis." For segregation in the schools based on housing patterns, see "Minutes of Regular Meeting, Compton City School District Board of Trustees, August 5, 1968," Ed-P.S.R. 85–87, box 2, CUSD Board Minute Files, CSA.

50. Richard M. Elman, *Ill-at-Ease in Compton* (New York: Pantheon, 1967), 122.

51. M. Filer, interview with author.

52. Lorraine Cervantes, interview with author, October 20, 2004, Compton, California, interview in possession of author; M. Filer, interview with author.

53. "Ross Miller Elected: Negroes Control Compton Council," *LAS*, June 8, 1967, A1.

54. Dorothy Townsend, "Compton to Elect first Negro Mayor Tuesday," *LAT*, 1 June 1969, C1.

55. In the late 1960s, African Americans began to be elected mayors in major

American cities. For in-depth analysis of this political transformation, see David R. Colburn and Jeffrey S. Adler, eds., *African-American Mayors: Race, Politics, and the American City* (Urbana: University of Illinois Press, 2001).

56. "Citizens Choose Dollarhide," *CHA*, June 5, 1969, 1; "Compton City Clerk in Race for 'Chace' Seat," *CB*, March 16, 1972.

57. "Elect Black Councilman Mayor of L.A. Suburb," *CDD*, June 21, 1969, 9; Steven R. Roberts, "Compton, Calif., 65% Negro, Believes in Integration and in Peaceful Change," *NYT*, June 8, 1969, 65.

58. Letter to John M. Brooks, National Director of Voter Registration, NAACP from Maxcy Filer, June 11, 1970, Undated 1955–1981, box 78, NAACP.

59. "Fourth Annual Achievement Award and Negro History Week Program," February 7, 1971, Undated 1955–1981, box 78, NAACP.

60. M. Filer, interview with author.

61. "Claims of 'Night Riders' in East Compton," *TB*, July 23, 1970, 1, 2, 4.

62. Michan Andrew Connor, "'Public Benefits from Public Choice': Producing Decentralization in Los Angeles, 1954–1973," *Journal of Urban History* 39(2013): 91; Michan Connor, "Creating Cities and Citizens: Municipal Boundaries, Place Entrepreneurs, and the Production of Race in Los Angeles County, 1926–1978" (Ph.D. dissertation, University of Southern California, 2008), 480.

63. Ray Zeman, "3 Cities Battling over Tax-Rich Area," *LAT*, January 29, 1970, OC_A1, A9; Davis, *Dead Cities*; Jack Jones, "Compton Annexation Foes Get 'Racist' Tag," *LAT*, March 25, 1969, C2; "City Battles Gardena Again," *CHA*, August 16, 1973, 1.

64. Jack W. Osman and John M. Gemello, "Revenue/Expenditure Limits and Override Elections: The Experience of California School Districts" (Stanford University, Institute for Research on Educational Finance and Governance, 1981), 3–5.

65. Frederick Alexander Kennedy, "An Analysis of the Effects of Decentralization upon Groups of Affected People in the Compton Unified School District" (Ed.D. dissertation, University of Southern California, 1973), 32.

66. "Compton Gets $6 Million in Grants," *LAS*, July 9, 1970, A12.

67. Bill Robertson, "Compton Admits Critical Problems; Pins Hope on Future," *LAS*, A15.

68. Marlene Walker, "Compton vs. Everybody," *CB*, July 25, 1973, A6. For in depth discussion on the loss of retail businesses in Compton, see Ahmed Mohammed Widaatalla, "Effect of Racial Change on the Tax Base of the City of Compton" (Ph.D. dissertation, University of California, Los Angeles, 1970), 115–59.

69. Nelson, interview with author; Steven C. Smith, "Shopping Center Plans Feasible, Compton Told," *LAT*, October 18, 1973, SE1, SE4.

70. "New Chamber Head Full of Hope," *CB*, January 9, 1974, 1.

71. Alberto M. Camarillo, "Chicano Urban History: A Study of Compton's Barrio, 1936–1970," *Aztlan* 2 (1971): 80–81.

72. Gilda Acosta-Gonzalez, interview with author, July 13, 2007, Downey, California, interview in possession of author.

73. Mae M. Ngai, "The Unlovely Residue of Outworn Prejudices: The Hart-Celler Act and the Politics of Reform, 1945–1965," in *Americanism: New Perspectives on the History of an Ideal*, ed. Michael Kazin and Joseph A. McCartin (Chapel Hill: University of North Carolina Press, 2006), 108–27.

74. Albert M. Camarillo, "Cities of Color: The New Racial Frontier in California's Minority-Majority Cities," *Pacific Historical Review* 76 (2007): 16; Passell, "Estimates of the Size and Characteristics of the Undocumented Population," *Pew Hispanic Center Report*.

75. Sandra Bass and Bruce E. Cain, "Introduction: Toward Greater Pluralism?" In *Racial and Ethnic Politics in California: Continuity and Change*, ed. Sandra Bass and Bruce E. Cain (Berkeley, Calif.: Berkeley Public Policy Press, 2008), 1.

76. Ibid.

77. *El Espejo 1977*, Manuel Dominguez Senior High, 1977.

78. Jose Ysidro Lopez, "Chicano Mobilization in Compton," *TB*, August 6, 1970, 7.

79. Deena R. Sosson, "History and Evaluation of the Compton-UCLA Urban Research and Development Project," in *Report on the Compton-UCLA Urban Research and Development Project*, ed. Sosson, 16.

80. Sides, "Straight into Compton," 591–93; Carl E. Martin, "The Black Community," in *The Employment Status of Los Angeles County's Minority Population*, ed. Carl E. Martin (County Commission on Human Relations, 1976), 14–15.

81. Howard William Edwards, "A Case Study of Compton Special Services Center" (California State University, Long Beach, 1972), 8

82. Brown et al., "Social and Economic Problems of the City of Compton."

83. L. M. Meriwether, "Surprise Switch: Enterprise School District Now Supports Unification," *LAS*, February 27, 1964, B1; "L. M. Meriwether, "School Unification Up to Voters," *LAS*, March 5, 1964, D1.

84. "Minutes of Regular Meeting, Willowbrook School District Board of Trustees, October 12, 1966," Ed-P.S.R. 85–87, box 3, CUSD Board Minute Files, CSA.

85. "Minutes of Regular Meeting, Willowbrook School District Board of Trustees, October 26, 1966," Ed-P.S.R. 85–87, box 3, CUSD Board Minute Files, CSA. Board members of the Enterprise district also unanimously rejected the idea of unification.

86. "Minutes of Regular Meeting, Enterprise School District Board of Trustees, October 12, 1966," Ed-P.S.R. 85–87, box 4, CUSD Board Minute Files, CSA.

87. Connor, "Creating Cities and Citizens," 23.

88. The Unruh School Act, Stats.1964, 1st Ex. Sess., ch.132.

89. "Minutes of Regular Meeting, Compton City School District Board of Trustees, February 24, 1969," Ed-P.S.R. 85–87, box 2, CUSD Board Minute Files, CSA.

90. Ibid; "Minutes of Regular Meeting, Willowbrook School District Board of Trustees, January 11, 1967," Ed-P.S.R. 85–87, box 3, CUSD Board Minute Files, CSA; "Minutes of Regular Meeting, Enterprise School District Board of Trustees, April 12, 1967," Ed-P.S.R. 85–87, box 4, CUSD Board Minute Files, CSA. In 1966, Enterprise City School District had an approximate population of 14,730. The population was 81.5%

African American, 8.7% white, 8.2% Latino, 1.1% Asian, and 0.5% other. See Regional Planning Commission, "Enterprise City School District Study, Phase No. 1" (Los Angeles County: Regional Planning Commission, 1967).

91. All quotations from "Minutes of a Special Meeting, Enterprise School District Board of Trustees, March 14, 1969," Ed-P.S.R. 85–87, box 4, CUSD Board Minute Files, CSA, emphasis original.

92. Ibid., emphasis original.

93. "Minutes of Regular Meeting, Compton Union High School District Board of Trustees, March 1, 1966," Ed-P.S.R. 81–94, box 6, CUSD Board Minute Files, CSA. The final vote for unification was 3,597 for and 2,941 against. Jim Cleaver, "Compton School Plan Wins," *LAS*, April 17, 1969, A1.

94. "Schools Approved," *CHA*, April 17, 1969, 1; "Superintendents React to Unification," *CHA*, April 20, 1969, 1; "Letter from John Lambie, County Engineer, to Martin Rohrke, State Board of Equalization, re: CUSD Formation," December 16, 1969, Compton Unified-correspondence folder, Los Angeles County Commission on School District Organization, LACOE; Richard Wales, "Certification of Election Results, Los Angeles County, 1969," Compton Unified correspondence folder, Los Angeles County Commission on School District Organization, LACOE.

95. Kennedy, "An Analysis of the Effects of Decentralization," 25.

96. Ibid., 4.

97. Ibid., 41.

98. "Minutes of Regular Meeting, Compton Union High School District Board of Trustees, May 27, 1969," Ed-P.S.R. 81–94, box 8, CUSD Board Minute Files, CSA; "Dr. Alonzo Crim Replaces Adamson as High School District Superintendent," *CHA*, June 5, 1969, 1.

99. Crim, "Educating All God's Children," 92.

100. Ibid., 93.

101. "Enterprise Schools Can't Pay Employees," *CHA*, 29 June 1969, 1; Susan Stocking, "School District in Watts Area Broke, Teacher Pay Held Up," *LAT*, June 27, 1969, 1, 28.

Chapter 5. Unyielding Problems

1. Morrison, interview with author.

2. "Compton Student Killed on Campus," *CHA*, September 24, 1972, 1; "High School Student Shot, Self Defense Says Guard," *CB*, November 8, 1972, 1.

3. Morrison, interview with author.

4. "Compton Rated Second in County Crimes," *CB*, January 17, 1973, 3.

5. Steven C. Smith, "Crime in Compton: Campaign to Combat Intensifies," *LAT*, October 1, 1973, SE1.

6. Bob Welkos, "'Horatio Alger' Fights for His Political Life," *LAS*, May 10, 1973, A3.

7. As quoted in Leanna Y. Ford, "Davis Beats Dollarhide," *LAS*, June 7, 1973, A9.

8. For conservatives' use of "law and order," see Michael W. Flamm, *Law and Order:*

Street Crime, Civil Unrest, and the Crisis of Liberalism in the 1960s (New York: Columbia University Press, 2005); Lisa McGirr, *Suburban Warriors: The Origins of the New American Right* (Princeton, N.J.: Princeton University Press, 2001), 188–216. For liberals' use, see Heather Ann Thompson, "Why Mass Incarceration Matters: Rethinking Crisis, Decline, and Transformation in Postwar American History," *Journal of American History* 97 (2010): 729–30.

9. "Woman Mayor in Compton More for 'the Man,'" *Sun Reporter*, June 16, 1973.

10. As quoted in Ford, "Davis Beats Dollarhide," A9.

11. Alejandro A. Alonso, "Racialized Identities and the Formation of Black Gangs in Los Angeles," *Urban Geography* 25 (2004): 659, 666–69.

12. K. Filer, interview with author; Alonso, "Racialized Identities," 669; Operation Safe Streets (OSS) Street Gang Detail, "L.A. Style: A Street Gang Manual of the Los Angeles County Sheriff's Department," in *The Modern Gang Reader*, ed. Malcolm W. Klein et al. (Los Angeles: Roxbury, 1995). For personal accounts of the gang culture, see Léon Bing, *Do or Die* (New York: HarperCollins, 1991) and Sanyika Shakur, *Monster: The Autobiography of an L.A. Gang Member* (New York: Penguin, 1994.)

13. Gisele Hudson, "Compton Police: Gangs Are Family Affair," March 1990, CUSD Folder, Compton File, CPL; Smith, "Crime in Compton," SE1. For discussion of Davis's job program see Cervantes, interview with author. For the growth of gangs in Compton, see James Diego Vigil, *A Rainbow of Gangs: Street Cultures in the Mega-City* (Austin: University of Texas Press, 2002), 75–77.

14. Jose Ysidro Lopez, "Community Control of Our Compton Schools," *CB*, December 10, 1970, 8.

15. "Chicano Youth Killed in School," *CB*, December 10, 1970, 1; "Parents Aroused by Stabbing Death," *CHA*, December 10, 1970, 1.

16. "Chicano Youth Killed in School," 1.

17. Lopez, "Community Control of Our Compton Schools," 8.

18. "Local School Test Results Rank Low," *CHA*, March 1, 1973, n.p.

19. Acosta-Gonzalez, interview with author.

20. "Centennial Students Picket School Board," *CHA*, October 29, 1970, 1; "Minutes of Regular Meeting, CUSD Board of Trustees, March 2, 1971," Ed-P.S.R.- 81–94, box 9, CUSD Board Minute FilesCSA.

21. Sharon Taylor, "Battle Looms Between Compton Parents and School Administration," *LAS*, February 3, 1972, A14.

22. "Compton Schools: A Report by the California Teachers Association Survey Team," Saul Halpert Papers, SCLSSR.

23. Ibid.

24. "Compton Schools: A Report by the California Teachers Association Survey Team."

25. "School Investigators' Motives Questioned," *CHA*, April 16, 1972, 1, 2; "Dr. Crim Attacks CTA Investigation," *CHA*, April 27, 1972, 1; "City Council Minutes, April 25, 1972," CCH.

26. "City and School Officials Answer Charges Levied by CTA," *CB*, May 11, 1972, 1; "Government Board Censures CTA," *CHA*, May 11, 1972, 1.

27. "Fire Crackers Blamed for School Turmoil, as 46 Teachers Call in Sick," *CB*, June 7, 1972, 1; "Teachers Boycott Centennial," *CHA*, June 4, 1972, 1; "Centennial HS like 'War Zone,'" *LAS*, June 8, 1972, A1.

28. "Assault Charged by Teacher," *CHA*, June 15, 1972, 1; "Compton Teacher Alleges Attack by Girl Students with Umbrella," *CB*, June 14, 1972, 1.

29. Judith Kafka, *The History of "Zero Tolerance" in American Public Schooling* (New York: Palgrave Macmillan, 2011), 98; Jeffrey Mirel, *The Rise and Fall of an Urban School System: Detroit, 1907–81* (Ann Arbor: University of Michigan Press, 1999), 333.

30. Ad Hoc Committee, "Final Report of the Ad Hoc Committee on the Prevention and Management of Conflict and Crime in the Schools" (1975); Kafka, *The History of "Zero Tolerance,"* 100–101; Gerald Grant, *The World We Created at Hamilton High* (Cambridge, Mass.: Harvard University Press, 1988), 45–76.

31. As quoted in "Student Journalists Grill Compton Schools' Chief," *CHA*, March 29, 1973, 1.

32. Celeste Durant, "L.A.'s Truants: Problems in Schools, Homes," *LAT*, October 1, 1973, A1.

33. Joyce A. Baugh, *The Detroit School Busing Case: Milliken v. Bradley and the Controversy over Desegregation* (Lawrence: University Press of Kansas, 2011).

34. "Minutes of Regular Meeting, CUSD Board of Trustees, November 28, 1972," Ed-P.S.R.- 82–93, box 2, CUSD Board Minute Files, CSA; "School Finance Trouble," *CHA*, November 30, 1972, 1; "Compton Schools Eroding," *LAS*, September 13, 1973, A1.

35. "Classes Canceled at Troubled School," *LAT*, April 3, 1973, E1; "Troubled School in Compton Reopens," *LAT*, April 4, 1973, C1; "Teachers Walk Out, Parents Take Over," *CB*, April 4, 1973, 1, 4; "Security Tightened, Classes Resume at School in Compton," *LAT*, April 5, 1973, D1; "Whaley Teachers Protest Disturbance," *CHA*, April 5, 1973, 1.

36. "Board Approves District Budget," *CHA*, August 16, 1973, 1; "School Attendance Shows Local Drop," *CHA*, September 27, 1973, 1.

37. *El Espejo 1973*, Manuel Dominguez Senior High, 33.

38. Quoted in Bob Allison, "Compton Schools: 'Tragic Decay,'" *LAS*, December 6, 1973, A12.

39. Ibid., A1; "Salaries, Violence, Substitutes at Issue, Compton Teachers Say," *LAS*, December 13, 1973, A1.

40. Jack McCurdy, "Compton Schools $600,000 in Red; Poor Management Blamed," *LAT*, December 5, 1973, 28.

41. Jack McCurdy, "Report Urges Closing of 5 Compton Schools," *LAT*, December 19, 1973, A3, 23; "Minutes of Regular Meeting, CUSD Board of Trustees, January 8, 1974," Ed-P.S.R.- 82–93, box 3, CUSD Board Minute Files, CSA.

42. "Minutes of Regular Meeting, CUSD Board of Trustees, December 11, 1973," Ed-P.S.R.- 82–93, box 3, CUSD Board Minute Files, CSA. The teacher also pointed to

"the kind of schools we have, not having any teachers or staff or programs in a majority of the schools for students who don't speak English, having only seven ESL teachers for the whole district, having teachers with books and maps that show Prussia."

43. Steven C. Smith, "Compton Schools: Is Unified Better?" *LAT*, February 3, 1974, SE1, SE3.

44. Jeffrey R. Henig, Richard C. Hula, Marion Orr, and Desiree S. Pedescleaux, *Color of School Reform: Race, Politics, and the Challenge of Urban Education* (Princeton, N.J.: Princeton University Press, 1999); Clarence N. Stone et al., *Building Civic Capacity: The Politics of Reforming Urban Schools* (Lawrence: University Press of Kansas, 2001); Wilbur C. Rich, *Black Mayors and School Politics: The Failure of Reform in Detroit, Gary, and Newark* (New York: Garland, 1996).

45. Mike Goodman and Harry Bernstein, "Teachers' Strike Shuts Down 41 Schools in Compton District," *LAT*, November 30, 1973, 3A, 24; "Teacher Strike Hits Compton," *CHA*, December 6, 1973, 1; "Agreement Reached in Teachers' Strike," *LAT*, December 20, 1973, A1; "Teacher Strike Settled," *CB*, December 26, 1973, 1; "Compton Teachers, Board Reach Strike Settlement," *LAS*, December 27, 1973, A1. Teachers would receive a 6 percent pay increase in January 1974 and a 7 percent additional increase in July.

46. Steven C. Smith, "Compton Schools: Is Unified Better?" *LAT*, December 20, 1974, SE1, 3; Bob Allison, "Compton Schools Ask State for $2 Million," *LAS*, March 14, 1974, A9.

47. "Compton School Board Tightens Budget Belt," *LAS*, March 7, 1974, A3; "District Rehires Fired Teachers," *CHA*, October 17, 1974, 1; "Compton Reinstates Last of 325 Teachers," *LAT*, October 10, 1974, C1. Six months following the furor caused when Compton school officials dismissed 325 classroom teachers in a series of cutback measures, most of the fired teachers were back on the job. The rehiring came after a state hearing officer recommended against the district position that the firings were done properly. Most had already been rehired to fill spots vacated by resignations or retirements. By the beginning of school, the number of unemployed teachers was down from 325 to 50. Compton Unified sent a letter to the 50 saying they could return to the district if they wanted to do so; 23 said they did.

48. Special Committee, California Grand Jury, Los Angeles County, "Public Hearing, City of Compton" (Los Angeles, 1975), 1.

49. Ibid., 7.

50. Ibid., 26.

51. William Farr, "Inner-City Problems Grow, Panel Warns," *LAT*, July 9, 1975, C1, C8.

52. Ibid.

53. Ibid., 8.

54. Ibid., 2–3; "Superintendent Gets Pact; Jury Blasted," *CHA*, April 10, 1975, 1; "Report Based on Hearsay, Superintendent Charges," *LAT*, July 17, 1975, SE1, SE6; "Grand Jury Finds Area Youths Pray," *CHA*, April 17, 1975, 1; Jim Cleaver, "Compton Officials Blast Grand Jury's Report," *LAS*, April 10, 1975, A1, C11; "Compton Officials Rip Grand Jury Report," *LAS*, July 24, 1975, A4.

55. "Minutes of Regular Meeting, CUSD Board of Trustees, September 10, 1975," Ed-P.S.R.- 82–93, box 5, CUSD Board Minute Files, CSA; "Minutes of the Los Angeles County Committee on School District Organization, October 1, 1975," Compton Unified Reports Folder, Los Angeles County Commission of School District Organization Papers, LACOE; "LA County Board of Education Public Hearing Proposed Transfer of Territory, November 10, 1975," Compton Unified Reports Folder, Los Angeles County Commission of School District Organization Papers, LACOE.

56. "School District Gets $3.5 Million in Aid," *CB*, March 24, 1976, 1, 2.

57. Compton was not alone in this phenomenon. In his book *Barrio-Logos*, literary scholar Raúl Homero Villa charts the cultural production of Latino spaces, arguing that Chicano culture and community have grown around contests over these spaces. Villa asserts that the relationship between cultural production from inside and outside the barrio come together to make meaning of the space. Raúl Homero Villa, *Barrio-Logos: Space and Place in Urban Chicano Literature and Culture* (Austin: University of Texas Press, 2000) Also looking at the relationship between culture and the definition of place, historian Eric Avila examines the making of white identity in popular culture and how this process helped create the divide between the "chocolate cities and vanilla suburbs." Eric Avila, *Popular Culture in the Age of White Flight* (Berkeley: University of California Press, 2004). Historian Andrew Wiese's work on black suburbia documents how blacks kept their racial identity after settling in the suburbs but also details how the perceived racialization of space led whites to flee such areas. Andrew Wiese, *Places of Their Own: African American Suburbanization in the Twentieth Century* (Chicago: University of Chicago Press, 2004).

58. Richard M. Elman, *Ill-at-Ease in Compton* (New York: Pantheon, 1967), 144, 179. Elman first became aware of Compton's changed racial composition when he was sent to Compton during the Goldwater-Johnson election. The television station for which he worked had chosen two mainstream California towns for study—one that voted Republican and one that voted Democrat. Compton was the latter. When Elman reported to his supervisors at the station that Compton voted Democratic because it was largely African American, they were surprised, and asked him and the camera operators to "shoot around some of those Negroes" because a majority town did not represent to them Main Street America. He and the crew did what they were instructed. Compton, and its increasingly black population, stuck with Elman and he returned a couple of years later to research a book about the community. See, Elman, *Ill-at-Ease in Compton*, 13–16.

59. Sides, "Straight into Compton," 596.

60. Douglas Dollarhide, "Dollarhide Reviews Book about Compton," *CHA*, October 1, 1967, 2.

61. R. Elman, "Author of Book on Compton Hits Critical Review by Dollarhide," *CHA*, October 8, 1967, 2. In his book, Elman had devoted a chapter to discussing Colonel Smith, the *Herald American*'s publisher, and his influence on Compton. In this chapter, Elman did not portray "the Colonel" kindly, painting him to be a modern-day

plantation owner who was losing his power. See Elman, *Ill-at-Ease in Compton*, 177–36.

62. Arnold Hano, "Who's No. 1? C-O-M-P-T-O-N! . . . ," *Boys' Life*, January 1970, 57.

63. "Compton: A Restless Dream," *LAS*, June 20, 1974, B7; "City Council Minutes, July 2, 1974," CCH; Steven C. Smith, "Compton Expands Renewal Area," *LAT*, July 21, 1974, SE1, SE4; "City Council Minutes, June 18, 1974," CCH.

64. "City Council Minutes, June 17, 1975," CCH; "Compton Mayor Sues TV," *LAS*, June 19, 1975, A3, C15.

65. Bruce Henderson, *Ghetto Cops* (Chatsworth, Calif.: Major Books, 1975), 19; "First Black Police Chief Joins New Compton Mayor," *LAS*, July 5, 1973, A1.

66. "City Council Minutes, June 17, 1975," CCH.

67. Letter to Virna Canson, West Coast Region, NAACP from Doris Davis, 13 November 1975, Folder 34, Compton Ca., 1975–1977, box 38, NAACP.

68. John Kendall, "A Ghetto Is Slow to Die," *LAT*, March 23, 1975, B1, B8; "County District Reading Scores," *LAT*, December 3, 1974, B8.

69. "Minutes of Regular Meeting, Compton Unified School District Board of Trustees, November 26, 1974," Ed-P.S.R.- 82–93, box 4, CUSD Board Minute Files, CSA.

70. Tom Gordon, "Compton Armed with Federal Funds on Crime," *LAT*, October 19, 1975, SE1, SE3.

71. "Hamm, Woolfolk Each Get 3 Years in Jail," *CB*, June 9, 1976, 1, 2; "Ex-Officials Get Prison Terms," *CHA*, June 24, 1976, 1; Tom Gordon, "2 on Compton Council Get Jail terms in Extortion Plot," *LAT*, June 22, 1976, C1, C2; Cressel, interview with author.

72. "Public Outraged at City Councilmen," *CB*, June 9, 1976, 1, 2; "Residents Shout 'Resign!'" *CHA*, June 3, 1976, 1; Tom Gordon, "Compton Clergy Mixes Power of Prayer with Politics," *LAT*, July 25, 1976, SE1, SE3; "Clergy and Citizens Unite for Strength," *CB*, August 4, 1976, 1, 2. The group endorsed Maxcy Filer and Johanna Carrington to replace Hamm and Woolfolk on the council. Filer won, but Carrington did not.

73. Miller, *Cities by Contract*, 180.

74. Ibid., 179.

75. "Petition Calls for Car Dealer Move to Plaza," *CHA*, May 25, 1978, 1; "Compton Opens New Auto Mall," *LAS*, April 28, 1977, A13; Kevin Fox Gotham, ed., *Critical Perspectives on Urban Redevelopment* (Oxford: Elsevier Science, 2001); June Manning Thomas, *Redevelopment and Race* (Baltimore: Johns Hopkins University Press, 1997).

76. Tom Gorman, "Compton CRA Sells $11 Million Bonds," *LAT*, January 26, 1978, SE5.

77. "Block Grant Funding Application Approved," *CB*, September 1, 1976, 1, 2; "Revenue Sharing Gets Extended for Compton," *CB*, June 16, 1976, 1.

78. "School District Gets $4.8 Million Funding," *CB*, January 3, 1977, 1.

79. Tom Gorman, "Compton Economy: Can $140 Million Heal It in 5 Years?" *LAT*, September 4, 1977, SE1, SE10. For test scores see "Reading Scores in L.A. County," *LAT*, November 14, 1977, 4.

80. In November 1973, California voters rejected Proposition 1, which would have limited state taxes and expenditures to a percentage of California's net product. Mickey D. Levy, "A Comparison of Voting Behavior on Tax Initiatives with Different Perceived Distribution Consequences," *National Tax Journal* 32 (December 1979): 551.

81. Jon Sonstelie, Eric Brunner, and Kenneth Ardon, *For Better or for Worse? School Finance Reform in California* (San Francisco: Public Policy Institute of California, 2000), 6.

82. *Serrano v. Priest*, 584 5 Cal. 3rd (1971) and *Serrano v. Priest*, 728 18 Cal. 3rd (1976).

83. Lawrence O. Pincus, "A Quarter Century of Turmoil: School Finance in California on the 25th Anniversary of *Serrano*," *Educational Considerations* 25 (1997): 5.

84. John Mathews and Mark Paul, *California Crackup: How Reform Broke the Golden State and How We Can Fix It* (Berkeley: University of California Press, 2010); Natalia Mehlman-Petrzela, "Origins of the Culture Wars: Sex, Language, School, and State in California, 1968–1978" (Ph.D. dissertation, Stanford University, 2009), 289.

85. Robert O. Self, *American Babylon: Race and the Struggle for Postwar Oakland* (Princeton, N.J.: Princeton University Press, 2003), 317.

86. California Secretary of State, *Statement of Vote, June 1978* (Sacramento: California Secretary of State), 1978.

87. Morrison, interview with author.

88. Sonstelie et al., *For Better or for Worse?* ix–xi; Dymally oral history interview, vol. 1, 228.

89. "School District Publication Budget Adopted by Trustees," *CB*, August 9, 1978, 1; Joel Cohen, "School Facility Financing: A History of the Role of the State Allocation Board and Options for the Distribution of Proposition 1A Funds" (Sacramento: California Research Bureau, 1999), 12.

90. James S. Catterall and Emily Brizendine, *Proposition 13: Effects on High School Curricula, 1979–1983* (Stanford, Calif.: Institute for Research on Educational Finance and Governance, School of Education, Stanford University, 1984), 9.

Chapter 6. A Rapidly Changing City

1. "Latino Voted to City Commission," *CHA*, December 20, 1984, 1.

2. Jeffrey R. Henig, Richard C. Hula, Marion Orr, and Desiree S. Pedescleaux, *Color of School Reform: Race, Politics, and the Challenge of Urban Education* (Princeton, N.J.: Princeton University Press, 1999), 118.

3. Wilbur C. Rich, *Black Mayors and School Politics: The Failure of Reform in Detroit, Gary, and Newark* (New York: Garland, 1996), 120.

4. Jorge N. Leal, "Las Plazas of South Los Angeles," in *Post-Ghetto: Reimagining South Los Angeles*, ed. Josh Sides (San Marino and Berkeley: Huntington Library and University of California Press, 2012), 11–32; James J. Connolly, ed., *After the Factory: Reinventing America's Industrial Small Cities* (Lanham, Md.: Lexington Books, 2010); Jon C. Teaford, *The Rough Road to Renaissance: Urban Revitalization in America,*

1940–1985 (Baltimore: Johns Hopkins University Press, 1990); Alison Isenberg, *Downtown America: A History of the Place and the People Who Made It* (Chicago: University of Chicago Press, 2004).

5. "Being Black, Poor Hurts Compton with HUD, City Aide Says," *LAT*, June 17, 1979, SE6; Gerald Faris, "Compton Loses Bid for Renewal Grant," *LAT*, June 28, 1979, SE4.

6. "Petition Calls for Car Deal Move to Plaza," *CHA*, May 25, 1978, 1.

7. Ibid.; "Compton Questions Volvo," *LAS*, May 25, 1978, A5; Gerald Faris, "Compton Will Add Two Dealerships to Auto Mall," *LAT*, January 4, 1979, SE2.

8. Gerald Faris, "Compton Auto Plaza off to Sputtering Start Despite High Hopes, $21 Million," *LAT*, August 12, 1979, SE1, SE7; David Einstein and Dave Cooper, "Car Dealer Shut Bankruptcy," *LAT*, February 26, 1984, SE1; David Einstein, "Dealer's Debts Top $1 Million," *LAT*, April 8, 1984, SE1.

9. Mike Davis, *City of Quartz: Excavating the Future in Los Angeles* (New York: Verso, 1990), 304.

10. Dwight L. Johnson, "We, the Black Americans" (Washington, D.C.: U.S. Department of Commerce, Bureau of the Census, 1986), 5.

11. Nora Hamilton and Norma Stoltz Chinchilla, *Seeking Community in a Global City* (Philadelphia: Temple University Press, 2001), 38, 73; Davis, *City of Quartz*, 304–5; James H. Johnson, Jr., Walter C. Farrell, Jr., and Chandra Guinn, "Immigration Reform and the Browning of America: Tensions, Conflicts, and Community Instability in Metropolitan Los Angeles," in *The Handbook of International Migration: The American Experience*, ed. Charles Hirschman, Philip Kasinitz, and Josh DeWind (New York: Russell Sage, 1999), 394–95, 403–6; Jonathan Musere, "Southern Californians' Attitudes to Immigrants: Blacks Compared to Other Ethnics" (M.A. thesis, University of California, Los Angeles, 1991), 29; Sides, "Straight into Compton," 593; Michael I. Lichter and Melvin L. Oliver, "Racial Differences in Labor Force Participation and Long-Term Joblessness Among Less Educated Men," in *Prismatic Metropolis: Inequality in Los Angeles*, ed. Lawrence D. Bobo et al. (New York: Russell Sage, 2000).

12. Lee Harris, "'We are trying to change the demand for drugs . . . the earlier we start the better chance we have to be effective,'" *LAT*, 28 May 1987, CUSD Folder, Compton File, CPL.

13. L. Allen, interview with author.

14. Mike Davis, *Dead Cities and Other Tales* (New York: New Press, 2002), 280.

15. As quoted in Gisele Hudson, "Program Offers Hope for Pupils School District's 'New Start,'" July 1989, CUSD Folder, Compton File, CPL; James Diego Vigil and Steve C. Yun, "A Cross-Cultural Framework for Understanding Gangs: Multiple Marginality and Los Angeles," in *Gangs in America III*, ed. C. Ronald Huff (Thousand Oaks, Calif.: Sage, 2002), 165.

16. Raftery, "Implementing Public Education," 580.

17. U.S. Senate Committee on the Judiciary, Subcommittee on Juvenile Justice, "Gang Violence and Control," Hearings before the Subcommittee on Juvenile Justice of

the Committee on the Judiciary, United States Senate, 98th Cong., 1st sess., on Gang Violence and Control in the Los Angeles and San Francisco Areas with a View to What Might be Done by the Federal Government, Westwood, California, February 7, 1983, San Francisco, California, February 9, 1983 (Washington, D.C.: Government Printing Office, 193), 2.

18. Josh Sides, "Straight into Compton: American Dreams, Urban Nightmares, and the Metamorphosis of a Black Suburb," *American Quarterly* 56 (September 2004): 593.

19. Davis, *Dead Cities and Other Tales*, 276.

20. Jack Katz, "Metropolitan Crime Myths," in *in New York and Los Angeles: Politics, Society, and Culture, a Comparative View*, ed. David Halle (Chicago: University of Chicago Press, 2003), 203; Eric C. Schneider, *Vampires, Dragons, and Egyptian Kings: Youth Gangs in Postwar New York* (Princeton, N.J.: Princeton University Press, 1999), 313n 3; Michelle Alexander, *The New Jim Crow: Mass Incarceration in the Age of Colorblindness* (New York: New Press, 2010), 133.

21. Katz, "Metropolitan Crime Myths," 198.

22. Ibid., 213; "City Council Minutes, August 16, 1979," CCH; "City Council Minutes, September 8, 1981," CCH; "City Council Minutes, November 3, 1981," CCH. The schools had anti-gang programs. See Gisele Hudson, "Program Offers Hope for Pupils School District's 'New Start,'" July 1989, Compton Unified School District Folder, Compton File, CPL. For discussion of girls in gangs (and about how scholars have viewed gangs as a male enterprise), see Jody Miller, *One of the Guys: Girls, Gangs, and Gender* (New York: Oxford University Press, 2001).

23. Gerald Faris, "Covering Compton: The P.D. Is P.D.Q.," *LAT*, July 19, 1979, SE1, SE2.

24. "School District Takes Hard Line on Vandalism," *CHA*, July 19, 1979, 1.

25. *Norbert Flores v. Anselmo Renoso, et al.*, 91793 Compton Judicial District (1979), Folder 11, box 27, BCP.

26. James H. Cleaver, "Compton Council Nixes Gambling," *LAS*, May 15, 1980, A8; Steve Tamaya, "Compton Third City in Year to OK Card Clubs," *LAT*, July 15, 1982, SE1; Tamaya, "Ministers Seek Reversal of Card Club Ordinance," *LAT*, July 22, 1982, SE1; "City Council Minutes, July 27, 1982," CCH; Steve Tamaya, "Compton Council Poker Advocates to Study Vote," *LAT*; Tamaya, "Compton Council Rescinds Its Ordinance," *LAT*, August 5, 1982.

27. Leal, "Las Plazas of South Los Angeles," 16–17.

28. Jon C. Teaford, *The Rough Road to Renaissance: Urban Revitalization in America, 1940–1985* (Baltimore: Johns Hopkins University Press, 1990), 261.

29. As quoted in "Update: Compton Plaza Hotel," *CW*, Fall 1987, 11.

30. "Compton Hotel Construction Progressing Rapidly," *CW*, Summer 1987.

31. Michele Fuetsch, "New Orleans-Style Complex Compton Unveils Plan for New Bourbon Street," *LAT*, October 6, 1988, 3; Michele Fuetsch, "Compton Hotel Debut Delayed," *LAT*, August 10, 1989, 1; Michele Fuetsch, "Key Compton Hotel Quietly Becomes a Ramada Urban Renewal," *LAT*, October 11, 1990, 3.

32. "Compton Low Percentage of Residents Among Hotel Hires Noted," *LAT*, July 13, 1989, 2; Fuetsch, "Compton Hotel Debut Delayed."

33. Fuetsch, "New Orleans-Style Complex Compton Unveils Plan for New Bourbon Street"; "Compton Approves Bourbon St. Study," *LAS*, October 27, 1988, D1.

34. Michele Fuetsch, "Compton Acts to Recover Part of Loan," *LAT*, March 12, 1989, 2.

35. Gisele Hudson, "Compton's Year Financially Frustrating Though Police Find Ways to Beef Up Arms," January 1990, Compton Unified School District Folder, Compton File, CPL.

36. Terry Spencer, "Compton Auto Mall Proposed as Site for New Brokerage Lot," *LAT*, March 13, 1988, 1.

37. As quoted in John H. Lee, "Compton Groups Urge Support for Housing," *LAT*, November 20, 1989, 8.

38. "City Council Minutes, November 21, 1989," CCH.

39. Michele Fuetsch, "2 Offers to Buy Land on Plaza Turned Down by Compton," *LAT*, December 14, 1989, 1; Frank Allen, interview with author, October 18, 2004, Compton, California, interview in possession of author; Michele Fuetsch, "Compton OKs Sale of Land to Mack Truck Redevelopment," *LAT*, December 28, 1989, 1; "Compton Council Rescinds Franchise for Truck Dealer in Default," *LAT*, June 21, 1990, 2.

40. Samoans lived in a concentrated area in the Carson-Wilmington-Long Beach area, but several hundred lived in one complex on Compton on the border of this concentration. Allen and Turner, *The Ethnic Quilt*, 161.

41. Josh Sides, "Renewal Through Retail? The Impact of Corporate Retail Investment in South Los Angeles," in *Post-Ghetto*, ed. Josh Sides, 44; 1980 Census; Camarillo, "Black and Brown in Compton," 365–66. For discussion of the changing demographics of Los Angeles County's Latino population see Raymond A. Rocco, "Latino Los Angeles: Reframing Boundaries/Borders," in *The City: Los Angeles and Urban Theory at the End of the Twentieth Century*, ed. Allen J. Scott and Edward W. Soja (Berkeley: University of California Press, 1996).

42. Hamilton and Chinchilla, *Seeking Community*, 50.

43. Susan Anderson, "A City Called Heaven: Black Enchantment and Despair in Los Angeles," in *The City: Los Angeles and Urban Theory at the End of the Twentieth Century*, ed. Scott and Soja, 345; M. Filer, interview with author; James H. Johnson, Jr., and Curtis C. Roseman, "Increasing Black Outmigration from Los Angeles: The Role of Household Dynamics and Kinship Systems," *Annals of the Association of American Geographers* 80 (1990): 205–22; Josh Sides, "Introduction: A Brief History of the American Ghetto," in *Post-Ghetto*, 3.

44. Mike Davis, *Magical Urbanism: Latinos Reinvent the U.S. Big City* (London: Verso, 2000), 139. For analysis of the demographic shift in Compton see Albert M. Camarillo, "Black and Brown in Compton: Demographic Change, Suburban Decline, and Intergroup Relations in a South Central Los Angeles Community, 1950 to 2000," in *Not Just Black and White: Historical and Contemporary Perspectives on Immigration, Race,*

and Ethnicity in the United States, ed. Nancy Foner and George M. Fredrickson (New York: Russell Sage, 2004), 365–67. For Los Angeles County as a whole, see David M. Grant, "A Demographic Portrait of Los Angeles County, 1970 to 1990," in *Prismatic Metropolis*, ed. Lawrence D. Bobo et al.

45. "City Council Minutes, July 24, 1973"; "City Council Minutes, March 19, 1974," CCH.

46. "Compton Asked to Boost Latino Representation," *LAT*, September 26, 1976, SE1. Also see "Group Questions City on Hiring Practices," *CHA*, October 14, 1976, 1; "Compton Latinos Demand City Data on Hiring, Jobs," *LAT*, October 7, 1976, SE1.

47. "Latinos to Picket Rites," *LAT*, February 17, 1977, SE8.

48. Cervantes, interview with author.

49. For discussion of internal solidarity in African American communities, see Marion Orr, *Black Social Capital: The Politics of School Reform in Baltimore, 1986–1998* (Lawrence: University of Kansas Press, 1999).

50. "Bilingual Act of 1968," in *Latino Education in the United States: A Narrated History from 1513–2000*, ed. Victoria-Maria MacDonald (New York: Palgrave Macmillan, 2004), 249–52.

51. Mark Brilliant, *The Color of America Has Changed: How Racial Diversity Shaped Civil Rights Reform in California, 1941–1978* (New York: Oxford University Press, 2010), 237.

52. Abdul Karim Bangura and Martin C. Muo, *United States Congress & Bilingual Education* (New York: Peter Lang, 2001); Bilingual Act of 1968," in *Latino Education in the United States*, ed. MacDonald, 252.

53. Gaynor Cohen, "Alliance and Conflict Among Mexican Americans," *Ethnic and Racial Studies* 5 (1982): 179.

54. "Presentation to the Board of Directors, CUSD, re: the Special and Unique Needs of Mexican American Students, and the Urgent Need for a United and Effective School System," n.d., folder 8, box 7, BCP.

55. Tom Gorman, "Compton Trustees to submit Bilingual Education Proposal to Federal Officials" *LAT*, January 22, 1978, SE9; "Compton 'Bilingual' Plan Leaders Named," *CB*, April 5, 1978, 4; "Group Plans Improved Bilingual Programs," *CHA*, April 6, 1978, 1.

56. William Trombley, "Can Bilingual Education Do Its Job?" *LAT*, September 4, 1980, B1.

57. Mario T. García and Sal Castro, *Blowout! Sal Castro and the Chicano Struggle for Educational Justice* (Chapel Hill: University of North Carolina Press, 2011).

58. "Minutes, Compton Unified School District Board of Trustees, September 13, 1988," CUSD.

59. Victoria-María MacDonald, John M. Botti, and Lisa Hoffman Clark, "From Invisibility to Autonomy: Latinos and Higher Education in the U.S., 1965–2005," *Harvard Educational Review* 77 (2007): 474–504; "Minutes of Regular Meeting, Enterprise School District Board of Trustees, October 11, 1961," Ed-P.S.R. 85–87, box 4, CUSD Board Minute Files, CSA.

60. Quoted in Davis, *Dead Cities and Other Tales*, 282.

61. Michele Fuetsch, "Affirmative Action Plan Urges Compton to Triple Number of Jobs for Latinos," *LAT*, April 6, 1989, 1. For discussion of affirmative action plan and resistance to it, see Johnson, "Immigration Reform and the Browning of America," 403–6.

62. M. Filer, interview with author.

63. Such tests were often biased against newcomers and outsiders to the system. See Christina Collins, *Ethnically Qualified: Race, Merit, and the Selection of Urban Teachers, 1920–1980* (New York: Teachers College Press, 2011).

64. Scott Harris, "Schools' Bilingual Funds Imperiled," *LAT*, November 17, 1984, B14; "Minutes, Compton Unified School District Board of Trustees, July 9, 1985," CUSD; "Minutes, Compton Unified School District Board of Trustees, July 23, 1985," CUSD; Michele Fuetsch, "Latino Aspirations on Rise in Compton Demographics," *LAT*, May 7, 1990, 1.

65. Cecilia Menjívar, "Educational Hopes, Documented Dreams" Guatemalan and Salvadoran Immigrants' Legality and Educational Prospects," *Annals of the American Academy of Political and Social Science* 620 (2008): 177–78; James P. Allen and Eugene Turner, *The Ethnic Quilt: Population Diversity in Southern California* (Northridge, Calif.: Center for Geographic Studies, 1997), 109–10.

66. As quoted in Michel Fuetsch, "Compton Latinos Allege Hiring Bias in Education," *LAT*, September 9, 1990, 7; "Minutes, Compton Unified School District Board of Trustees, September 5, 1990," CUSD.

67. Hamilton, *Seeking Community*, 56.

68. K. Filer, interview with author.

69. "Bias Suit Filed on 7 Demotions," *LAT*, July 29, 1980, C1; "Compton Teachers Claim Reverse Discrimination," *LAS*, July 31, 1980, 5; "Wade Denies Bias in Work Lawsuit," *LAS*, October 1, 1981, A2; Scott Harris, "White Officials Demoted by Compton Schools Win Case," *LAT*, November 21, 1981, E1; "Judge Assails Demotion of 7 Educators," *LAT*, November 23, 1981, OC_A4.

70. Bill Farr and Anne La Riviere, "Compton Downplays Diploma Issue," *LAT*, July 24, 1980, C1; Kevin Roderick, "State to Act on School's Disputed Teaching Degrees," *LAT*, August 9, 1980, B1; Cervantes, interview with author.

71. K. Filer, interview with author.

72. Kevin Roderick, "State Probing Nepotism in Compton School District," *LAT*, October 8, 1980, 22.

73. Anne La Riviere and George Reasons, "Compton's Schools: Sea of Troubles," *LAT*, July 1, 1981, B1.

74. Ibid.

75. Kathleen Martin, "State Takeover of the Compton Unified School District (Impact on Curriculum, Professionalism, and Leadership Styles)" (Ed.D. dissertation, University of Southern California, 1997), 89; Baenen, *Banking on Blight*, 9.

76. Quoted in Mary Barber, "Results of State Testing in Compton Schools Voided; Tampering Discovered," *LAT*, October 17, 1980, C3.

77. Rebecca Trounson, "Students Below State Averages: But 11 of 18 District Scores

Show Improvement," *LAT*, November 8, 1981, SE1; James H. Cleaver, "Compton School Board Fires Aaron C. Wade," *LAS* July 9, 1981, A1; La Raviere, "Compton's Schools: Sea of Troubles."

78. Kevin Roderick, "Test Stymies 1st Class of Seniors—But for Long?" *LAT*, June 21, 1981, A3; "Surplus of Teachers Becoming Shortage," *LAT*, April 20, 1981, SB2; Maura Dolan, "School Districts Worry About Diminishing Supply of Teachers," *LAT*, August 29, 1982, SE1.

79. All quotations from Laurel Leff, "Blackboard Jungle: In Inner-City School, Getting an Education Is Often a Difficult Job," *WSJ*, February 5, 1980, 1, 24.

80. Aaron C. Wade, "Letter to the Editor: A School District like Any Other?" *WSJ*, March 10, 1980, 27.

81. Ibid.

82. La Raviere, "Compton's Schools: Sea of Troubles"; Scott Harris and Anne La Raviere, "U.S. To Probe Compton Use of School Aid," *LAT*, September 3, 1981, F1.

83. Wilson Riles, "Detailed Information Regarding the Petition to Transfer Territory from the Compton Unified School District to the Los Angeles Unified School District," 1982, Compton Unified Reports Folder, Los Angeles County Commission of School District Organization Papers, LACOE.

84. Los Angeles County Superintendent of Schools, "Statement of Official Information and Statistics Prepared Pursuant to Education Code Section 35757," Compton Unified Reports Folder, Los Angeles County Commission of School District Organization Papers, LACOE; Gerald Faris, "School Transfer Bid Sent to State for OK," *LAT*, September 17, 1981, SB1.

85. Daryl Kelley, "Parents Keep Children Home in Protest of Compton School Conditions," *LAT*, November 15, 1984, SE17; Daryl Kelley, "Student District-Hopping Costs Compton $5 Million," *LAT*, February 24, 1985, SE5; L. Allen, interview with author; Cervantes, interview with author.

86. "Minutes, Compton Unified School District Board of Trustees, November 26, 1985," CUSD; Daryl Kelley, "Bargaining in Compton District Collapses," *LAT*, April 25, 1985, SE1.

87. Ivan Browne, "Willowbrook Junior High: A High Record of Continuing Excellence," *CHA*, January 21, 1982, 1, 2; Cervantes, interview with author.

88. Frank Clifford, "Highly Praised Compton School Accused of Waste," *LAT*, October 17, 1982, C1; Frank Clifford, "$80,000 Compton School Contract Questioned," *LAT*, November 21, 1982, SE1.

89. "Principal's Demotion Riles Public," *LAS*, May 12, 1983, A2; "School District Rebuts Finding of Federal Audit," *LAT*, December 16, 1982, SE2; David Einstein, "Compton Schools Chief Defends District Shakeup," *LAT*, May 5, 1983, SE1.

90. William Nottingham, "Trustee's Hearing Reveals Bitter Fruit Stress Claims by Woods Illuminates Rancor, Divisions in Compton Schools Leadership," *LAT*, November 23, 1986, 1; "Feds Probe School Dist. Spending," *LAS*, December 16, 1982, A3; "FBI Takes Control of CUSD," *LAS*, April 28, 1983, A1.

91. National Commission on Excellence in Education, *A Nation at Risk: The Imperative For Educational Reform* (Washington, D.C.: National Commission, 1983).

92. James Andrew LaSpina, *California in a Time of Excellence: School Reform at the Crossroads of the American Dream* (Albany: State University of New York Press, 2009); Janice Lowen Agee, "California Public Education: 1983–1994" (Sacramento: California Department of Education, 1994), 1, 17; George D. King, "Educating Minority Students in California: Descriptive Analysis and Policy Implications" (Sacramento: California Legislature Assembly, Office of Research, 1990), 1.

93. Jal Mehta, "How Paradigms Create Politics: The Transformation of American Educational Policy, 1980–2001," *American Educational Research Journal* 50 (2013).

94. "School Guard Hit by Shot from Auto," *LAT*, April 17, 1983, A33; Michael Seiler, "Bullets Hit 5 at Compton School, *LAT*, September 13, 1983, B1; Sandy Banks, "Security Tight at School After Shooting Spree," *LAT*, September 14, 1983; Chico C. Norwood, "Gunfire Mars School Opening," *LAS*, September 15, 1983, A1; "Compton High School Shooting Spurs Rally," *LAS*, October 13, 1983, A2.

95. A couple of weeks later, ABC Unified lifted its ban on home games at Dominguez High but allowed its individual principals to decide whether they would send their teams to Dominguez.

96. Jomarie Leone, "Dominguez Security OK'd," *CHA*, December 27, 1984, 1.

97. Shirley A. Thorton and Gerald H. Kilbert, "California Department of Education Report on the Compton Unified School District" (Sacramento: California Department of Education, 1992), 13; Compton Senior High for the 1988–89 school year had 1,701 enrolled (1,045 African American, 609 Latino), 217 graduated (149 African American, 52 Latino), 58 completed a–f requirements (40 African American, 18 Latino), 15 were U.C. Entrants (8 African American, 7 Latino). Dominguez High for 1988–89 had 1,867 enrolled (947 African American, 871 Latino), 291 graduated (165 African American, 122 Latino), 75 completed a–f requirements (41 African American, 33 Latino), 6 were U.C. Entrants (3 African American, 2 Latino). For the 1989–90 school year the statistics were also similar. Compton Senior High had 1,756 enrolled (1,016 African American, 712 Latino), 208 graduated (164 African American, 38 Latino), 57 completed a–f requirements (29 African American, 27 Latino), 8 were U.C. Entrants (2 African American, 6 Latino). Centennial High had 1,409 enrolled (840 African American, 553 Latino), 227 graduated (171 African American, 56 Latino), 40 completed a–f requirements (32 African American, 8 Latino), 2 were U.C. Entrants (0 African American, 1 Latino). Dominguez High had 1,785 enrolled (847 African American, 894 Latino), 365 graduated (200 African American, 161 Latino), 112 completed a–f requirements (67 African American; 40 Latino), 7 were U.C. Entrants (4 African American, 3 Latino).

98. Ibid., 11. Similar characteristics meant, for example, parent occupation index, parent education index, AFDC percentage.

99. Frank M. Sifuentes, "Letter to the Editor: Conflicts Surface in Compton as Latino Population Increases," *LAT*, May 17, 1990, 6.

100. Thorton and Kilbert, "California Department of Education Report," 12–13.

Compton High sent the most with nine, while Centennial and Dominguez sent two and three respectively.

101. David Einstein, "Compton Teachers Picket for Pay Hike," *LAT*, October 27, 1983, LB1; Einstein, "Compton Teachers Stage 1–Day Walkout to Back 5% Pay Hike," *LAT*, December 1, 1983, A1.

102. "Compton Raises Pay for Substitute Teachers," *LAT*, March 8, 1984, LB3.

103. "Compton," *LAT*, February 21, 1985, SE2; Daryl Kelley, "6% Raise for Teachers Rejected in Compton," *LAT*, April 11, 1985, SE1; "Compton Teachers OK New 2–Year Contract," *LAT*, May 3, 1985, A29.

104. William Nottingham, "Stress Test Cost of Workers Compensation Soars at Compton Schools," *LAT*, August 24, 1986, 1.

105. Kelley, "6% Raise for Teachers Rejected in Compton."

106. K. Filer, interview with author.

107. Quoted in Kenneth M. Ritter, "Compton Students 'Robbed,'" *CHA*, January 15, 1986, 1, 3; Henig et al., *Color of School Reform*.

108. "Minutes, Compton Unified School District Board of Trustees, March 25, 1986," CUSD; Nottingham, "Stress Test Cost of Workers Compensation Soars at Compton Schools."

109. L. Allen, interview with author.

110. "Schools Combat Arson," *LAS*, December 25, 1980, A18; "Schools Fight Vandalism," *LAS*, April 30, 1981, A5; Ritter, "Compton Students 'Robbed.'"

111. Richard Walker, "Urban Aid Cuts Come Under Fire," *CHA*, July 16, 1986, 1, 3.

112. "Minutes, Compton Unified School District Board of Trustees, September 23, 1986," CUSD.

113. Ibid.

114. Ibid.

115. Sheryl L. Thomas, "Teachers Return to Classes," *CHA*, July 16, 1986, 1.

116. Ibid.

117. Ibid.

118. "Striking Teachers Arrested," *CHA*, January 15, 1987, 1; Ralph Bailey, Jr., "Compton Teachers Arrested," *LAS*, January 15, 1987, A1; "Compton Teachers' Strike Barred," *LAS*, March 19, 1987, A1.

119. Sheryl L. Thomas, "Teachers Hit Picket Lines Again," *CHA*, January 29, 1987, 1, 3; William Nottingham, "Bitter Lessons: Compton School Labor Standoff Has Ugly Edge," *LAT*, February 1, 1987, 1.

120. As quoted in Mike Mills, "Classrooms in Compton Cited as 'Horrible' by NEA Chief," *LAT*, May 28, 1987, 1; Darlene C. Donloe, "Futrell Appalled at Conditions in Compton," *LAS*, May 14, 1987, A4.

121. Arnold Adler, "Teacher-District Talks Still Stalled," *CHA*, May 14, 1987, 1, 2.

122. William Nottingham, "Compton Teachers Ratify Pact Granting 7% Retroactive Raise," *LAT*, June 18, 1987, 1; "Compton Teachers, District In Accord," *LAS*, June 25, 1987, A1; "CTA Head Says Compton Teachers Are 'Suffering,'" *LAT*, June 4, 1987, A5.

123. Michele Fuetsch, "Compton Schools Near Teacher Quota Despite Turnover, Higher Rolls," *LAT*, September 28, 1989, 1; "Poor Working Conditions Cause Teacher Shortage," *LAS*, August 24, 1989, A10; Michele Fuetsch, "Inner City Teachers: Well, It Isn't the Paycheck," *LAT*, November 5, 1989, 1.

124. "Minutes, Compton Unified School District Board of Trustees, October 24, 1989," CUSD.

125. "Minutes, Compton Unified School District Board of Trustees, February 23, 1990"; "Minutes, Compton Unified School District Board of Trustees, March 27, 1990," CUSD; Michele Fuetsch and Tina Griego, "50% of School's Teachers Call in Ill," *LAT*, March 3, 1990, 4.

126. "Compton Parents Join Students to Protest Poor Conditions," *LAT*, May 13, 1990, 2; "Minutes, Compton Unified School District Board of Trustees, March 27, 1990," CUSD; "Parents Blast Compton Board, Picket Meeting," April 1990, Compton Unified School District Folder, Compton File, CPL.

127. As quoted in Michele Fuetsch, "Compton High Parents Group Urges Reforms," April 1990, Compton Unified School District Folder, Compton File, CPL.

128. Michele Fuetsch, "Report Says Compton Can Afford Hike in Teacher Pay," *LAT*, April 19, 1990, 1; Joe Segura, "Study Blasts Compton's School District Budgeting," April 1990, Compton Unified School District Folder, Compton File, CPL.

129. "Minutes, Compton Unified School District Board of Trustees, April 30, 1990," CUSD; Michele Fuetsch, "Latest Ideas for School Cuts Touch Off Uproar," *LAT*, May 13, 1990, 3.

130. As quoted in Hector Tobar and Michelle Fuetsch, "School Assaults Bring Tragedy to Compton," *LAT*, April 25, 1991, 1; "Student Shot on Campus," *LAT*, February 28, 1991, 2.

131. Pierre DeVise, "The Geography of Wealth and Poverty in Suburban America: 1979–1985," Committee on Population and Demographics, City Club of Chicago, 1987.

132. Ibid., 7, 18.

133. "City Council Minutes, August 11, 1987," CCH; William Nottingham, "Compton Council Rejects Tax Increase, Tough Gun Law," *LAT*, August 20, 1987, 1; M. Filer, interview with author.

134. "Minutes, Compton Unified School District Board of Trustees, April 10, 1990"; "Minutes, Compton Unified School District Board of Trustees, March 12, 1991"; "Minutes, Compton Unified School District Board of Trustees, April 23, 1991," CUSD.

135. Eithne Quinn, *Nuthin' but a "G" Thang: The Culture and Commerce of Gangsta Rap* (New York: Columbia University Press, 2005), 73–74; Herman Gray, *Watching Race: Television and the Struggle for Blackness* (Minneapolis: University of Minnesota Press, 1995), 23.

136. Quinn, *Nuthin' but a "G" Thang*, 72.

137. Gail Hilson Woldu, *The Words and Music of Ice Cube* (Westport, CT: Praeger, 2008), 15; Jeff Chang, *Can't Stop Won't Stop: A History of the Hip-Hop Generation* (New York: St. Martin's, 2005), 303, 306, 317.

138. As cited in Cross, *It's Not About a Salary*, 201.

139. NWA "Fuck Tha Police," *Straight Outta Compton* (Ruthless/Priority Records, 1988). For discussion see Tricia Rose, *Black Noise: Rap Music and Black Culture in Contemporary America* (Hanover, N.H.: Wesleyan University Press, 1994), 128–30.

140. Woldu, *The Words and Music of Ice Cube*, 20–21.

141. Dan Charnas, *The Big Payback: The History of the Business of Hip-Hop* (New York: New American Library, 2010), 223.

142. Verna Griffin, *Long Road Outta Compton: Dr. Dre's Mom on Family, Fame, and Terrible Tragedy* (Philadelphia: De Capo Press, 2008), 136.

143. Compton's Most Wanted, "Raised in Compton" (Epic/Sony, 1991); DJ Quik, "Born and Raised in Compton," *Quik Is the Name* (Priority Records, 1991).

144. Quinn, *Nuthin' but a "G" Thang*.

145. As cited in Cross, *It's Not About a Salary*, 198.

146. Murray Forman, "'Represent': Race, Space and Place in Rap Music," *Popular Music* 1 (January 2000): 83.

147. Rose, *Black Noise*; Brian Cross, *It's Not About a Salary*; Murray Forman, *The 'Hood Comes First: Race, Space, and Place in Rap and Hip-Hop* (Middletown, Conn.: Wesleyan University Press, 2002).

148. As cited in Lee Harris, "Paramount Erases 'Compton' Boulevard, Draws Fire," *LAT*, November 27, 1986, 1.

149. Adrianne Goodman, "'Street Wars' over Name Compton Blvd. Faces Identity Crisis," *LAT*, October 23, 1988, 10; Aubry, "Compton: A Backdrop to the Challenge and the Controversy," A7; Shawn Hubler, "Racism Seen in Street Name Change: Redondo Beach: Move to Rename Stretch of Compton Boulevard Considered a Swipe at the Predominantly Black City of Compton," *LAT*, December 31, 1989, 6; Dirk Breersma, "Hawthorne Is 3rd City to Change Street Name," July 1989, Compton Unified School District Folder, Compton File, CPL; "City Council Minutes, July 17, 1990," CCH; Michele Fuetsch, "East Compton's Name Change Riles Officials," *LAT*, August 9, 1990, 1.

150. As cited in Alida Brill, "Lakewood, California: 'Tomorrowland' at 40," in *Rethinking Los Angeles*, ed. Michael J. Dear et al. (Thousand Oaks, Calif.: Sage, 1996), 110.

Chapter 7. Enter the State

1. "Simi Valley Bound," *CB*, April 22, 1992, A1.

2. *Understanding the Riots: Los Angeles Before and After the Rodney King Case* (Los Angeles: Los Angeles Times, 1992), 45; Greg Braxton and Jim Newton, "Looting and Fires Ravage L.A.," *LAT*, May 1, 1992, A1, A10, A29; Seth Mydans, "Storm of Anger Erupts—National Guard Is Called into City," *NYT*, April 30, 1992, A1; Laurie Becklund and Stephanie Chavez, "Beaten Driver a Searing Image or Mob Cruelty," *LAT*, May 1, 1992, A1, A14.

3. *Understanding the Riots*, 74; James D. Delk, "Military Assistance in Los Angeles," *Military Review* (1992): 13.

4. Louise L. Hornor, ed., *California Cities, Towns, & Counties: Basic Data Profiles for*

All Municipalities & Counties, 1992 (Woodside, Calif.: Information Publications, 1992), 83; Bureau of the Census, "Twenty-First Census of the United States, 1990: Area and Population" (Washington, D.C.: Government Printing Office, 1990), 645; Shirley Thorton and Gerald H. Kilbert, "California Department of Education Report on the Compton Unified School District," (Sacramento: California Department of Education, 1992), 2. According to City of Compton, "City of Compton General Plan-Vision 2010" (Compton: City of Compton, 1991), 9–10, "The 1990 population of Compton is reported by the U.S. Census to be 90,454, ranking 15th among the 85 cities in Los Angeles Country. However, based on evidence of unit overcrowding and illegal garage conversions, the actual count of persons in the City may likely be higher. Estimates of population growth can be made using a variety of methods. To estimate the City's population at build-out, (assuming that build-out means less than 100 percent of the maximum possible number of dwelling units permitted under land use policy), the number of permitted units can be multiplied by the average household size reported by the 1990 U.S. Census. This method yields a build-out population in the City of 112,445 persons, assuming 28.906 total dwelling units and an average household size of 3.89 people." For further discussion see F. Allen, interview with author; L. Allen, interview with author; Stan Bosch, interview with author, October 18, 2004, Compton, California, interview in possession of author.

5. "City Council Minutes, April 30, 1992," CCH; "City Lifts Emergency," *CB*, May 6, 1992, A1.

6. California State Assembly, State of California: Assembly Bill Number: AB 33, 1993; Harold Blume, "School District Requests Bailout of $18.4 Million," *LAT*, March 25, 1993; "Compton Schools in Trouble Again," *LAS*, March 25, 1993, A1; P. Pascual, "State Appointee Takes Over Compton Schools," *LAT*, July 10, 1993.

7. "Excerpts from Bush's Speech on Los Angeles Riots: 'Need to Restore Order,'" *NYT*, May 2, 1992, 50; *Understanding the Riots*, 98.

8. *Understanding the Riots*, 108; Manual Pastor, Jr., "Latinos and the Los Angeles Uprising: The Economic Context" (Claremont, Calif.: Tomas Rivera Center, 1993), 11–12.

9. D. O. Sears, "Black-White Conflict: A Model for the Future of Ethnic Politics in Los Angeles," in *New York and Los Angeles: Politics, Society, and Culture: A Comparative View*, ed. David Halle (Chicago: University of Chicago Press, 2003), 384.

10. "Of 58 Riot Deaths, 50 Have Been Ruled Homicides," *NYT*, May 17, 1992, 26; "U.S. Looks into Korean Grocer's Slaying of Black," *NYT*, November 26, 1992, A18; "City Lifts Emergency," A1; "DAC Loans Available," *CB*, May 13, 1992, A1, A2; "Richards Tells of Rebuilding Plan," *CB*, May 6, 1992, A1.

11. "Investigation Continues into Missing Police Funds," *CB*, July 29, 1992, A1, A2; "Legislation Aids Compton Civil Unrest Recovery," *CB*, October 20, 1993, A2; "City Council Minutes, October 12, 1993," CCH.

12. As cited in, *Understanding the Riots*, 117.

13. Carla Rivera, "Riots' Causes Same as in '60s, State Panel Says," *LAT*, October 2, 1992, A1, A34.

14. Assemblyman Willard H. Murray, Jr., to Governor Pete Wilson, September 4, 1992, GCBF-vetoed, AB2043, 1992, CSA.

15. "Compton Unified School District: Facts at a Glance," Murray, AB 2043, 1992, CSA.

16. Stephen G. Blake to Assembly Member Willard Murray, memorandum, 8 January 1991, A/C Ed., AB33, 1993, CSA.

17. "State May Take Over Local School District," *CB*, September 2, 1992; "Unofficial Board Meeting Actions, Compton Unified School District Board of Education, September 2, 1992," CUSD; "City of Compton General Plan-Vision 2010, Facilities Element," 5.

18. Governor Pete Wilson to Members of the California Assembly, n.d., Murray Papers, AB 33, 1993, CSA.

19. As cited in Howard Blume, "Compton Schools Face Twin Crises," *LAT*, October 2, 1992, B1, B4.

20. K. Filer, interview with author; James Bolden, "Compton Education System under Fire," *LAS*, October 29, 1992, A1, A14; "City May Lose CUSD," *CB*, August 12, 1992, A1, A2; "Final Meeting Today," *CB*, September 23, 1992, A1, A11.

21. Maureen Saul to Kelvin Filer, February 23, 1993, A/C Ed., AB33, 1993, CSA.

22. K. Filer, interview with author; Bolden, "Compton Education System Under Fire," A14; "Harold Cebrun New Acting School Head," *CB*, December 16, 1992, A11.

23. "State Posts Call for Administrator," *CB*, April 28, 1993, A2; "Compton Schools in Trouble Again"; "CUSD Faces Bankruptcy," *CB*, March 24, 1993, A1, A2; "CUSD Financial Woes," *CB*, March 31, 1993, A1, A2; "Murray Legislation Offers Bailout Loan," *CB*, April 7, 1993, A1, A2; Harold Blume, "School District Requests Bailout of $18.4 Million," *LAT*, March 25, 1993, Compton Unified School District Folder, Compton File, CPL; "Agenda, Special Meeting, Compton Unified School District Board of Trustees, March 30, 1993," CUSD.

24. Los Angeles County Office of Education, "Report of Priority Corrective Actions for the Compton Unified School District," May 4, 1993, Senate Committee on Education, AB 33, 1993, CSA.

25. See, e.g., Kelvin Filer to Delaine Eastin, 23 February 1993, A/C Ed., AB33, 1993; Hourie Taylor to Delaine Eastin, 14 May 1993, Murray, AB 33, 1993, CSA; Harold Cebrun to Gary Hart, 29 June 1993, Murray, AB 33, CSA.

26. "CUSD Gets Bailed Out," *CB*, July 7, 1993, A1, A10.

27. "Concurrence in Senate Amendments," A/C Ed., AB33, 1993, CSA.

28. "State Takes Over CUSD," *CB*, July 14, 1993, A1, A2; Pascual, "State Appointee Takes Over Compton Schools."

29. "Compton Gets New School Chief," *LAS*, August 25, 1993, A1; "Search Continues for School Administrator," *CB*, August 25, 1993, A1, A2; James Bolden, "Compton Stepping Up School Chiefs Search," *LAS*, September 2, 1993.

30. K. Filer, interview with author.

31. Kevin Bushweller, "Under the Shadow of the State," *American School Board Journal* 185 (1998): 17.

32. "City/Schools Unite to Quell Mounting Tension," *CB*, September 8, 1993, A1, A2; Bolden, "Compton Stepping Up School Chiefs Search"; Fiscal Crisis and Management Assistance Team, "Compton Unified School District AB52 Assessment and Recovery Plans, February 1999," 1. The two appropriations bills, AB 657.Stats 1993, Chapter 78; AB 1708.Stat 1993, Chapter 924, were in July 1992 and October 1993. The idea of selling off district lands continued. See "New Bill Would Help Compton Pay Debts," *LAS*, January 25, 1996, A8.

33. Omar Bradley to Delaine Eastin, n.d., Senate Committee on Education, AB 33, 1993, CSA.

34. Juan Carrillo, interview with author, June 22, 2007, phone interview, interview in possession of author; Malaika Brown, "Compton Unified School District Awaits Arrival of Superintendent," *LAS*, January 27, 1994, A3.

35. Erin Aubry Kaplan, "The King of Compton," *LAW*, April 4, 2001.

36. F. Allen, interview with the author.

37. Mike Davis, *Dead Cities and Other Tales* (New York: New Press, 2002), 282; Cervantes, interview with author; Kaplan, "The King of Compton."

38. Kaplan, "The King of Compton."

39. "Audit Confirms Charges," *CB*, February 3, 1993, A1, A12; "Board Clarifies Action," *CB*, June 9, 1993, A1, A4; "Board Fired Washington," *CB*, March 17, 1993, A1, A16; "New Head for College," *CB*, March 3, 1993, A1, A2; " 'No Confidence' Vote," *CB*, February 24, 1993, A1, A2; "Official Admits Wrongdoing," *CB*, February 3, 1992, A1; "State Queries College," *CB*, March 10, 1993, A1, A2; Bolden, "Compton Stepping Up School Chiefs Search"; "Cronies Spare Jones; Dean Willard Is Sacrificial Lamb," *CB*, June 2, 1993, A1, A2.

40. As cited in Sabrina Hockaday, "Bringing Compton Together at Summit," *LBPT*, April 29, 1994, Compton-Race Relations Folder, Compton File, CPL; "City Council Minutes, April 19, 1994," CCH.

41. "California Department of Education Report on the Compton Unified School District," 3.

42. As cited in, "If Compton Schools Were in South Africa, They'd Be Closed Down," *CB*, May 4, 1994, A1.

43. Los Angeles County Office of Education, "Report of Priority Corrective Actions for the Compton Unified School District," May 4, 1993, 4–5; Senate Committee on Education, AB 33, 1993, CSA.

44. Senate Committee on Education, AB 33, 1993, CSA. For information on Harris see "State-Appointed Administrator Now at Helm," *CB*, February 9, 1994, A1.

45. "Minutes of Regular Meeting of the State Administrator and Advisory Board of Trustees, Compton Unified School, February 10, 1998," CUSD; "Unofficial Board Meeting Actions, Regular Advisory Meeting of State Administrator, CUSD, March 14, 1995"; "Minutes of Regular Meeting, CUSD Board of Education, April 26, 1988"; "Minutes of Regular Meeting, CUSD Board of Education, May 8, 1990"; "Minutes of Regular Meeting, Compton Unified School District Board of Education, November 10, 1987," all CUSD.

46. Sarah Sentilles, *Taught by America: A Story of Struggle and Hope in Compton* (Boston: Beacon Press, 2005), 5.

47. "Rally Protest Police Beating of Teen-Ager," *NYT*, August 7, 1994, 25; Davis, *Dead Cities and Other Tales*, 276–77; "Activists Cry for Unity, Criticize Compton Officer," *LAS*, August 11, 1994, A1; "Latinos Picket, Want Investigation," *LAS*, September 1, 1994, A3.

48. Bryan Cotton, "Hispanics Boycott Compton School," *LAS*, September 22, 1994, A1.

49. Ibid.

50. R. Michael Alvarez and Tara L. Butterfield, "The Resurgence of Nativism in California? The Case of Proposition 187 and Illegal Immigration," *Social Science Quarterly* 81 (2000): 167.

51. Sekou M. Franklin and Richard Seltzer, "Conflicts in the Coalition: Challenges to Black and Latino Political Alliances," *Western Journal of Black Studies* 26 (2002): 75.

52. Steve Farr, "Prop. 187: Some Blacks See Illegal Immigrants as Competition" *LAS*, October 20, 1994.

53. Jim Newton, "Compton's Racial Divide," *LAT*, May 16, 2011.

54. Farr, "Prop. 187."

55. F. Allen, interview with author.

56. L. Allen, interview with author.

57. Nelson, interview with author.

58. Cervantes, interview with author.

59. As cited in, Sam Roberts, "Hispanic Population Outnumbers Blacks in Four Major Cities as Demographics Shift," *NYT*, October 9, 1994, 34. Similar tensions can be seen in other areas. In Miami, for example, tensions arose between blacks and Latinos over competition for jobs and government contracts. For more information, see William Julius Wilson, "The Political Economy and Urban Racial Tensions," *American Economist* 39 (1995): 5.

60. "Compton Schools," *City News Service*, June 8, 2000.

61. California AB 474 1994

62. Ibid.

63. Willard H. Murray, "Prison Will Improve Compton's Image and Create New Jobs," *CB*, October 5, 1994, A10; "Committee Studies New Proposal for Compton Prison," *LAS*, April 14, 1994, A1.

64. Thompson, "Why Mass Incarceration Matters," 733; "Senate Panel Rejects Plan for Prison Facility," *LAT*, June 23, 1994.

65. Murray, "Prison Will Improve Compton's Image."

66. Pysche Pascual, "Voters to Advise City on Prison Proposal," *LAT*, January 5, 1995.

67. Emanuel Parker, "Compton Prison: Tucker, Murray Argue over Proposed Jail," *LAS*, February 1, 1995, A1.

68. As quoted in ibid.

69. HoSang, *Racial Propositions,* 161.

70. "City Council Minutes, February 22, 1994," CCH; Pascual, "Voters to Advise."

71. Emily Adams, "Assemblyman Gives Up on State Prison Plan," *LAT,* May 4, 1995.

72. Davis, *Dead Cities and Other Tales,* 280.

73. Thompson, "Why Mass Incarceration Matters," 703; Alexander, *The New Jim Crow.*

74. Thompson, "Why Mass Incarceration Matters," 703.

75. "Southern California Edison Pledges $35 Million to Rebuild Compton," *LAS,* June 4, 1992, B7; "Conference Held on Area Revitalization," *LAS,* July 22, 1993, B7.

76. "Robbins, Green Face Runoff: Voters Want Fresh Leadership," *CB,* April 26, 1995, A1, A2. For further discussion see, Cressel, interview with author.

77. Emily Adams and Tina Daunt, "Compton Getting a Bad Rap, Residents Say," *LAT,* August 12, 1994, A24.

78. "Compton get [sic] $536,000 Grant," *LAS,* December 1, 1994, A8; "Casino/Hotel Set for Compton," *LAS,* September 21, 1995, A3; Jim Cleaver, "Some Odd Things at Compton Poker Parlor," *LAS,* November 28, 1996, A1, A7.

79. Wilson, "The Political Economy and Urban Racial Tensions." For a more extensive explanation, see William Julius Wilson, *When Work Disappears: The World of the New Urban Poor* (New York: Knopf, 1996); James D. Smith, "Measuring the Informal Economy," *Annals of the American Academy of Political and Social Science* 493 (1987): 83. For discussion of informal economy, see, e.g., Alejandro Portes, Manuel Castells, and Lauren A. Benton, eds., *The Informal Economy: Studies in Advanced and Less Developed Countries* (Baltimore: Johns Hopkins University Press, 1989); M. Estellie Smith, ed., *Perspectives on the Informal Economy* (Lanham, Md.: University Press of American, 1990); Jeffrey Fagan, "Drug Selling and Licit Income in Distressed Neighborhoods: The Economic Lives of Street-Level Drug Users and Dealers," in *Drugs, Crime, and Social Isolation: Barriers to Urban Opportunity,* ed. Adele V. Harrell and George E. Peterson (Washington, D.C.: Urban Institute Press, 1992), 99.

80. As cited in Murray, "Prison Will Improve Compton's Image and Create New Jobs," For discussion of gang activity in Compton, see Cervantes, interview with author; Deborah Hastings, "Compton Residents Still face Crime and Racial Tension," *LAS,* February 22, 1996, A4; Adams and Daunt, "Compton Getting a Bad Rap, Residents Say."

81. Sentilles, *Taught by America,* 12.

82. Ibid., 154.

83. "Walter Tucker Hit with Extortion, Fraud Charges," *LAS,* August 18, 1994, A1; Michael Janofsky, "California Congressman Is Indicted by U.S.," *NYT,* August 12, 1994, A12; Jim Newton and Emily Adams, "Rep. Tucker Is Indicted; Denies Bribery Charges," *LAT,* August 12, 1994, A1, A24; Ron Russell and Robert J. Lopez, "Rep. Tucker Indicted on New Charges," *LAT,* June 2, 1995, B1, B3; Davis, *Dead Cities and Other Tales,* 277. This was not the first time Tucker had been involved with legal scandals. In 1988, as a prosecutor in the Los Angeles County District Attorney's office, he was charged with tampering with the date on photographs he was using as evidence in a narcotics case in

an effort to cover up his having withheld evidence from the defense. Tucker pleaded no contest to these charges and served 3 years probation. Despite these marks on his record, in April 1991 he became Compton's youngest mayor and after less than a two-year term as mayor, he was elected to the U.S. Congress with 86 percent of the vote. See Carla Hall, "Tucker's Career Blossomed Despite Scandal," *LAT*, August 12, 1994, A24; Janofsky, "California Congressman Is Indicted by U.S."; Davis, *Dead Cities and Other Tales*, 277.

84. "Tucker's Troubles Continue," *CB*, August 17, 1994, A1, A12; "Tucker Retains Seat," *CB*, November 16, 1994, A1, A2.

85. Kenneth B. Noble, "Congressman Heads to Trial in California," *NYT*, September 25, 1995, A10; David Rosenzweig, "Rep. Tucker Found Guilty of Bribery and Tax Evasion," *LAT*, December 9, 1995, A1, A22; "Tucker Indicted Again," *CB*, June 7, 1995, A1, A2; "Tucker's Star Comes Crashing Down," *CB*, December 13, 1995, A1; Emanuel Parker, "Tucker Convicted on Nine Felony Counts," *LAS*, December 14, 1995, A1.

86. Jim Newton and Henry Weinstein, "Rep. Tucker to Be Indicted Sources Say," *LAT*, August 11, 1994, A1, A23; "Moore Indicted on 23 Counts," *CB*, September 6, 1995, A1, A2.

87. "Moore Indicted on 23 Counts," CB, September 6, 1995, A1, A2; "Pat Moore Cries Foul Claims 'Railroaded,'" *CB*, November 23, 1994, A1, A13.

88. Rosenzweig, "Rep. Tucker Found Guilty of Bribery and Tax Evasion"; "The Pat Moore Saga Continues and Continues and Continues," *CB*, April 23, 1997, A1; "Pat Moore Gets 33 Months in Texas Prison," *CB*, May 14, 1997, A1, A2; Emanuel Parker, "Ex-Councilwoman Gets 33 Months," *LAS*, May 15, 1997, A1.

89. "School Administrator Responds to Charges," *CB*, September 28, 1994, A1, A2; "Workman's Comp Fraud Investigated," *CB*, September 21, 1994, A1, A2; "CUSD Director Investigated," *CB*, February 1, 1995, A1, A2; "Monk Pleads Guilty," *CB*, April 26, 1995, A1; "School Official get 16 Months," *LAS*, April 20, 1995, A1; Cressel, interview with author. In October 2004, former board trustee Basil Kimbrew was charged with misuse of funds while in office. The charges were for actions after the state takeover.

90. Sentilles, *Taught by America*, 111.

91. Ibid., 114.

92. "CUSD Board to File Federal Lawsuit," *CB*, December 20, 1995, A1; Michael Datcher, "Trustees Try to Regain Control," *LAS*, June 27, 1996, A1; Eric Moses, "Compton Officials Tell It to the Judge," *LAS*, February 27, 1997, A1.

93. Cervantes, interview with author.

94. F. Allen, interview with author; L. Allen, interview with author.

95. As cited in Michael Datcher, "Compton School Chief Will Retire; An 'Agent for Change,'" *LAS*, February 22, 1996, A3.

96. Ibid.

97. "Compton Gets New School Chief," *LAS*, March 28, 1996, A1; "New State Administrator to Take over CUSD Reins," *CB*, February 7, 1996, A1, A14; Datcher, "Compton School Chief Will Retire."

98. "District Advisory Board Holds Special Meeting," *CB*, February 21, 1996, A1.

99. Daniel de Vise, "Compton Schools Get D+," *LBPT*, May 30, 1996, CUSD Folder, Compton File, CPL.

100. "Schools to Get $13 Mil Facelift," *LAS*, June 6, 1996, A1; "Compton Teachers Return to Classrooms," *LBPT*, June 2, 1996, Compton Unified School District Folder, Compton File, CPL; "Teachers Settle Strike," *CB*, June 12, 1996, A1, A5; "Minutes of Special Meeting of the State Administrator and Advisory Board of Trustees, Compton Unified School, August 6, 1996," CUSD; "City Council Minutes, June 11, 1996," CCH; Daniel de Vise, "Compton Strike Cripples Schools," *LBPT*, June 1, 1996, Compton Unified School District Folder, Compton File, CPL; Peter Y. Hong, "Compton Teachers to Strike After Talk Fails," *LAT*, June 6, 1996, 1.

101. "Minutes of Special Meeting of the State Administrator and Advisory Board of Trustees, Compton Unified School, September 24, 1996," CUSD; "Minutes of Special Meeting of the State Administrator and Advisory Board of Trustees, Compton Unified School, June 10, 1997," CUSD; "Minutes of Special Meeting of the State Administrator and Advisory Board of Trustees, Compton Unified School, June 10, 1997," CUSD.

102. Dan Olmos, Commentary: Affirmative Action Should Be About Equality (*All Things Considered*, NPR, 24 June 2003).

103. Jeff Leeds, "State Fails to Stop Compton Schools' Slide into Decay," *LAT*, January 26, 1997. Parents had been continuously complaining about the conditions of Compton Unified's schools. See, e.g., "Minutes of Special Meeting of the State Administrator and Advisory Board of Trustees, Compton Unified School, October 15, 1996," CUSD; "Minutes of Special Meeting of the State Administrator and Advisory Board of Trustees, Compton Unified School, November 19, 1996," CUSD.

104. Bushweller, "Under the Shadow of the State," 17.

105. "The Lions in Compton," *LBPT*, November 15, 1996 Compton Unified School District Folder, Compton File, CPL.

106. "CSBA Officials to Visit Compton School District," *CB*, July 16, 1997, A2; Fiscal Crisis and Management Assistance Team, "Compton Unified School District, *Serna v. Eastin* Consent Decree Six Month Report, February 2002."

107. "California Parents Sue State over Schools in Their City," *NYT*, July 14, 1997, A12; "CSBA Officials to Visit Compton School District," A1, A2; Fiscal Crisis and Management Assistance Team, "Compton Unified School District, *Serna v. Eastin* Consent Decree Six Month Report"; Heather Wood, "Parents File Suit over Schools," *LBPT*, July 10, 1997, Compton Unified School District Folder, Compton File, CPL. Examples of state approval for fixing of damages, see: "Minutes of Special Meeting of the State Administrator and Advisory Board of Trustees, Compton Unified School, August 31, 1993," CUSD; "Minutes of Special Meeting of the State Administrator and Advisory Board of Trustees, Compton Unified School, March 14, 1995," CUSD; "State, Compton School District Settle with ACLU, Other Groups," *LAS*, December 25, 1997, A4.

108. "School Trustees Lose Lawsuit against State," *CB*, March 5, 1997, A1, A2; "Justice Department Investigates Compton School District Takeover," *CB*, April 2, 1997, A1;

Johnston, "Justice Dept. Investigates Takeover of Calif. District." For state takeovers possibly violating the voting rights act, also see: Lynn Olson, "State Takeovers Run Afoul of Voting Rights Act," in *Education Week on the Web* (1996).

109. If passed, the state would match the $107 million in funds to renovate the schools. "City Council Minutes, September 1, 1998," CCH.

110. Shirley Allen, "Bond Issue Support," *CB*, April 8, 1998, A2.

111. "City Council Minutes, January 13, 1998," CCH.

112. "Minutes of Regular Meeting of the State Administrator and Advisory Board of Trustees, Compton Unified School, January 13, 1998," CUSD. Emphasis in original document.

113. For details on the conflict between the city and state over the appointment, see: "Bradley-Jordan Fails to Stop Sanchez Appointment," *CB*, March 18, 1998, A1, A2; "Bradley, Lankster Petition for Special Election," *CB*, February 25, 1998, A1, A2; "City Files Suit on School Appointment," *CB*, February 11, 1998, A1, A2; "CUSD Board Appointment Process Reopened," *CB*, January 28, 1998, A1; "Leslie Irving Named to School Board," *CB*, January 14, 1998, A1; "Restraining Order Filed on State Appointment," *CB*, January 21,1998, A1, A2; Deborah Belgum, "Compton Schools Feud Flares Anew; Education," *LAT*, March 12, 1998, B1; "Compton Mayor's Sister Arrested," *LAS*, March 19, 1998, A3; "Minutes of Regular Meeting of the State Administrator and Advisory Board of Trustees, Compton Unified School, March 10, 1998," CUSD; Mariko Thompson, "City, School Board Clash," *LBPT*, March 17, 1998, Compton Unified School District Folder, Compton File, CPL.

Epilogue: Out from Compton's Past

1. As quoted in Ian Hanigan, "Compton Reclaims Its Schools," *LBPT*, December 13, 2001, A1. See also "Back from Bankruptcy," *LBPT*, December 13, 2001.

2. Dennis Freeman, "Local School Districts Behind in Hiring 'Highly Qualified' Credentialed Teachers," *LAS*, October 9, 2003, A1; Dennis Freeman, "Struggles in Schools Continue Even Beyond Brown vs. Board," *LAS*, May 27, 2004, A1.

3. "Eastin Labels Compton School Board 'Corrupt,'" *CB*, July 23, 1997, A1; "School Recovery Plan Passes Senate," *CB*, June 11, 1997, A1, A14; "School District Stays Under State Control," *CB*, October 15, 1997, A1, A2.

4. Fiscal Crisis and Management Assistance Team, "Compton Unified School District AB52 Assessment and Recovery Plans, February 1999," 2; "AB52 Goes Through Changes," *CB*, June 25, 1997; "School District Stays Under State Control." Assemblyman Washington tried to bypass this bill in 1999 by proposing alternative legislation to restore all legal rights, powers, and duties to the district immediately. His constituents, who implored other lawmakers not to return the district to local control, derailed this attempt. Washington assembled his own panel of impassioned supporters to counter these assertions, but the legislature voted against his bill and redirected the focus on the implementation of the 1997 legislation. Fiscal Crisis and Management Assistance Team, "Compton Unified School District AB52 Assessment and Recovery Plans, August 1999,"

1; Dorothy Korber, "Schools' Return Denied," *LBPT*, April 9, 1999, CUSD Folder, Compton File, CPL.

5. "Minutes of Regular Meeting of the State Administrator and Advisory Board of Trustees, Compton Unified School, December 9, 1997," CUSD.

6. "Students Must Pass before Being Passed," *LAS*, April 2, 1998, A1, A13; "Compton Schools Turn to Private Sector," *LBPT*, February 24, 1998, CUSD Folder, Compton File, CPL; "Compton Students Get Boost from New Partnership," *CB*, March 4, 1998, A1, A2; "Minutes of Regular Meeting of the State Administrator and Advisory Board of Trustees, Compton Unified School, February 13, 2001," CUSD; "Minutes of Regular Meeting of the State Administrator and Advisory Board of Trustees, Compton Unified School, July 10, 2001," CUSD; "Minutes of Regular Meeting of the State Administrator and Advisory Board of Trustees, Compton Unified School, September 25, 2001," CUSD.

7. Richard Less Colvin, "District Hires Tutors, Raising Questions," *LAT*, February 23, 1998,; Ted Shelsby, "Sylvan wins Calif. Deal worth $5.4 million Math, reading for Compton district," *BS*, January 22, 1998.

8. Randolph E. Ward, *Improving Achievement in Low-Performing Schools: Key Results for School Leaders* (Thousand Oaks, Calif.: Corwin Press, 2004).

9. "Academic Performance Index," California Department of Education, http://www.cde.ca.gov/ta/ac/ap/, accessed March 30, 2013.

10. Patricia Burch, *Hidden Markets: The New Education Privatization* (New York: Routledge, 2009); Julie A. Marsh, Ron W. Zimmer, Deanna Hill, and Brian P. Gill, "A Brief History of Edison Schools and a Review of Existing Literature," in *Inspiration, Perspiration, and Time: Operations and Achievement in Edison Schools*, ed. Brian P. Gill et al. (Santa Monica, Calif.: RAND, 2005), 7; Heinrich Mintrop and Tina Trujillo, "The Practical Relevance of Accountability Systems for School Improvement: A Descriptive Analysis of California Schools," *Educational Evaluation and Policy Analysis* 29 (2007): 320; Heinrich Mintrop and Tina Trujillo, "Corrective Action in Low Performing Schools: Lessons for NCLB Implementation from First-Generation Accountability Systems," *Education Policy Analysis Archives* 13 (2005).

11. Ward, *Improving Achievement in Low-Performing Schools*.

12. "Enterprise Zone Program," California Department of Housing and Community Development, http://www.hcd.ca.gov/fa/ez/EZoverview.html, accessed April 1, 2013; "Gov. Davis Announces Employment and Job Training Grant for Compton," *LAS*, January 31, 2002, A16.

13. "Gov. Davis Announces Employment"; "Compton to Benefit from HUD Housing Grant," *LAS*, August 15, 2002, A18.

14. Fiscal Crisis and Management Assistance Team, "Compton Unified School District, *Serna v Eastin* Consent Decree Six Month Report, February 2002," 1; Betty Pleasant, "Court Orders State to Improve Education in Compton Schools," *LAS*, March 23, 2000, A1, A14; "Minutes of Regular Meeting of the State Administrator and Advisory Board of Trustees, Compton Unified School, October 10, 2000," CUSD.

15. "Schools in Local Hands," *LBPT*, September 20, 2000, Compton Unified School District Folder, Compton File, CPL; "City Council Minutes, April 4, 2000," CCH.

16. Kalem Aquil, "Letter: The State and the Compton Schools," *LAS*, April 27, 2000, A6; Tracy Manzer, "Compton Schools May Out Janitors," *LBPT*, October 7, 2000, Compton Unified School District Folder, Compton File, CPL.

17. "City Council Minutes, January 16, 2001," CCH; "City Council Minutes, January 23, 2001," CCH; Mary Hancock Hinds, "Compton Funding School Texts," *LBPT*, December 23, 2000, Compton Unified School District Folder, Compton File, CPL.

18. Ian Hanigan, "Compton Regains Its Schools," *LBPT*, December 13, 2001, A9.

19. "Minutes of Regular Meeting of the State Administrator and Advisory Board of Trustees, Compton Unified School, August 28, 2001," CUSD; "Minutes of Regular Meeting, Board of Trustees, Compton Unified School, December 11, 2001," CUSD; Reid, "Calif. Returns Compton District to Local Control"; "Control of Schools Returned to Compton; New Board Seated," *LAS*, December 20, 2001, A4; Hanigan, "Compton Regains its Schools;" Ian Hanigan, "Compton Regains School Control," *LBPT*, June 2, 2003.

20. Fiscal Crisis and Management Assistance Team, "Compton Unified School District AB52 Assessment and Recovery Plans, February 2001," 10–11.

21. Ian Hanigan, "'Centennial' Students Pondering Their Future," *LBPT*, September 1, 2003; Dennis Freeman, "Stripping of Accreditation Hits Parents by Surprise," *LAS*, August 28, 2003, A1.

22. F. Allen, interview with author.

23. Bosch, interview with author. For further discussion of Centennial's loss of accreditation, see F. Allen, interview with author.

24. See Bosch, interview with author; Cervantes, interview with author. For examples of interethnic fighting see "Compton Students fight on Campus and at Football Game," *Associated Press State and Local Wire*, October 11, 2003. This article describes how a fight between two girls at Compton High triggered a "race-related melee" that involved at least fifty students and school officials to lock down the campus for approximately two hours.

25. Kevin K. Kumashiro, *The Seduction of Common Sense: How the Right Has Framed the Debate on America's Schools* (New York: Teachers College Press, 2008), 37.

26. Diane Ravitch, *The Death and Life of the Great American School System: How Testing and Choice are Undermining Education* (New York: Basic Books, 2012), 93–94; Kumashiro, *The Seduction of Common Sense*, 28.

27. Kumashiro, *The Seduction of Common Sense*, 19.

28. Jennifer Booher-Jennings, "Below the Bubble: 'Educational Triage' and the Texas Accountability System," *American Educational Research Journal* 42 (2005): 233.

29. Angela Valenzuela, "Introduction: The Accountability Debate in Texas: Continuing the Conversation," in *Leaving Children Behind: How Texas-Style Accountability Fails Latino Youth*, ed. Angela Valenzuela (Albany: State University of New York Press, 2005), 1.

30. "Governor Applauds Bunche Elementary School, a 2006 California Distinguished School," CUSD, http://www.compton.k12.ca.us/www/documents/Governor%20Applauds%20Bunche%20Elem%20news%20release%205-16-06.pdf.

31. Patrick Range McDonald, "California's Parent Trigger," LAW, December 9, 2010. In 2012, Laurel Elementary became the third Compton school to be named a California Distinguished School. That same year it was named a Nation Title I Distinguished School, denoting its ranking among the country's top Title I schools.

32. Kristina Rizga, "The Battle over Charter Schools," Mother Jones, April 7, 2011"; Theresa Montaño, "Obama, Eschucha! Estamos en la Lucha!: Challenging Neoliberalism in Los Angeles Schools," in The Phenomenon of Obama and the Agenda for Education: Can Hope Audaciously Trump Neoliberalism, ed. Paul R. Carr and Brad J. Porfilio (Charlotte, N.C.: Information Age, 2011), 176.

33. School turnarounds were an integral part of the Obama administration's education policy. See http://www2.ed.gov/programs/sif/sigoverviewppt.pdf; http://www.ed.gov/category/program/school-improvement-grants, accessed December 2, 2012. For analysis of the effectiveness of school turnarounds, see Tina Trujillo and Michelle Renée, Democratic School Turnarounds: Pursuing Equity and Learning from Evidence (Boulder, Colo.: National Education Policy Center, 2012).

34. Patrick Range McDonald, "California's Parent Trigger," LAW, December 9, 2010; Janelle T. Scott, "Market-Driven Education Reform and the Racial Politics of Advocacy," Peabody Journal of Education 86 (2011): 580–99, 586.

35. Scott, "Market-Driven Reform," 586.

36. McDonald, "California's Parent Trigger"; Scott, "Market-Driven Reform," 586.

37. "Lessons of 'Parent Trigger,'" LAT, editorial, November 14, 2011.

38. Simone Wilson, "Compton's Parent Trigger Feud," LAW, December 30, 2010.

39. "Examining California's Parent Trigger Law," National Public Radio, May 8, 2011.

40. Ravitch, Death and Life, 122; Scott, "Market-Driven Reform," 581.

41. Simon Wilson, " 'Parent Trigger' Plan B," LAW, May 26, 2011.

42. Martin Carnoy, Rebecca Jacobsen, Lawrence Mishel, and Richard Rothstein, The Charter School Dust-Up: Examining the Evidence on Enrollment and Achievement (Washington, D.C.: Economic Policy Institute, 2005), 3.

43. Christopher Lubienski, Janelle T. Scott, John Rogers, and Kevin G. Welner, "Missing the Target? The Parent Trigger as a Strategy for Parental Engagement and School Reform," NEPC Policy Memo (2012).

44. Wilson, "Compton's Parent Trigger Feud"

45. As cited in Wilson, "Compton's Parent Trigger Feud."

46. Wilson, "Compton Parent Trigger Feud."

47. Kristina Rizga, "The Battle over Charter Schools," Mother Jones, April 7, 2011.

48. "Our Work: McKinley Elementary," Parent Revolution, http://parentrevolution.org/content/mckinley-elementary, accessed November 1, 2012.

49. Wilson, "Compton's Parent Trigger Feud."

50. Simone Wilson, "Why Compton Unified Rejected the Parent Trigger (and Why It's in No Position to Do So)," *LAW*, February 25, 2011.

51. "Lessons of 'Parent Trigger.'"

52. Ibid.

53. Philip E. Kovacs, ed., *The Gates Foundation and the Future of U.S. "Public" Schools* (New York: Routledge, 2011).

54. Ravitch, *Death and Life*, 133.

55. Janelle T. Scott, "Market-Driven Education Reform and the Racial Politics of Advocacy," *Peabody Journal of Education* 86 (2011): 581; Carnoy et al. *The Charter School Dust-Up*.

56. Lubienski et al., "Missing the Target," 2.

57. Patrick Range McDonald, "Parent Trigger Movie *Won't Back Down* Inspired by L.A. *Weekly* Feature Story," *LAW*, September 18, 2012; Kenneth Turan, "'Won't Back Down' Doesn't Let Up on Unions," *LAT*, September 27, 2012; Andrew O'Hehir, "'Won't Back Down': Why Do Teachers' Unions Hate America?" *Salon*, September 26, 2012.

58. Kelly-Anne Suarez, "Tennis Star Serena Williams Addresses Half Sister's Killer," *LAT*, April 7, 2006; "Tennis Stars' Eldest Sister Shot in Compton Dispute," *LAS*, September 18, 2003, A1.

59. "Straight into Compton," *LAT*, March 24, 2006; Matthew Wells, "LA Suburb Sees Murder Rates Soar," *BBC News*.

60. Wells, "LA Suburb Sees Murder Rates Soar"; "The Gangs of Compton, Part 1," *Day to Day*, NPR, March 6, 2006; "Terror, Hope on the Streets of Compton, Part 2," *Day to Day*, NPR, March 7, 2006

61. "The Gangs of Compton, Part 1."

62. "City Council Minutes, April 4, 2000"; "City Council Minutes, May 9, 2000"; "City Council Minutes, May 16, 2000," CCH. Mayor Bradley had already had disagreements with police over some suspensions of officers, which many observers felt had personal rather than professional motivations.

63. Bosch, interview with author.

64. Erin Aubry Kaplan, "The King of Compton: Mayor Omar Bradley and His Reign of Chaos," *LA Weekly*, April 4, 2001; Bosch, interview with author.

65. "City Council Minutes, April 4, 2000"; "City Council Minutes, May 9, 2000"; "City Council Minutes, July 11, 1998," CCH; Erin Aubrey Kaplan, "No More Omar," *LAW*, June 13, 2001; "Judge Rules Compton Can Disband Its Police Dept.," *LAS*, August 31, 2000, A1; "Supervisors OK Sheriff Deputies for Compton," *LAS*, September 21, 2000, A3.

66. "The Gangs of Compton, Part 1."

67. Ibid.

68. As quoted in Wells, "LA Suburb Sees Murder Rates Soar."

69. Wells, "LA Suburb Sees Murder Rates Soar."

70. Scott Hamilton Kennedy, OT: *Our Town*, DVD, dir. Scott Hamilton Kennedy (New York: Film Movement Series, 2001).

71. Sentilles, *Taught by America*, xviii.

72. Ibid., 191–92.

73. Jeff Benedict and Armen Keteyian, "Straight Outta Compton," *Sports Illustrated*, December 5, 2011, 82.

74. Ian Thornton, "Cricketers in the Hood," *The Guardian*, October 9, 2011.

75. "A Special Election for Rediscovered Players," *NYT*, February 26, 2006.

76. While the number of pastors involved did not come close to matching the approximately 174 churches in the city, it represented a major change because the churches had previously existed in their own "self-serving, small communities." Bosch, interview with author; F. Finley McRae, "Bradley Faces Critics at Compton at Compton Forum," *LAS*, December 7, 2000, A3. The post-election period turned into a circus, with Bradley contesting the election, a judge overturning the results and appointing Bradley mayor, only to have that overturned and Perrodin reinstated. F. Finley McRae, "Ousted Mayor Calls Compton Election 'Worse Than Florida,'" *LAS*, June 14, 2001, A1; McRae, "Bradley Sues to Regain Control of Compton," *LAS*, August 23, 2001, A4; Alex Coolman, "No Election Fraud 'Smoking Gun' Found in Compton Ballot Inspection," *LAS*, November 22, 2001, A3; Alex Coolman, "Bradley Ousted Again; Perrodin Reinstated Compton's Mayor," *LAS*, February 28, 2002, A1; "Perrodine is the Mayor!" *LAS*, March 13, 2003, A1. In 2003, police arrested Bradley, city manager John Johnson, and councilmember Amen Rahh for misusing municipal funds while in office. The three were convicted in February 2004 of using city-issued credit cards to pay for such expenses as golf shoes, clothing, and tooth repair. Dennis Freeman, "Three Convicted in Trial of Compton Officials," *LAS*, February 12, 2004, A1; "Compton City Councilman Investigated for Alleged Misuse of City Credit Card," *LAS*, August 8, 2002, A3; Keven Herrera, "Compton Officials Arrested," *LAS*, March 6, 2003, A1; Erin Aubry Kaplan, "Arrested Developments," *LAW*, March 6, 2003.

77. Jim Newton, "Compton's Racial Divide," *LAT*, May 16, 2011.

78. Abby Sewell, "Compton Finds Itself in Full Financial Meltdown," *LAT*, November 1, 2011.

79. Abby Sewell and Jessica Garrison, "Compton on Brink of Bankruptcy," *LAT*, July 18, 2012.

80. "CUSD Board of Trustees Takes Decisive Action to Balance Their Budget," Press Release, CUSD, http://web.compton.k12.ca.us/Components/UserControls/ResourceMgr/rsrcView.aspx?rsrc=nfdOvAqhws5bQEPUJn4BBA%3D%3D, accessed April 2, 2013.

81. Orfield, *American Metropolitics*.

82. "Examining California's Parent Trigger Law," *NPR*, May 8, 2011.

83. Richard Harris and Michael E. Smith, "The History in Urban Studies: A Comment," *Journal of Urban Affairs* 33 (2011): 99–105; Richard Harris and Robert Lewis, "How the Past Matters: North American Cities in the Twentieth Century," *Journal of Urban Affairs* 20 (1998): 159–74.

INDEX

Acknowledgments

I have lived with this project for a very long time. While I am responsible for any mistakes, the book is a product of much collaboration. Though I fear that I will not be able to thank all who have touched it, I am pleased to have the opportunity to try.

I am indebted to the people of Compton who have aided me in understanding their town and its history. I would first like to thank the students, parents, and educators at Willowbrook Middle School, who first introduced me to Compton and its schools, when I was a teacher there in the mid-1990s. During the course of my research I had the opportunity to interview several people who lived or worked in Compton. These people opened their lives to me, giving me their time, trusting me with their life stories, and offering perspectives I could not have gotten through my other sources. Thank you to Gilda Acosta-Gonzalez, Frank Allen, Linda Allen, Stan Bosch, Juan Carrillo, Lorraine Cervantes, Savannah Chalifoux, Fred Cressel, Charles Davis, Kelvin Filer, Maxcy Filer, Ron Finger, Pamela Grimm, Jane Harris, Shirley Knopf, Dennis Kroll, Sydney Morrison, Katherine Nelson, Pamela Samuels-Young, Charles Self, and Otis Skinner.

After five years of teaching both in Compton Unified and in Los Angeles Unified, I received a Rose and Irving Crown Fellowship from Brandeis University. I am grateful for this fellowship, along with those from the Spencer Foundation and the Brandeis University Graduate School of Arts and Sciences. A two-year fellowship at Rice University's Kinder Institute for Urban Research allowed me to complete this book. At various stages, grants funded my research. At SUNY Fredonia, I received a Scholarly Incentive Research Grant and the Amy Elizabeth Everett Memorial Award. I also received funding from the Southwest Oral History Association, the Historical Society of Southern California, and the Haynes Foundation, as well as the Brandeis history department and provost's office.

At Brandeis I had the honor of working with several wonderful scholars. The amazing Jacqueline Jones taught me to think broadly about history but also supported me as an individual. She has been my greatest cheerleader while remaining an insightful critic. She is beyond generous with her time, advice, and support. Jackie has been a role model and I cannot thank her enough for her dedication to me and my work.

Michael Willrich and I have worked together for many years. He became a part of the early stages of this book, and his tough questions were instrumental in helping me shape my own. David Engerman has provided much insight into our profession. Jane Kamensky served as a model researcher, writer, and colleague. I thank her for her advice and friendship. As a member of the Brandeis Spencer program, I had the opportunity to learn from education scholars across disciplinary boundaries, including Joyce Antler, Sharon Feiman-Nemser, Marya Levenson, and the late Ted Sizer.

At Brandeis, I was also fortunate to be a part of a remarkable group of colleagues who have become lifelong friends. I especially want to thank Lindsay Silver Cohen, who has been a phenomenal friend and ally for over a decade. She has read more drafts of this work than I can count, and her careful and insightful comments have made it much stronger. Rob Heinrich has always been available in a moment's notice to work through an idea, edit a draft, or talk baseball, all of which I am extremely thankful for. Since my arrival at Brandeis, Hilary Moss encouraged me to pursue the history of education and her enthusiasm has never waned, including when she invited me to share my manuscript with her seminar on race and education at Amherst College. I thank her and her amazing students for their close reads and suggestions. I also want to thank David Soll, William Walker, Eric Schlereth, Gabriel Loiacono, Jessica Lepler, Lynda Yankaskas, Denise Damico, Ju Zhang, and Paul Ringel for their help and friendship.

SUNY Fredonia has offered a supportive working environment, including, but not limited to, my colleagues in the history department. Amy Cuhel-Schuckers worked with me to best articulate what my project was about, as did the members of the Professional Development Center's multidisciplinary research colloquium, who read and commented on a draft of my introduction. Dave Kinkela, Steve Fabian, Zhao Ma, and Emily VanDette all went well beyond the bounds of collegiality and friendship in supporting this project. My hours of conversation with each of them, and their readings of various chapters, have improved the book immensely.

Rice University's Kinder Institute for Urban Research was an amazing place to work. The Institute and the University gave me the time, space, and resources to complete this book. The members of Rice's history department also welcomed me into their halls and their seminars. The untenured writing group graciously read and commented on my introduction before many of its members even met me, and on my epilogue as we got ready to say goodbye. Thanks also to Allen Matusow and Jim Sidbury for providing thoughtful comments. Sara Stevens gave invaluable advice on images, and Jean Aroom and Kim Ricker, at Rice's GIS/Data Center, patiently tried to teach me GIS. I am deeply indebted to Jean, who made magic with the book's maps.

Alexander Byrd was instrumental in bringing me to Rice and served as my go-to person on all things Houston. His enthusiastic support, close readings, and sage advice have all been tremendous, and I do not have the words to thank him enough for being so wonderfully supportive. Alex also shared my manuscript with his students in his Post-*Brown* seminars and I thank him and his students for their insights on how to make this a stronger book. One student, Morgan Anthony, came to my aid in the last legs of this marathon, helping me complete several final tasks, and I thank her for all her work.

My intellectual community has reached beyond institutional boundaries. Bethany Rogers has remained my point person on the history of education, and she has served as both a wonderful editor and friend. In the earliest stages of this project, Becky Nicolaides offered suggestions on how to approach metropolitan history in general, and Los Angeles history in particular. John Rury and Timothy Gilfoyle graciously read and commented on the entire manuscript at a critical juncture in its development. Benjamin Shaykin offered help with the maps and gave invaluable advice on fonts. At a late stage Michan Connor and Hilary Jenks offered important comments that helped me to clarify my argument and sharpen my prose. I have also received invaluable help from Lisa Boehm, Michael Fein, Sheryl Kaskowitz, Marc Lerner, Courtney Shah, and Tina Trujillo.

I had the opportunity to try out some of my ideas at conferences, talks, and in print. Thank you to the discussants, panel participants, and audience members in the myriad conferences where I presented portions of this work. Portions of this research also appeared in somewhat different form in the *History of Education Quarterly*. I thank Wiley for granting permission to reproduce this work.

My research in California was aided by the many friends who opened up their homes, even for extended stays. For this hospitality, friendship, and support, my thanks go to Alison Miller, Kim Pollock, Darren Pollock, Learka Bosnak, Whitney Moss, Ryan Currier, Hanh Le, and Traci Verardo-Torres. For over two decades Barry Bienstock has encouraged me to pursue my love of history. For that and his quiet pride, I thank him.

My study of Compton has had me spending many hours in libraries and archives. I benefited from the help of many, unfortunately too many to name here, but I would like to highlight a few. At the California State Archives Lucy Barber helped me find much needed treasures. Francisco Garcia at California State University, Dominguez Hills, kept the archives open for me, always with a friendly smile. I would like to give special thanks to those at Compton's office of the city clerk—Charles Davis, Alita Godwin, and Donesia Gause—who opened their office to me, gave me a desk, and took interest in my research. At Rice, Anna Shparberg was instrumental in procuring important materials, as were the interlibrary loan departments at Brandeis, SUNY Fredonia, and Rice.

Many thanks to my University of Pennsylvania Press editor, Robert Lockhart, whose unfailing support and wise advice guided this project into being. His edits were amazing and made this book stronger. Rachel Taube answered all my questions and helped get the manuscript ready for production. Once in production, Alison Anderson skillfully ushered the project through the process. I would also like to thank Margot Canaday, Glenda Gilmore, Michael Kazin, and Thomas J. Sugrue for including this book in the Politics and Culture in Modern America series. And, I would especially like to thank the once anonymous reviewers, Eric Schneider, and John Spencer, who encouraged me to write a stronger book.

My family has been my foundation. The Singers and the Butlers have become my family and have given much support. My father David Straus has always enjoyed talking history with me. My sister Jennifer Norman and her family, Ax, Samantha, and Jack, have offered love and support. My grandparents Naomi and Edward Bassuk always offered their enthusiasm, from listening to stories of Compton to offering frequent flyer miles for research trips. I can only imagine how proud they would have been if they had lived to see this book. I suspect most of Manhattan, and the outer boroughs, would have heard about it if they had. My mother, Karen Bassuk, and her partner, Doug Feeley, have been my boosters, supplying continuous love and enthusiasm.

To my children, Etta and Desmond, and my husband, Todd Singer, I thank you. Todd has lived with this project since its inception, and Etta and Desmond came along in the middle. Etta and Desmond remind me every day of both why we need equity in schools and that there is life outside school, even for professors. Their joy and enthusiasm constantly amaze me. Todd has been the most patient of partners, listening to me talk about Compton, reading every word of this project many, many times, and in the process becoming, in his words, "the world's second leading expert on Compton and its schools." I believe him. I dedicate, with love, this book to him.